Virgin or Vamp

By the same author

Portraits in Print

A World Like This *(a novel)*

Safe, Strong, and Streetwise

Recovery: How to Survive Sexual Assault

*V*IRGIN *or* *V*AMP

How the Press Covers Sex Crimes

HELEN BENEDICT

New York Oxford
OXFORD UNIVERSITY PRESS

Oxford University Press

Oxford New York Toronto
Delhi Bombay Calcutta Madras Karachi
Kuala Lumpur Singapore Hong Kong Tokyo
Nairobi Dar es Salaam Cape Town
Melbourne Auckland Madrid

and associated companies in
Berlin Ibadan

First published in 1992 by Oxford University Press, Inc.,
200 Madison Avenue, New York, New York 10016

First issued as an Oxford University Press paperback, 1993

Library of Congress Cataloging-in-Publication Data
Benedict, Helen.
Virgin or vamp : how the press covers sex crimes / Helen Benedict.
p. cm. Includes bibliographical references and indexes.
ISBN 0-19-506680-4
1. Sex crimes in the press—United States. 2. Press—United States—Public opinion. 3. Public opinion—United States. 4. Mass media—United States—Objectivity. 5. n-us. I. Title.
PN4888.S49B46 1992
364.1'53—dc20 92-3821
ISBN 0-19-508665-1 (PBK.)

The author gratefully acknowledges permission to reprint excerpts from:

Against Our Will by Susan Brownmiller. Copyright © 1975 by Susan Brownmiller. Reprinted by permission of Simon & Schuster, Inc.

Time magazine, with permission.

The Oregonian, with permission.

"Oregon Husband–Wife Rape Law" by Betty Liddick, December 23, 1978. Copyright © 1978, *Los Angeles Times*. Reprinted by permission.

The Village Voice, with permission.

"Leap Up Social Ladder for Woman in Rape Inquiry," by Fox Butterfield and Mary Tabor, April 17, 1991 and "Darkness Beneath the Glitter: Life of Suspect in Park Slaying," by Samuel G. Freedman, August 28, 1986. Copyright © 1986/91 by *The New York Times* Company. Reprinted by permission.

"Ain't love grand?" by Mike Royko. Reprinted by permission of Tribune Media Services.

"East Side Story" by Michael Stone, *New York*, November 10, 1986. Copyright © 1992 K-III Magazine Corporation. All rights reserved. Reprinted with the permission of *New York* magazine.

2 4 6 8 10 9 7 5 3 1

Printed in the United States of America

Preface

I first took an interest in how the press treats sex crimes as a result of my twelve years of research on rape. As a magazine and newspaper reporter, I had written articles and, later, two books about how rape affects the victim and her loved ones and how teenagers and children can protect themselves from assault. I had also trained as a rape counselor at St. Vincent Hospital's Rape Crisis Center in New York. I learned from the dozens of interviews I conducted with women, men, and children who had been raped, and with their counselors and families, just how deeply terrible a crime sexual assault is. I learned how it destroys the fundamental sense of autonomy and privacy of the victim—one's body is used as an object, one's humanity degraded; how it introduces trauma and distrust between the victim and those close to her, often destroying marriages and families; and how little the police, the press, and the public at large understand or even sympathize with these troubles. I learned how rape victims become trapped in a cycle of injustice: having fallen victim to a violent crime through no fault of their own, they are blamed for it, sometimes mocked for it by neighbors, friends, family, and the law. I also learned that, even after two decades of feminist attempts to educate the public about rape, women are still screamed at or even beaten by their fathers and lovers for having been raped, are still stigmatized or run out of town for it, and are still commonly portrayed as promiscuous liars by the press and the public, as the rape case against William Kennedy Smith recently illustrated.*

When I became a professor of journalism, I began to look at the subject from a different view. Knowing all I do about rape, I became

---

*See Helen Benedict, *Recovery: How to Survive Sexual Assault* (New York: Doubleday, 1985), for cases illustrating these points.

concerned about the lack of such knowledge in the press. Indeed, the press, it seemed to me, was a prominent part of the cycle of injustice that traps victims. My journalist colleagues, I found, tended to perpetuate rather than debunk the myths and misunderstandings that so hurt victims, not intentionally, perhaps, but through habit and ignorance. With this hypothesis in mind, I set out to research this book, by both analyzing press accounts of sex crimes and by interviewing the reporters and editors who worked on the original stories.

My research would not have been possible without the help of various institutions and individuals. I thank the Columbia Graduate School of Journalism and the Gannett Foundation's National Research and Publications Program for Journalists in Education for time and money to pursue my research; to the Cummington Community and School of the Arts for summers of peace and support; to the research assistants who have helped me so diligently over the years: Marego Athans, Viva Hardigg, Claire Holt, Molly McCarthy, Twig Mowatt, Emile Wilbekin, and Ken Wolf; to Regina Freitas for her translations from the Portuguese; to the reporters who gave of their time and consciences, allowing me to interview them, often at length; to Bell Gale Chevigny, so generous with her time, knowledge, and encouragement, who helped me so much with the history chapter; to Rachel Toor, the first to believe in and help me with this book; to my duaghter, Emma, who had the grace to be born as I finished writing this book, reminding me, as her brother Simon had done, that there is innocence and joy; and, above all, to my husband and perennial editor, Stephen O'Connor, who has endured this disturbing subject for many years with unceasing faith and encouragement.

New York H. B.
February 1992

Contents

INTRODUCTION, 3

1. *Rape Myths, Language, and the Portrayal of Women in the Media* 13
2. *Sex Crimes in the Press: A Recent History* 25
3. *"A Policeman in Every Bedroom": The 1978–1979 Greta and John Rideout Marital Rape Case* 43
4. *"She Should Be Punished": The 1983–1984 New Bedford "Big Dan's" Gang Rape* 89
5. *"How Jennifer Courted Death": The 1986 Killing of Jennifer Levin* 147
6. *The Jogger and the Wolfpack: The 1989–1990 Central Park Jogger Case* 189
7. *Conclusion: How the Press Should Cover Sex Crimes* 251

NOTES, 267
BIBLIOGRAPHY. 295
INDEX, 301

Virgin
or
Vamp

Introduction

This book is first and foremost a critique of the way the print press covers sex crimes. In it, I will demonstrate that the pervasiveness of rape myths and the habits of the newsroom have led the press to consistently cover these crimes with bias and, sometimes, even cruelty.

I have chosen this subject not only as an exercise in press criticism, however, but as a way of examining public attitudes toward women, sex, and violence, and the role the press plays in establishing or reinforcing those attitudes. Sex crimes have a unique ability to touch upon the public's deep-seated beliefs about gender roles. Whereas people may put on a tolerant front when discussing those roles in marriage or the job market, their true opinions are often shocked out of them by the news of a rape or sex-related murder. For example, the very person who declares that a woman has a right to be paid as much as a man for the same work might well blurt out, "Well, what did she expect?" upon hearing of a gang rape in a seedy bar. Sex crimes have the ability to evoke such beliefs because they involve aggressive, sexual interaction between men and women, and call into play age-old myths and assumptions about rape and sex.

As has been well documented (Ericson, Graber, Gitlin, and others), the press both reflects and shapes public opinion.[1] Sometimes, by reporting events and echoing what is said out in the field, it merely reinforces established opinions by mirroring them.[2] At other times it takes a more active role, suggesting new views and challenging old ones.[3] It usually does both, in a constant give and take with the public. When the press reports a sex crime, therefore, it is also reflecting the public opinions elicited by that crime. In this book, I will show how sex-crime reporting exposes the press and the public's view of both the crime[4] and of sex roles and women in general.

Method

The book is based on an examination of four specific sex-crime cases, all of which were among the most prominent of the past decade. Each case became a major event for print and television, and they were all either analyzed in books or magazines after they were over, or turned into motion pictures.[5] The fact that these crimes were so widely reported and therefore so frequently discussed make them particularly useful as vehicles for public opinion about sex roles.[6]

The cases are the 1979 Greta and John Rideout marital rape case in Oregon, which provoked national debate about the rights of husbands over wives; the 1983 pool table gang-rape of a woman in a New Bedford, Massachusetts bar, which resulted in clashes between feminists and local residents; the 1986 sex-related killing of Jennifer Levin by Robert Chambers in New York, which outraged feminists and press critics; and, finally, the 1989 gang rape and beating of the Central Park jogger in New York, which divided men against women, blacks against whites in the furor that accompanied it.

Each case symbolizes a critical factor in public opinion about gender roles. Marriage (the Rideouts), ethnicity (New Bedford), class (Levin), and race (the jogger) are revealing windows through which to look at press and public attitudes toward sex crimes and women. (The rape case against William Kennedy Smith, very much on the public's mind during 1991 and 1992, will be referred to in the conclusion. I did not include it as one of my major four cases because it was primarily a story about celebrities—its notoriety was entirely due to the Kennedy name—and thus it does not play the symbolic role of the other cases.)

I analyzed the language of the original newspaper and magazine stories about each case, and interviewed the reporters and editors responsible for those stories. For background, I conducted research in the fields of media analysis, history, press ethics, the sociology of crime, rape and sexual assault, and linguistics.

I concentrated on the local and national papers that devoted the most coverage to each case, and managed to interview a fair sample of reporters from each one of those papers. My findings, of course, were greatly affected by the types of newspapers that covered the crime, the location of those papers, and the time that had elapsed between the case and my interviews. The Rideout case, for example, was covered primarily by traditional, family-oriented newspapers, which are staid and careful and not subject to much competitive pressure. The New Bedford and New York cases, on the other hand, were covered by splashy tabloids as well as by big city broadsheet newspapers in a much more competitive atmosphere.

Likewise, the Rideout and New Bedford cases both occurred many years ago, ten and five, respectively, at the time I interviewed the reporters who had worked on the original stories. This lapse of years, I found, had a twofold effect upon the interviewees: their memories of details were more inexact but, at the same time, their distance from the cases enabled them to analyze their own performances with less emotion and defensiveness than the reporters interviewed about more recent stories.

As I went through the clips about each case, reading the day-to-day coverage, I looked for certain specifics: The attitudes toward women brought to bear on the case by the reporters, how they were expressed and how they interplayed with public reaction to the story; the public and local attitudes toward sex and violence, race, and class reflected by the coverage; the sort of vocabulary used; which issues raised by the case were picked up by the papers and which were ignored; how the accused were treated; and, above all, how the victims were portrayed.

Because I approached my research as a social critic rather than as a social scientist, I did not use formal methods of content analysis, although I sometimes referred to others' work that did. However, I did count the number of male versus female reporters on each case, and found that all the cases except the Rideouts were covered predominantly by men. This points to an irony intrinsic to the newspaper coverage of rape and sex crimes: Because rape is a crime, and because crime reporters are traditionally male, rape is covered mostly by men. In addition, as most editors are still men, rape stories tend to be edited by men.[7] (The Rideout case was an exception because it was not covered until it reached trial, and trials, unlike crime stories, are not primarily the domain of male reporters. The editors on the story, however, were almost all men.) The paradoxical fact that rape, a crime that happens overwhelmingly to women, is usually covered by men may partly explain why the press has been so slow to change its approach to sex crimes.

My examination of the way men and women report sex crimes, however, did not show that women automatically do a better job. More important than the reporter's gender, I found, was that reporter's understanding of sex crimes and rape myths. A myth-saturated woman will be just as insensitive to the subject of rape as a myth-saturated man, especially given the conditions and habits of newsroom behavior. Women, however, are more likely to have read about rape than are men, who do not usually consider themselves at risk of an attack and so are simply not as interested in the subject as women.[8] (Beneke and others have shown that men are often reluctant to understand rape and unable to empathize with victims.[9]) Also, women, especially newspaper women, are more likely to have a relatively modern attitude toward women's role in society than are their male counterparts, perhaps because of the battles they have had to fight to get their jobs. Nevertheless, opinion pieces and columns were the only forums in which I found women consistently more enlightened than men in their treatment of rape cases.

Television

Robinson and other television analyists have found that television tends to be a summarizing and highlighting medium while newspapers provide broader, more substantive coverage of the news.[10] I did not include television coverage in this analysis, therefore, because I am interested in how the print press interprets sex crimes for its public. The analytical, in-depth coverage of the print press served my purpose better than did the superficial flashes of television news.[11] I also left out television for practical reasons. The years I have taken to read through every clip about each case would have been doubled, if not tripled, had I tried to tackle television as well. I therefore have restricted myself to mentioning television when it played such an influential role on the coverage of these cases that it was mentioned in the print press as part of the wider story.

Habits of the Newsroom

It is only too easy, when criticizing the press, to portray reporters and editors as cynics, ready to sacrifice all fairness to a racy headline. As my interviews reveal, and as Ericson has pointed out, reporters are not always so unfeeling.[12] The circumstances under which they write and the set of societal and journalistic clichés with which they work often lead them to unfair reporting quite unwittingly. The primary factors that affect the way a news story is written are as follows:

Competition

Because of the intrinsically competitive nature of newspapers, when a "hot" story breaks, the papers must desperately try to outdo each other and their broadcast rivals in scoops and timing. This is particularly true in the media-saturated city of New York, where two of my cases took place. This competition puts such pressure on editors and writers that they tend to take short cuts and fall back on well-tested clichés without stopping to think about the subtle implications of what they write.

Deadlines

Due to the necessity of printing a newspaper once, maybe twice a day, regardless of whether a rival exists, all daily news reporters are under pressure to meet deadlines, and all of them must, therefore, report and write faster than they should for the good of a story. This again drives them to depend on clichés and habits, rather than taking the time to think out the careful, unique approach each story deserves.

Reporters' Ambitions

An individual reporter's eagerness for a byline, the glory of a front-page story, and the glamor of stardom create another kind of pressure, increasing that reporter's likelihood to cater to what Arthur Brown, metropolitan editor of the *New York Daily News*, called the "baser instincts" of the press and the public to go for sexy, sensational stories rather than careful, in-depth reporting. Indeed, it could be argued that the single most powerful cause of a reporter's insensitivity to sources is his or her ambition to outshine rivals.

What Sells

Studies have repeatedly shown not only that crime stories sell more papers than any other type of news (except, perhaps, war), but that violent crime wins the most attention from readers, and sex-related crime the next most attention.[13] Brown of the *News* detailed other categories of news stories that sell papers, as well: sex, scandal, "pretty girls," decadence, and, as he put it, "classy people doing things they aren't supposed to." Thus events like the Jennifer Levin murder and the Central Park jogger rape attracted the press in droves not only because these young women were killed or raped, which happens all the time, but because they were white, good-looking and wealthy—they fit the formula that sells papers. Further reasons why these cases were so well covered while other, similar cases were not are part of the analysis I will give in each chapter.

Journalistic Traditions

By this I mean the traditional criteria that define events as worthy of reporting in newspapers, as identified by Katz, Ericson, Graber, and others: Stories must tie in to a current event or preoccupation in the news; crime stories must point to some kind of moral; and news must be about something that is new or unusual. These criteria have survived unchanged for decades, and every one of them has a profound effect on the way sex crimes are covered. For example, that news must be the unusual, never the usual, virtually guarantees that the press will ignore typical rapes or assaults (the rape of a young, single, poor woman by someone of her own race, whom she knows[14]) in favor of the bizarre, sensational, or gory. Furthermore, because news must be new, the elements that are usual or typical within the extraordinary sex crime also tend to be denied or ignored—"It's the first time this ever happened," as a veteran *Daily News* reporter inaccurately said of the Central Park jogger rape. With its eye firmly fixed only on the new and original, the press often fails to inform the public, accurately, of what really goes on in the world. *Time* magazine writer Joe Queenan pointed this out in his comments on the media obsession with the 1992 William Kennedy Smith rape trial: "Deep in their hearts, most journalists know that it's a waste of resources to have 300 reporters covering a murky rape trial in Southern Florida while the economy is disintegrating, the tropical rain forest is vanishing, the Bush Administration is stumbling, and the AIDS crisis is worsening. But the public seemingly can't get enough of the Kennedys. . . . 'I am here because of the Kennedy name, says Yvon Samuel of *France-Soir*.' Willie Smith is a nobody."[15]

Racism

One of the most pervasive traditions of the mainstream press is to assume that crime against whites is newsworthy while crime against blacks and other minorities is not.[16] The result of this racism is twofold: rapes by black men against white women receive a disproportionate amount of coverage, even though they represent only 4–20 percent of rapes in this country;[17] the rapes of black women are largely overlooked, even though they are significantly more likely to be raped than women of any other race.[18] The crimes described in this book, for example, received inordinate attention while similar murders and rapes of black or Latino women went ignored. This bias in the press is why, in my choice of the four cases, I was unable to include one in which the victim was black or a member of another minority group. I have referred to other cases with minority victims for comparison, but the mere fact that I could find no such case as prominent as these four is revealing. The only exception was the 1988 Tawana Brawley case, which I will discuss in the jogger chapter. I decided not to use the Brawley case as one of my main four, however, because evidence indicates that her rape was an elaborate hoax—the authors of two books on the subject concluded that the rape never happened—and so was not, properly speaking, a sex crime at all.[19] The fact, however, that the mainstream press defines crime news essentially as crimes that happen to white people is a major point in this book and is discussed at length in the history, Levin, and jogger chapters.

Sexism

The press has a long tradition of slighting women, which, compounded by the antifemale bias in our language and the myths about rape determine more than any other factor how sex crime victims are portrayed by the press. This will be discussed in the next chapter.

Class Prejudice

Newspapers reflect the class biases of American culture, which, along with racial and sexual biases, determine why some crimes are chosen for attention over others, and dictate to a large extent how victims and suspects are portrayed. I will illustrate this with each case.

Bias of Sources

Reporters and their editors are not subject to the preceding prejudices alone, of course. Indeed, I found that many of them proved to be more aware of the sexist, racist, and class biases of society and more well-informed about sex crimes than were average members of the public.

They are, however, still subject to journalistic rules governing accuracy and are obliged to quote sources as they speak. If sources tend to describe a rape victim in terms of her sexual appeal, for example, then reporters have to quote what they hear—and so, in turn, those sorts of descriptions tend to dominate the printed stories. The Levin story, therefore, not only revealed the sexism of the reporters and editors working on the case, but the sexism of the teenagers with whom Levin and Chambers spent their time.

Reporters' Opinions

No reporter is an empty vessel. Every one brings a set of opinions, peeves, and prejudices to his or her work, and these often leak into a story. As will be seen, if Jennifer Levin's lifestyle had not triggered such class envy, resentment, and annoyance among some reporters, then she might have received fairer treatment. Likewise, if John and Greta Rideout had not elicited such contempt among reporters because of their class and lack of sophistication, they might have been written about with more respect.

Manipulation

The habitual hurry and pressure under which reporters work render them particularly susceptible to manipulation by lawyers, public relations agents, interest groups, and press-savvy members of the public. Once a case goes to trial, for example, court reporters are usually prohibited from talking to defendants or witnesses by lawyers, and so are free only to report what one attorney or the other says each day in court. When reporters succumb to this without looking elsewhere for insight into the trial, they become nothing but mouthpieces for the attorneys. The media as a whole has not yet learned to cope with lawyerly manipulations, as will be seen.

Hierarchy in the Newsroom

No news story is produced by one reporter alone. He or she is subject to the whims of copy editors, rewrite people, headline writers, and editors. A careful, well-informed reporter can be utterly undermined by an insensitive headline writer—the frequent difference between the promise of a tabloid headline and the actual story inside attests to that. On one hand this group endeavor means that not all the flaws in a newspaper story are one person's fault; on the other hand, it allows everyone concerned to pass the buck. For example, most of the *Daily News* reporters, as well as the editor, expressed disapproval of some of their paper's headlines during the Levin case, but would not take responsibility for them.

Some of these factors can be resisted by individual reporters; others can only be changed by a radical shift of priorities in the newsroom—but they are all present in every news story and must be recognized by any reporter trying to do a good job. My aim in writing this book has not been to point a critical finger at individual reporters, but to take these factors into consideration and to look at whether imbalanced coverage occurred. If it did, I tried to determine when the imbalance was in the sources, when in the reporters and editors, when in the newspaper system, and when, indeed, in society at large.

Ultimately, the purpose of my book is to show reporters and editors how to cover sex crimes without further harming the victims. Rape and sex-related murders represent the most extreme examples of human aggression and violence aside from war, yet many of the rape victims I have interviewed for my previous work have said the attack itself was only the first in a string of assaults upon them—people's reactions to their victimization and their treatment by the press and the courts being the others.[20] In the summer of 1990, the FBI released crime statistics showing that rape is the fastest rising crime in America—rape has been rising four times faster than the overall crime rate for the past decade.[21] Rape will therefore be a story that every news reporter will have to cover with increasing frequency. That is why the lessons to be learned from the four cases I have analyzed here are so important, to the journalists who covered these particular stories in the past, to reporters who will cover similar stories in the future, and to all editors and reporters who wish to cover sex crimes with consideration rather than cruelty. At the end of this book, therefore, I have included guidelines for reporting sex crimes without perpetuating the cycle of injustice against victims.

· 1 ·

Rape Myths, Language, and the Portrayal of Women in the Media

In spite of the attempts by feminists and psychologists to explain away rape myths over the last two decades, studies have found that those myths are still alive and well.[1] In his 1982 book, *Men On Rape*, Timothy Beneke interviewed a large sample of men and found that many not only blamed female victims for having been raped, but admitted to being tempted to commit rape themselves.[2] Other studies conducted in 1987 found that victims are still widely blamed for inviting rape, while perpetrators are seen as lustful men driven beyond endurance.[3] In 1991, *The New York Times* featured an article about rape victims who blame themselves.[4] A telephone survey of 500 American adults taken for *Time* magazine in May 1991, found that 53 percent of adults over age fifty and 31 percent of adults between thirty-five and forty believe that a woman is to be blamed for her rape if she dressed provocatively.[5] And at the end of 1991, *Newsweek* pointed out that the public's disinclination to believe either Anita Hill during the Justice Clarence Thomas hearings on sexual harassment or Patricia Bowman, who said she was raped by William Kennedy Smith, "show the lengths skeptics will go to deny the possibility of sexual offense."[6] Because rape myths continue to hold such sway, and because they lie at the root of my discussion in this book, they must be explained again.

The Rape Myths

Rape is Sex

This most powerful myth about rape lies at the root of all the others. It ignores the fact that rape is a physical attack, and leads to the mistaken belief that rape does not hurt the victim any more than does sex. The idea that rape is a sexual rather than an aggressive act encourages people not to take it seriously as a crime—an attitude frequently revealed in comments by defense attorneys and newspaper columnists. ("If it's inevitable, just relax and enjoy it," said Clayton Williams in 1990, when he was candidate for governor of Texas.[7]) Rape crisis counselors and researchers define rape as an act of violence in which sex is used as a weapon, and point out that a woman would no more "like" rape than she would like being mugged or murdered.[8] (As a teenage victim of rape once said to me, rape is to sex like a punch in the mouth is to a kiss.) I prefer to characterize rape simply as a form of torture. Like a torturer, the rapist is motivated by an urge to dominate, humiliate, or destroy his victim. Like a torturer, he does so by using the most intimate acts available to humans—sexual ones. Psychologists and researchers in the field have discovered that rape is one of the most traumatic events that can happen to a person. Most rapists, whether they know the victim or not, threaten murder and other tortures, and many beat, stab, or otherwise harm their victims. During the attack, therefore, the victim is terrified of being killed or mutilated. Also, forced vaginal or anal penetration is painful and humiliating. Afterward, a victim may have to live with years of phobias, suspicion, fear, and instability. Psychologists have likened "rape trauma syndrome"—the long process of reaction and recovery—to the postwar traumas men experience after living through combat.[9] It can take some women decades to recover; others never recover at all.

The Assailant is Motivated by Lust

Because rape is seen as sex, the assailant is assumed to be a hot-blooded male driven beyond self-control by lust. (In the 1989 gang rape and battery of a female jogger in Central Park, one of the suspects reflected his belief in this myth when he said about another, "He had all the girls; he didn't need to rape anybody."[10]) In fact, research has shown that far from being frustrated men with no other sexual outlet, most rapists have normal sex lives at home, and many of them are married.[11]

The motivation to rape stems most commonly from anger, the need to dominate and terrify, or more rarely, from sadism, not from pent-up sexual desire.[12] The rape of men illustrates the point: Men who rape other men are rarely gay and do not rape out of desire—they rape to dominate, punish, or degrade, as do the rapists of women. As one man who had raped another in prison explained, "Beating him up wasn't enough. If you rape him, you degrade his manhood, too."[13] These motivations apply as much to assailants who know or are married to their victims as to those who rape strangers.[14]

The Assailant Is Perverted or Crazy

The image of a rapist as perverted, ugly, seedy, or insane contradicts the preceding hot-blooded-male myth, but it is held in reserve, as it were, for times when the sex crime is extremely grotesque or when the victim cannot easily be pegged as having provoked it. Yet repeated studies have found that rapists usually have normal psychological profiles compared to other criminals.[15] The majority of rapists are known to their assailants—they are relatives, boyfriends, husbands, teachers, doctors, neighborhood friends, colleagues, therapists, policemen, bosses—not seedy loners lurking in alleyways.[16]

The Assailant Is Usually Black or Lower Class

This essentially racist perception leads to the widely held misconception that most rapes are committed by black men against white women, or by lower class men against higher class women—a conception bolstered by the press, which tends to give these stories more play than other kinds of rapes (see the next chapter). It is true that proportionally more rapes are committed by the urban poor, but the majority of rapes occur between members of the same class and race.[17] According to a U.S. Department of Justice study conducted between 1973 and 1987, 68 percent of white women and 80 percent of black women are raped by men of the same race. The study also found that 57 percent of all rapists are white, 33 percent black, and the rest are either of mixed or other races.[18]

Women Provoke Rape

Because rape is believed to be sex, victims are believed to have enticed their assailants by their looks and sexuality. This belief is so established that not only lawyers, reporters, and policemen accept it, but victims and perpetrators do, too.[19] In fact, interviews with rapists have revealed that they barely notice the looks of their victims. The only exception is when a rapist attacks a woman who, in his eyes, represents a race or class he hates, or reminds him of a person on whom he wants revenge.[20] Most commonly, rape is a crime of opportunity: the victim is chosen not because of her looks or behavior, but because she is there.

Women Deserve Rape

Because rapists, like all men, are believed to find women irresistible, this myth assumes that women bring on rape by behaving carelessly prior to the crime—it was not the rapist who "caused" the rape, it was the woman who failed to prevent herself from enticing him. The myth is in use every time a police officer asks a victim a question like, "What were you doing out late at night on your own?" Even the Central Park jogger was subject to the "she deserved it" myth because she "failed," as several reporters wrote, to protect herself by shunning the park at night. Every time a woman has knowingly or carelessly taken a risk before she was attacked, such as going home with a man, going to a party alone, or taking a walk at night, this myth is brought in to blame her. The facts that everyone takes such risks at times and that acting foolishly does not mean one "deserves" an attack are often forgotten, as is the fact that a behavior that may have seemed normal, such as jogging alone, can appear dangerously risky in retrospect if it was followed by an attack. This myth makes it particularly difficult for women who were taking an obvious risk such as hitchhiking when they were attacked to escape blame.

Only "Loose" Women Are Victimized

The myth that women invite sexual assault naturally leads to the belief that only overtly sluttish women are raped. This belief denies sex crime victims their innocence, forgetting that they committed no crime, and ignores the facts that babies, children, and elderly women are assaulted, that most rapes are committed by people known to the victim, and that 7–10 percent of all rape victims are boys and men raped by other men.[21] The loose-woman idea is also part of a larger, widely held myth that bad things do not happen to good people—a thought that comforts nonvictims, but forces victims to blame themselves. The myth results in a cyclical trap for a sex crime victim: The woman becomes "bad" by virtue of having been raped because one myth holds that she would not have been attacked if she had not provoked the assailant with her sexuality, while another myth holds that only "loose" women are sexual.

A Sexual Attack Sullies the Victim

Because rape is seen as sex rather than violence, and a woman's sexuality is still seen largely as the property of her present or future husband, a rape victims is seen as having been "spoiled" or "dirtied" by an assault. Among Muslims, for example, a woman who has been raped is sometimes disowned by her fiancé or family for having brought them shame by becoming sullied and thus unmarriageable. St. Vincent's Hospital Rape Crisis Center in New York has had to shelter rape victims from the threat of murder by their families for these reasons.[22] Victims of nonsexual crimes are never seen in this way.

Rape Is a Punishment for Past Deeds

This myth applies to all sorts of victims, of both crimes and accidents. It is as ancient as the idea of fate itself, yet plays a living part in people's thinking about tragedy. The myth may be a defense mechanism: If we believe that victims bring on their misfortunes because of past bad behavior, then we can convince ourselves that we are immune by virtue of having been "good." This is not rational thinking, of course, but therapists and counselors who work with victims of tragedy find this sort of protective mythologizing very common. The truth is that almost all crimes and accidents happen entirely at random and have nothing whatsoever to do with the past behavior, personality, or beliefs of the victim. Yet over and over again, the victim of a rape is accused of having brought on the crime, if not because of her actions at the time of the assault, then because of her lifestyle before it.

Women Cry Rape for Revenge

The idea that women like to use accusations of rape as a tactic for revenge, or simply to get attention, has been popular for thousands of years. In Susan Brownmiller's definitive history of rape, *Against Our Will,* she pointed out

> The most bitter irony of rape, I think, has been the historic masculine fear of false accusation, a fear that has found expression in male folklore

> since the Biblical days of Joseph the Israelite and Potiphar's wife,[23] that was given new life and meaning in the psychoanalytic doctrines of Sigmund Freud and his followers, and that has formed the crux of the legal defense against a rape charge, aided and abetted by the set of evidentiary standards (consent, resistance, chastity, corroboration) designed with one collective purpose in mind: to protect the male against a scheming, lying, vindictive woman.[24]

The tendency of women to lie about rape is vastly exaggerated in popular opinion. The FBI finds that 8 percent of reported rapes are unfounded, but other researchers put the figure at only 2 percent.[25] A recent police study of three California cities disclosed that the rate of unfounded rape reports ran at less than 1 percent, half the FBI's count.[26] The reality is that the usual reaction of a woman to her rape is not to report it at all because she is afraid of not being believed and because it brings down upon her such injustice and insensitivity on the part of the police, her friends, the judicial system, and the press.[27] The media's invasive treatment of Patricia Bowman, the woman who accused William Kennedy Smith of rape, is a case in point. (Women also refuse to report rape out of fear of retaliation from the assailant.[28]) A woman willing to risk such humiliation and trauma for a lie is rare indeed.

One function of all these myths, and perhaps the reason why they persist to this day, is to protect nonvictims from feeling vulnerable.[29] If people can blame a crime on the victim, then they can find reasons why that same crime will not happen to them. A way to do this is to hold a crime victim up to a set of old-fashioned moral standards far more rigid than are normally applied in everyday life, so that the victim is bound to fail and look like a "bad" woman. For example, Jennifer Levin was widely blamed for going into Central Park at night with Robert Chambers for sex as if young men and women had not been sneaking off to the park together for decades. Indeed, sex crimes in general have the power to bring out some of the most hypocritical of double standards about the behavior of men and women, victims ("them") and nonvictims ("us").

As a result of the rape myths, a sex crime victim tends to be squeezed into one of two images—she is either pure and innocent, a true victim attacked by monsters—the "virgin" of my title—or she is a wanton female who provoked the assailant with her sexuality—the "vamp." These two puritanical images are at least as ancient as the Bible. They can be found in the story of Eve as temptress and corruptor (the "vamp"), and in the later Victorian ideal of woman as pure and uninterested in sex (the "virgin"). Indeed, rape is often seen as a punishment for women who dare to be sexual at all.[30]

Whether any one victim is labeled a "virgin" or a "vamp," and which myths are brought into play, depends both on the characteristics of those who are discussing the case and on the circumstances of the crime itself. Going over the vast amount of sociological literature on this subject—studies of how people react to rape scenarios—I have identified eight factors that lead the public, and the press, to blame the victim for the rape and to push her into the role of "vamp."

1. If she knows the assailant. (Victims receive more sympathy if the assailant is a stranger.[31])
2. If no weapon is used. (Studies show that the public is more inclined to believe a rape happened if a weapon was used.[32])
3. If she is of the same race as the assailant. (Victims traditionally attract the most sympathy if they are white and their assailants black. Blacks raped by whites tend to receive more press attention than black-on-black crime, which receives the least of all.[33])
4. If she is of the same class as the assailant. (She will be blamed less if the assailant is of a lower class than she.[34])
5. If she is of the same ethnic group as the assailant. (If prejudices to do with ethnicity or nationality can be called in to slur the assailant, the victim will benefit.[35])
6. If she is young. (Older women tend to be seen as less provocative.[36])
7. If she is "pretty." (Studies have found that although people tend to be biased against attractive rape victims, they are biased *in favor* of attractive assailants.[37] The idea is that an attractive man does not need to rape because he can get all the women he wants, a reflection of the "assailants are motivated by lust" myth. This finding applied tellingly to the Chambers/Levin case.)
8. If she in any way deviated from the traditional female sex role of being at home with family or children.[38] (People blame the victim more if she was in a bar, hitchhiking, at a party, or out on her own anywhere "good girls" are not supposed to be preceding the attack.)

Language

The myths about women, sex, and rape are, of course, much helped by the gender bias of our language. Dale Spender, Robin Lakoff, and other linguists have documented the inherent sexism in English and their findings are essential to the examination of newspaper language about sex crime victims.[39] Here are some examples:

- There are more words for men than women.
- There are more positive words for men than women.
- Many more words for women have sexual overtones than words for men.
- There are 220 words for a sexually promiscuous female and only twenty for a promiscuous male.
- There are no words in English for a strong female—no semantic equivalent of "hero," for example. Think of the difference between "hero" and "heroine." A hero is active, strong, brave. A heroine more often waits to be rescued by the hero. One rarely says, "She's a real heroine" when someone does something noble, the way one says, "He's a real hero." Likewise, think of the difference between "master" and "mistress." That mistress carries the double meaning of boss and sexual servant, whereas master does not, typifies the difference between the way male and female words are used in our language.[40]

This linguistic set of facts is highly pertinent to the way sex crimes are portrayed by the press. The press habitually uses words to describe female crime victims, especially sex crime victims, that are virtually never used for men. Those words are consistently sexual, condescending, or infantilizing. For example, look at the effect of changing "she" to "he" on these words used by *The New York Times* to describe Jennifer Levin, victim of the 1986 "Preppy Murder": "He was tall and beautiful; a bright, bubbly, young man about to start college and pursue a career."

Men are never described as hysterical, bubbly, pretty, pert, prudish, vivacious, or flirtatious, yet these are all words used to describe the female victims of the cases I have examined here. Imagine, "Vivacious John Harris was attacked in his home yesterday."

Male crime victims are rarely described in terms of their sexual attractiveness, while female crime victims almost always are. "An attractive male athlete was found beaten up in an alleyway" sounds absurd. In both the Central Park jogger and the New Bedford cases, even policewomen and female detectives were described as "attractive" or "pretty." Imagine, "Handsome, blond detective Paul Robinson took the witness stand today."

Women are habitually defined in terms of their relations to men rather than as separate individuals.[41] Men are never identified as "Mr. Sarah Wilkins"; male college students are never called "coeds"; divorced men are not usually described as "divorcees."

Women are often described as having been "beaten" when men are described as "beaten up." The first connotes punishment, the second pure violence. Young women are often described as merely "bright," whereas young men tend to be allowed "intelligent." And, of course, young men in their late teens or early twenties are called men or youths, not boys, whereas the jogger, at twenty-eight, was not only occasionally referred to as a girl, but even as a "little girl."

The cumulative impact of sexist vocabulary may be subtle, but linguists have demonstrated that it is powerful. As Bea Bourgeois, a writer who has commented on sexism in newspapers pointed out, "Words are the tools we use to communicate our perceptions of each other and our world. They draw the roadmaps of the mind."[42]

The Portrayal of Women in the Media

The press's portrayal of female crime victims is not only shaped by language and rape myths, but by the view the media has of women in general. In a 1980 study of the mass media for the United Nations, Margaret Gallagher discovered several pertinent facts about the way women are treated by the press both in the United States and abroad.[43] A more recent study has shown little improvement:[44]

- Women, who make up 52 percent of the U.S. population, rarely appear in the news at all. The percentage of women in newsmaking roles in the United States in 1977 was only 7 percent.[45] By 1989, only 11 percent of people quoted in a sample of ten newspapers were women.[46]
- When women are in the news, their role is often trivialized. World leaders are described in terms of their hats or dress designers, and successful career women are put on magazine covers declaring, "I want a child."
- The most common portrayal of women by the visual media (television, magazines, film, and advertisements) is as sex object and glamour girl, the alluring siren.

- Women are usually portrayed at home, whereas men are seen in the outside world and at work.
- Underlying the media's portrayal of women is an inescapable virgin–whore dichotomy. The women at home are the virgin types. The alluring sirens of the ads are the whores. As Gallagher pointed out, "Throughout the imagery of the 'virgin' runs a consistent stress on subordination, sacrifice and purity. The 'whore' imagery is connected with cruelty, inhumanity, insensitivity and unscrupulousness." This finding is particularly relevant to the portrayal of sex crime victims, for it fits right in with the rape myths described earlier: Not only rape victims are categorized as virgins or vamps, but women in general are as well.
- All media underrepresent women workers. For example, in the United States and Canada in 1978, almost half the labor force was women. In television portrayals, however, working women were only 12–30 percent of the total women shown. Men, meanwhile, were typically shown at work or about to go to work, not washing dishes or kitchen floors.
- The media presents women as being rewarded for the characteristics of passivity, dependence, and indecisiveness, while they are punished for showing characteristics that are considered "good" in men—decisiveness, independence, forcefulness, tenacity.
- Advertising is the worst of all forms of media for presenting women as powerless sex objects, subordinate to men. Magazines and entertainment shows such as soap operas are the next worst. As Gallagher said,

> Numerous studies around the world report consistently on this fact: women are shown as dependent, foolish, indecisive, deceitful, incompetent and so on. More worrying, however, may be the fact that often these flaws are presented as being desirable or even funny . . . better to be wide-eyed and pretty than a forceful blue-stocking.

Most of the studies that revealed these findings were completed a decade or more ago, but new evidence suggests that surprisingly little has changed. A February 1991, study analyzing the representation of women in U.S. newspapers found that more than 85 percent of front-page news and 70 percent of local, first-page news was devoted to men.[47] The researchers also looked at the coverage of the Persian Gulf war and found that women soldiers were almost always depicted as mothers and were virtually never shown with weapons or performing their duties, while men were never shown with pictures of their children. A 1989 conference on Women and the Media, sponsored jointly by the United Nations and the Columbia University Graduate School of Journalism, released more revealing statistics:

- Women still only hold 6 percent of top media jobs and 25 percent of midmanagement jobs in the media. "Men determine what is news," the researchers concluded. (In a 1982–1983 study, the number of women working full-time in the American media was found to be 33.8 percent, a decade behind the number of women in the workforce as a whole.[48])
- Women working in the media are paid less than men—64 cents to every dollar.
- Even though the number of women reporters is increasing, they still receive fewer bylines than do men. A study of photos, bylines, and story sources in ten newspapers in March, 1989, revealed that only 27 percent of the front-page bylines were women's.
- Only 24 percent of the photographs in those ten newspapers included women, who were usually shown with their families.[49]

Obviously, women fare badly at the hands of the press. Pushed into subordinate roles of sex objects, wives, mothers, or crime victims, they have little opportunity to be portrayed as self-determining individuals. When a reporter sits down to write a story about any woman, therefore, let alone a woman who has been victimized in a sex crime, he or she has an enormous burden of assumptions, habits, and clichés to carry to the story. Not only are the conventional images of women so limited, but our very language promotes those images. It is not surprising, therefore, that the public and the press tend to combine the bias in our language, the traditional images of women, and rape myths into a shared narrative about sex crimes that goes like this:

The "Vamp" version:

The woman, by her looks, behavior or generally loose morality, drove the man to such extremes of lust that he was compelled to commit the crime.

The "Virgin" version:

The man, a depraved and perverted monster, sullied the innocent victim, who is now a martyr to the flaws of society.

Both of these narratives are destructive to the victims of rape and to public understanding of the subject. The vamp version is destructive because it blames the victim of the crime instead of the perpetrator. The virgin version is destructive because it perpetuates the idea that women can only be Madonnas or whores, paints women dishonestly, and relies on portraying the suspects as inhuman monsters. Yet, my research has shown that reporters tend to impose these shared narratives—which are nothing but a set of mental and verbal clichés—on the sex crimes they cover like a cookie-cutter on dough, forcing the crimes into proscribed shapes, regardless of the specifics of the case or their own beliefs. They do this through their choice of vocabulary, the slant of their leads, and the material they choose to leave out or put in, and they often do it unconsciously. The problem with this shared narrative, however, as Joan Didion put it in an April 1989 lecture at the Columbia School of Journalism in New York, is that it "gets between the reporter and the actual situation." It leads, she said, to telling "tiny lies."

Journalists continue to portray sex crime victims in these two false images because they are forced to by the rape myths. If a reporter publishes less-than-flattering details of a rape victim, then those details are immediately used against her. If a reporter chooses to suppress those details in order to protect the victim from being persecuted by them, then the reporter is buying into the virgin image and committing biased journalism at the same time. As long as the rape myths hold sway, journalists are going be continue to be faced with the excrutiating choice between painting victims as virgins or vamps—a choice between lies.

· 2 ·

Sex Crimes in the Press

A Recent History

Violent crimes have been the meat and potatoes of daily American newspapers since the mid-1800s. It was then that the penny presses first produced their lurid accounts of violence and murder and it was then, in 1833, that the first crime beat was established by a newspaper, the *New York Sun.*[1] Once the popularity of crime stories was discovered, the press quickly began to prefer violent crimes to all other types of news.[2] Until the 1930s, however, sex crimes were written about relatively little,[3] with one glaring exception—when they occurred as the supposed reason for a lynching.

The lynching of black men by white mobs grew out of slave owners' methods of controlling slaves, but was most common between 1890 and 1910, peaking in 1890–1895, a time when rural white Southerners were threatened by black emancipation, economic instability, Reconstruction, and the Populist revolt.[4] The two most common excuses for lynchings were accusations of murder and miscellaneous crimes, but the third most usual "reason" given by the lynchers for their actions was that the victim had been accused of rape, rape-murder, or of a perceived sexual insult to a white woman.[5] As Jacqueline Dowd Hall has written, the lynchers used the honor of white women to justify their violence because "white women were the forbidden fruit, the untouchable property, the ultimate symbol of white male power."[6] Hall also wrote

> Only a small percentage of lynchings, then, revolved around charges of sexual assault; but those that did received by far the most attention and

> publicity—indeed, they gripped the white imagination far out of proportion to their statistical significance. Rape and rumors of rape became the folk pornography of the Bible Belt. As stories spread the rapist became not just a black man but a ravenous brute, the victim a beautiful young virgin.[7]

Because rape was used so often to justify mob violence, and because it had such a hold on the public imagination, lynching stories were among the most frequent vehicles for sex crime reporting of the time.

As the century progressed, assaults against white women were given less and less often as the excuse for lynchings, largely due to the refusal of the Association of Southern Women for the Prevention of Lynching to allow the violence to be carried out in women's names [8]; nevertheless, rape remained the main justification in the minds of many.[9] The history of sex crime coverage in this country, therefore, is inseparable from the history of lynching. Stories of lynchings became the main vehicle for rape coverage, it was through the stories of lynchings that the press first focused on rape as a crime that mirrored racial tensions, and it was in those stories that the press indulged most freely in the virgin version of the rape myth.

In 1942, Jessie Daniel Ames, a suffragette and founder and executive director of the Association of Southern Women for the Prevention of Lynching, pointed out the virgin narrative and its language in the newspapers of the time:

> In describing the victim of an assault, newspapers use such words as "young, lovely, innocent, devout in her religious life, loving, affectionate; now broken and ruined, a glorious future of proud womanhood destroyed and blasted." . . . This method of propaganda has been used successfully over a long period of years—that all white women of the South are categorically pure and noble and sacred, and all white men of the South are defenders of this purity, nobility and sacredness against spoilation by a Negro.[10]

As this brief history will show, ever since the days of lynching and its corresponding dependence on the virgin version of the rape narrative, the public has been obsessed with interracial rape,[11] and the press has tended to cover the rape of white women by blacks more than any other type of sex crime. An early example:

> The negro locked the door on the inside. Mrs. Lashbrook became frightened and screamed. Coleman threw pepper in her eyes, struck

> her on the head and knocked her down, but did not stop her cries. He then seized a razor, cut her throat and assaulted her. He then left the room, but returning and hearing her groaning, he struck her repeatedly on the head with an axe until he was sure she was dead.
>
> (*New York World*, Dec. 7, 1899.)

The obsession with interracial rape may reflect the historical preoccupation of the nation, but it does not reflect the statistics—numerous studies have consistently found throughout several decades that the majority of rapes are committed by men against women of their own race.[12]

The 1930s

Other than in stories about lynchings, the practice of which more or less came to an end by the early 1940s, the press ran few stories about rape or other sex crimes between the 1930s and the 1950s. In a study of magazines published from 1900 to the present, researchers found only a handful of articles on rape before 1956.[13] The articles that did appear continued to feature stories of black men accused of raping white women,[14] however, or tended to cover only the most bizarre of sex crimes. Researchers have found that when the press covered a rape during this period, it paid more attention to the suspects, who were seen as threats to society, than it did to the victims, who were mere symbols of the white property under attack.[15] (White-on-white rape was covered rarely enough, but black-on-black rape was entirely ignored by the press during this period. As for the rape of black women by white men, I found no such story covered by the mainstream press until the 1950s.)

The most notorious rape case of the 1930s was that of the "Scottsboro Boys." This case, which occurred in the Depression year of 1931, became an important landmark in the history of civil rights and in the history of rape coverage. In brief, the story went as follows: two young women, poor, white, and recently laid-off from their jobs as millworkers, took a ride, hobo-style, on a freight train to Chattanooga, Tennessee. On that train were many other youths, black and white, also seeking employment. Somewhere along the route, a fist fight broke out between the men and the whites were forced off the train. When news of the fight reached the next town, in Alabama, along with the knowledge that two white women were still on the train, a posse of seventy-five white men quickly formed, already talking of rape. As soon as the train arrived, nine of the black youths, aged thirteen to twenty, were arrested. The two women tried to run away but were cornered by the posse. Asked if they had been raped, one of the women replied, "yes."

The women were put in jail on possible vagrancy and prostitution charges, and it is thought that they may have testified to having been raped in order to protect themselves.[16] The nine black youths barely escaped a lynching, protected by the local sheriffs and the National Guard. Eventually, after a three-day trial in a packed courtroom, eight of them were sentenced to death for the rape by an all-white, male jury. The ninth, Roy Wright, was given life imprisonment because he was under fourteen.

At this point, the American Communist Party, the International Labor Defense, and the civil liberties movement became interested in the case and organized worldwide demonstrations on behalf of the accused. The supporters managed to raise enough money to hire good lawyers for the defense, who were able to appeal and eventually to get the convictions overturned on the grounds that the jury was all white and that black men had been systematically excluded from Alabama juries throughout history. A second trial was set and one of the women dramatically recanted her story, saying she had lied about being raped. (The other women stuck by her original claim.) Nevertheless, the second jury convicted the youths again. The judge, James E. Horton, set aside that verdict, too, and ordered yet a third trial on the grounds that both women had been lying and that women of that "character" tended to lie in general. In his concluding opinion, he wrote

> History, sacred and profane, and the common experience of mankind teach us that women of the character shown in this case are prone for selfish reasons to make false accusations both of rape and insult upon the slightest provocation, or even without provocation for ulterior purposes. These women are shown, by the great weight of the evidence, on this very day before leaving Chattanooga, to have falsely accused two negroes of insulting them.[17]

The third trial resulted in a conviction yet again for some of the accused, but after more appeals and trials, the death penalty was finally revoked for all but one, and three of the defendants were released. The remaining five "Scottsboro Boys" still had to serve long sentences, however, and although none, in the end, was executed, the last man was not freed until 1951.

The Scottsboro case spawned a good deal of press about lying women, and as a result it has always been a thorn in the sides of feminists.[18] Although history has forgotten that the youths were convicted by an all-male jury and that one of the women recanted her story and testified for the defense, the fact remains that the women did lie and that innocent men suffered as a result. That fact has never been forgotten.[19] In *Against Our Will,* Brownmiller argued that, as a result of the history of lynching, Scottsboro, and similar cases after it, black and leftist activists have unfairly held white women responsible for the persecution of blacks ever since. Like Jessie Ames and other suffragettes, Brownmiller wrote that the cry of rape was usually concocted by white men in women's names. Brownmiller also pointed out that white women were not allowed on juries and thus were powerless to determine the fate of black men anyway. (Women did not win the right to sit on juries until 1966.) Nevertheless, these cases have resulted in a long history of white women being blamed in the pages of the press for the persecution of blacks in the name of rape—a blame that came up again as recently as 1990, when Peter Noel, a writer for the black-owned and oriented paper, *The City Sun* in New York, tried to draw an analogy between the Central Park jogger case and Scottsboro, as will be seen in Chapter 6.

The 1940s

During the early part of the 1940s the press was, of course, preoccupied with war and the job of keeping up American morale. Once the war years were over and the soldiers were back home, however, formerly accepted gender roles in this country underwent a change, for women had become used to holding jobs outside of the home and living without men, while men had become used to easy sex and living without the responsibility of wives and children. In the period of adjustment that followed, pressure rose to force women out of the workplace, where they were competing with men, and back into the home, where they were a threat to nobody. At the same time, the rate of violence rose in this country and with it rape, which, feminists have theorized, may have been a result of increased male–female tensions, of female—or feminist—challenge to male dominance, and of a resulting impulse by men to keep women in their place.[20] Meanwhile, as white American society was struggling to maintain its prewar status quo, black America was fighting for its freedom, too—so white, male dominance was doubly threatened by women and blacks. One result was a preponderance of stories in the white-owned press featuring black men accused of rape or rape-murders, pictured scared and in handcuffs, while their white victims were depicted in innocent-looking high-school photographs—images, Brownmiller suggested, that functioned, like the lynching stories, to keep white women in their place by exacerbating their fear of rape, and functioned to keep black men in their place by depicting them as dangerous, subhuman, and prone to arrest.[21] These same images, designed to exploit racial fears and stereotypes, can often be seen today—they were rife in the Central Park jogger case in New York.

The Early 1950s

By the early 1950s, America had plunged into McCarthyism and news reporting duly reflected the anticommunist mood of the time. This was particularly the case for sex-crime reporting because American Communists were leaders in the civil rights movement and champions of black suffrage, so tended to become active in rape cases involving black men and white women, which were still the main kind of sex crime featured by the press. When the leftist press covered interracial rape cases, therefore, it tended to pit women, as the accusers, against blacks, as the falsely accused. Meanwhile, when the mainstream press covered such cases, it tended to give as much space to discrediting communists and the leftist press as to following the story of the rape. An example of both these approaches can be seen in the 1951 case of Willie McGee, another southern black man accused of raping a white woman, this time in Mississippi.

The story was that the wife of a postal worker, "Mrs. Troy Hawkins," as the press tended to call her, said she was awakened in the middle of the night by a man "crawling up to the bed in the darkness." After threatening to cut her throat, she said, the man raped her and fled. Willametta Hawkins could not identify her assailant; all she could say was that he was a "Negro who had been drinking." Through a series of circumstantial clues, however, McGee, who knew Hawkins, was arrested. According to a deputy sheriff, he confessed to the attack.

After a long trial, the jury found McGee guilty in two-and-a-half minutes and sentenced him to death. The conviction was later reversed on the grounds that he had been tried in "so electric an atmosphere" that State Guardsmen had been compelled to patrol the courthouse with bayonets and that the jury, therefore, had to have been biased.

McGee was tried and sentenced again in a different town, and this time the sentence was reversed on the grounds that blacks were excluded from grand jury lists. At that point the defense suggested that Hawkins had pursued McGee for years, that he had no choice but to succumb because of her power as a white over him, and that she had cried rape because he had tried to end the relationship—a contention that was widely supported by independent researchers at the time. "People who don't know the South don't know what would have happened to Willie if he told her no," Rosalee McGee told sympathizers in support of her husband. "Down South, you tell a woman like that no, and she'll cry rape anyway. So what else could Willie do? That's why I never got angry at Willie."[22] That defense was also urged by the communists and their newspaper, the *Daily Worker*, which vilified Hawkins and urged McGee's innocence. As Jessica Mitford, who campaigned diligently on McGee's part and traveled South with other members of the Civil Rights Congress to appeal for him, wrote, "At the heart of the case was the fact that no white had ever been condemned to death for rape in the deep South, while in the past four decades fifty-one blacks had been executed for this offence."[23]

The mainstream press reacted to McGee's support among communists and leftists with McCarthyist rhetoric.

> **JUSTICE & THE COMMUNISTS**
>
> To communists all over the world, "The case of Willie McGee" had become surefire propaganda, good for whipping up racial tension at home and giving U.S. justice a black eye abroad. Stirred up by the Communist leadership, Communist-liners and manifesto-signers in England, France, China, and Russia demanded that Willie be freed. . . . Not only Communists took up the cry. In New York, Albert Einstein signed a newspaper ad protesting a miscarriage of justice. Mrs. McGee, *a captive of the Communists*, addressed party rallies, staged an "all-night vigil" in front of the White House.
>
> (My emphasis, *Time*, May 14, 1951, p. 26.)

After five years and five months of agitation and retrials, the defense was rejected in the courtroom and McGee was sentenced to death yet again. This time he was executed in the electric chair. Some members of the press blamed the communists and their reputation:

> The Communists vigorously espoused McGee's cause, but their support nowadays is rather a kiss of death . . . The Communists and fellow travelers have been so thoroughly and rightfully discredited that

> no decent American wants to have any share in their crocodile tears and phony indignation. (John Gogley, *Commonweal*, 1951.)[24]

Others blamed racism and McCarthyism:

> Willie McGee was convicted because he was black and supported by Communists, not on any conclusive evidence.
> (Mary Mostert, *The Nation*, 1951.)[25]

The language used by *Time* and other mainstream publications about this case was revealing: McGee was called by his first name, "Willie," and "Mrs. Hawkins" was denied a first name at all—two of the methods, linguists would point out, by which our language denigrates second-class citizens; the alleged rape victim was named because in those days newspapers had not even thought of shielding victims; and Communists were blamed for everything, especially for pointing out the racism in the American judicial system.[26] The McGee case, however, is significant for other reasons, too. It was a case of burning importance for civil rights advocates, who had plenty of evidence that McGee was innocent. It has been brought up by black activists and the leftist press throughout the years as an example of unequal justice in America. Furthermore, like the jogger case in 1990, it pitted the interests of black men against those of white women. A few quotes from "ordinary people" in the communist paper, *The Daily Worker*, which called Willametta Hawkins a Potiphar's wife, show how this case was used to protest injustice toward blacks by trivializing rape:

> "I've always been skeptical about this rape business."
> "I'm convinced it is almost impossible to rape a woman if she doesn't really want it."
> "If there was any raping done, it was Mrs. Hawkins who raped my husband." (Quote from Rosalee McGee.)[27]

Willie McGee was far from the only black man to be executed for the rape of a white woman in the early 1950s. In February 1951, seven men were executed at once in Virginia for gang-raping a white Jehovah's Witness. Known as the "Martinsville Seven," that was another rape case that was a cause célebre for leftists concerned with racism and civil rights. Although the Martinsville Seven did not receive as much press attention as did McGee, their case became a further occasion for the leftist newspapers of the time to set black men against white women.

In 1951, another notorious rape case occurred, this time in Florida. It involved two black men accused of raping a seventeen-year-old white housewife. (Evidence that the accused had been brutally beaten by police during questioning was thrown out of court.) These men were also sentenced to death, amid much publicity, but the sentence was reversed because, once again, no blacks had been allowed on the jury.[28]

The fact that the most notorious sex crimes between the 1800s and 1950s were cases of black men accused of raping white women not only reflected the history of lynching and racist preoccupation of the press of the time, but is still informing black reactions to sex crime coverage today. Every time a case like the Central Park jogger reaches the press, every time blacks are accused of raping or attacking whites, it raises the specter of this bitter history—of the parade of black men going to their deaths for raping white women—while guilty white men go free. One only has to pick up black-oriented papers like the *Amsterdam News* and the *City Sun* to see how that bitterness turns black men against white women—as if white women were responsible for the justice system in America—while ignoring black women altogether.

The Mid- and Late 1950s

By the second half of the 1950s, the civil rights movement had graduated from the fringe to the mainstream press, and the media had at last become more aware of how it wrote about blacks. The result was a sudden change in the press's choice of rape stories. The press still showed a preference for bizarre sex crimes and blacks accused of raping whites, but now it tended to emphasize false accusations, miscarriages of justice, lynching, and even crimes with black victims. The only rape stories to appear in *Time* and *Newsweek* in the mid-1950s, for example, were about the case of a woman who had her rapist's baby, and about four white men accused of raping a young black woman.

The most notorious lynching case of this time was the 1955 "wolf whistle murder" of Emmett Till, a black fourteen-year-old from Chicago who was visiting his uncle in the tiny Mississippi village of Money for the summer. Till, an only child, was known among his friends and family as a prankster who had a severe stutter as a result of a bout of polio when he was three.[29] Stories vary about exactly what happened, but on the whole they indicate that Till, on a dare from his friends, entered a white-owned store and either asked Carolyn Bryant, the young, married, white woman behind the counter for a date, said "bye-bye baby" to her on his way out, grabbed her around the waist, or merely wolf-whistled at her. (Till's mother, Mamie Till Bradley, said that Till had only whistled as a consequence of his speech defect.) In any event, Bryant was maddened enough to chase him out of the store with a gun. Contrary to popular belief, she did not tell her husband of the incident, but one of Till's cousins did.

The woman's husband, Roy, and his half-brother, J. W. Milam, were so enraged by Till's audacity that they sought him out at his grandfather's home, forced him into a car, and drove him to the river intending, they said later, only to scare him by pistol whipping him and threatening to throw him in. Instead, they told a reporter, because Till refused to show the proper remorse, they beat him severely, shot him in the head and dumped his body in the river with a heavy fan tied around his neck—a fact they never denied. "What else could we do?" Milam told a white journalist. "He was hopeless. I'm no bully; I never hurt a nigger in my life. I like niggers in their place. I know how to work 'em. But I just decided it was time a few people got put on notice."[30] Till's mother was called to identify her son's mutilated body, only recognizable by its ring, but an all-white, male jury ignored her evidence and acquitted the accused men on the grounds that Till's body was so badly damaged that no one could be sure it was actually his.

The acquittal horrified most of the national and international press. The case demonstrated that "the life of a Negro in Mississippi is not worth a whistle," as *Das Freie Volk* in Dusseldorf, Germany, declared.[31] Mississippi and its courts were denounced as racist by hundreds of newspapers, conservative, liberal, and communist alike. The only exception were the local white-run papers in Mississippi, which considered the case flimsy, the jury fair, and the state capable of handling "its affairs without any outside meddling."[32] On the whole, however, that case, followed by the Mississippi lynching of Mack Charles Parker, who was pulled from a jail cell and hanged two days before his trial for rape, marked a turn in the press away from the antiblack slant of its previous sex crime coverage.

The tendency to blame white women for the persecution of black men was as strong as ever, however, and is worth mentioning here because of its effect on the left and because it reveals the power and pervasiveness of the "women provoke rape" myth. In *Soul on Ice,* a highly influential book among radicals of the 1960s, Eldridge Cleaver described his reaction to seeing a magazine picture of Carolyn Bryant, the woman at whom Till supposedly whistled:

> Here was *a woman who had caused the death of a black*, possibly because, when he looked at her, he also felt the same tensions of lust and desire in his chest . . . and in spite of everything and against my will and the hate I felt for the woman and all that she represented, she appealed to me. I flew into a rage at myself, at America, at white women, at the history that had placed those tensions of lust and desire in my chest.[33] (My emphasis.)

In other words, it was not the fault of Bryant's husband and his brother for killing Till, it was not Milam's chillingly racist words justifying his deed that enraged Cleaver—it was the woman he blamed for being desirable. Cleaver's answer to his rage at white women, reached only a few days after he saw Bryant's picture, was to become a rapist.[34]

The most famous sex crime of the late 1950s was the "Florida Tobacco Roaders" case of 1959. This was another interracial rape, only this time it became a landmark because the accused were four white men and the victim was a black college student. The *Time* magazine story about the case embraced the "rapists are seedy loners" myth, while patting whites on the back for overcoming their racist legacy and achieving justice. Even the headline was self-congratulatory.

> PASSING THE TEST
>
> In a legal sense, it was four young, white Florida Tobacco Roaders who were on trial last week in a sweltering Tallahassee courtroom. They were charged with abducting a 19-year-old coed at Florida A. & M. University (for Negroes), forcing her at shotgun and knifepoint into a lonely stand of pines . . . and, between them, raping her seven times. But in a broader and more important sense, the Southern, segregated State of Florida was being tested in its ability to render equal justice under the law. *Florida passed the test with dignity and a fine regard for law and justice.* (My emphasis, June 22, 1959, p. 18.)

The story went on to describe the accused in terms of their class:

> The defendants . . . made up a sorry lot of delinquents, victims as well as products of their squalid environments. Collinsworth (23), an illiterate telephone lineman, is a chronic drunk, son of a sadist who beat him habitually throughout his childhood. Scarborough (20), an air force en-

> listed man, is an orphan whose mother was shot to death in a barroom brawl when he was seven and whose father committed suicide the same year. Stoutamire (16) quit school after the eighth grade, [and] has had a brush with juvenile authorities. Beagles (18) is a high-school senior, the son of a truck driver and a waitress.

The crime itself was described in sexual, sensational terms. Note how frequently the race of the victim is mentioned.

> **Ugly Pleasure.** Early last month, after an evening of boozing, the four went out deliberately looking for a Negro girl to ravish. They found their victim (Florida law prohibits the publication of names of rape victims), who had just been to a college dance, with her escort and another couple in a parked car behind a drive-in theater. Hours later, their ugly pleasure taken, the rapists gagged the Negro girl, flung her on the floor of their car and sped off. . . . The case came to trial only 39 days later. Circuit Judge W. May Walker *presided as though the defendants and their victim had skins of the same color.*
>
> (My emphasis.)

The all-white, male jury found the defendants guilty, but unlike cases when the accused were black, and in contradiction to the claim of racial fairness trumpeted at the beginning and end of the story, they recommended mercy. That meant the rapists could be sentenced to life imprisonment, but not to death.

All in all, the notorious sex crimes of the 1930s, 1940s, and 1950s reveal the give and take between the press and public opinion. As the mores of the time gave way from racism to civil rights, so did the press turn from depicting blacks as criminals to depicting them as victims. Meanwhile, the women in sex crime cases were still being described according to the rape myths—as vengeful liars, promiscuous or disreputable if sympathy was with the assailants (Scottsboro, McGee, Till), or as virginal innocents if the sympathy was with the victims (Florida Tobacco Roaders). Then came the 1960s.

The 1960s

In the 1960s, the civil rights movement became a central concern in America and so, following the trend, the press continued its tendency to feature stories about miscarriages of justice due to racism. The press's sensitivity to race was long overdue, and it provided a welcome contrast to the stories of the 1940s and early 1950s, but it was still untempered by any awareness of sexism. Thus the press tended to fall right into the hands of the people who liked to defend accused rapists by denigrating the victims, rather than by criticizing the American judicial system.

One way the press manifested its suspicion of sex crime victims was by simply ignoring them. Throughout the 1960s, attention to victims was scant in rape stories, and the adjectives used to describe them still tended to hint that they were unrespectable or alluring—almost all the rape stories carried by the mainstream press at this time described the victims as "pretty" or "attractive." A 1962 story on the Boston Strangler in the *Boston Globe,* for instance, began: "An attractive divorcée was found strangled. . . ."[35] A 1969 story about St. Louis's "Phantom Rapist" described one of his victims as "a pretty woman's page writer for *The St. Louis Post-Dispatch.*"[36]

The language used about sex crime victims was also often infantilizing and mocking. Young victims were almost always called "girls" or "coeds," rather than young women or students; and middle-aged victims were often denigrated as "spinsters." Male crime victims, on the other hand, were never called boys (unless they were children), coeds if they went to coeducational colleges, and rarely bachelors if they were unmarried. An example of the mocking tone the press could take toward women in those days was a wrap-up story about the Boston Strangler—one of the most notorious rape cases in that decade and one that, atypically, did not involve a black man—published in *Newsweek.*

> [T]he ladies of Boston were badly frightened. Women who had never fancied pets were suddenly acquiring watchdogs. Chain latches sold briskly at hardware counters. The taxicab business was up; Fuller Brush sales were down. Jittery spinsters reached for their telephones and dialed the police at the first sight of a stranger in the neighborhood; on one such call, officers dashed into a Beacon Hill alley and flushed their man—a detective working on the same case they were.
>
> (Sept. 24, 1962, p. 24.)

Given that the Strangler (Albert DeSalvo) had murdered and sometimes raped thirteen women in Boston, often by posing as a salesman or repairman to get into their homes, the fear of these women was justified. The mocking tone of the *Newsweek* piece was not. DeSalvo, incidentally, used the "rape is sex and motivated by lust" myths himself to justify his numerous rapes and murders. *Newsweek* played right along with him in this astonishing paragraph:

> Albert DeSalvo . . . a hypersexual type who fit none of the patterns, who merely needed more sex than most—he claims more than 1,000 rapes—and who had a cold wife. (Oct. 31, 1966, pp. 118–19.)

The case that attracted the most attention in the early 1960s, however, was yet another interracial rape-murder—the killing of Kitty Genovese, a white woman, by Winston Moseley, a black man, in 1964. It was a story that pricked the conscience of New York so deeply that it is still brought up whenever a similar rape or murder occurs. The press drew Genovese analogies in both the New Bedford and Central Park jogger gang rapes, for instance, because her case came to symbolize the corruption of modern city life—a life in which everyone is too frightened or too selfish to help another person, a life in which the value of humanitarianism has been forgotten.

Genovese, a twenty-eight-year-old bar manager, was walking toward her home from work shortly after 3:00 A.M. on March 13, 1964, when she was attacked. Moseley, a twenty-nine-year-old business machine operator, had gone out that evening expressly to "find any girl that was unattended" and kill her, as he later told the court during his trial.

Moseley jumped Genovese and stabbed her several times. She screamed, "Oh, my God, I've been stabbed! Please help me." Lights turned on in her building and a man stuck his head out of the window and shouted, "Let that girl alone!" Moseley went back to his car and Genovese staggered around the corner toward her apartment building, bleeding from four stab wounds. Moseley came back, found her lying in the vestibule of her building, stabbed her again until she was "quiet" (i.e., dead), tore at her clothes and raped her. Moseley, who had raped and tortured several other women before, was arrested and sentenced for life. In 1968 he escaped from prison, kidnapped a couple at gunpoint and raped the woman before he was caught again. In 1989 he sought a retrial on technical grounds and hit the headlines once more.[37]

The crime particularly horrified the nation because thirty-eight of Genovese's neighbors watched the attack from their windows, and did nothing to help. One man called the police, but no one came down to her aid or even tried to frighten the assailant away. As *The New York Times* put it when it first covered the case on March 27, 1964:

> For more than half an hour 38 respectable, law-abiding citizens in Queens watched a killer stalk and stab a woman in three separate attacks in Kew Gardens.[38]

In *Against Our Will,* Brownmiller pointed out that not many people remember that Kitty Genovese was raped by her killer as she lay dying of stab wounds. Indeed, the crime is not remembered as a sex crime at all; however, it is an important case to keep in mind during the analyses of the other crimes in this book because of the various ways they echoed it. In the New Bedford gang rape onlookers also stood by, doing nothing to help. In the Central Park jogger gang rape, the victim also received an unusual amount of sympathy in the press, largely because, like Genovese, she was white and her assailant(s) were black. In addition, the press periodically still brings Genovese up as "a story that shook this city's soul" when it wants to indulge in scolding or bemoaning the moral corruption of city life.[39]

In general, women in the 1960s were still seen as the property of men by conservatives and radicals alike. The mainstream press depicted them as the wives, daughters, or "coeds," symbols of white America, "taken" from their men by rapists. Activists like Eldridge Cleaver saw white women as the property and pride of white men, on whom they could wreak revenge. As Cleaver wrote, "Rape was an insurrectionary act. It delighted me that I was defying and trampling upon the white man's law, upon his system of values, and that I was defiling his women . . . I felt I was getting revenge."[40] (Cleaver's attitude toward black women was even more frightening: "I started out by practicing on black girls in the ghetto . . ."[41]) It took the rise of the women's movement in the early 1970s to bring society to an awareness of rape as a crime that mattered not as a violation of male property or of white dominance, but as a violent act that caused human beings harm.[42]

The 1970s

In the 1970s, as the modern women's movement arose, women themselves finally took control of information about rape. "Speak-outs" on rape were held and the first books on the subject were published. In 1974, Connell and Wilson edited *Rape: The First Sourcebook for Women,* an oral history of rape victims talking about their ordeals.[43] That same year Medea and Thompson came out with *Against Rape,* which documented women's fury and fear and dealt with prevention.[44] The next year Brownmiller's feminist history and analysis of rape, *Against Our Will,* was published. The first comprehensive studies of rape came out at this time, too, among them Amir's *Patterns in Forcible Rape* (1971) and Burgess and Holmstrom's *Rape: Crisis and Recovery* (1979). Indeed, most of the significant studies on rape were conducted in the 1970s and early 1980s, and most of the books on the subject were written then, too. As a result of all this public discussion, rape coverage changed radically. The press reported many more rape stories in the 1970s than it had earlier, shifted its focus from the suspects to the victim, and, for the first time, printed articles on the aftereffects of rape, on how victims can be helped, on the anger of victims, and on rape as a societal rather than an individual problem.[45]

The press also revised the way it portrayed rape suspects. Before 1971, newspapers and magazines had depicted rapists either as stereotyped monsters (especially if they were black) or as victims of sordid environments (if they were white)—both versions of the "weird loner" myth. As studies came out revealing that rapists did not tend to have pathological or sociopathic profiles, however, it became harder for the press to fall into these clichés. By 1973, therefore, the press began to allow rapists different profiles, although the blame for their actions often fell on their mothers. By the end of the 1970s, according to Gordon and Riger, enough studies of convicted rapists had appeared to offer the press complex, substantiated alternatives to the myths that had dominated the picture of rapists for decades.[46]

Rape was also getting into the news during the 1970s because of widespread reforms in the legal and social treatment of rape cases. Rape-crisis centers were set up to offer counseling and help victims go through the court process, victim trauma treatments were developed, victim assistance organizations were founded, and programs were put in place to sensitize police and doctors to the issue. By the late 1970s, the press was focusing on topics such as whether victims' names should be reported in newspapers and police treatment of rape victims.[47] Even press discussions of the death penalty were occasionally paying attention to the victim and her safety as well as to the suspects and their rights.

An example of this new kind of coverage can be seen in a 1977 *Time* magazine story on the notorious "L.A." or "Hillside Strangler," a man who had sexually assaulted and murdered at least ten women. The story was far from a feminist dream—female college students were still defined in relation to men by the word "coed" and the race of minority women was mentioned while that of white women was not—but it was certainly an improvement over *Newsweek*'s Boston Strangler story fifteen years earlier.

> In life the ten victims were very different from each other. They ranged in age from twelve to 28. One was black. Two were Chicanos. Three

> were thought to be prostitutes . . . four were drifters. Two were coeds. One was a waitress who, according to friends, was "very cautious" with strangers. Their deaths, however, were frighteningly similar . . . all ten were found sexually molested, strangled and flung down desolate ravines or roadside gullies . . . In nine of the murders the bodies were nude. (*Time*, Dec. 19, 1977, p. 24.)

The story went on, as had the article about the Boston Strangler, to talk about the fear these crimes had torched in women. Unlike that earlier story, however, it did so without references to "jittery spinsters" or mockery, revealing, perhaps, that the press was now willing to take rape more seriously.

> So far . . . all the publicity has only deepened the fear in Glendale and other communities in the Los Angeles area . . . sporting goods stores are ringing up large sales in guns of all types. . . . At Glendale High School . . . a note on the bulletin board warns single teachers not to go unaccompanied to or from the faculty Christmas party . . .
>
> Many residents, particularly women, are rushing to sign up for classes in self-defense.

Newsweek did less well in its follow-up story on the L.A. Strangler the next month. With the headline "Strangler's Grip," the story, by Dennis A. Williams, raised some of the old sexist specters.

> It was raining steadily and Carolyn, a pretty, 21-year-old prostitute working Hollywood's Sunset Strip, seductively twirled a lavender umbrella over her shoulder. She was wearing brown leather boots and a navy raincoat—and she was nervous. "I'm more cautious now. I ask them a lot of questions," she said . . .
>
> Since last October, a sexual psychopath known as the Hillside Strangler has terrorized Hollywood and other parts of Los Angeles. He has murdered eleven young women after raping some of them, then discarded their naked bodies, usually in hilly roadside areas, like so many broken dolls. (Jan. 9, 1978, p. 24.)

Opening a rape and murder story with the image of a "pretty" prostitute "seductively" twirling an umbrella played too readily into the "bad women are raped" and "rape is sex" myths. Also, likening murdered women to broken dolls was crude, but the story, in contrast to the rape stories of the 1950s and 1960s, at least went on to profile each victim in some depth in an effort to make them human, not just symbols or statistics.

At the same time as the women's movement was changing public attitudes toward rape, Americans were turning against the death penalty. There was still an enormous discrepancy between the sentences that black and white men were getting for rape, as there is today in many states, but black rapists were no longer being sent so readily to their deaths. A case in 1970 illustrated the beginnings of this change, when even conservative southern juries were showing a preference for life sentences over execution. The length of the sentence, however, also illustrated the continuing racism of the American justice system.

> The all-white Oklahoma City jury took only six minutes to decide on a guilty verdict for the black man accused of abducting and raping a white woman at knife point. . . . The astonishing sentence for Charles Callins, 22, an ex-con with no previous sex offenses on his record: 1,500 years, the longest known prison term for a single offense ever ordered in the U.S.
>
> The gigantic sentence was the latest indication of a growing trend in the Southwest. In September, two Oklahoma blacks were sentenced to 500 years each for assaulting a white woman; in October, a similar Oklahoma conviction drew 1,000 years. Juries in neighboring Texas have also meted out sentences of 1,000 and 1,001 years. . . .
>
> Callins in practice may very well be treated as a lifer and so could be paroled in 15 years. (*Time*, Dec. 28, 1970.)

In general, during the 1970s, the focus of the press shifted from the suspects to the victim. After 1971, rape stories not only discussed racial prejudice but, for the first time, examined prejudice against victims, too. Most important of all, the press at last paid some attention to minority women and the injustice they were experiencing at the hands of the police and the criminal court system.[48]

By the end of the 1970s, rape laws had progressed far enough to include the first attempt at prosecuting a husband for raping a wife with whom he still lived. How the press covered that case, and others after it in the 1980s and 1990s, will be the subject of the rest of this book.

· 3 ·

"A Policeman in Every Bedroom"[1]

The 1978–1979 Greta and John Rideout Marital Rape Case

During the Christmas week of 1978, an unlikely young couple in the small city of Salem, Oregon, became famous overnight. Reporters from all over the country and from as far away as Germany and England descended on the bewildered pair and on the modest courthouse of Salem and stayed for over a week, exciting and disturbing the natives and creating what one local reporter called "a spectacle."

John and Greta Rideout, who were both twenty-one-years old, were sudden celebrities, but not for any reasons of glamor. John Rideout was standing trial on the charge of rape, and the victim was his wife.

A year before the trial, in 1977, Oregon had become the third state in the nation to make marital rape illegal. Until then, in Oregon—and in most other states—a man could not be charged with raping his wife because, under seventeenth-century British common law, she was his to have whenever he wanted.* The "marital rape exemption law," as it

*By June 1991, only nineteen states had made marital rape illegal in this country. In North and South Carolina, Oklahoma, and Missouri, a husband could not be prosecuted at all for raping his wife. In the twenty-seven remaining states, a husband could be prosecuted for raping his wife *unless* he only used "simple force" rather than a weapon and unless she was judged legally unable to consent because of temporary or permanent mental or physical impairment or disability. In other words, while a nonhusband could be prosecuted for forcing intercourse on a woman unable to consent, a husband still had the right to force sex on his drunk, unconscious, comatose, or otherwise helpless wife. Source: The National Clearinghouse on Marital and Date Rape, Berkeley, California.

is known, was created by an English seventeenth-century chief justice named Matthew Hale, who was famous for his hunting and hanging of witches.[2] As America's legal system is largely based on British common law, the law passed into the American system.* The Rideout case, therefore, instigated the first national look at a law that astonished much of the public by its very existence: a law upholding the notion that a woman is the property of her husband.

The case also reflected a new interest in rape and spousal violence. Brownmiller's *Against Our Will* had come out three years earlier to much attention. Del Martin's book, *Battered Wives,* had appeared in 1976 in paperback and, by the late 1970s, articles on battered women were appearing regularly in women's and family magazines. Public awareness about rape and battered women had not yet reached its peak—that did not happen until the early 1980s—but the information was available and in the public discourse.

The Rideouts, therefore, to their evident confusion, brought into every home the question of which rights, if any, a husband has over his wife. The implications of the case on marital relations and the law were so powerful that attorneys on both sides reported receiving hundreds of letters and contributions from across the country.[3] The story triggered many a clash of opinion, especially between traditional men and feminist women; a clash that was reflected in newspaper columns, in the coverage itself, and in the posttrial follow-ups.

The Case

Greta and John met when she was nineteen and he was eighteen in Portland, Oregon. John, one of six children, came from a poor, fatherless family in Silverton, a small farming and bedroom community between Portland and Salem. Greta was one of four children of a secretary and a draughtsman in Phoenix, Arizona. She had dropped out of high school, earned an equivalency diploma, and moved to Oregon with her sister.[4]

---

*In March 1991, the "marital rape exemption law" was finally invalidated by a British Court of Appeal. The court ruled that "the time has now arrived when the law should declare that a rapist remains a rapist irrespective of his relationship with his victim." *Ms.* magazine, June 1991, p. 11. The effect of this ruling, if there is one, on American law has yet to be seen.

"I was pretty lonely," Greta told *L.A. Times* reporter, Betty Liddick in an interview two weeks before the trial. "I didn't know anybody. I had to get a job. After a month, I met John, and I got a big crush on him right away."[5]

The couple began living together in Portland. John worked as a cook, Greta as a waitress. When Greta became pregnant John proposed marriage, but she refused him because, she told Liddick, she thought he was "irresponsible."

John joined the army and left Greta alone with her daughter. Later, John proposed again and this time, driven by loneliness and poverty, Greta flew to Georgia to marry him. "I was on welfare. I didn't have a car. It seemed exciting, flying to Ft. Stewart in Georgia to get married," Greta told Liddick. Soon their fights—over money, over responsibility, over sex—escalated.

> Ms. Rideout paused and bit her lip. Yes, there were good times, she said, like the day after a fight when John would bring her roses. "But if I remember the good times . . . I just wish there had been more of them." She began to cry.

Greta left John again to live with her parents, but he followed her and won her back, saying he wanted to be a good husband and father. They moved to Salem. Still, as Greta told Liddick, their relationship did not improve. "We just didn't get along. The more I expressed myself, the worse it got. I was trapped. I had no money, no way to leave."

Greta tried leaving again, twice, but each time she returned, driven by fear of loneliness, by lack of money, by the struggle to bring up her child alone and by, as she later told an *In These Times* reporter, her hope that she could change John.

On October 10, 1978, the Rideouts had their biggest fight to date. Greta said John hit her in the face, almost breaking her jaw, choked her, dragged her home from a neighboring field, and forced her to submit to sex in front of her daughter. John said they quarreled, she kneed him in the groin, he slapped her, and then they made up and made love.

After the fight, Greta ran to a neighbor's house, hid under the table, and called a women's crisis hotline, saying she had been beaten and was being chased by her husband. Two days later, she pressed charges of rape. John was arrested, indicted, and the trial was set. Greta told Liddick,

"If I hadn't called, I would have sunk into the gutter . . . I didn't want to live my life like that. My mother taught me to think a lot of myself. If I hadn't called, if I had stayed . . . I might have been brainwashed into thinking I had deserved it."

The Reporting

Given the potentially prurient nature of this case, the Rideout story was covered in surprisingly discrete language. The headlines, on the whole, were reserved; neither Greta nor John were described when they appeared in the courtroom; there were no references to Greta's behavior in court, and the traditional barrage of suggestive adjectives used about rape victims (vivacious, bubbly, blonde, sweet, pert, naïve, etc.) were absent.* It is possible to attribute this discretion to the fact that, unlike the other cases described in this book, the Rideout story was covered largely by women. Of the main local newspaper and wire reporters on the case, three were women and two were men. Of the national reporters covering the story in person, two were women and one was a man. Of the significant bylined stories I collected from the Associated Press, United Press International, *Time, Newsweek, In These Times, The Washington Post, The Los Angeles Times, The New York Times, The Oregonian, The Statesman Journal,* and its afternoon paper, *The Oregon Journal,* seven were by women and four by men. (The totals were twelve women to seven men.) Women were also well represented among the local radio and television reporters. Only the columnists who wrote on the case and the editors were predominantly men. As unusual as this preponderance of women was, however, I found the discretion could not be attributed to that alone.

Linda Kramer, who covered the case for the AP, said to me in an interview that the Oregon papers were too staid to run sensational headlines. "It wouldn't play there to have headlines about Bizarre Case in bold letters. . . . I think the coverage was completely different than it would have been in San Francisco or Seattle. *The Oregonian* was the great gray lady!"

Janet Evenson, who covered the case for the local Salem *Statesman Journal* agreed, adding that her restrained language was a result of her

*In my 1991 interview with Greta, she said the only time she recalled being described was by Walter Cronkite on the national television news, who called her "the pretty Greta Rideout" in an update of the trial—au.

training to write about trials as neutrally as possible. "Traditionally, our attempt is to keep from tainting the potential jurors," she said.[6]

The discretion can also be attributed to the local reporters' relative lack of experience. Salem, Oregon, is a place where most reporters start out rather than end up, and this was true of three of the five main newspaper reporters who covered the case. Kramer now works for *People* magazine; Timothy Kenny, who covered the case for UPI, is a reporter for *USA Today;* and Sandra McDonough, the main reporter for *The Oregonian* on the case, is now a lobbyist in Washington, D.C. Local reporters, I found, were more conservative in style and less likely to go for color and personal details than were their more experienced colleagues from out-of-town papers.

Finally, the discretion was a reflection of the times. The year of the Rideout trial, 1979, was the peak of the feminist 1970s, a period when the press and public at large had been sensitized to women's issues. Had the case occurred in the prefeminist 1950s or 1960s, or in the backlash 1980s or 1990s, it probably would have been written about in much more sensational language.

The First Stories: A Quiet Response

The Rideout story initially belonged to local reporter Janet Evenson, who stumbled across it during a routine check of indictments at the district attorney's office. She wrote a short, plain story that was published inside the paper under a small headline:

> **WIFE ACCUSES HUSBAND OF RAPE**
>
> A Salem man was charged Wednesday with raping his wife.
>
> His indictment by Marion County Grand Jury is believed to be the first such charge in Oregon—and possibly in the nation.
>
> (*Statesman Journal,* 10/14/78).

Evenson, who was then thirty-four and had been covering courts for the *Statesman Journal* for ten years, said she had to argue with her editors in favor of naming Greta because the paper had a "staunch policy" not to use victims' names in rape stories. She won the argument. "I strongly advocated using the name because it was the first case like this," she told me. "The victim was over twenty-one—not a minor. She knew her attacker, obviously. It was generally felt that she probably knew what she was getting into when she brought the charge. We had no idea that the publicity was going to go the way it did . . . I guess to be really dramatic about it, the publicity never would have happened had we not identified her in the first place." The decision to use Greta Rideout's name was followed by all the other papers without a word of debate.

On the same day as Evenson's first story, *The Oregonian*, a larger paper based in Portland, also ran a small story about the case and it was not long before the story went out on the wires, but there was no hint of the attention to come. For the first month of the case, Evenson was still the only reporter to cover the early details of the case, the defense attorney's pretrial moves.

> **HUSBAND CHARGED WITH RAPE DISPUTES LAW**
>
> A man charged with raping his wife challenged Friday the constitutionality of Oregon's recently revised rape law.
>
> He maintains the law attempts to invade a fundamental right retained by the people—private marital relations.
>
> (*Statesman Journal*, 11/4/78.)

In Evenson's follow-up front-page story, she quoted the judge as saying, "I don't think there's a contractual consent to forceful intercourse just because a person's married."

The story later quoted the prosecutor, D.A. Gary Gortmaker: "It is absurd to claim that the victim of this crime, by her unfortunate marriage to this defendant, has irrevocably subjected herself to brutal sexual attack by her husband" (*Statesman Journal*, 11/30/78).

These first stories reflected the fundamentally feminist nature of the case and why the nation became so fascinated by it: It dealt with a man's sexual rights over a woman, with the rights of women over their own bodies, and with the place of the law in domestic relations.

The AP and UPI were running stories in regional newspapers all along the west coast by the end of the first month of coverage, but national attention was still lacking. The first stories were only what Timothy Kenny, the UPI reporter, called "curtain raisers," explaining the new law and how this case would relate to it. Only one reporter paid any attention to Greta herself during this early stage of the case; Betty Liddick of the *L.A. Times*.

Liddick was then a thirty-seven-year-old feature writer who had been reporting for the *L.A. Times* for six years. "I had a particular interest during those years in women's issues and I wanted to do [that story] very badly," she told me. Liddick flew to Salem and conducted a remarkably candid interview with Greta, which ran two weeks before the start of the trial. In contrast to the plain and unemotional language of the other reporters, Liddick used some New Journalism techniques to set a scene, create a mood, and to draw a sympathetic picture of Greta as a long-suffering, lonely, and poor single mother—a victim:

> Early winter snow came during the night, covering the tall forest high in the mountains . . .
>
> Greta Rideout watched the soft snow shower from an open window and suddenly felt a chill beyond the weather. A panic. She had begun to realize only in the past few weeks the importance of a phone call she had made—one that women's rights advocates predict may have a national impact on their fight for legal rights.
>
> That cold afternoon, Oct. 10, she had given no thought to political consequences. She reacted out of personal terror, Ms. Rideout said. She called Salem police to report she had been raped and beaten. (*L.A. Times*, 12/3/78).

The story, Liddick said, was based on preliminary research, two days of reporting, and detailed questioning of Greta. "I wanted to write those details, not just the cold facts of the case," she said. She also tried to interview John to get his side, but his attorney had advised him not to speak to reporters. Instead, Liddick interviewed his mother.

> She walked through the yard filled with dogs, chickens and haystacks the other afternoon, explaining that bad weather had forced the plowing under of the barley crop, the well had gone dry and now she faced the stress of her son's legal troubles.
>
> "We're starving to death," Mrs. Fennimore said, tears welling in her eyes. She could talk no more about the case except to add, "It's a nightmare."

In spite of this touching moment with John's mother, the piece sounded unmistakably pro-Greta. I asked Liddick what her impression of Greta had been. "I felt that she was somebody who was pretty unsophisticated and without skills who somehow had the courage to say, 'I'm not going to take anymore of this kind of life,' " Liddick replied. "And I felt admiration for her."

Liddick's story illustrates the freedom reporters have to interpret a case before the attorneys take possession of it during a trial. Liddick not only helped the reader picture Greta alone and thoughtful in her apartment—she even had us feel Greta's chill—she reconstructed Greta's day, checked on the weather as a backdrop, and wrote the story as if she had access to Greta's intimate thoughts.

> She turned off the light and lay on the floor pallet in her near-empty apartment and, for the first time in a long while, feeling the pressures of the past weeks slip away, slept as peacefully as the snow falling outside her window.

Most significantly, Liddick was one of the only reporters during the entire case to think of putting Greta's troubles in the context of battered women:

> At the women's Crisis Service Center here, where Greta Rideout has been provided counselors and advocates . . . staff counselor Norma Joyce predicted, "Perhaps more women now will realize they are not property in a marriage."
>
> Said board director Nancy Burch: "The value of the case is that as it becomes more publicized, women will react—speak out—against the violence they receive from men."

In the same story, Liddick also gave a colorful example of the conflicts the case unearthed:

> Testifying at a committee hearing on the bill, Lawrence Smith of the state public defender's office said, "This (bill) puts a policeman in every marital bedroom. If the wife says, 'Not tonight, John,' or if she is slightly intoxicated after a party and the couple has intercourse, the husband could be convicted of rape."

I asked Evenson why she did not write a story like Liddick's—following up Greta, filling in background, describing her and her life. "Oh God," she said, laughing, "that's not quite my style of writing. I'm real straightforward. I don't get into a lot of the personal things. I guess that could be a defect in some people's eyes."

Sandra McDonough, who covered the case for *The Oregonian*, said much the same thing. "I was really green at the time. I felt under pressure to beef up my leads, but I was not a flashy kind of reporter."

The difference between Liddick's reporting and that of her local colleagues revealed not so much a defect as a different approach to reporting. Evenson, McDonough, Kenny of UPI, and Kramer of the AP were writing for editors of the old school, who demanded balanced, impersonal, terse reporting. These reporters saw their job as an obligation to record the facts of the case and its legal repercussions, not to examine its subtler and more slippery implications. Liddick, on the other hand, who was writing in the school of New Journalism, went after the color, the psychology, and the emotion. Also, as Kramer pointed out, Evenson and the other local reporters were swamped by the daily details of the case, whereas Liddick was able to sweep in with some perspective and write just one feature.

In spite of Liddick's revealing story, which was carried to other newspapers through the *LA Times–Washington Post* news service, local reporters still dominated the coverage. As a result, at this early stage of the trial, their careful but unexciting style set the tone for the coverage—a tone that the majority of national reporters tended to reflect once they descended upon the town.

The Pretrial Calm: Missing the Story

Even though the national media was arriving in Salem in droves by early December, the pretrial hearings were mostly ignored. The few stories that were printed focused on jury selection and the case's legal background, but the press as a whole was silent, waiting for the trial itself to begin. As McDonough said of her paper, *The Oregonian*, "I can't even explain why, but we sort of missed the story right up till the trial."

The lack of reporting at this stage was certainly affected by the fact that the pretrial hearings were closed to the press, but that ruling need not have silenced reporters to the degree it did—Evenson had to rely on interviews with attorneys for her information, but she, at least, found stories. The rest of the reporters' lack of interest at this time was extremely unfortunate, for it meant that they missed one of the most important developments in the case when, during those hearings, the presiding judge decided that evidence of Greta's prior sexual conduct was admissible at the trial. That decision allowed John's defense attorney to bring up evidence damaging to Greta, while leaving her with no legal recourse to deny or explain his allegations. The decision also meant that Greta's sex life, and even her alleged sexual fantasies, could be heard in court. Essentially, the judge's decision, largely missed by the press, resulted in Greta being put on trial as much as John.

Furthermore, it was at the pretrial hearing for the grand jury that Gortmaker dropped his original charge of beating and rape in favor of rape alone. (There was little question on either side that John had beaten up Greta—photographs existed of the bruises.) That decision, which changed the entire nature of the case, also went unnoticed by the press. Evenson was the only reporter who questioned Gortmaker's decision, but even she never obtained an answer. Kramer said she remembers wondering about the charge at the time. "It left the jury no way out," she said. "As old colleagues and adversaries, Burt and Gortmaker could well have worked something out—Burt might have thought he had a much better chance of getting his client off if the charge was just rape. I'm more sophisticated now and if I were covering that trial today, I would have asked what the other charges were and what went on between the attorneys beforehand."

That these secret negotiations went unexplored by the press was particularly unfortunate in the light of D.A. Gortmaker's reputation. "Gortmaker was a very dominant person," Evenson said, "but he was not known as a person who successfully prosecuted a lot of sex crimes. He would rather plea-negotiate than go to trial, so the feminist movement would not have been too thrilled with the guy. I'm not sure Gortmaker even had his heart in the case as far as believing that she was raped."

The Trial: A Spectacle

On the day the trial started, December 19, 1978, the national and world media crammed into the hitherto peaceful and unassuming Salem courthouse in such untoward numbers that, according to Evenson, who still works at the *Statesman Journal*, Salem judges have refused to allow television crews into courtrooms ever since. The effect of this barrage was both to carry the Rideout case all over the country and to dazzle local newspapers so much that they began to write almost as many stories about their media cousins as they did about the case.[7]

"By the time the case got to trial, Greta and John weren't really the center of the story," commented McDonough. "The story was the fact that it was a trial about a man accused of raping his wife. . . . It was more the sensationalism of the trial than them. They became pawns in an important test case."

McDonough and Kenny described the way they saw the circuslike atmosphere in the courtroom: The jury, eight women and four men, were packed in by the public and the press. Television cameras, lights, and wires were everywhere. Reporters from all the major networks, from local television and radio stations, from the wire services, and from newspapers and broadcast stations in Canada and elsewhere were crammed into every crevice. And there in the middle sat skinny John, nervous in his unaccustomed suit, next to his attorney, the frail but charismatic Charles Burt. (Greta was not allowed in the courtroom except to give testimony.)

Evenson described John: "John was a kind of product of his attorney's imagination. The first time I saw him in court, he was greasy-haired, lots of pimples, a sloppy dresser—nobody that I'd want to have around, frankly. And Charlie Burt, I guess, gave him some kind of hormone shots and whisked him off right away to clean him up, which is typical. Attorneys do that with their clients. But John came off looking far more the home-grown boy than the first time I saw him."

Even the attorneys were flamboyant. Gary Gortmaker, the prosecutor, was a heavyset man of about six feet, four inches, who basked in the spotlight and played up to his audience with dramatic gestures and statements. In Dickensian contrast, Charles Burt, the defense attorney and one of the most important lawyers in the state, was small and hunchbacked, and manipulated the jury with quiet, mesmerizing skill. Through it all, the lights glared and the crowds shifted. As UPI's Kenny said, "It was real entertainment!"

McDonough wrote a column about the amount of attention attracted by the case.

> If the importance of trials were rated according to the amount of media play they attract, then the Rideout case would place somewhere under some of the more sensational cases in American legal history, including the trials of Patty Hearst and the Chicago Seven.
>
> (*Oregonian*, 12/31/78, B3.)

McDonough recalled that story: "I've always wondered how much the fact that the trial became a spectacle affected the jury. Even though they weren't reading the newspapers, they were in the room and there were so many reporters there and this was Salem, Oregon—we don't see that kind of thing! It was a spectacle. That's what it was all about, the spectacle, and I probably as much as anybody else got caught up in that."

Kenny said he thought the media attention certainly affected D.A. Gortmaker. "This was the most important case he had prosecuted as a lawyer, I'm sure, and I saw him become enamored of the attention. He had that kind of personality anyway—the kind of guy who enjoyed attention. I saw him become sort of impressed with himself as the trial went on."

The story of the trial's opening ran in the national press from one coast to the other. "Salem hits the big time," as Evenson said. With this attention, she and other local reporters suddenly found themselves in demand. McDonough sold stories to the Los Angeles *Herald Examiner* and to the briefly revived *Look* magazine. Evenson sold stories to the *Washington Star* and the *Chicago Tribune*. Her *Tribune* story ran at the top of the front page, under the headline, "Landmark rape case: man vs. wife." (Note the semantics of this familiar phrase: While John was allowed the dignity of his gender, Greta was only defined in her relation to him. Similarly, elsewhere, John was called Rideout and Greta only Mrs. Rideout. In the context of marital rape, this tradition of defining women in relation to men was particularly ironic. Furthermore, legally speaking the case was not man versus wife, but John Rideout versus The People—in rape cases, the state is the accuser, the victim is only a witness.) On either side of the story, which was set off in a box, were pictures of Greta and John looking inappropriately happy—pictures that were to run in almost every paper all week. Evenson's text however, emphasized the feminist and legal interest in the case.

> Tuesday, in a county courthouse in Salem, Ore., one of those fixed ideas in the law will begin to change.
>
> John Joseph Rideout is going on a trial on a charge of rape—specifically, for raping his wife.
>
> The mere fact of the charge goes against legal tradition. Although the law has few absolutes, one, certainly, has been that forced sexual relations between a married couple was no crime. . . .
>
> As women's rights advocates see it, a couple's interest in privacy is not so great that violence can occur in the sex life without any criminal charge resulting. No theories of privacy prevent prosecution for other types of violence within the family, feminists note.
>
> On the other side, those who oppose "spousal rape" laws argue that no aspect of marriage is more entitled to be shielded from government interference than sexual relations.
>
> (*Chicago Tribune*, 12/19/78, p. 1.)

The era of this story is reflected by the fact that it mentions women's rights advocates and feminists in respectful, unremarkable tones. There is not the implication seen so often today that the word *feminist* denotes man-hating extremism. Nor is there evidence of the even more recent shunning of the term *feminist* altogether.[8]

The Defense: Serious Sexual Problems

Once both attorneys had made their opening statements on the first day of the trial, the press had a new job: It had to reflect the arguments of the attorneys instead of explaining the legal implications of the case, as Evenson had done in her *Tribune* story. This meant reporters were now more subject to manipulation by attorneys and less free to interpret the case themselves. How they fared under this pressure can be seen by their choice of leads in the very first trial stories.

> **DEFENSE IN SPOUSE-RAPE TRIAL**
> **CLAIMS WIFE HAD SEXUAL PROBLEMS**
>
> SALEM, Ore. Dec. 21 (UPI)—The attorney for a man accused of raping his wife has told jurors he intends to prove the witness "has severe sexual problems," and that the publicity from the case is a "source of gratification" to her . . .
>
> Defense attorney Charles Burt told jurors in opening remarks Wednesday the couple's marriage was unstable, with a history of "quarrel, make up, have sex; quarrel, make up, have sex." In addition, said Burt, Mrs. Rideout once told her husband she was raped by another man, later denying the story.
>
> She also told Rideout that "she had a lesbian sexual relationship," Burt said. "She told John that she later abandoned it."
>
> (by Timothy Kenny, *The Washington Post*, 12/22/78, p. A10).

Kenny's decision to make the defense's attack on Greta his lead turned out to be typical of the press that day. McDonough made the same choice for *The Oregonian* and Evenson for the *Statesman Journal* and *Washington Star*. The neglect of the prosecution's side was blatant—Kenny devoted only his last paragraph to it, without even mentioning the alleged rape.

> District Attorney Gary Gortmaker told the jury in the Marion County Circuit Court case the couple quarreled the afternoon of the alleged incident, with Rideout chasing his wife outside.

The only exception to this bias against Greta's side was Kramer's first AP story of the day (she switched to the prosecution's side in a second story):

> Greta Rideout will testify that her husband repeatedly struck her on the face and then raped her as their 2½-year-old daughter watched and cried, "Mommy, Mommy," the prosecution said in opening statements Wednesday.

I asked Kenny why he chose to emphasize the defense's arguments over the prosecution's in his story. He replied: "I don't recall having one bias or another, or not one that I was aware of. It must have been the thing I thought was the most interesting or sexiest part of the story. . . . Linda's [Kramer] was better. She had a lot more experience as a wire service reporter at that point."

Kenny added that he may have filed that story by telephone after hearing Burt's opening remarks and before returning to the courtroom to hear Gortmaker's. The contrast between his story and Kramer's, however, points to a difficulty every reporter has when covering a trial: Which side do you put in the lead, and how do you avoid sounding biased?

One answer to that question was provided by *The Washington Star*, the only paper to make a real attempt at a balanced account of the trial's opening. The *Star* used Evenson's story from the *Statesman Journal*, but although it opened with the "serious sexual problems" lead, the editors balanced the story with a careful, if unexciting headline, a bold typeface layout, and an introductory paragraph:

> **RAPE JURY HEARS 2 VERSIONS OF EVENTS.**
>
> SALEM, Ore.—A woman who has charged her husband with rape has "a very serious sexual problem" that neither she nor her husband "could understand or solve," a defense attorney contends. . . .
>
> During the opening statements, Burt and District Attorney Gary Gortmaker gave differing accounts of what they believe happened at the apartment.
>
> GORTMAKER SAID Greta Rideout's testimony will show that John Rideout woke up from a nap around 2:30 or 3 P.M. that day and indicated he wanted to have sexual intercourse.
>
> She resisted and left the apartment, running to a neighbor's house, Gortmaker said. . . .
>
> The defendant found her, "grabbed her by the arm," and took her back to the apartment, he said. There she resisted him again, she screamed, he struck her on the left side of her face, put his hand over her mouth and applied pressure to a vein on her neck, Gortmaker said.
>
> Soon after, they had sexual intercourse as "he kept one hand on her throat," he said.
>
> BURT TOLD THE jurors his client did not force his wife to have intercourse. "He honestly believed that if you are married to a woman, you have a right to sex," Burt said.
>
> The attorney said the Rideouts did have an argument that day. "She had kneed him in the groin . . . he slapped her on the face."
>
> The couple later made up and had intercourse, he said.
>
> (12/22/78, p. 2.)

Thanks to the attention reporters had given to Burt's accusations against Greta, the defense's case was looking strong by the end of the second day of the trial: Newspaper readers had now been told that Greta had sexual problems (never defined), that her sexual behavior was corrupt (her alleged lesbian and extramarital affairs, including one with her husband's half brother, were mentioned later in every story, even though these allegations were based on statements by John that Greta was never allowed to refute), and that she often lied (she retracted her accusation that this brother-in-law had raped her). All the reader knew about John, however, was that his wife had accused him of "slapping" and raping her.

Later, posttrial stories revealed more: John had also had extramarital affairs and admitted as much in court—a story that did not make it into most papers. In an interview with *In These Times,* Greta said she was indeed raped by her brother-in-law but had retracted her story when he threatened to hurt her. In another interview, she explained that she had told John about lesbian fantasies, which she made up, because she was worried he had homosexual leanings and wanted to encourage him to talk about them.[9] We cannot know if these last two statements are true, but the slant against Greta in the printed stories early in the trial was so unmistakable that when McDonough read her stories from the perspective of ten years later, she was shocked: "Boy, these stories here certainly aren't very sympathetic to Greta!" she exclaimed. "I was just covering what Charlie Burt said!"

Several of the reporters I interviewed echoed McDonough's reaction and admitted that they had allowed themselves to be manipulated by the charismatic Burt. Their gullibility was probably exacerbated by their inexperience. McDonough was only twenty-four and this was her first trial. Kramer was twenty-eight and had five years experience with AP, but this was the first trial she had covered on a day-to-day basis. Kenny, although thirty with about five years experience as a reporter and editor, was new at his job as a wire service reporter and overwhelmed at having to cover the case alone. "It was too difficult," he said. "I never had the sense that I was on top of things. I was kind of scrambling around. Everybody else had other people helping them. It was just too tough to keep up with."

Burt's control of the reporters and the courtroom was so complete that when he declared in his opening statements that Greta had "serious sexual problems," neither Gortmaker nor the reporters challenged him to define what he meant. Without anyone forcing him to clarify the phrase, he managed to leave the impression that Greta's sexual problems consisted partly of frigidity, and that John, therefore, was driven to aggressive sex (the "rapist is motivated by lust" myth)—or, as Burt might have had it, to exercising his husbandly rights—an impression the press helped to promote. I asked Kenny and the others why no one challenged Burt to define the vague and damaging phrase, "serious sexual problems."

"I'm surprised that nobody did," Kenny said. "It certainly would have been possible." But, he added, because the phrase was part of Burt's opening remarks, and because Burt was not holding press conferences, it was hard to find a chance to ask him any direct questions. Also, Kenny said, the crowded courtroom made interviewing all the principles in the case difficult: "I didn't do a very good job, frankly," Kenny said. "I did the best I could, but in retrospect I can see the sort of job I could do now with more experience. There were definitely holes, and I think that was true of all the reporting, partly because it was the first marital rape case. People didn't know the kinds of things to ask, so we were lead pretty much around by the lawyers on both sides."

Kramer said it would have been possible to challenge Burt to define the phrase in the halls during trial recesses or outside the courtroom but that there was no guarantee he would have answered. "But the stories still could have included a line about he was asked and didn't answer," she added.

Pursuing the matter of Burt's manipulations, I asked the reporters if they had formed opinions during the trial about whether John Rideout was guilty: If they were all secretly on Burt's side, that might explain his sway over them. That is not, however, what I discovered.

"I had no question about [his guilt] all the way through," McDonough said. "It was pretty obvious."

"I thought the evidence was clear that he was guilty," said Evenson.

Kenny said, "I guess my inclination was that he was guilty and that it was his fault and that she was the victim. I came to sort of understand what his predicament was. He was a kid who was largely uneducated, he was in his early twenties and didn't really know what the heck was going on. Not to excuse his behavior, but he was raised in an environment where it was, I suspect, almost acceptable to treat women this way."

Kramer was the only one who said she does not even recall whether she believed John was guilty. She was trying to be objective, she said, and she was mostly interested in whether marital rape would be recognized as a crime in general.

On one hand, these reporters deserve credit for showing their opinions so little in their reporting. "I tried not to let my reactions affect what I was writing," said Kenny, and he succeeded. On the other hand, the reporters must be criticized for leaning so far in the opposite direction, perhaps in their eagerness not to appear biased, that they allowed the side they did not agree with, the defense, to dominate.

Burt's charisma and ability to produce quotable phrases—it was generally acknowledged that he was the more effective of the two lawyers—may well have been why he so successfully won over the reporters, but there was another reason his argument attracted, as well. Burt was relying on three well-worn rape myths to appeal to his audience: "Rapists are motivated by lust," "only bad women are raped," and "women cry rape for revenge," concepts easily understood by everyone. Gortmaker, on the other hand, had to tread the controversial, sordid, and untried ground of rape within the sanctity of marriage. Given the inexperience of the reporters, the newness of the subject, the competition of the packed newsroom, and the tendency of the press to fall into clichés in the rush of deadline, it is not surprising that they fell into Burt's mythmaking like wasps into honey.

Midtrial: Greta as Feminists' Pawn

Over the next two days, December 22 and 23, the prosecution called twenty-seven witnesses to the stand: neighbors who had heard the couple fight, friends and strangers who had seen Greta's bruises, the crisis center volunteers who had taken Greta's call for help, and the police who had arrested John.

The defense called only four witnesses, but they were effective. One said Greta had nothing but a "slight black eye" after the fight with John, another said John was a nice boy, and a third testified that Greta had boasted about the money she would make selling her story to the movies. One of the defense witnesses was John's half brother, the very man Greta had said had raped her, and another was his wife. They both called her story of the two rapes lies.

> Rideout's sister-in-law, Nancy Hinkle . . . described Rideout as a "gentle person." She also testified she never had seen him get mad or physical in the seven years she has known him.
>
> (*Statesman Journal*, 12/22/78.)

The jury also heard a friend of Greta's say that Greta had claimed to have had a lesbian affair with her but that the claim was a lie. In addition, several papers quoted the same witness saying that Greta was an honest person but tended to lie about sex. (Greta's refutations of these statements were never allowed in court—her rebuttal was confined to posttrial interviews.)

Perhaps the most damaging evidence against Greta, however, was Burt's wily suggestion that she had become a pawn in the hands of feminists. Burt planted this idea by mentioning that, when Greta had visited the local rape crisis center, she had seen a sign on the wall that read, "When a woman says no, it's rape." That, he hinted, along with the urging of the rape crisis center advocates, had given Greta the idea of charging her husband with rape. (Burt was ignoring the glaring question of what Greta was doing in the rape crisis center in the first place. She had gone, she later told reporters, to seek help as a battered woman.) She had even threatened John with the charge just before the alleged incident, witnesses said.[10] (Greta denied this, but again went unheard.) Burt used these pieces of evidence to suggest that Greta was looking for a chance to accuse John of rape as a way of wielding power over him—the old "women cry rape for revenge" myth. A quote at the bottom of the story from a friendly witness revealed the view of women that Burt was relying on to bolster his antifeminist argument:

> [The witness] added that she never has known Mrs. Rideout to be dominant nor vindictive. "I like Greta," she said.[11]

By the time the trial adjourned for Christmas, the jury and the public were left with an overwhelmingly negative impression of Greta. They had heard utterly convincing evidence that she had been beaten by John badly enough to give her a black eye and a noticeably bruised face, and that she had been afraid enough to call the crisis center and the police, but that was irrelevant because the charges of battery had been dropped. They had also heard a good deal about how much she lied, about her unconventional sexuality, and about how excited she supposedly was over the money she might get for selling her story. (John also sold his story rights to the movies, but nothing was ever made of that.) Above all, they had heard the idea that Greta was incited by feminists to cry rape for revenge, an idea that, in this marital rape case, plugged into the old myth with a new twist: the "rape lie" as a weapon with which to subordinate that foundation of society, the institution of marriage.

The trial, and the press, took a break over Christmas and reconvened on December 27.

The Final Testimony

After two days of wrap-up stories, quoting fresh witnesses and reiterating what had gone before, the long-awaited moment arrived: John and Greta themselves were to take the stand. As with the opening statements, the press was left to choose which testimony to put first—hers or his—and which to give the most space. This time, the choice was more varied.

> Greta and John Rideout told their separate and different versions Tuesday of what happened in their Salem apartment the day Mrs. Rideout claims her husband raped and beat her.
>
> (McDonough, *The Oregonian*, 12/27/78.)

Michael Seiler, who had been covering the case for the *L.A. Times* after Liddick's solitary story, emphasized Greta's side:

> Greta Rideout, who has accused her husband of rape, testified in court here Tuesday that her enraged husband chased her around their apartment, caught up with her in an adjacent public park and threatened to beat and rape her there if she did not return home with him.
>
> (*L.A. Times*, 12/27/78.)

Kramer switched away from her usual allegiance to Greta:

> John Rideout testified Thursday he slapped his wife after she kneed him in the groin, but that he did not force her to have sex.

Evenson wrote four huge stories on the case that day, giving both sides, but her main wrap-up story attempted balance:

> Greta Rideout said Tuesday her husband "beat me into submission" Oct. 10.
>
> John Rideout later testified his wife voluntarily had intercourse with him that day. (*Statesman Journal*, 12/27/78.)

These stories allowed Greta's side to come across as more convincing than it had earlier. Several papers quoted her testimony at length (one paper said it was twenty-seven minutes long, another said almost two hours), for it was dramatic and moving. McDonough said: "When I think about it now, I don't think I could go through what Greta went through. It was pretty gruelling for her. The story she told about John storming through the house while she ran to a neighbor's house and hid under the table—it was a pretty horrible thing to have to be recounting to a crowded, standing-room only courtroom, with people in line to get in." The reporters were sympathetic toward Greta, and they said there was a feeling in the courtroom that she had won over a lot of the public. It therefore came as a shock when, the next day, right after the public had read Greta's detailed account of John's brutality, the jury announced his acquittal.

The Acquittal

The announcement of the acquittal came on Thursday, December 28, the same day the court heard the attorneys' closing statements. The news stories, therefore, had to include both reactions to the verdict and an account of the closing statements.

Most of the acquittal stories took the same form: The fact that John was acquitted, a reiteration of the charge and its historical significance, the make-up of the jury, quotes from jury members saying they were neither sure of his innocence nor sure enough of his guilt to convict him, quotes from John saying he was not certain of how he felt, quotes from Greta saying she was disappointed and hoped the verdict would not discourage other women in her position from pressing charges, and a summary of the attorneys' arguments. The slant of the stories, however, was affected by how much of the final testimony the reporters decided to include, and by whether they emphasized John's story or Greta's.

Many of the stories, such as Seiler's for the *L.A. Times,* reiterated the defense's stand, once again running over Greta's alleged "sexual problems" and affairs and even mentioning her supposed abortions. Seiler's story, which stood out as among the most slanted against Greta, ran on the front page under the head "Husband Innocent of Rape." After including only a three-line mention of the defense's case, it concluded with two paragraphs about Greta's lies and promiscuity—reinforcing the oft-remarked fact that in rape cases it is the victim who is put on trial, not the accused—and brought up further besmirching and unsubstantiated details about her life by quoting Burt at length.

> Burt also reminded the jury of Mrs. Rideout's two abortions, at least one of which was the result of a relationship with another man while she was married to John, according to the attorney.
>
> (*L.A. Times,* 12/28/78.)

The acquittal stories by the news magazines and *The New York Times* were more balanced than the local stories, but they shared one flaw: They gave the impression that the jury had nothing to judge by but Greta's word against John's, neglecting any mention of the testimony by the twenty-seven prosecution and four defense witnesses, or of the photographs of Greta's battered face. Jerrold K. Footlick's story in *Newsweek* serves as an example:

> In the end, the case turned into what lawyers call a swearing contest. "I was crying . . . he was pulling my pants down," Greta Rideout said on the witness stand. "I didn't force her in any way," said John Rideout under oath. (1/8/79.)

I asked McDonough if the out-of-town press ignored the witnesses because their evidence was so contradictory as to be of no help to the jury. "No, I remember thinking that the witnesses were very strong," she replied, "especially the neighbors, who recounted the violence that was going on in that house. It made an impression on me that's lasted till this day. When you mentioned the trial, my first thought was that he was guilty."

The press's neglect of the witnesses, which either came about because of sloppy reporting or overediting, resulted in an unintentional bias, for it played into the hands of the marital rape law critics by reinforcing the notion that the new law should be dropped because rape cases never amount to more than the accuser's word against the accused's, and so can never be proved. The argument that marital rape laws are no good because you cannot prove rape became increasingly heard in the debate about the case, as will be seen shortly.

The acquittal stories that stood out as the most unusual and colorful, although also by far the most unrepentantly sympathetic to Greta, were two stories by Cynthia Gorney for *The Washington Post*. The balance of her information was markedly different from Seiler's and the local reporters' and included a revealing quote from John that was not seen anywhere else.

In the first story she wrote,

> The jury's unanimous verdict was met with a burst of applause in the courtroom. John Rideout . . . got up slowly, looking too stunned to smile, and shook his attorney's hand . . .
>
> John Rideout was asked when it was over how he felt, and he stood in front of the television cameras in the courthouse hallway, speaking

> slowly, looking scared. He said he was pleased, of course. "I don't believe this has happened to me, to start with," Rideout said. "You have a lot of mixed-up confused ideas in your head. I'm only 21 years old and I have a long way to go."
>
> (*Washington Post*, 12/28/78, p. A2.)

Even though it could be argued that Gorney's article was infused with personal opinion—her description of John looking stunned does make him sound a bit guilty—she brought up a point that few others had: the Rideouts' youth. The theme came up again in Gorney's second, bigger story the next day, under the head "The Rideouts: Case Closed, Issue open." Here, she conveyed a sense of John and Greta as people and how they had been affected by this gruelling case.

> No, Greta Rideout said afterward, over and over, she did not feel like a martyr. She would be all right. She was stunned and disappointed and she thought the jury did wrong in acquitting her husband . . .
>
> "Justice was not done," she kept saying—but she would be all right. She would probably go back home to Spring Park, Minn. . . . and be close to her family for a while. Her father had seen her on television, seen the face of his skinny 23-year-old daughter while reporters spoke about her sexual history and this violent rape she had described, and he wept. He broke down crying on the telephone. Greta said, "I've never seen my father cry, never."
>
> (*Washington Post*, 12/29/78, p. D1.)

Gorney also quoted John saying something so revealing that his lawyer ordered him to stop talking to the press shortly afterward:

> John Rideout said he figured he'd take a day off from work, thank you, and then go back to cooking at the Silverton Sambo's. "I think the jury—wasn't looking—at the moral side of it," he said slowly, his voice cracking once or twice. "I think they looked at the evidence. I don't know why I say it, but that's what I truly believe."

McDonough and Evenson both said they took this statement by John as tantamount to a confession. "In one of the stories he admitted that he thought the law was right and good and all that stuff," Evenson said. "He almost as much as admitted what he did was wrong." Kramer also put another quote from John in a January 11 story that revealed a hint of his guilt.

> "I said a few things to the press this morning to get rid of them, but my attorney said I'd better shut up," Rideout said. "We've been though a traumatic experience and I don't want to end up in jail . . . I don't understand it, but it has to do with the testimony at the trial."
>
> Rideout was asked: "Do you mean that something you might say now could conflict with your testimony at the trial?"
>
> "Something like that," Rideout replied, refusing to elaborate.

Gorney went on to give perhaps the frankest description of the Rideouts that had yet reached print:

> They seemed so much smaller than the questions they had unleashed—one thin blond woman with the face of a determined teenager, gazing at the jury with her hands clasped on her knees; and one thin dark-haired man, the traces of acne still on his cheeks, staring up at her with wide brown eyes that rarely blinked . . . A man in the courtroom watched the two of them and said softly, "I think they're both a couple of losers, personally."

The most remarkable achievement of Gorney's stories, even if their somewhat melodramatic language was not to everyone's taste, was that she managed to get across the view of the Rideouts that everyone, including the reporters, seems to have held at the time: That Greta and John were young, inexperienced, unimpressive people—as the man in the courtroom said, losers.

"The way I saw it at the time was two really young people who emotionally weren't ready for this marriage," said McDonough. "My impression of Greta was, well I don't think I would have called her particularly brilliant. I thought she was really sad. When I think of Greta I think of her on the stand, crying, describing the rape and getting beaten up by the lawyers. I had the sense that she had a sad life and was going to have a sad life."

Evenson had the same impression: "They were pretty ding-y, really."

Kenny felt sorry for them. "They were young, unsophisticated people. The attention from the media and from the general public had put them in the spotlight, and they weren't able to handle that."

Kramer saw them as rather pathetic. "Real people have blemishes," she said, "and Greta and John had blemishes, both of them."

The reporters' perception of Greta and John as unsophisticated losers was significant. "Reading some of the stuff I wrote now," McDonough said, "I'm wondering if I took it seriously. My newspaper didn't take that story very seriously. Just look at how we covered it! We were more interested in the spectacle of the trial than in the story of what was really going on."

If John and Greta had been rich, glamorous, or merely upper class, the press probably would have taken their story more seriously; it certainly would have paid much more attention to the two of them as individuals, as the Jennifer Levin case will amply illustrate.

The Early Opinions

While local reporters were filing day-by-day accounts of the trial, the issues raised by the case were being busily discussed at dinner tables, in barrooms, in letters to the editor, and in opinion columns: The rights of husbands over wives, and whether the law should be allowed into the privacy of the marital bedroom.[12]

On one side were columnists such as Richard Cohen, Carl R. Rowan, Ellen Goodman, and Colman McCarthy, who stood up for the protection of women against rape in or out of marriage. They argued that the law was already used to intervene in families for the protection of children, and so should be allowed to do so for women. On the other side were columnists such as George Will and Mike Royko, who were worried about women using the rape law for revenge and about the law interfering with marital privacy.

At the start of the trial, Richard Cohen published a long column in *The Washington Post* under the title, "Lack of Law Bolsters Male Fantasy, Myth." He began by mocking the myth that women like rape by depicting himself as a teenage boy watching the movie, *Gone With the Wind:*

> She squirmed and fought, but in the morning she awoke with a smile. She was happy at last. Her husband had finally raped her.
>
> Oh boy! In the balcony we understood. . . . What she needed was a good you-know-what and her husband, as was his right, had given it to her. Women were like that—fighting, but then giving in. Sometimes you had to be a little rough. In the balcony we knew that. We knew that in this sense, at least, a man could do what he wanted with his wife.
>
> It turns out we were right. This is almost beyond comprehension because we were right on almost nothing else. . . . But on the marital rape business we were right. You can do it. The law, it turns out, is still in the balcony. (*Washington Post*, 12/21/78.)

Cohen went on to explain the Rideout case and its legal pros and cons, but he came down clearly in favor of the new law:

> In the end, the marital status of the victim should not matter.

Syndicated columnist George F. Will took a different view:

> The idea that marriage implies or requires perpetual consent, under all circumstances, to sex is grotesque. And a partner in a marriage must have recourse to the law when the other partner resorts to violence. But it is a grave business when the law empowers one partner to charge the other with a felony punishable by 20 years in prison.
> (*Washington Post*, 12/28/78).

After the acquittal, columnists and editorial writers fiercely debated whether the jury was right, the case worth it, and the law sound. The day after the acquittal was announced, one of the few syndicated female columnists of the time, Judy Mann, lamented the verdict and charged that the jury had avoided the larger, constitutional questions the case raised. Like Will, she also pointed out how hard rape cases are to prove in general and suggested that other types of charges might work better.

> "Quite frankly, I was shocked at the verdict because that particular case had more corroborating evidence of rape than most rape cases ever have," says Mary Ann Largen of the Health, Education and Welfare Department's rape task force.
>
> If the Rideout case proves anything, it is that spousal rape cases are going to be the hardest rape cases to prosecute. And it raises the question of whether violence in marriage, which takes the form of rape, should be prosecuted as assault—a crime that "traditionally" has carried life and death penalties. (*Washington Post*, 12/19/78.)

Even though Mann, like other national reporters, neglected to take into account either the evidence from the witnesses at the Rideout trial or the mores of the traditionalist, rural jury,[13] she did go on to make a point that had been sorely missing in the discussion of the case so far—that marital rape is a form of domestic violence. She also turned out to be right in predicting how reluctant women would be to press rape charges against their husbands. In spite of the dire warnings by the new law's opponents that women would now be crying rape whenever they wanted, in Oregon, at least, at the time of this writing, there have been no marital rape cases since the Rideouts', according to Evenson. Instead, Evenson said, prosecutors are relying on the more easily proved charge of assault and battery—the very solution Mann suggested.

The Oregonian ran both columns and letters about the case, many of which concerned fundamental questions of male–female relations and women's rights. One woman wrote:

> "It was hard to assess the truth in the Rideout case, but Greta Rideout appears to have, to some extent, attempted to provoke her husband into abusing her so that she might accuse him." (1/6/79, p. A19)

Another woman wrote an attack on "radical women" and "libbers."

> "Surely, neither spouse must be beaten or subjected to cruelty; but the case Ms. Rideout lost will be only one of a series of attacks on that which is a bugaboo to the 'libbers'—marriage." (1/7/79, p. C2)

A man from Lake Oswego mocked the new law:

> "Now that the Oregon Legislature has made marital rape a crime, it would seem the next logical step would be the crime of theft. If either of the spouses were to remove money from the other's possession without that spouse's approval, then that spouse could be cited for theft." (1/23/79, p. B6).

Ellen Goodman, the only other female columnist besides Judy Mann to write about the case, came out for the marital rape law. Like Mann, she made the essential point that rape, "in or out of marriage" is "a crime of violence rather than . . . a crime of sex."[14] That only three columnists, two of them women, made this point, even though the majority of columnists supported the marital rape law, was revealing. (Colman McCarthy was the sole man.) Without an understanding that rape is an act of violence, there could be little understanding of what Greta was doing in court and, indeed, of why there was a law against marital rape at all.

On the whole, however, these early columnists were sympathetic to Greta and to the notion that men should not have the right to rape their wives. Therefore, when John and Greta announced their reconciliation, it came as a nasty shock.

The Reconciliation

On January 10, 1979, only two weeks after John was acquitted and Greta was quoted as saying justice had not been done, the couple appeared in Charlie Burt's office and announced that they had reconciled. The press, feminists, and antirape advocates were not amused.

The reconciliation, or at least the way it was reported, gave fodder to those on the side of husbands' absolute right over wives and fed all the speculation that Greta had been crying rape for revenge and attention, that the law did not belong in the marital bedroom, and that Greta was nothing but a hysterical woman. Even moderate people, as reflected by the columnists and letter writers, chose to take the reconciliation as evidence that Greta either was not raped or did not mind being raped. No one saw her any longer as a victim, no one really understood why it had happened, and the press clearly felt "had."

"John and Greta became local celebs, as much as you can be that in Salem," said McDonough. "I used to see them at the Inn Restaurant where all the legislators would eat, and there was always a twittering around them. And they loved it! They courted the press, they'd have little press conferences. . . . They went out and posed. They were getting a lot of publicity and I think we were all feeling a little bit used."

The Oregonian took the couple to task in an editorial published on January 11: "Even in charity, it could not be said that the Rideout case was worth the wide attention it received or the hopes it raised for abused women."

A letter, published on January 17, reiterated the point: "I think the Rideouts should be sent a bill by the state for reimbursement of tax money wasted on their publicity joke."[15]

By the time of the reconciliation, the out-of-town publications had withdrawn their own reporters from the case and had to depend on the wire services and local reporters for the story. This meant that, once again, as at the beginning of the trial, McDonough, Evenson, Kenny, Kramer, and Don Jepson (of *The Oregon Journal*) were virtually the only reporters covering the Rideouts, which gave them a good deal of control over the national view of the story. Perhaps as a result, the feelings that they described earlier about the case—their lack of respect for Greta and John, their unwillingness to take the story seriously, their fatigue with the entire subject, and, now, the fact that they felt conned—may have contributed to the mercilessness of the coverage in general.

McDonough, for instance, interviewed the Rideouts and discovered they had just gone out and bought a huge, round bed. She sold that story to *Look* magazine. "And that was the lead, with a picture of John and Greta by their round bed," she said. "I was really kind of embarrassed when I read it." Evenson wrote a piece for her own paper and for *The Washington Star* playing up the "romance" in somewhat facetious language. Her story ran under the blatant headline:

> **RAPE TRIAL SAVED US, COUPLE SAYS**
>
> John and Greta Rideout are unemployed and in debt up to their ears, but they say they are happier than they've ever been.
>
> "We have something now that we never had before," John said.
>
> (*Washington Star*, 1/11/79, p. 1)

Evenson went on to quote them talking about finding God and planning to go to marriage counseling and to help other women in violent relationships. The story was highlighted by a box, and ran under a photo of the couple laughing, John's arm around Greta; Greta, in a new hairstyle, smiling at John.

The reconciliation began, said the Rideouts, when Greta had called John to arrange a meeting to discuss custody of their daughter. Evenson quoted Greta:

> "We were paranoid about being seen together. We were afraid someone would see us and think the wrong thing," Greta said.
>
> They met on a streetcorner and drove around together, her with the hood of her coat drawn up over her head. They ultimately drove 45 miles to Portland and parked their car in a lot.
>
> They giggled recalling "the big deal we went through deciding whether we could kiss each other" as they sat in their car, Greta said.

None of the reporters made an attempt to find an explanation for the reconciliation (see "The Cycle of Violence" below). They interviewed no counselors for battered women, no experts on violent marriages, no person with any perspective on the case. The reporters had their own ideas about it, as will be seen, but none of them looked any farther than the Rideouts themselves for an explanation, and the Rideouts were so confused and bedazzled by their newfound fame that they did not know what they were doing, either.

If the local reporters failed to find explanations for the reconciliation, the national columnists did no better. In fact, fed perhaps by the facetious attitude of the local reporters, they were downright hostile.

The Later Opinions

The first syndicated columnist to write about the reconciliation was William Raspberry, whose piece ran in the *Washington Post* and elsewhere. Raspberry expressed both the disgust that the press felt about the reconciliation and its sense of having been used.

> I suppose that nearly everybody believes it is theoretically possible for a man to rape his wife: to make her believe that he will do her serious bodily harm unless she acquiesces to his sexual demands.
>
> But nearly every man knows (or thinks he knows) of women who say no, no, no when what they mean is: Force me. A few men still believe that every woman wants to be raped, that "gentle" and "considerate" equal namby-pamby.
>
> These men will likely see the Rideout reconciliation as proof that they were right all along, that she really must have liked it.
>
> (*Washington Post*, 1/15/79, p. A21).

Raspberry went on to argue that accusations of marital rape are, at best, suspicious. He concluded with a quote he said he agreed with from another man, George Nodelman, who had written a letter on the subject to *The New York Times*. The quote revealed a total lack of awareness that rape is an act of violence:

> In a situation where a husband compels a wife to have sexual intercourse against her will, there cannot be the same traumatic experience. There may be resentment or injured feelings, but the overall effect cannot be compared to rape by a stranger.

In fact, as Nodelman and Raspberry would have discovered had they interviewed rape experts or read any of the books on the subject available at the time, rape by an intimate is often more traumatic for the victim than rape by a stranger. Not only is the victim terrified, abused, and humiliated by the rape itself, but she has been betrayed by the very person she thought she could trust.[16]

If Raspberry's column was unkind to the Rideouts, Mike Royko's, which ran in papers all over the country two days later, was cruel. In it, Royko revealed the extent to which this case elicited deep-seated beliefs about marriage and sex roles.

AIN'T LOVE GRAND?

It's always nice to see a happy ending to a love story.

Thus, it was happy news that Greta and John Rideout . . . have patched up their much-publicized differences and are going to remain married . . .

As most people know, Greta, 23, recently accused her husband, John, 21, of raping her. She also said he hardly ever brushed his teeth and did not bathe regularly . . .

Women's groups howled that Greta was only the tip of the oppressed iceberg, that wives were being raped in droves by their husbands.

Luckily for John, the jury believed him. Or at least it did not believe Greta. In either case, John was found not guilty and avoided being sent to Oregon State Prison, where he surely would have suffered the humiliation of other prisoners pointing at him and teasing: "He raped his wife; he raped his wife, the sissy." . . .

Most women would not want to live with a man who rarely bathed or brushed his teeth, and raped her. And most men would not want to live with a woman who would try to have him sent to a state penitentiary.

But somehow they have worked things out. . . .

During the trial, Greta considered selling her story to the movies.[17] It would probably make an even better movie now that is has a happy ending.

You can almost do the touching dialogue yourself as it may have taken place in the lawyer's office:

"Hello, John."

"Hello, Greta."

"John, I notice that you do not have a peculiar odor."

"Yes, Greta. I have been washing my feet lately."

"Oh, John, if you had only washed your feet and brushed your teeth before, things might have been different for us."

"Greta, do you think that there is a chance that we might . . ."

"I don't know, John. After all, you did rape me."

"Greta, we have been in this room together for 10 minutes, and I have not tried to rape you, have I?"

"No, I have to give you credit for that."

"And all during my trial, did I once lunge at you across the courtroom, like a sex-crazed fiend?"

"No, you didn't. And I was touched by your consideration."

"Then let us walk off into the sunset together, Greta."

"Yes. And remember to change your underwear every day, John."

Royko went on to further attack Greta and feminists:

> Many women's groups are going to be disappointed at the way this has turned out, because they believed that Greta was a symbol of the oppressed female-person . . .
>
> On the other hand, the story of Greta and John might be the answer to the age-old problem of how to get some husbands to reform their nasty ways.
>
> Science tells us that nagging is bad because it gives men ulcers and heart attacks and drives them to drink.
>
> But if John has really changed, then Greta might have found the answer. Not nagging. Not marriage counselors. Maybe the way to turn a man into a model husband might be to threaten him with a prison sentence for rape. (*The Oregonian*, 1/17/79, p. D5.)

Royko's column did not go unnoticed. One man wrote an outraged response to the *Oregonian*.

> "Royko, perhaps in an attempt at humor or perhaps in an effort to distract readers from the focus of that trial, suggests that violence within a marital framework is a joking matter, and that what was really at issue were the personal habits of the Rideouts.
>
> "However, rape was the issue, and rape is not a joke."
>
> (1/24/79, p. D10.)

Art Buchwald's column on the Rideouts, widely syndicated like Royko's, was no less mocking. He took the same position and a similar tone. The column ran in several papers on January 21, under the head, "Get Rideoutta Here you Crazy Maniac, I Love You."[18] It opened with a tongue-in-cheek claim: "I don't know anyone in this country who has taken a stronger position on rape than this columnist. I've been against it."

Buchwald wrote of his indignation at John's acquittal, then tackled the reconciliation, drawing on the myth that rape is sex and women like it:

> After attempting to send her husband to the prison farm, Greta decided it was all a big mistake and she loved him in spite of what he had done to her, or maybe because he had . . .
>
> I must admit that all during the well-publicized trial, my wife kept

> saying, "You're being too hard on John Rideout. There is more to this story than Greta is admitting."

What does Buchwald's wife supposedly bring up? *Gone With The Wind.* Only this time, instead of decrying the myth that women like rape glorified by the film, as Richard Cohen had done in his earlier column on the case, Buchwald used it to explain Greta's actions.

> "The next scene showed Vivian in the morning in a rumpled bed with the happiest smile she had on her face during the entire picture."
>
> "Are you trying to say John Rideout is Clark Gable?"
>
> "Not necessarily," she said, "but Greta Rideout could be another Vivian Leigh."

Buchwald concluded with the very statement feminists watching the case must have feared the most: "I'll never take sides in another husband–wife rape case again without thinking of *Gone With the Wind.*" In other words, he will never hear of another wife rape case without thinking that women like to be raped.[19]

The lack of understanding on the part of these columnists was certainly due to their attitudes toward women and marriage, but it was also fed by the mocking tone of the reporters covering the case and by the absence of any explanation for why the couple was back together. With no one willing to explain why Greta had returned to John, there was nothing to contradict the "women like rape" and "women cry rape for revenge" myths that dictated the general view of the reconciliation.

The Cycle of Violence: Missing the Story Again

To those knowledgeable in the field of domestic violence, Greta's return to John was not only unsurprising, but expected. The Rideout's reconciliation was part of the pattern of fighting and making up that characterizes violent relationships—the "cycle of violence," as it has been dubbed by psychologists.

Researchers and counselors describe domestic violence as typically following this pattern[20]: The woman, usually in a rigidly traditional role as wife, is financially and emotionally dependent on the man, often with children to support. She may have been abused as a child, and thus know of no other type of intimate relationship than a violent one. She may suffer from low self-esteem, or she may simply have fallen into a trap that financial and emotional circumstances prevent her from escaping.

The man in this pattern is typically possessive, jealous, and yet insecure. He may feel or actually be powerless in the world and he bolsters his faltering self-esteem by dominating the woman. He usually begins to assert his power over her with emotional abuse—he constantly denigrates her, tells her she is no good as a mother or as a sexual partner and that she is neither smart nor attractive nor interesting. He tries to isolate her from friends and family, and often discourages her from having a job by telling her she is not intelligent enough to hold one. He gradually escalates his abuse to hitting, beating, and sometimes to raping her. It is common that when she becomes pregnant his attacks on her increase—battering men usually aim for the pregnant woman's abdomen—a reflection, probably, of his need to hold her in subjugation to him and him only and his fear of rivals.

As the woman's self-esteem sinks even further under this treatment, she becomes too ashamed of herself to reach out for help. Meanwhile, after each spell of violence, he expresses remorse, apologizes, and promises never to do it again—often feeling genuinely full of self-hatred for his actions—and they bask in the pleasant aftermath of forgiveness. The woman hangs on, hoping she can believe him and that she can save the relationship and not have to face life alone, struggling to support a child and a job—something she by now feels incapable of doing. The man continues to be adoring and remorseful one day, resentful and jealous of her the next. Thus, the "cycle of violence" is set—a fight, remorse, reconciliation, another fight, and so on.[21]

Greta and John fit this pattern perfectly, as was proven both by the events that unfolded after the trial, and by the descriptions of their relationship Greta gave to the few reporters who listened. She was financially dependent on him, isolated from her family, and burdened with a small child and no job. He was jealous, possessive, deeply insecure, constantly denigrating to her, and increasingly violent.

Greta first described the violence in her marriage in her early interview with Liddick of the *Los Angeles Times*, the story that was published two weeks before the trial. In it, she said that John had beaten and threatened her several times and that she had left him twice before. "Let's just say there was a lot of violence in our marriage," Greta said. "When I tried to express my opinion, he couldn't stand it. He couldn't understand I wanted to be my own person."

Greta's account of John's violence was so convincing to Liddick, especially once it was backed up by the crisis counselors to whom Greta had gone for help, that Liddick said she became terrified of John herself. "I was told that he was living with his Mom," she said. "So I drove out to this country farmhouse, hoping for the story that I would get to meet him and interview him, but at the same time thinking, 'God I hope he's not home. He scares me to death.' "

Even though Liddick's story was widely syndicated and one of the first to attract the press's attention to the case, her description of the violence between John and Greta was ignored both by the trial attorneys and the rest of the mainstream media. Greta was never widely described as a battered wife, nor was the alleged rape linked to the pattern of violence she claimed to have suffered at John's hands. (Columnists Ellen Goodman and Judy Mann, and even McDonough of *The Oregonian*, did mention domestic violence in connection with the case, but they never recognized Greta as a battered wife trapped in the cycle of violence.) The only exception to this silence was a posttrial interview by Michelle Celarier, which ran in the alternative newspaper, *In These Times*. Celarier ignored the fact of John's acquittal in this story, accepting only Greta's side of the story, which was certainly biased, but she nevertheless provided important information missed by the rest of the press:

> It seems his violence against her has increased since they were married two years ago, from slaps and mental abuse to beatings which left her face bruised and swollen. Their sexual activity, too, had become increasingly violent, finally turning into rape on Oct. 10, a day when her resistance initially was the strongest.

Later in the story, Celarier quoted Greta describing John's violence in more detail:

> "At times I'd be laying there, watching TV, and he'd walk up and kick me. I started feeling, god, he's weird . . ."
>
> "He was in love with me when I was weak, but when I showed any strength, he hated my guts . . ."
>
> "He would see pretty women, strong career women, on TV or in magazines, and they seemed 'prudish' to him. He'd get worked up and say, 'jeez, I'd like to rape that bitch's ass.' "

Finally, Celarier put Greta in the wider context of battered women.

> Like most battered women, Greta Rideout had been afraid to fight back. The relationship became one of "love–hate, love–hate." John even

> threatened to sexually manipulate their daughter and told his wife he would show Jenny "what sex is all about" when she became an adolescent.
>
> "At times he'd turn to me and say, 'I'm sick, aren't I?' " Greta said, and her love began to turn to pity. "I kept thinking maybe I can help him." (*In These Times*, 1/10–16/79, pp. 3, 8.)

I asked Janet Evenson why so few of the local reporters recognized that Greta was a battered woman. She said that she could not recall any discussion in the newsroom on the subject. "Unfortunately, feminism is something I have never written much about," she mused. "And unfortunately, as a newspaper, we ignored it rather badly. We just focused in on this as a trial, not looking at the bigger picture." Evenson said she had attributed the couple's reconciliation to their youth.

"They were very young and thrust into this public eye. Even at the time when I wrote the story, I thought, 'Gee some of the things these kids are saying are so inane, but they're saying it and I'm paid to report it,' so I did. But their youth is what struck me more than the thought of the battered woman syndrome. Of course now I look back and, yes, it was classic."

Kenny of the UPI said he interpreted the reconciliation in much the same way as Evenson. "They were young, unsophisticated people and the pressure or attention from the media and from the general public had put them in the spotlight and they weren't able to handle that. They knew each other best of anyone else that was around them—the lawyers, the reporters—so they naturally gravitated towards each other." Kenny added that he, too, was unaware of the material on battered women available at the time, and that it never occurred to him to link the Rideouts' case with it. "In general the whole topic of battered women and violence in the family is more public now," he said. "I don't recall it being discussed in the legislature or anywhere when I was a reporter in Salem, Oregon."

McDonough said she, also, was unaware of the issue of battered women. "I don't recall my editors ever even talking to me about the story or how we would cover it. We were a classic large but small-town newspaper with men at the top, and they just didn't think about things like [women's issues]. And I just wasn't trained to look beyond what my job was."

Linda Kramer of the AP was more experienced. She, at least, had read parts of *Against Our Will* and was aware of the issue of rape from being a reporter in the San Francisco Bay Area, which was ahead of much of the world on this matter. Nevertheless, Kramer said, the concept of the "cycle of violence" and the link between rape and violence were not known to her at the time. She said that even the local women's crisis center workers, who at least saw Greta as a battered wife, failed to recognize—or were not quoted as recognizing—the reconciliation as part of the cycle of violence. In her AP story about the reconciliation, she quoted the crisis workers as saying only that John had a new, "converted" point of view about rape, revealing that they were making the same mistake battered wives make—accepting the man back in the hope that he has reformed:

> "He said he had a brand new view of the problems women have and that he felt the rape law is right," the worker said. "A man should not be able to rape his wife. I was very impressed with what he was saying. He seems real sincere." (*L.A. Times*, 1/10/9, p. 1)

Yet the subject of domestic violence was not, in fact, so obscure. Articles about "wife battery" were appearing regularly in the Sunday magazines of newspapers and in mainstream women's magazines at the time; references to battered women were sprinkled throughout the Rideout coverage by *Washington Post* reporter Cynthia Gorney, by Betty Liddick of the *L.A. Times,* and even by Kramer herself. In addition, among the alternative press the subject was well known, as the *In These Times* article revealed. Indeed, Liddick said she initially approached the story because she saw it as an example of domestic violence: "I did stories about abortion, childbirth, rape and battered women because they reflected the times, satisfied my social conscience and were exciting to write about and to help educate the public." Liddick said she had no trouble understanding the reconciliation, although, unfortunately for Greta, she was no longer writing about the story by then. "I thought it was typical of people in that kind of situation," she said. "There is a terrible link, each person psychologically is getting something from that relationship and it's hard to let go. It's unhealthy and it feeds a lot of less than healthy needs." Even the local crisis workers were quoted saying they hoped Greta's case would help abused women everywhere. Yet the link between the Rideouts' reconciliation and the cycle of violence was never made in print.

The reason I emphasize this lack of insight is because a recognition of the link between Greta as a battered woman and her return to John would have gone a long way toward rescuing her from ridicule and toward educating the public about battered women in general. That was not to be, however, even when events bore out that link just a few months later.

The Dark Side

Even before the Rideout saga moved on to its next chapter, there was one clue that all was not as well with the couple as the press assumed. At the same time as the reconciliation was reported, so was the fact that Greta had been evicted from her apartment two weeks after the trial. The reason she was evicted, according to all reports, was that her brother-in-law, the one she had accused of raping her, had arrived at her apartment in an apparent fury at the reconciliation, and upon not being admitted, had kicked down her door. Shocked at the damage, the landlord evicted Greta. This strange piece of extraneous violence was reported by the press in the most casual of tones: "Mrs. Rideout was evicted from the apartment Monday because of a door allegedly kicked in by the brother-in-law, the crisis worker said."[22] (This sentence is an amusing example of the lengths reporters have to go to to sound neutral. The phrase she was evicted "because of a door" does not even make sense.)

No one seemed to have followed up this tidbit with a question about the brother-in-law's motives or an with an attempt to interview him or Greta about it. The incident was mentioned in passing as all but insignificant, another bizarre occurrence in this woman's sordid life. Later, however, more clues came out, foreshadowing what was to come.

On March 5, two months after the reconciliation and after the couple had retreated from the public eye, Kramer conducted her one major interview with Greta in the Rideouts' apartment.

> Tacked on the wall of John and Greta Rideout's sparsely furnished apartment is a hand-lettered sign: "Love can endure all things."
>
> But the Rideouts, who captured national attention when wife accused husband of rape then stunned everyone by kissing and making up, are still having their problems.
>
> Greta Rideout says the couple has yet to visit a marriage counselor.
>
> "We should," she said. "Things aren't peachy keen around here."
>
> The couple has other loose ends untied.

The piece went on say that the Rideouts had not followed through on any of the other good intentions they had declared to the world upon their reconciliation: They had not joined a church, they had not volunteered to work with a women's crisis center, and John had not found a full-time job. In short, the couple was broke, isolated, and worried.

On looking back at this story, Kramer said she remembered having a sense of the couple being unhappy. "I remember sitting with Greta and talking at the kitchen table, and John was supposed to be sleeping in the back room. Basically, I saw them as dressed up and put on display by interest groups and groomed for the trial, and those weren't the real people. They were blemished people. And away from what we'd now call the spin control doctors, the ragged ends were visible, which were that their marriage had always been on again off again. Everything had been on and off. Jobs had been on and off, the relationship had been on and off. But what I wouldn't have recognized at the time was the violence."

Kramer's piece ended, hauntingly, with this paragraph.

> "It would be nice to be settled and financially secure like everyone else," [Greta] said, smoking a cigarette and looking around the $300-a-month apartment she says they no longer can afford. "When we signed the six-month lease we thought John would be working fulltime."[23]

The Divorce

Four days after this story was published, Greta left John and filed for divorce. Reading Kramer's two stories in juxtaposition leaves the impression that Greta had fled the house only hours after Kramer left her.

> The on again, off again marriage of John and Greta Rideout was off again Friday. Mrs. Rideout, who accused her husband of rape and then reconciled with him, has filed for divorce.*
>
> Rideout said he hadn't seen his wife or their 3-year-old daughter, Jenny, since Tuesday. He said he received a note from her saying that she was leaving.
>
> Greta left all her clothes at their north Salem apartment, Rideout said.[24]

Later in the story, Kramer quoted Burt, John's clever defense attorney.

*Greta had actually filed for divorce a long time earlier and had left the papers active. This time she merely reactivated them—au.

"I wouldn't be surprised if they got back together again.

"I'm just talking about the history of their relationship. It's been an on-again, off-again thing."

I asked Kramer if she had foreseen the divorce. "I got a sense that they weren't very together people and that this isn't working," she said, "but I didn't have the context." Because she did not recognize the signs of violence in the marriage, Kramer explained, she did not see just how bad it had gone.

By the time of the divorce, both the national and the local press were clearly fed up with the Rideout story. Sandra McDonough did not cover the divorce at all—she was determined never to write another Rideout story again. Janet Evenson wrote a fairly small page one story on it for the *Statesman Journal*, under the modest head, "Rideout Reconciliation fails; divorce hearing date is set," quoting Burt as saying, "They're just youngsters with a lot of problems." (Prosecuting Attorney Gortmaker was not quoted on the reconciliation, so once again Greta's side was not heard.) *The New York Times* printed a two-inch item about it under their "Notes on People" column, and none of the other papers carried more than short versions of the wire stories. After all the vilification Greta received for the reconciliation, it seems odd that she got so little attention for leaving John after all. Evenson explained: "I think the story had literally written itself to death. They had unlisted telephones and finding them was a little bit difficult, but a lot of it was that everybody was tired of them . . . we were just doing a kind of perfunctory follow-up job without exploring any of the messages behind it."

John in Trouble

In spite of Burt's predictions, Greta did not return to John again, and the divorce was finalized in May 1979. Kramer remembered a story she did for the AP at the time: "Leafing through my clips, I noticed a lead about the divorce and it had the word amicable in it. An amicable divorce. I stopped and thought, 'Was that my word or New York's word [meaning the editor's]? If it was my word it sort of jumps out at me. It's probably an indication that I was not educated about the cycle of violence. I wrote pretty much what was happening without putting it in a context, which of course is a wire service tendency anyway. I see that context is lacking now. It would have been nice to have a quote from somebody like Del Martin [author of *Battered Wives*] saying this is typical of the cycle."

It would have been even nicer to have such a quote the following September, when John was found guilty of trespassing in Greta's apartment. As if he had read the textbook on the behavior of violent husbands, he had been pursuing Greta, threatening and harassing her until, once again, she filed charges against him.[25] This time, John was found guilty, charged with breaking into Greta's home (he had torn off the chain lock, damaging the molding around the door), and was sentenced to two years probation and a nine-month suspended sentence, provided he get some counseling and have no unsupervised contact with his ex-wife.

Three months later, John was in court again. Under the head, "John Rideout faces legal trouble," Evenson wrote:

> Among other things, Rideout stands accused of having contacted his ex-wife, who now goes by her former name, Greta *X*, without supervision . . .
>
> Rideout allegedly yelled obscenities at *X* outside a North Salem cocktail lounge, and later followed her when she left the lounge . . .
>
> Rideout had telephoned, "saying he was coming down to Salem and that when he found her, there would be 'a lot of hell.' "
>
> (*Statesman Journal*, 1/18/80.)*

John was also accused of violating his probation by refusing to cooperate with any program of mental health. He was found guilty and sentenced to nine months in jail. He served forty days.

Even at this point the press paid almost no attention. *The New York Times* picked the story up in a one-inch AP piece under a tiny head at the bottom of an inside page,[26] but the story was nowhere to be found anywhere else. Even the columnists were silent. Liddick, who is now managing editor of the *New Leader* in Springfield, Missouri, gave her view of the omission:

"I don't think that it's peculiar to sex cases that newspapers don't follow the story. Newspapers generally do a poor job in following stories. Our attention span is fairly short, we'll latch on to a good hot issue, go at it for all its worth and then a year later, when it's appropriate to do a whatever happened to so-and-so, we don't do a good job."

---

*I have excised Greta's maiden name from this story to protect her current privacy—au.

The lack of coverage at this stage was unfortunate because most people now thought of the Rideouts as a silly couple who had aired their marital troubles in public, instead of as a couple trapped in the nightmare of domestic violence. John finally served time for harming Greta, after the world had chosen to vindicate him and mock her, and virtually no one heard about it.

The Movie

During the years that the Rideouts had been in and out of the news, two women had obtained exclusive rights to the story from both John and Greta and had filmed a television movie about them. The movie, named *Rape and Marriage—the Rideout Case* was shown on CBS in October 1980, a year after John had served his short sentence. Although the movie did not explore what had eventually happened to John and Greta, when the reviews came out the case was revived briefly in the press and a few readers, at least, learned about the final chapters of Greta and John's lives.

The movie received mostly favorable reviews, although it was acknowledged that the couple and the case had been prettied up. Ron Cowan, who reviewed it for the *Statesman Journal,* said the film portrayed the Women's Crisis Center as having manipulated "the bewildered Greta into legal action"—the argument defense attorney Burt had made against Greta in court. In interviewing the local crisis counselor about the movie, however, Cowan did get across the long overdue view of Greta as a battered woman on the run: "She's out of the state right now and working," said Bibelheimer. "She wanted to get out of here. She was afraid. She was afraid of another run-in with John." (10/29/80, p. C1).

Howard Rosenberg also updated the public on the Rideouts in his review for the *Los Angeles Times* by mentioning two little-known facts: that John had been jailed and that Greta's attorney, Gary Gortmaker, had been sentenced to four years in prison and disbarred for life for theft of public funds.[27]

In spite of the movie and its reviews, however, the end of the Rideout case remained widely unknown. Today, I have found that people remember the rape and the reconciliation, but very few remember the divorce. Almost no one knows about John's jail term. Thus, Greta went down in history as a woman who accused her husband of raping her and then went back to him—a woman, like Scarlett O'Hara, who likes rape.

Epilogue

Through contacts in the field of rape and women's rights, I was able to interview Greta herself in June 1991, after this chapter was written. Because I was not able to contact the victims in any other case in this book (two of them are dead, the third in hiding from the press), in the interest of balance I have confined Greta's comments to this epilogue. They are recorded here for posterity.

Greta: "It's taken me eleven to twelve years to be able to sit and talk about this without getting angry or upset. Now I'm at the point where either way it doesn't matter, except the movie still irritates me. (The movie said terrible things about my parents throwing me out that just weren't true. They've been very supportive.) I've done a lot of reading and educating myself about battered women's syndrome now. I went to college for a year and majored in journalism in Salem afterwards. I was young and naïve and uneducated then, it's true, but now I think I can have a pretty objective point of view of the whole thing."

HB: Do you regret having gone through the trial?

Greta: "At first I thought the trial made my ordeal worse. I was literally put on trial. I was shamed in court and it took me a long time to get an objective view on that. I was only twenty-one, with not much of a past. I'm thirty-five now and have a big past. If it happened now, imagine what they would do!

"But now I'm glad I had the courage to do it. It gave me the impetus to get out of the relationship and to get a more objective insight on what was happening to me and John. And it helped me realize that no, I didn't deserve it.

"Also, I feel protected now with all of this behind me—and John has left me alone. I've not seen or talked to him since 1980. I took action after he raped me and I took action again after I'd left him and he broke down my door. He knows he cannot terrorize me for the rest of my life, or his daughter. Had I tried to deal with it on my own I might have ended up dead. He did threaten to kill me. After he beat me up and raped me that time, he dragged me into the bathroom and smashed my face up against the mirror and said, 'Everytime you disobey me this'll happen to you. If you go to the police, I'll kill you.' (The movie left that out. I think they were afraid he'd sue them.) But I went to the police anyway."

HB: How do you view your reconciliation with John now?

Greta: "I had a lot of guilt and low self-esteem about going back to John because people turned against me. But I think I did it because I didn't have anyone I was close to and nor did John. My sister was there, in Salem—she was never even called as a witness, even though John's half-brother and sister-in-law were—but my relations with her were not good then. And I had no money. I got fired from my job because of the trial. Then John kept saying he was sorry and he still loved me. We got into being reborn Christians—I was in a fantasy world, trying to look at the bright side. I remember thinking, 'Everybody is against me anyway, what do they care?' I went in and out of denial. I hoped he'd get help and change, and I was vulnerable and depressed. So I went back to him sincerely. I thought I was still in love, I was still drawn to him, and we had a high when we first got back together. That lasted a while. Then I could see the high dropping and the escalating potential violence again. He didn't abuse me during the two months we were back together, but then at the end he kept me prisoner for two days. That's when I knew he wasn't going to change—I knew that I'd leave him and never go back. So I escaped. But once I did I went through quite a depression. I remember reading in the Del Martin book *[Battered Wives]*, I think it was, that both members of the couple get depressed and withdrawn when they finally break up. Often the man, the batterer, has a breakdown because the pattern is very addicting."

HB: How has your life been affected by your relationship with John and all that happened during and after the trial?

Greta: "It definitely affected me in the area of marriage. I do have a fear of getting married. I'm afraid the man will change, and a violent or domineering side of him will come out that I didn't see before. I was engaged to someone for seven years who was real jealous and possessive, and I was afraid to marry him.

"I've been bringing up my daughter on my own and working. I've gone to counseling, I've been reading, getting psychological help, going to school on and off for ten years. After the trial, I lost so much weight from nervous tension that I got down to eighty-eight pounds. But now my mental and physical health are very good."

HB: How were you affected by the press reports of the case?

Greta: "I felt a lot of anger at the press, I got upset. You don't want people reading and believing things about you that aren't true."

Discussion

What could the reporters have done to avoid these untruths and to counteract the final, damning image of Greta as a woman who likes rape?

They should have recognized the case as one of domestic violence and educated themselves about the issue. Had they thought of looking up rape and domestic violence in the library, they could have portrayed John and Greta's reconciliation with insight instead of mockery.

They should have followed up when the divorce and John's subsequent troubles were announced, which would have enabled them to take the story more seriously and to recognize Greta's behavior as contrary to the Scarlett O'Hara stereotype fostered by the defense attorneys.

They should have resisted the temptation to laugh at Greta and John for their youth, class, and lack of sophistication. Their scorn for the couple was snobbery, which does not belong in responsible reporting.

Finally, they should have resisted the attorneys' attempts to manipulate them into portraying Greta as the vamp of the rape narrative.

The fact that the reporters, as well-intentioned and careful as most of them were, failed to meet these standards was a function of habits in the newsroom and the power of the rape narrative.

As Kenny of UPI pointed out, newsroom habits do not traditionally allow court reporters the time to research the background of a case, especially when that background falls into a fringe realm such as women's issues. Nor, as Liddick said, do newsroom habits encourage reporters to follow up on an old story—the search is always for the new, the hot, the scoop. Newsrooms also do not encourage reporters to be aware of their class, race, or gender biases, as the rest of this book will illustrate. Finally, court reporters tend to fall victim to attorneys because they are fettered by legal restraints and lack of time, and because many are ignorant of the legal system, intimidated by lawyers, and not enterprising enough to report independently of what goes on in court each day.

The tendency to turn against Greta was also, as discussed, a function of the rape narrative. A look at the rape myths and ingredients listed in Chapter 1, which bias the public against a sex-crime victim, reveals that Greta had seven of the eight myths against her. She not only knew her alleged assailant, she was married to him; no weapon was used to give the public or press a reason to pity her; she was of the same race, class, and ethnic group as her supposed assailant; she was young; and she was perceived as attractive. The only ingredient in her favor was that she was not deviating from her traditional womanly role when the rape was supposed to have occurred—she was at home with her daughter. The defense quickly took care of that by trumpeting her supposed lesbian and extramarital affairs, abortions, and "serious sexual problems" in court—by painting her as a social deviant. Those biasing ingredients enabled both the defense and the press to push Greta into the unsympathetic role of vamp in the rape narrative—the woman who teases and tempts the man, then cries rape for revenge. Greta thus fell victim both to the foibles of press habits and to the worst of the rape myths.

My belief that the reporters could have done a better job on this story is backed up by the fact that three of them did: Gorney of the *Washington Post*, Liddick of the *L.A. Times*, and Celarier of *In These Times*. These three all went beyond the obvious reporting and the manipulations of the attorneys to look deeper into the background of the story. Although they were not covering it on a daily basis, and Liddick, at least, had the luxury of time in which to research the story, they did show that there were other approaches possible. Unfortunately, no one else followed up on these approaches and the stories remained solitary and uninfluential, ignored either out of sheer busyness or because people were unwilling to hear the message behind them: That rape is battery, that battery is commonplace, and that this case was not about a foolish romance, but about domestic assault.

The reporters I interviewed about the Rideout case acknowledged the weakness in their coverage and talked about how they would cover it differently now. Kramer, for instance, said that any prosecuting attorney today would not only recognize that the case fit into the cycle of violence, but would bring in experts on wife battery to testify in court. She also said that she would challenge the attorneys now that she is more experienced. Still, would Greta be treated with more understanding today? Would the case be seen as one of domestic violence, or is the shared narrative of victim as bad girl still too strong? Would she be portrayed as a battered woman fighting back, or as the vamp in the rape narrative, seducing her assailant and then crying rape for revenge? One only has to look at more recent cases to see.

·4·

"She Should be Punished"

The 1983–1984 New Bedford "Big Dan's" Gang Rape

One Sunday night in March 1983, in the small city of New Bedford, Massachusetts, a young woman ran, screaming, out of Big Dan's Tavern. Wearing only a sock and a jacket, she flagged down a passing pick-up truck for help. Sobbing and shaking, she told the driver that she had been gang-raped.

The story was quickly labeled the "Big Dan's pool table rape" by the local press and became a national fixation within days. The case was disturbing not only because the woman had been attacked by at least six men in a public place, but because she had told police that a roomful of men had cheered during the rape instead of helping her. Virtually overnight, columns and letters appeared all over the country likening the Big Dan's rape to the killing of Kitty Genovese (described in Chapter 2) and chiding the accused men, society in general, and individual citizens for allowing such a brutal crime to occur.

The Genovese parallel, however, was only the beginning of the press's interest in Big Dan's. The case was taken up by feminists and a huge candlelight march was held in New Bedford protesting violence against women a week after the rape, Gloria Steinem sent a letter to be read to the crowd, local feminists spoke, and grandmothers, men, and children turned out to lend their support. The press covered the march at length and the country was reminded that this was no longer 1964, the year of Genovese's death, nor 1979, the year of Greta and John Rideout's misunderstood day in court—this was the 1980s and women were enlightened and angry about rape. Meanwhile, another vocal group was waiting in the wings with a very different point of view: the local Portuguese.

New Bedford is known as a home for first and second generation immigrants from Portugal. Their presence is so prominent (about 60 percent of the population) that the telephone book is thick with Portuguese names, and many of the local stores display signs in Portuguese only. It is not surprising, then, that most of the people involved in the case were Portuguese themselves: the six accused men were all first generation immigrants, the victim was of Portuguese descent, the district attorney, the police chief, and half the jury were Portuguese-Americans, and the leader of the local feminist protest had a Portuguese surname. Nevertheless, the New Bedford Portuguese saw the coverage of the case as a slight to their community and an instance of bigotry. Before long "Big Dan's" was as much about ethnic prejudice as it was about rape, a conflict that resulted in pitting the Portuguese and their traditionalist views against the victim and antirape activists.

The case also brought up another issue that is important to this book: the printing of a rape victim's name. Unlike the Rideout case, the use of the New Bedford victim's name became a huge source of contention in the press. Editorials and letters debated it, every argument was considered, and newspapers chose different solutions.

The New Bedford rape, therefore, is fascinating for several reasons. It evolved into a blatant example of the way women are regarded once they become rape victims; it revealed the inherent class prejudices of the press and the public; it exposed the raw nerves of downtrodden immigrants in America; and it put the press to an unusual test—a test of how to be fair in the light of violent feelings, extreme and opposing points of view, and vociferous criticism.

The Case

The victim of the Big Dan's rape had been born and brought up in the North End of New Bedford. Abandoned by her mother in infancy, she was raised by her great-grandmother in a Portuguese-speaking household until she was five, when she moved to her grandparents' big house in New Bedford. Although she saw her mother occasionally, she never knew her father. The family lived primarily on welfare.

The girl spent her whole life in New Bedford. She attended local schools until she dropped out of high school because she was pregnant with a son, and then moved into an apartment with her boyfriend and had two more children. Employed intermittently, she continued to depend on welfare.[1] She and her boyfriend fought constantly and ended up having what a neighbor called a "platonic relationship"[2]; however, they kept on living together.

On March 6, 1983, the woman, by now twenty-one, celebrated her older daughter's third birthday with a small party. That evening, after putting her children to bed, she left her boyfriend to watch over them and went out to buy cigarettes. She walked to Big Dan's Tavern, a bar two blocks from her home, and once inside ordered a drink and chatted with the waitress, whom she knew. She stayed for a while, drinking and talking to people in the bar.

Some time later, as she told it, she was pushed to the floor by several men, her jeans were forcibly pulled off, and she was carried, struggling, crying and shouting for help, to the pool table at the back of the small bar. There she was raped, forced into oral sex, hit, held down, and molested by at least four men while others watched and perhaps cheered. No one tried to stop the assault and no one called the police.

After so many assaults she lost count, the woman managed to break free and run out of the door. Screaming and only half dressed, she ran into the street waving for help. A pick-up truck stopped and the men inside covered her and took her to the police station, where she explained what had happened. The police took her back to the bar, with her consent, where she identified some of her assailants, who were still hanging around drinking and, some said, boasting of the rape.

Four men were arrested on charges of aggravated rape—gang rape—and two others were arrested on charges of joint enterprise, which means encouraging an illegal act and doing nothing to stop it. The men were brought to trial in the nearby town of Fall River, Massachusetts.

The Reporting

The Big Dan's case received meticulous attention from the local press for more than a year, from the beginning of March 1983, when the rape occurred, to April 1984, after the two tandem trials of the accused were over. The local papers I have examined are the New Bedford *Standard-Times*, which was the first paper to find the story; the *Portuguese Times*, a small, Portuguese-language weekly also located in New Bedford; the *Providence Journal*, the metropolitan newspaper of Rhode Island; the *Boston Herald*, a tabloid; and the *Boston Globe*.[3] The reporters who covered the story for these papers were mostly men—the ratio was twenty-five men to ten women—but several women covered the trials virtually by themselves.

On the out-of-state newspapers, I looked at the *L.A. Times* and *The New York Times,* whose stories on the case were all by men; at *The Washington Post,* which gave the case a lot of attention and assigned only women to the story; and at *Newsweek,* which contributed its usual one page to the case, with no byline. On the whole, the national news relied on wire stories, also mainly written by men, which were often rewrites of the local reporters' stories.

As in the Rideout case, television was a prominent presence. A cable station covered the trial live, local television was all over the courtroom, and the national networks gave the case a great deal of attention before and during the trial. The all-pervasive presence of television contributed to making the media part of the story itself, which elicited its own set of reactions among the public.

The First Week: The Crime and the Outrage

On the morning of March 7, 1983, Alan Levin, a twenty-six-year-old police reporter for the *Standard-Times* with two years' experience, arrived at the New Bedford police station to go through his routine check of the logs—the day-by-day record of reported crimes. When he stumbled upon an intriguing report of a gang rape in Big Dan's bar, he knew right away that the story was hot. "All we managed to get in were four paragraphs the next day," he said. "It was right on deadline. But I kind of made it a big deal because of the way the woman described it. It was so outrageous."

From the beginning, the story had all the makings of a hit. Katz (1987) found not only that crime news sells papers, but that newspapers prefer the kind of crime news that implies "some sort of teaching about the contemporary state of moral character," particularly of "personal moral competence."[4] Like the Genovese case, the New Bedford rape raised questions about the mores of urban society that made it a perfect vehicle for this sort of teaching. Cohen and Young (1973) also found that newspapers prefer covering solved rather than unsolved crimes, or at least those in which the suspects have been arrested, because a known suspect adds to the story, and this case fit that requirement, too[5]: Plenty of witnesses and neighborhood residents seemed eager to talk, even to brag about the event; several of the suspects incriminated each other in statements to reporters and to the police; and four of the suspects were arrested instantly. The New Bedford rape, therefore, was a news reporters' dream.

Levin's first story began:

> A young woman, surrounded by 12 to 13 jeering men Sunday night in a North End Bar, was brutally raped by at least four of them—so many times that she lost count, police said.
>
> (*Standard-Times*, 3/8/83, p. 1.)

He went on to give the elements of the crime that attracted so much attention and outrage.

> One witness said last night he did not intervene because the assault was none of his business. "Why should I care?" said the man, who spoke on the condition that he would not be named.
>
> The bartender, identified as Carlos Machado, told police he was afraid to call authorities. One of the men wielded a butter knife in the attack, Machado said.*
>
> The barroom was whipped into a lurid, cheering frenzy, as they watched the sexual assault, according to police and witness reports.

Levin's description of the "cheering" crowd and his choice of the words "lurid" and "frenzy" helped to attract other newspapers to the story. The very next day, March 9, the tabloid *Boston Herald* ran an enormous headline on page one: "BAR CROWD CHEERS AS WOMAN IS RAPED."

It was the cheering crowd, more than the actual rape, that inspired public horror and lent itself, like the Genovese murder, to gloomy examinations of societal mores.

> Take a look at the not-so-innocent bystanders in Big Dan's Tavern, folks. They're living proof that there is a level lower, and more to be despised, than absolute zero.
>
> They're occupying it.

---

*The existence of the knife was never substantiated in the trial, but another paper called it a kitchen knife. The difference between a butter knife—small and blunt—and a kitchen knife—large and sharp—is enormous: an example of how important a tiny detail of vocabulary can be.

> There's no excuse . . . not passion,* not booze, not an overwhelming desire to brutalize another . . . for the gang rape.
>
> But there's even less than that for the dozen or so drinkers who watched—and did nothing—while, police say, a woman who tried to leave the joint was stripped, thrown on a pool table, threatened with a knife, and repeatedly assaulted . . .
>
> The woman, whoever she was, must know how abandoned Kitty Genovese felt years ago, when her cries for help as she was being slain on a New York street went unheeded by apartment house tenants who heard her and did nothing—either out of fear or because they didn't want to get involved.
>
> As for the tenants, their counterparts drink in a New Bedford bar. (*Herald* editorial, 3/10/83, p. 27.)

A later *Boston Globe* editorial typified the mea culpa tone of many of the opinion pieces of the time:

> Are the patrons of Big Dan's much different from the rest of us?
>
> Probably not. That's the scariest part of this story . . .
>
> We all like to think we are different, of course. We must believe that we would stand alone in protest. . . . Still, this grim tale reminds us that failure is always a possibility, and of just how close we are to those who raped and those who watched and cheered.
>
> (3/16/83, p. 18.)

Once the public learned that the four suspects who had been arrested the day after the crime had been released on only $1,000 bail each, the outrage rose even higher. By the third day after the rape, the crime had been publicized enough to stir local women's groups to action: "Women on the march over barroom rape" (*Herald,* 3/11/83, p. 1).

Local feminist groups and the Women's Coalition Against Sexist Violence announced plans for a candlelight march to protest rape and "sexist violence." They were lead by a professor of political science at Southeastern Massachusetts University, Rita Moniz, who became the most quoted leader of the women's protest over the weeks to come. The protest, born of an era of feminist attention to rape, did much to help draw the sympathy of the nation to the victim and to the issue.

---

*The "rape is sex" myth, reflected by the suggestion that "passion" could motivate rape, is evident even in this piece sympathizing with the victim.

But amid all this high moral outrage was another element, at first a sleeper, that was later to explode: the Portuguese.

The Portuguese

Because of the location of Big Dan's Tavern in a Portuguese section of New Bedford, and because all the men accused of the rape were Portuguese, most of the newspapers included mentions of the Portuguese aspect of the case in their coverage. They did so, however, at very different stages of the story, and that timing had repercussions.

The *Standard-Times*, the leader in the initial coverage, was the first to mention that the rape had occurred in a Portuguese neighborhood. On March 9, its second day of covering the case, the paper ran a story by John Impemba, a twenty-eight-year-old reporter who had worked for two other dailies in Massachusetts before joining the paper a year before this case, describing the neighborhood as "a blue-collar community, only yards from a waterfront park where children play on sunny days. . . . The residents living nearby mainly speak their native tongue—Portuguese—or broken English . . ." (3/9/83.)

The next day, one of the suspects out on bail, Daniel Silva,[6] tried to escape by buying a ticket to his native Azores, a collection of islands off the coast of Portugal. His passport had expired, however, and a telephone call alerted the travel agent, who in turn notified the police. Silva was re-arrested, his and the other suspects' bails were raised, and all three suspects were jailed. (The fourth suspect had disappeared since his initial arrest but was found a few days later.) Yet even Silva's attempt to escape did not incite the rest of the papers to mention that he or the other suspects were Portuguese. Phil Kukielski, who reported the case for the *Providence Journal* and is now regional editor of three of the *Journal's* borough editions, explained why: "It's our conscious policy not to refer to race or ethnicity unless it's critical to the understanding of the story. Referring to someone in that community as Portuguese is odd because at least two-thirds of the people living in those communities are Portuguese. It's like writing a story out of Dublin and identifying someone as being Irish."

I asked James Ragsdale, editor of the *Standard-Times* why the Portuguese aspect of the case came up so often in his paper. His answer was very different from Kukielski's. "We abide by the standards that call for us not to refer to ethnic origin unless it is germaine to the story," he said, "but in this story it became germaine because it was part of the community itself. We had to explain, for example, why one of the defendants who was out on bail tried to skip town and couldn't because his passport had expired. The ethnic issue has to come into it there. But we didn't allow people to point derogatory fingers at the Portuguese as a whole."

The reason the *Standard-Times* emphasized the Portuguese aspect so much also may have been because, as the local paper, it felt obliged to cover local reaction to the case—and the local people reacting were Portuguese. In addition, the reporters on the *Standard-Times* got rather a shock when they discovered, it seems for the first time, just how Portuguese the North End of New Bedford was. Their surprise may have colored their reporting.

"The *Standard-Times* did not have any Portuguese-speaking reporters or editors," Impemba recalled. "When you went into the neighborhoods, started knocking on doors, and asking questions, it was an eye-opener to find out how heavily non-English speaking it was. I don't think until this incident that people at the newspaper, who were white, English-speaking people, fully understood how entrenched and foreign the North End neighborhoods were and still are."[7]

The dearth of Portuguese-speaking reporters at the *Standard-Times*, which has since been remedied, and its lack of concern for representing the local ethnic group on their staff could well have contributed to community resentment. It also could be argued that the editors and reporters on the local paper should not have been so surprised at the ethnicity of the area—they should have known that, as Impemba put it, "it wasn't just old-timers who couldn't speak English, it was people of all ages." That surprise suggests both some neglect on the newspaper's part and that the reporters on the case had really stumbled across two stories—the rape case, and the Portuguese-village aspect of New Bedford. Instead of covering the stories separately, however, they linked them, giving the impression that the Portuguese ethnicity of the defendants had something to do with the rape.

Whatever the reason for all this attention, the Portuguese community objected to it. Manuel Adelino Ferreira, editor of the local Portuguese-language newspaper, the *Portuguese Times*, located only a few blocks from Big Dan's, spoke to me about this. "The local press gave too much emphasis to the fact that [the suspects] were Portuguese immigrants," he said. "It became an ethnic issue which it should never have been. We were very angry because the press blamed an entire community for the action of a few."

I asked Ferreira how the press should have covered the case. "Maybe not mention the Portuguese at all," he replied. "They should cover that just like any story. We have a famous case here now, the Stuart case.[8] I don't know if they're English or Irish. Is that important?"

Ferreira's objection seems slightly odd in the light of the fact that one of the only two papers to mention the Portuguese during the first week of the case was the *Portuguese Times* itself. At the end of its first story on the crime was the sentence, "The 'Big Dan's Tavern' is located in an area of countless Portuguese families."[9] (The other paper to mention the ethnic angle was the *Boston Globe,* which described the neighborhood as "blue-collar, Portuguese-American.") Nevertheless, Ferreira was not alone in minding the ethnic emphasis, especially once a local radio station, WBSN, aired the comments of some New Bedford residents.

> Comments made over a New Bedford radio talk show throughout the week bothered many in this close-knit area. Some callers said the woman deserved what she got. Some pointed the finger at the entire Portuguese community. One Portuguese man said those comments were made by "animals." (Impemba, *Standard-Times*, 3/13/83, p. 1.)

This description was mild compared to what had actually been said on that radio show. Ragsdale and Ferreira explained that the WBSN show was run as a free-for-all, in which anyone could call up and say whatever they wanted. Many of the calls attacked the victim, but just as many attacked the Portuguese. "Some of these people would call up and say terrible things about the Portuguese," said Ragsdale. " 'Ship them all back on a boat,' and that kind of stuff. I recall listening at the height of everything. The venom and evil that was being poured out over the radio waves!"

Oddly, little more than the quote above was written about the radio show, so when the Portuguese began to criticize the media, it was hard for readers to understand why. First, they saw stories about the ethnic neighborhood in which the crime took place, and next they saw that the Portuguese were outraged about the coverage—but they were never told what had happened in the interim. This gap in the reporting, which occurred because of the editors' unwillingness to print ethnic slurs, even in quotes, contributed to the lack of understanding among the American press and public about why the Portuguese were so angry—a lack of understanding that exacerbated the Portuguese sense of being isolated and misunderstood.

The Press and the Victim

During the early stages of reporting this case, before much was known about the victim or the circumstances of the crime, the press treated her with care. Sensitized to rape by the women's movement, and appalled by the reports of the cheering crowd in the bar, the papers refused to name her, even though her identity had been revealed on police records and in court. Several papers ran stories about rape trauma and the new rape shield laws, designed to protect a victim from having her sex life dragged through court in a trial.[10] Columnists wrote many sympathetic pieces about rape victims and society's responsibility for the crime. In general, the first month's coverage revealed the relative enlightenment of the time, resisting the temptations of the rape narrative, treating rape as a societal rather than an individual problem, and attempting to recognize the victim's need for sympathy without blame.[11]

One of the best of these background stories was "Understanding gang rape patterns," by *Boston Globe* writer Gary McMillan. McMillan referred to research by leading people in the field of sexual assault, particularly Menachim Amir's oft-quoted 1971 study of rape[12] and Nicholas Groth's valuable work on sex offenders,[13] to explain to the reader just how common gang rape is and the forms it usually takes: McMillian wrote that one third of all rapes are committed by gangs; most victims are between twelve and nineteen; despite gang rapists' supposed strength in numbers, they are as likely to beat their victims as are lone rapists, although less likely to kill or mutilate them; and that a victim of gang rape is "far more likely to suffer from a variety of sexual acts and degradation" than the victim of a lone rapist. McMillan offered a profile of the typical rapist and went further than most other accounts in describing just how traumatized the victim would be, and why. He also explained the legal aspects of prosecuting gang rapes, and ended,

> [T]he violence and sheer numbers involved in gang rapes spreads a sharp and strong miasma of fear among all women. As one 14-year-old girl in Easton said last week after watching a television program about gang rape, "Mommy, this means I have to be afraid all my life."
>
> (*Globe*, 4/11/83, p. 1.)

Another example of the sympathetic coverage of this time was a well-intentioned but contradictory editorial in the *Providence Journal*, bemoaning the tendency of society to blame the victim while quoting someone doing it:

> "I've been a cop for 18 years," said Sgt. Ronald A. Cabral . . . "but I have never seen anything like this." He said the victim did not know any of the attackers and did not provoke the assault. "I checked it out, this girl was decent," he said. . . .
>
> Does an attitude prevail that women often invite attacks and therefore deserve what they get? Such insensitivity cries out for public attention and organized steps to counter it. (3/16/83, p. A16.)*

An early piece in the *Standard-Times* by Margaret Charig, the paper's main female reporter on the case, provided another example of the willingness of the press at this time to approach rape as a societal rather than only as an individual problem. Entitled, "The victim: Where can she find aid, support?," the story chronicled the reactions of victims to rape in general, quoted the district attorney on the case, Ronald A. Pina, saying the Big Dan's victim was "not in good shape," and explained the medical and psychiatric treatments available to rape victims. The piece was overly optimistic—it made the official treatment of victims sound too perfect and kind—but it provided useful information for rape victims, responded responsibly to the fear the stories about the crime must have awakened in the paper's female readers,[14] and reminded readers to consider the victim's point of view. It was the kind of story that should accompany rape accounts more often.

The initial sympathy for the rape victim was allowed not only because of the enlightenment about rape at the time but also, ironically, because of the rape narrative. None of the rape myths had been pulled out to use against the victim yet, but the defendants, on the other hand, fit all the worst stereotypes about rapists. They were not married to the victim, like John Rideout; they were not rich, upper class, particularly handsome, or "nice"—the men were foreign, lower class, and sleazy (even Manuel Ferreira said so†) and as such, they were easy to

---

*The editors were apparently unaware of the way they had perpetuated rape myths in this piece by insisting on the victim's "decency." It took a reader to point it out. "As quoted in the media, New Bedford police officials indicate that the victim of an alleged gang rape 'was a decent girl,' a fact that they had 'checked out' to their satisfaction. Such statements reinforce the concept that victims in such situations need somehow to be vindicated of complicity. . . . Only two paragraphs after quoting these police statements . . . a Journal editorial asks, 'Does an attitude prevail that women often invite attacks and therefore deserve what they get?' It appears that the editorial writer has, unwittingly perhaps, answered the very question posed." *Providence Journal*, 4/2/83, p. A11.

†"Two of them should be in jail—they're terrible kids," Ferreira said to me in an interview.

perceive of and depict as criminals. Because the defendants fit the weird stranger myth, therefore, the victim was at first allowed her innocence, as a rather odd headline in the *Standard-Times* reflected: "After tragedy, 'she'll never be innocent again.' "

The Second Week: The Candlelight March and the Portuguese Reaction

On Monday March 14, eight days after the rape, local women's groups prepared for a New Bedford march against sexist violence. The event was important to local people, but most significantly it was a showcase for feminists. It was a reminder to the public that rape had become a politicized crime, that awareness of rape was widespread, and that coalitions had been formed to fight victim-blaming myths. Rita Moniz was quoted saying, "New Bedford has had a long history of trivializing the role of women," and that she was determined to stop that from happening again.[15] Signs were waved declaring "Rape is Violence," and outrage was expressed at the men who watched the crime and did nothing to prevent it. The papers predicted that 1,500 people would show up for the march. They were wrong:

> **4,500 CHANT IN PROTEST OVER GANG RAPE IN BAR**
> More than 4500 men and women rocked the streets outside City Hall last night with a chant of "No More Rapes" in protest of the gang rape of a woman last week in a downtown bar.
>
> The crowd stood shoulder-to-shoulder, back-to-back . . . many of them carrying signs such as "Rape is Hate" and "Rape is Not A Spectator Sport." . . . There were almost as many men as women in the crowd and some demonstrators carried signs proclaiming "Men Against Rape."
> (*Herald*, 3/15/83, p. 3.)

The march both awakened the local public to the horror of sexual violence and attracted the national media. The Massachusetts papers were joined by the *L. A. Times, The New York Times,* and all three national television networks. "News reports of the protest are expected to be seen by nearly 50 million people on network news shows tonight" declared the *Standard-Times*.

Like any political protest, however, the march produced its empty slogans—"There's more anger here tonight than if a zoo had been bombed"—and its inflammatory statements—"Castration without anesthesia." It also produced its enemies; particularly, some of the local Portuguese. Their objection was the same one that Ferreira had raised.

> The New Bedford Portuguese community unfortunately has been associated with the case. The "local news," the American news, is identifying the supposed perpertators as elements of our ethnic group. . . .
>
> How could they attribute the responsibility to us or anybody from the Portuguese community?
>
> (*Portuguese Times*, 3/24/83, pp. 1–3.)

The *Portuguese Times* was particularly critical of the *Standard-Times* for continuing to emphasize the ethnic side of the story, even in its coverage of the candlelight protest, and of *The New York Times* for stories like this one by Dudley Clendinen:

> **BARROOM RAPE SHAMES TOWN OF PROUD HERITAGE**
>
> [T]he story . . . has caused great pain in a city that has been economically and psychologically depressed for two generations. The search for an explanation has stirred speculation about the character of the woman, the character of the bar and the character of the Portuguese community. (3/17/83, p. A16.)

"The perception I saw," said Ferreira, "was that this terrible thing happened here on account of the culture these people were from. That this was no part of American society because we in America don't do those terrible things. That this was a bunch of Portuguese immigrants who did this. That's what the media tried to portray. And it's not true. The United States is the most violent society in the world, and the rape rate is the highest."

The press, however, would not leave the ethnic issue alone. As the days went on, it grew to such proportions that it took on a life of its own, quite apart from the crime and from attention to the victim. Ragsdale said television was responsible for first waking up the national media to the ethnic side of the story. "When ABC brought in the news crew, they were all scrambling all over the city to find interpreters," he said. "Some of them got good interpreters and some of them got bad ones. There was a lot of bad information going out. That's when the ethnic issue became so enmeshed in the coverage that it never did get out of it."

In reaction, the *Portuguese Times* continued to run editorials and statements decrying the treatment of the Portuguese. As the Portuguese got angrier, an unfortunate development occurred: The community began to polarize into the local Portuguese for the defendants versus outside people for the victim.* Even more unfortunately, the Portuguese began to identify with the defendants and to blame the victim for all their troubles.

> CITY AGONIZES OVER "WHY?" IN POOL TABLE GANG RAPE
>
> The search for an explanation . . . has spawned dozens of rumors, many floated on a local radio station. . . . Several anonymous callers have claimed to know the victim and charged that (in one young man's words) "she was no innocent girl." But the police department, which has kept the victim's identity confidential, has told reporters that she is a "decent" young woman.
>
> Others callers have suggested that, by going into the bar alone, the victim brought her fate on herself. "I didn't think there were people who still thought that way," Moniz said, "but there are."
>
> (Doyle McManus, the *L.A. Times*, 3/16/83, pp. 1, 22.)

The Press as Detective: The Suspects' Story

The backlash against the victim, already strong in the community by mid-March, received an enormous boost when the suspects got a chance to tell their side of the story. This happened when local reporters, free to play detective before attorneys had clamped down on their clients, interviewed two witnesses to the crime, Jose Medeiros, twenty-two, an unemployed landscaper, and Virgilio Medeiros, twenty-two, an unemployed boat builder. (They were not related.) The *Boston Herald* ran the interview as a front page story by Joe Sciacca.

> The eyewitnesses said they saw the woman with one of the defendants at another end of the bar, hugging and kissing.
>
> The defendant suddenly grabbed the woman and pushed her to the floor, removing her pants and unbuckling his own. She did not appear to be resisting, the witnesses said, as the suspect got on top of her.
>
> The defendant was too intoxicated to have intercourse, they said, but picked up the woman and carried her to a green felt pool table at the back of Big Dan's.
>
> Two other men, who have also been arrested, went over to the pool

*Two defense funds were set up for the defendants at this point, which emphasized the polarization even more—some people were donating to the funds for the defendants, others to a fund for the victim.

table and forced themselves on the woman. One of them made her perform oral sex.

A fourth man has been charged in the incident, but the two witnesses said he was not involved.

When the other two men became involved, the woman began to cry and scream, the witnesses said.

"She kept saying, 'What did I do to you guys? What did I do to you guys?' " said Virgilio Medeiros.

The story went on to quote the witnesses claiming to have tried to help the victim and comfort her. Then, it added: " 'After the attack, the woman got off the table, hugged one of the defendants, and ran out the door,' Medeiros said." (*Herald*, 3/17/83, pp. 1, 15.)

One Medeiros was quoted as saying he wished he had helped her more. The other said, "At first I thought it was just a free show."

The very day the interview was published with the Medeiroses, they were arrested and charged as accessories before the fact. Even though their reliability as witnesses thus might seem compromised, their versions of the story were nevertheless quoted by the *Providence Journal*, the *Standard-Times*, and most of the other papers as a credible alternative to the victim's account.

The press made much of the differences between the victim's version of the rape, as recounted by the police, and that of the Medeiroses largely because the witnesses suggested that the original aspect of the crime that had so horrified the public—the cheering voyeurs—had never happened. Indeed, when antivictim sentiment increased during the trial a year later, many people were quoted as saying the cheering was a fabrication of the press. The seeds of that opinion were in the Medeiroses' testimony, as self-serving as it might have been. When I asked Alan Levin which version he thought the most accurate—the victim's crowd of cheering bystanders or the Medeiroses' five silent onlookers—he said:

"Frankly, I think sources confirmed the cheering. There was an older reporter at the paper at the time, who has since retired, who spoke Portuguese. He went up there on the second day, took off his tie and sat in the bar and asked what had gone on. He prepared a memo from what the bartender said which was shocking. It described twenty-two to twenty-four people in this scene of pandemonium, screaming. It made the woman's account pale. But none of that stuff ever got in the paper directly." (The reason that account was not printed, editor Ragsdale explained, was because the older reporter's Portuguese was not good enough for the paper to trust.)

Levin, too, had interviewed Virgilio Medeiros before he was arrested. He met him in Big Dan's during the first day or so after the rape. Levin said, "He confirmed a lot of this stuff then. He confirmed the shouting and he said people were yelling, 'Go for it, go for it!' He, of course, didn't see anything wrong with it and insisted that this woman had given him consent initially. But clearly the initial reports suggested that there were a lot of people in the bar."

Impemba, Levin's colleague on the *Standard-Times*, disagreed. He, too, said he went into Big Dan's on the day after the rape. "There were very few people in there and few could speak English," he said, "but my impression was that there was not this large group of cheering people that witnessed and participated in the event. The person who I think was single-handedly responsible for creating that image was Ron Pina, the district attorney. It was the language he used and the description he used that catapulted this situation into the limelight."

Impemba went on to say that, in retrospect, he does not trust the early press accounts because of the language barrier. "I, clearly, as a white, English-speaking reporter didn't fit into a heavily ethnic neighborhood like that. You stick out like a sore thumb. People are leery of your intentions down there. I think if there could have been more trust between the community and the press, we may have had more success getting the real facts of the case."

The new version of the rape by the Medeiroses was harmful to the victim and the reporters knew it, but their attempts to reach her for a statement failed. "We tried to get to talk to her but she wouldn't speak under orders by the cops and the D.A.," said Levin.

Impemba had the same trouble. "I remember going up to her third floor apartment," he said. "Her kids were playing outside the door. I made a very sympathetic approach—you know, not even with a notebook in hand. She said nothing and closed the door gently. It was clear that I wasn't welcome. It was unfortunate. The victim was traumatized, but if her family or someone close to her understood a little better that the press was only trying to ferret out the story, I think we would have been more successful at presenting a balanced account of things."

The only answer the victim did give to the Medeiroses' accusations was a statement issued through her lawyer.

> The woman who police say was raped by four men in a bar here charged yesterday that "there have been a lot of lies told and printed about me and this incident." . . .
>
> Alluding to some press reports and court testimony questioning her

> reputation and the circumstances surrounding the alleged rape, the woman said in her statement, "I wish people would not believe them and wait for the trial for the truth to come out."
>
> (Wendy Fox and Jonathan Kaufman, *Boston Globe*, 3/20/83, p. 21.)

While people waited, however, venom against the victim increased.

The Portuguese Attack the Media

During the flurry over the Medeiroses' interviews and arrests, the local Portuguese were organizing. They set up two defense funds for the accused men, and a group called The Portuguese Americans United (PAU) issued a statement declaring that the media attention had created "a psychological state of siege toward a particular ethnic group."[16]

> Due to the attention that this case has been getting, we are inclined to believe that inexcusable amounts of racial prejudice and discriminatory innuendoes have surfaced against the Portuguese throughout the area.[17]

By March 18, only twelve days after the rape, nearly every paper in the area was carrying stories about the PAU statement, and some of the editors were appearing on television in response to it.[18] Ferreira went on national television saying, "There is a resentment against the Portuguese. It may be hidden, but now it has resurfaced"[19]; Ragsdale rose to his paper's defense on ABC's "Nightline."[20]

I asked the *Standard-Times* reporters if there had been any inkling in the newsroom of the criticism that would be leveled at them by the Portuguese. "None at all," said Impemba. "If there was anything that flabbergasted me about the entire incident it was that bitter reaction in the Portuguese community."

Charig, however, had a different answer. "I think we knew that this had the potential to be a very volatile issue in the community. Even within the Portuguese community there were differences of opinion among immigrant populations: The second and third generation Portuguese, the fourth generation Portuguese, the more established ones. From the outset we knew that it was going to be a hot issue."

As a result of the PAU's statement, the press engaged in extensive self-examination over its handling of the ethnic issue during the next few days. Ragsdale chose to tackle the criticism head-on in an editorial, "The Story at Big Dan's: why we covered it as we did."

> [T]here was an awareness in our newsroom that reasonable minds in the community wanted to speak out on how the story affected the predominantly Portuguese neighborhood. Stories were published to allow expression for those views. . .
>
> [T]he community's reaction to such as incident—right down to a neighborhood's reaction—was fundamentally fused to the event itself.
>
> (*Standard-Times*, 3/27/83, p. 14.)

I asked the reporters who covered the case if they thought the Portuguese criticism fair. Some were as certain of their infallibility as Ragsdale sounded in his editorial, and attributed the Portuguese rage to a bottled up sense of discrimination that had been going on for decades and to the bigoted callers on the radio talk shows. For example, Kukielski of the *Providence Journal* said all the press was blamed for those calls. "After the arrests, every closet bigot who had some standing grudge against new immigrants went anonymously on the radio and said, 'You know the problem here is that we should get rid of all these immigrants. Everyone with a green card ought to be deported.' These are the radio talk shows that were on in all the factories, where so many of the local people work. All of a sudden everybody with a green card felt vulnerable.

"I suspect that somehow or other the press was at fault for not being sensitive enough," Kukielski added. "But what we should have done differently escapes me. [After the trial] there were 10,000 people marching on the streets of Fall River to protest the unfairness of something that, by my rights, was manifestly fair. Something got lost in the translation there."

Other reporters were less sure of whether they had been fair. Impemba, for example, said that the language barrier and being an outsider may have hampered his reporting and understanding of the Portuguese.

Ferreira seemed to disapprove of the media's approach to the story as much now as he had in 1983. He especially disliked the *Boston Herald's* coverage, he said, which he characterized as "very conservative on political and social issues, and very sensational about crime—a [Rupert] Murdoch paper." When I asked him to explain his objections further, he said: "The press portrayed the woman as very innocent. For example, I remember the reports saying 'the woman, mother of two.' It wasn't relevant but the image portrayed throughout the country was of a very innocent mother who decided one night to buy cigarettes. It was nothing like that."

I asked Ferreira how he saw the case, then, as he so disagreed with the press accounts of it. "The press portrayed her as a very innocent woman, which she was not," he replied. "She was a prostitute."

"How do you know she was a prostitute?" I said.

"It was a known fact."

"You mean she slept with men for money?"

"Yes. They tried to prove this in court but decided it was irrelevant. She was never married, she had two kids from different men and she was known by one of the men [in the bar]. She used to hang around in bars and stuff, you know. This doesn't make it right what they did." (Ferreira's memory is cloudy on this issue. In his own paper, in a story quite probably written by himself, since he wrote most of them, he quoted an unidentified witness to the rape as saying that "he didn't know the woman, and neither did the rest of the people at the bar that night.")[21]

I asked Ferreira again how he knew she was a prostitute.

"Well, I don't know," he conceded. "This was a common saying. The common word was that she was like a prostitute."

When I mentioned Ferreira's view to Kukielski of the *Providence Journal*, he strongly disagreed. "We looked into that to a certain extent," he said. "She had not been arrested as a prostitute and I never found any evidence for it. I don't believe she was." It is clear from this interview, however, that Ferreira shared his community's perception of the victim as a bad woman who brought the rape upon herself: the vamp. That perception was revealed in a *Washington Post* story three days after the PAU issued its statement.

> Indeed, during a recent lunch at the Café Mimo, where patrons debated the issue among themselves in Portuguese . . . sentiment ran more in favor of the accused than the victim.
>
> "She went there for one reason—not cigarettes," speculated one customer, who refused to identify himself. "She was asking for it," he said, expressing a sentiment fairly common among many patrons interviewed.
>
> "I know this group: they do crazy things, but nothing like this. For them to do it, she had to do something to them," he speculated further. As for the spectators who did nothing to prevent the incident, he said, 'Why stop something that has nothing to do with you?" . . .
>
> "The girl's no good if she goes to that bar," said David Arruda, owner of Haurico Hardware next door. (3/21/83, p. A1.)

Unfortunately, like Ferreira, many of the Portuguese expressed their valid objections to the press treatment of the community as resentment of the victim.

Pretrial Moves: The Columnists Versus the People

By the third week of the case, during various pretrial moves, the press was having a field day. The courtroom was jammed with people eager to express their opinions. D.A. Pina was giving colorful quotes whenever, it seems, he was asked. Hundreds of threatening and passionate letters were being sent to the defendants and the editors, and the ethnic furor gave a whole new angle to the story that could fill pages when there was nothing else new to report. Meanwhile, victim-blaming quotes from the locals were proliferating and, in reaction, columnists were springing to the victim's defense.

Anne Taylor Fleming, for example, wrote a strongly worded column for the *Boston Herald* lamenting the morals of a society that watches rape without doing anything to stop it: "We are talking . . . about a deadness, about an inability to feel horror at something and therefore an absolute inability to react to stop it." (3/26/83, p. 26.)

Richard Cohen and Judy Mann, who had both written about the Rideout case, condemned the rapists and the sexist attitudes toward the victim. Cohen wrote:

> What is remarkable about the whole exercise is how nothing much has changed. For all the talk about rape recently, for all that has been written, for all the progress supposedly made by the women's movement, people are still trying to explain the rape by wondering what the victim did to provoke it. (*Washington Post*, 3/22/83, p. B1.)

Mann brought up the valuable point that rape is glorified by popular culture—the same point Cohen had made with *Gone With the Wind* in the Rideout case.

> In "Falcon Crest" . . . a husband and wife . . . hated each other. After he slaps her around at a party, she tells him he's "incredible," and the two are shown heading to bed. In "General Hospital," a heroine falls in love with her rapist. In the movie "Getaway" a woman who is raped is shown enjoying it. (*Washington Post*, 3/25/83, p. B1.)

Ellen Goodman criticized the blame-the-victim tendency of the public in her syndicated column and, like Mann, tackled media images of rape.

> From High Falls, N.Y., a teacher forwarded to me a "photo fantasy" from the January *Hustler* magazine. In a series of photographs that might have served as a blueprint for the New Bedford rape, a waitress is sexually assaulted, graphically and in living color, on a pool room table by four leather-clothed men. Only, she enjoys it . . .[22]
>
> I don't know whether the men in New Bedford read this seamy magazine. I don't know how great a distance it is from the reader to the voyeur to the cheering squad. But in our world, the real world, a woman cried out and four men were arrested for rape.
>
> (*Globe*, 3/31/83.)

Mary Kay Blakely wrote a stirring piece about the case for *Ms.* magazine under the title, "The New Bedford Gang Rape: WHO WERE THE MEN?" In the article, Blakely joined the Kitty Genovese analogists and decried the indifference and hostility of the men who watched and cheered. She then used the case to make a plea to men:

> I want you to feel fear. I want you to understand that every two-and-a-half minutes, another woman in this country is raped, that one third of all rapes are committed by two or more "offenders." I want you to imagine that you have only 20 seconds to think what to do. And, if you don't want to be among the anonymous bystanders in Big Dan's, if you are horrified that more than a dozen men could actually cheer for a rape in progress, then imagine that you have only another two minutes to act. I want this fear to give you the courage to take risks, to object, to do something. (*Ms.* July, 1983, pp. 50–101.)

Even conservative columnist Pat Buchanan jumped in to defend the victim, only he used the case to attack the decay of religion and morals in America, and to call for a return to the death penalty: "As the external protections of women—the scaffold and the law—collapsed, the internal ones were likewise crumbling." (*Herald*, 3/31/83, p. 28.)

The role of the columnists in this case provides an example of how the press at times differs from the public. The columnists, on the whole, were much more enlightened about rape than were the New Bedford residents who were giving quotes to the papers and calling in to radio shows. As a result, these columnists took on a role that members of the press sometimes deny—that of teacher.

Jury Selection

During the rest of that spring and summer of 1983, coverage of the Big Dan's case was sporadic—the press was waiting for the trial. The most excitement during this hiatus occurred in August, when *Hustler* magazine played right into the Portuguese objections to the coverage of the story by publishing a picture of a mock postcard featuring a smiling, nude woman lying on a pool table, brandishing a cue stick. The caption read, "Greetings from New Bedford, Mass. The Portuguese Gang-Rape Capital of America."[23]

The press woke up to the case again at the beginning of February 1984, with the start of jury selection. The trial was going to be complicated. It had to be moved out of New Bedford because of the amount of pretrial publicity it had received; the six defendants had to be tried in two separate trials, four in one, two in the other, because some of them had incriminated each other in statements to the police; and the jurors had to be strictly sequestered in order to keep them ignorant of the media's coverage.

At this pretrial stage the *Providence Journal* put in the most coverage. Even though its circulation area did not include New Bedford, it did include Fall River, where the trial was to be held, and the paper thus saw its role as the newspaper of record on the case. A team of three reporters were assigned to the story full time—one reporter per trial, Neil Downing and Karen Ellsworth, and a "team leader," Phil Kukielski. On the day before jury selection was to begin, the team wrote two stories that ran on the front page of the second section, giving valuable background on the case and preparing readers for the coverage to come. One was headed "Why tandem trials, and how they will work," and described the defendants, the attorneys and the judge. The other was headed "Big Dan's rape case puts many issues on trial" and gave a full history of the case. It read almost like the program notes to a play:

> Women's groups see what happened in Big Dan's as a symptom of the "sexist violence" that infects society and a particularly graphic example of some men's insensitivity to the crime of rape.
>
> The Portuguese community in southeastern Massachusetts is torn between feelings of shame and anger. Some feel embarrassed that the case has put their city in such an unfavorable light. Others suspect that the defendants have been singled out for public vilification because of their ethnic origins. (2/5/84.)

The *Washington Post* jumped in at this point, running a dramatic story by Ruth Marcus headed "Rape Trial: A City and Its Agony" (2/8/84, pp. F1–2). The piece recapitulated the crime and set the scene for the trial, but the prose, which leant toward sympathy for the victim, was an example of what Ferreira and the local Portuguese found so offensive:

> Six men, *all resident Portuguese aliens,* have been charged with aggravated rape and face life imprisonment if convicted. . .
>
> From the start, the case has generated strong feelings among residents of this historic whaling port, *which has one of the highest rates of unemployment in the state.* (My emphasis.)

The jury selection was monitored both by women's groups looking out for sexism and by Portuguese groups looking out for bigotry. The *Boston Globe* in particular paid attention to the gender balance among the jurors. "Men Outnumbering Women Two-to-One as Potential Jurors in Big Dan Rape Case" (2/15/84, p. 3.) (In the end, the juries were more balanced, although they still favored men.) The *Portuguese Times* complained about the questions asked of potential jurors.

"I think the judge was biased," Ferreira told me. "He asked a very stupid question of the jurors. The question was this: 'Do you think that the Portuguese are more prepared to commit crimes than any other group?' It is a prejudiced question. If a person's a bigot, he's a bigot. He could say yes or no. I don't think you can identify bigotry with yes or no." (For the record, the judge asked potential jurors a series of *voir dire* questions designed to weed out prejudice, not just the one Ferreira quoted, most of which had been suggested by the defense lawyers, not the prosecution.[24] The judge also conducted an exhaustive three-stage interview with each juror. Unfortunately, the news accounts mentioned the process but did not list all the questions, which perhaps contributed to the local perception that only one question had been relied on to expose the bigoted.)

On the whole, the concerns of women's groups at this stage received less coverage than did those of the Portuguese. A mention was made of a member of the Coalition Against Sexist Violence who was attending the trial, she said, "to see whether the media are covering it fairly and whether any 'innuendoes' about the alleged victim are made in the courtroom,"[25] but she was never mentioned again. This was particularly odd in the light of a pretrial motion made by a defense attorney a few days later, which was a clear attempt to smear the victim.

> **BIG DAN VICTIM'S BACKGROUND AN ISSUE**
> The alleged victim in the Big Dan's rape case has had sex-related psychiatric treatment, a defense lawyer asserted in Superior Court yesterday. (*Providence Journal*, 2/15/84, p. 15.)

In spite of this troubling headline and lead, which to a casual reader makes the victim sound like a nutcase, the allegation itself was based solely on the report of one of the defendants, Joseph Vieira, who claimed that the victim had told him that she was seeing a psychiatrist in the bar on the night of the rape. Vieira's lawyer, David Waxler, saw this as an opportunity to undermine the victim's credibility, but as the story went on, it became clear that the accusation had little ground.

> Prosecutors continued to maintain that there is no proof the victim ever received psychiatric treatment. But Waxler insisted that there is proof . . .
>
> The issue apparently was resolved late in the day, when the victim signed a consent form allowing the judge to privately review any records a state agency may have regarding her.
> (*Providence Journal*, 2/15/84, p. 15.)

This small event illustrates perfectly the essence of rape trials. On the one side is the defense lawyer, relying as his main tool on undermining the credibility and reputation of the victim. On the other side is the prosecution, recognizing and fighting that fact. I asked Neil Downing, who wrote the preceding story, if he had any qualms about reporting an unsubstantiated accusation by a defendant against his accuser. Did the story, I asked, not amount to reporting hearsay? Downing replied: "Certainly I would have a problem if [the accusation] occurred outside of a courthouse. Clearly then it would have been hearsay. But it came up in a public forum at the courthouse and it was part of the defense's arguments. It behooves us to report it. After all, we don't want to make decisions for or against the victim or the defense in our news columns."

The irony is, when trial reporters put a statement about a victim or defendant in the lead without attributing it until later, that is exactly what they are doing. By allowing themselves to become a direct, unfiltered pipeline from the attorneys to the public, court reporters in effect argue for or against the victim or defendants every day. Both the *Providence Journal* and the *Washington Post*, for example, put Vieira's allegation about the victim in their leads without making it clear until later that the source of this slur was one of the men accused of raping her. Reporters obviously rely on this format to make a lead sensational, but it has the effect of using the pages of the press to put defendants and victims on trial.

That a trial need not be covered with this format was demonstrated by Jonathan Kaufman of the *Boston Globe.* Kaufman took care to attribute the information he was giving high up so that it did not sound like irrefutable fact, and reminded the reader that a trial is not so much a forum for truth as an attempt by both sides to dress up the facts to put their clients in the best light. In one story, for example, he wrote that the attorneys "drew a harsh picture" of the scene in the bar.[26] By depicting attorneys as drawing a picture, rather than by merely quoting them, Kaufman was telling the reader that a trial relies on selected and highlighted evidence, not on facts.

Using the Victim's Name

During the weeks of jury selection, the press was crowding the courtroom in ever-increasing numbers. Ellsworth wrote in the *Providence Journal* that at least two dozen reporters were inside the courtroom and that, outside it, camera crews from Channels 4, 5, 6, 7, 10, 12, NBC, ABC, and the Cable News Network were following the defendants each time they entered or left the courthouse.[27] All the reporters in this crowd knew the victim's name. They heard it every day, many times. (David Waxler, one of the defense attorneys, made a point of referring to the victim by name whenever he could.[28]) As the reporters heard her name, they had to grapple with the question of whether to use it.

Up until the trial, no newspaper or television station had revealed her name. Every one of them adhered to the policy of preserving a rape victim's anonymity for the sake of her dignity and safety. When a cable television station decided to cover the trial live, however, it declared that it would "break with the practice of other media covering the trial by broadcasting the name of the woman who was allegedly raped."[29] The cable station was owned by the Providence Journal Company.

The victim's lawyer, Scott Charnas, asked the judge to prevent the station from broadcasting her name, but although the judge prohibited the use of her photograph during the trial (in order to protect her privacy and her children's), he said he did not have the power to forbid the use of her name—he could only *ask* the media not to use it. It turned out later that the judge had hoped her name would be bleeped out over the air, but was unrealistically optimistic. As Kukielski said, bleeping out her name would have required a technological sophistication that the cable company simply did not have.*

Once cable television declared it would use her name, news editors struggled over whether to follow suit. Most chose not to: The *Globe*, the *Standard-Times*, the big out-of-town papers, television channels 10 and 12, and the Associated Press never used her name. United Press International took a middle ground and passed along her name to its clients but left it to them to make the decision and did not put it in its own stories. Three of the main newspapers and one of the television stations covering the case, however, did decide to use her name: the local *Fall River Herald News*, the *Portuguese Times*, the *Providence Journal* itself, and the local television channel 6, which also unsuccessfully challenged the judge's ban on photographs of the victim.

The *Journal* was ill at ease with its decision. In a prominent editorial, Charles McCorkle Hauser, who was then editor but is now retired, tried to explain his position in a column headed "Rape, privacy and the press" (3/4/84, p. B1). In it, Hauser depicted an imaginary conversation between himself and a reader. The reader was questioning him about the paper's policy not to print rape victims' names with the following oft-heard arguments:

1. What right do newspapers have to withhold information from the public? (Answer: Newspapers cannot print everything that happens, so they naturally have to make choices. Sometimes these choices are made to protect the innocent.)
2. Why do papers shout about their First Amendment rights if they are going to practice censorship? (Answer: Exercising our right of free press carries with it certain responsibilities such as protecting innocent people from unfavorable publicity.)
3. If a rape victim should have no reason to be ashamed, because rape is a crime of violence, not sex, and is not her fault, do you not perpetuate the stigma against her by hiding her name? (Answer: Yes, but the stigma is still there and so she needs protecting until attitudes change.)[30]

*The technology seems to have improved little in eight years. During the 1991 rape trial of William Kennedy Smith, the alleged victim's name was inadvertently broadcast several times, in spite of media attempts to bleep it out—au.

Finally, Hauser gave the reason for choosing to break the policy in the Big Dan's case: "Because of live broadcasts from the courtroom. Suddenly the name was going into living rooms all over the area on radio and television."

In other words, Hauser broke the rule because everyone else was breaking it. This reasoning was an evasion, however. He was publishing the name because cable TV was publishing the name (and reaching about 44,000 homes in New Bedford while doing it)—but the cable TV was owned by his own paper's company. In short, his right hand was doing it because his left hand was doing it.

In an effort to get to the bottom of this circular reasoning, I asked Kukielski to explain the decision. He had two answers. The first was that the *Providence Journal* sees itself as a paper of record and a champion of the First Amendment. "Names are attached, as a matter of policy, to all our news stories," he said. Nevertheless, he acknowledged that this has not been true for rape victims except in this one case, which led him to the second reason. "It wasn't like we wanted to publish the name," he said. "I went into this expecting we would adhere to the normal practice and not publish the name. I think everybody did. But people started to complain about the unfairness of the proceeding. There was this inequity developing. The names and pictures of the defendants were nationally known. The victim, on the other hand, was cloaked in anonymity. Normally, both the victim and the accused stay relatively anonymous."

In a sidebar on the use of the victim's name by the cable stations, the *Boston Globe* quoted the owner of the station giving another justification that was not based on principle, fairness, or the First Amendment: "Paul Silva, regional manager of Colony Communications, which runs the cable stations, said last week that the company is broadcasting the name because it wants viewers 'to see and hear everything they would see and hear if they attend the trial.' "[31] That is, the station used the name simply to give the viewers the illusion that they were in the courtroom—for reasons of entertainment. (The tendency of television to broadcast this trial as a soap opera resulted in misgivings about allowing cameras into the courtroom in both the Levin and jogger cases, as will be seen.)

The decision of these papers and television stations to use the victim's name did not go uncriticized. Throughout and after the trial, letters poured in objecting to it and editorialists took the subject up at length.

"BIG DAN'S JUDGE ASSAILS MEDIA FOR NAMING RAPE COMPLAINANT" (*Providence Journal*, 3/22/84, p. A9).
"PRESS BLASTED FOR PUBLICITY ON RAPE CASE" (*Standard-Times*, 3/24/84, p. 1).
"BIG DAN'S JUDGE RUES NOT TELLING CABLE TV TO 'BLEEP' VICTIM'S NAME" (*Providence Journal*, 4/7/84, p. A5). Superior Court Judge William G. Young said he "sticks by" his position that use of the victim's name by the media was "a grave injustice to her and a grave error in editorial judgment."

The *Globe* devoted pages to the debate, beginning with a letter to the editor from Alan M. Dershowitz, professor of law at Harvard Law School.

> The Globe's policy of not publishing the names of alleged rape victims (as in the Big Dan's case) raises several implications dangerous to civil liberties. It contributes to an atmosphere of presuming that the unnamed person was indeed a victim—thus undercutting the presumption that the defendants are innocent . . .
>
> Moreover, the policy of not identifying alleged rape victims, unlike other victims, contributes to the stereotype that there is a worse stigma attached to being a rape victim than a victim of other crimes of violence.
>
> It may well be true that such increased stigmatization exists today in the minds of some, but a widespread media policy of treating rape differently from other forms of brutality will only help to reinforce and magnify that perception. (3/2/84, p. 10.)

Dershowitz's editorial triggered a flood of letters to the editor, most of them disagreeing with him. Several arguments for not using the name were made:

1. Since defense tactics are always to put the victim on trial, not publishing her name spares her further violation. She ought to have the right to be presumed innocent, too.
2. Publicity so terrifies rape victims that fear of it discourages them from reporting their rapes. (This contention was supported by the local rape crisis center, which reported that many local rape victims were telling their counselors that they were afraid to press charges because of the way the Big Dan's victim was being treated by the trial attorneys and the press.[32])
3. Rape is not like other crimes. It is a sexual violation and so

is more humiliating than any other kind of crime, and therefore the victim's identity should be hidden to protect her, not from shame, but from a further violation of her privacy.

The issue of whether to use a victim's name is not simple, which the *Providence Journal* and other papers recognized at the time. As will be seen, two more recent cases, in 1990 and 1991, raised the issue again, and many of the arguments listed here were repeated. The arguments always boil down to a basic conflict: The principle of freedom of speech and the right of the accused to be presumed innocent until proven otherwise sit on one side. The well-being and privacy of the victim sit on the other. As Judge William G. Young, who presided over the Big Dan's case, put it:

> Balanced against the public's right to access to court proceedings . . . was the victim's right to privacy, the probability that she would be subject to a large amount of "immediate, continued" public attention, the effect that attention would have on "her children and her children's future," and "the sufficiently significant chance that she would be intimidated and distracted while testifying."[33]

The fact is, most sex crime victims do not want to be named. That is an irrefutable obstacle to the press and one that forces editors and reporters to make unpleasant and often unsatisfactory decisions, as Kukielski expressed. "It was not our intention to exploit the victim in this case, though it may have been the result. I think we would have been criticized either way for what we did."

The Defendants

By the time the trial was due to begin, the defendants were well known to the public by name and sight because photographs of them had been displayed in the media almost every day. Like the victim they were young; four of them in their early twenties. In alphabetical order, they were:

John M. Cordeiro, twenty-four, unemployed, known as "the bearded" one. He was accused of holding the woman down and trying to force her to have oral sex. In court, he claimed that the victim had enjoyed herself, but before the trial the press revealed that he had implicated himself and Raposo right after the rape by apologizing to the victim in front of police. He was charged with aggravated (i.e., gang) rape.

Virgilio Medeiros, twenty-four, an unemployed boat builder. Witnesses said he shouted "Do it! Do it! That's how it's done" and blocked the bartender's way through the door when the latter tried to go for help. He was charged with joint enterprise for aiding the others in the rape.

Jose Medeiros, twenty-three, an unemployed landscape worker, known as "the blond one." He was also charged with joint enterprise for supposedly touching the victim while she was held down, and for shouting encouragement to the others.

Victor M. Raposo, twenty-three, a handyman. He was supposed to have tried to force the victim to have oral sex. The press revealed that Raposo had two prior convictions, one for indecent exposure a year before this case, and one for assault with a dangerous weapon, but those convictions were not admissible in court. He was charged with aggravated rape.

Daniel C. Silva, twenty-seven, a part-time factory worker and farm hand. He was the one witnesses said had actually raped (i.e., vaginally penetrated) the victim. He was also the one who tried to flee to the Azores after his arrest. He was charged with aggravated rape.

Joseph Vieira, twenty-eight, had worked on local dairy farms and was known as "Joe from Connecticut." The victim said he had helped Silva carry her to the pool table, had held her down and had raped her himself. He was also reported to have tickled Silva's "rear end" with a straw while Silva was raping the victim. Vieira was the only married defendant, and was the man who claimed the victim had told him she had psychiatric problems. He was charged with aggravated rape.

Four of the men were being tried together in the morning trial: Cordeiro, the two Medeiroses, and Raposo. Silva and Vieira were being tried in the afternoon.

The Trials: Opening Day

The tandem trials opened on February 23, 1984 and lasted a little over a month. Nowhere was the impact of using the victim's name more apparent than in the opening story by Neil Downing of the *Providence Journal.*

> FALL RIVER, Mass.—A twenty-one-year-old mother of two was grabbed from behind as she left Big Dan's bar in New Bedford last March 6,

> and was sexually assaulted on a pool table while other patrons cheered her attackers, ignoring her cries for help . . .
>
> Veary and Asst. Dist. Atty. Robert J. Kane said that the woman, Maria A. Bianco, squirmed free and, naked from the waist down, ran into the street. (2/24/84, p. 1.)*

After weeks of reading about the victim as an anonymous figure, the shock of seeing her name linked to a description of such brutality was strong enough, but that shock was exacerbated by Downing's choice of words. By using the phrase *squirmed free* rather than *struggled, escaped,* or *broke free,* he suggested an action that sounded not so desperate as intimate, a bit slimy, and decidedly sexual. (In other accounts, she was described as escaping during a moment when the men had let go of her to change places. There was no squirming—she simply leapt off the table and ran. Would a man ever be described as "squirming free" from an assailant?) Also, by using the phrase *naked from the waist down,* Downing suggested something stripteaselike rather than terrifying.

The phrase *naked from the waist down* was first used by Levin of the *Standard-Times.* It was picked up by all the reporters on his newspaper during the first month after the crime, and again a year later during the trial, as well as by the *Portuguese Times* and the AP; however, there were other, less purient ways of describing the scene. Robert Silva, one of the men who actually witnessed the victim in this state, used the phrase: "I seen a woman in the middle of the street with one sock on and a jacket and nothing underneath."[34] Jonathan Kaufman of the *Boston Globe* managed to describe the same event without using the words *squirmed* or *naked from the waist down:*

> At one point, Veary said, the woman broke free and ran into the street wearing only a sock and a sweater. She stood in the middle of the street, a prosecution witness testified, and waved down a passing pick-up truck carrying three men. (2/24/84, p. 15.)

Downing and Levin were by no means the only reporters to use suggestive vocabulary during their coverage of the trial. Wendy Fox of the *Boston Globe* described the victim as having been "stripped" from

*Not her real name. I have changed the victim's name, even though it is widely available now in records and news reports, because I have no wish to perpetuate the pain of the rape and its memory on her family—au.

the waist down, for instance, a phrase then picked up by other papers. (Would a man be described as stripped or only as having his clothes torn off?) Other reporters repeatedly described the victim in terms that would never be used for a man: ***brunette, bubbly, hysterical,*** and ***unwed mother of two.*** (Fathers are never described as "unwed," with all it implies about illegitimate children. Rather, they are described as "single fathers" if their parenthood is mentioned at all, indicating a sort of heroism.)

Karen Ellsworth, the other *Journal* reporter covering the case, spoke about why reporters sometimes choose the wrong words. "The nature of the newspaper business is that you don't have a lot of time to think about your choice of words," she said. "You'll use a word that, when you're writing the story, appears not to have any kind of connotation. It's only later that you stop and think about it." Perhaps reporters could avoid this pitfall if they were less willing to appropriate the words of attorneys, who always have an ulterior design (the word "squirmed" originated in the mouth of Attorney Kane), were more aware of the implications of the words typically used to describe rape and sexual assault, and were more resistant to clichés in general. (See Conclusion for further discussion.)

The *Portuguese Times* was another paper inconsiderate of the victim in its opening trial story, for it not only printed her name, but her *address* as well. The paper also gave a negative slant to its headline: "VICTIM CONTRADICTS HERSELF" (3/1/84, pp. 1, 2).

The other papers covering the trial's opening day spared the victim from the use of her name, but they were hardly circumspect when it came to lurid details. The *Boston Herald,* in classic tabloid manner, ran exaggerated headlines and dwelled on the most sordid aspects of the case:

> **BIG DAN'S OPENING DAY SHOCKER**
>
> **'THEY WERE CHEERING LIKE IT WAS A BASEBALL GAME'**
>
> INSIDE: Four pages on the rape case that stunned the nation

The reporter, Andrea Estes, who was thirty-one at the time and had been at the paper for about a year, quoted D.A. Veary at length:

> "She was kicking, she was screaming, she was pushing that man away. Finally she began to cry, begging for help that never came . . .

> "The men at the bar were cheering, cheering like at a baseball game." (3/1/84, p. 1.)

Inside, another female reporter, Gayle Fee, took a more responsible line and reminded readers of the feminist and ethnic antagonisms bubbling underneath the case:

> **FEMINISTS & PORTUGUESE ACTIVISTS CRAM COURT**
>
> Cheryl Followwill, 27, said she came to support "the victim."
>
> "I really felt there ought to be some women here to stand by this poor lady," she said.
>
> "Over and over again you keep hearing the argument, 'What was she doing in that bar?' Well, she has her rights; she's a person, too."

Then the other side:

> "Too many people are already presuming these men are guilty," said Alda Melo of the New Bedford Committee for Justice [one of the two fundraising committees for the defendants] . . . there's a good possibility that these men won't get a fair trial." (3/1/84, p. 3)

Fee's story was accompanied by two photographs that drove home the opposition between feminist groups and the local Portuguese. The first was headed "Flashback to protest," and showed a crowd of women from the candlelight march carrying a sign saying "New Bedford Women's Center in unity-strength." The picture was captioned, "A week after the alleged rape, angry women marched through New Bedford." The second photograph showed a crowd of people holding signs saying "Proud to be Portuguese" and was captioned, "Shamed by the bad publicity, the Proud Portuguese community fought back." Even if feminists and the Portuguese protesters had not yet regarded each other as enemies, coverage like this portrayed them as such.

The Victim Exposed

As has been well documented, testifying in court is the most traumatic experience for a rape victim other than the rape itself.[35] This is so not only because she has to face her assailants and endure cross-examination, which often makes her relive the assault and which questions her reputation, but because she becomes subject to scrutiny by the press.

The victim in Big Dan's had to testify twice, at the beginning of each of the tandem trials, and she had to do so standing up (there was no seat in the witness box) for a total of fifteen hours over three gruelling days in a row. While testifying, she faced all six defendants, a courtroom packed with people, constantly whirring television cameras, and a barrage of news reporters eager for a hot story.

To make things harder for her, this was the kind of rape trial in which the defense lawyers' only strategy was to discredit her. There are two kinds of rape cases, legally speaking. The first is a rape that everyone agrees happened—the only question is whether the police have the right culprit. The second involves the question of whether there was a rape at all, and that brings in legal standards of consent and evidence. Big Dan's was the second kind of case (as was the more recent Kennedy Smith case.) Because there were so many witnesses to the fact that the men had been in the bar, and because the men had no alibis, the defendants' lawyers could not rely on misidentification as a defense. They therefore had only one strategy left—to prove that the woman had sex with the men willingly. (John Rideout's lawyer used the same strategy, successfully, as did Kennedy Smith's lawyer.) To prove that, they had to portray her in the worst possible light.

At the beginning of the trials, when the victim took the stand, the coverage sounded sympathetic, if sensational, because she was telling her side of the story. Her account was powerful and had a profound effect on the jury and the public:

> "I could hear yelling, laughing, down near the end of the bar," she said ". . . My head was hanging off the edge of the pool table . . . I was screaming, pleading, begging . . . One man held my head and pulled my hair. The more I screamed, the harder he pulled . . ."
>
> (*Washington Post*, 2/25/84, p. A3.)

Even though her words were strong, however, and invited sympathy, the press quickly found something to criticize: her calmness on the witness stand. Her lawyers were later quoted praising the victim for her self-control, but several of the trial reporters described her stance as "dispassionate" and "almost clinical," making her sound cold and tough, untroubled by what had happened.[36] (The defense attorneys recognized this and later tried to turn it against her in their cross-examinations.) The press's reaction to her manner illustrated a paradox that rape experts have long pointed out: If a victim is calm in court, she is seen as not having suffered enough, which indicates she is not a genuine victim;

if she is sobbing and frightened, she is seen as hysterical, unstable, and thus unreliable. By falling for this Catch 22, the press played into the hands of the defense lawyers.

Another subtle point that came up in the first testimony stories was that the victim was described, over and over again, as having left her children in bed while she went out to the bar. The fact that her boyfriend was at home with them was only mentioned in one story by one paper. This omission, unintentional as it probably was, gave the inaccurate impression that the victim was prepared to leave her small children unattended.

Of all the aspects of the early—and continuing—trial coverage, however, the one that most humiliated the victim was the explicit testimony, especially when it was coupled with her name.

The testimony in the courtroom had to be explicit because of the nature of the crime. Some of the men had been charged with aggravated rape, which meant under Massachusetts law that the prosecution had to prove actual sexual penetration; the other men had been charged with joint enterprise, which meant determining in detail what they had physically done. The court therefore had to hear about oral sodomy, about Vieira tickling Silva's rectum with a straw as Silva was raping the victim, about the sperm found in her vagina and on a defendant's underwear, and about other such graphic evidence.

The *Standard-Times* chose to cover all this with discretion. "We had a conversation to remind everybody about our policy with regard to profanity," recalled Ragsdale, the paper's editor. "The issue had to be extremely important for that profanity or vulgarism to find its way into the story." The *Providence Journal*, however, took the opposite stand:

> When Kane asked her if she felt anything inside her mouth while she was on the pool table, she said she could not remember, but under cross-examination . . . she said she did feel something in her mouth when Cordeiro was standing next to her. She was forced to open her mouth because another man was pulling her hair, she said.
>
> (2/28/84, pp. A1–14.)

> Silva got on top of her. Neither had pants on. Pacheco said one of the pool players had his hand on her head, unzipped his pants, and tried to engage her in oral sex . . . Pacheco said Vieira then took a straw from the bar, walked over to the pool table and inserted it in Silva's rear end. (3/8/84, p. 8.)

> Raposo "denied having any involvement with the girl at first . . . then said he remembered holding the girl's legs and taking his penis out," Gormely said. (3/13/84, p. A4.)

Kukielski spoke about his paper's decision to be so graphic. "We were constantly torn between providing a full and uncensored report of a proceeding that people were watching in their living rooms [on cable television every day], and adhering to our normal standards about taste and references to sexual contact. It was a daily dilemma. . . . We weren't happy about writing these stories. We weren't happy about ruining people's breakfasts.

"Karen [Ellsworth] was a key player in the decision. "She was fresh out of law school and she was a very strong advocate for using more anatomical detail than we were normally comfortable with. She was saying it was absolutely critical to judging the guilt or innocence of these people to have this information here."

Downing agreed with Ellsworth's reasoning. The problem with sanitizing rape reports, he said, is that you prevent the reader from understanding just what kind of crime rape is.

In many ways, Ellsworth and Downing's argument was valid. Graphic descriptions of sex crimes do force readers to realize their brutality, while sanitizing them does perpetuate the myth that rape is sex and does not hurt. However, the fact that the *Journal* used more explicit descriptions than any other paper, was one of the only papers to name the victim, and named her *against her will* changed the stakes. The reader was suddenly seeing Maria Bianco, by name, linked with images of her being raped and orally sodomized, screaming, crying, and "squirming." There can be no question that the result invaded her privacy, humiliated, and stigmatized her.

The Arguments

After the victim had finished testifying, both sides called their witnesses. The prosecution called the bartender, the police, the men who had rescued her in the street, and the doctor and nurses who had examined her after the rape. The defense produced a drunken man who had been in the bar during the rape but was unconscious almost the whole time, another customer who had witnessed the rape but was not charged, and the waitress to whom the victim had talked early that evening. In summary, the attorneys' strategy boiled down to arguments that undermined the victim's credibility versus evidence that corroborated the rape.

The testimony corroborating the rape was this: Some of the defendants had confessed when arrested; the bartender said he had seen the victim resist the attack, and that one of the defendants had threatened to kill him if he told of what he had seen; one defendant apologized to the victim in front of the police; semen was found in the victim's vagina after the rape,[37] bruises were seen on her by doctors after the rape; the men who rescued her testified to her traumatized condition; her own account of the attack.

The testimony used by the defense can be boiled down to the following points, made by the defendants, defense lawyers, and witnesses: The victim wanted sex with the defendants; no rape happened because she did not resist; she was a liar, exaggerating the number of men in the bar and changing her story later; she was drunk, wild, and promiscuous, sitting naked on the pool table smoking marijuana; she was a habitual accuser of men because she had filed a rape complaint some years earlier; the main witness for her, the bartender, was crazy and unreliable; she was a "welfare cheat" because she had accepted welfare payments for her children even though her boyfriend worked; and she was pursuing the trial out of avarice because she had tried to sue the bartender for not coming to her aid and because she had been offered a book contract for her story.

Several of the defense's contentions could not even hold up in court, although that did not stop the press from splashing each one across its pages. She had been drinking, but later laboratory evidence cast doubt on the blood alcohol test she had been given, and the nurse and police officer who had seen the victim after the rape both said she had not acted drunk.[38] She had been approached by publishers interested in making a fast buck out of her story, like any principal in a notorious crime, but had not invited the approach nor encouraged it—in fact she turned it down. She had filed a suit against the bartender, but that was standard procedure and entirely within her rights—she told the court she did it on principle, and the lawyers dropped the matter. The stories of her sitting naked on the bar smoking marijuana were too unlikely for anyone to take seriously. Finally, the fact that she continued to draw welfare for her children, even though her boyfriend was employed (she was not) had nothing to do with the rape, although its use in court shows how ineffective rape shield laws are to really protect a victim from irrelevant slurs to her character.[39]

Some of the other accusations the defense brought up however, were more problematic. The question of the number of men in the bar was never resolved and the victim was thoroughly mocked for changing her count. (The *Washington Post* was one of the only papers to give her explanation for this change: ". . . Speaking calmly, with her hands folded on the wooden bar of the witness stand, the woman said that she may have given police the higher numbers initially because she was traumatized and hysterical after the March 1983, incident."[40] Without this explanation, the victim seemed to have been lying. With it, she only seemed too traumatized to have remembered—a significant difference of interpretation.) The evidence that she had been talking to the men and perhaps flirting with them before the attack looked convincing, and that was bad for her because it fed so perfectly into the "women provoke rape" myth that it lost her much sympathy. Also, her denial of all knowledge of the prior rape claim, even though it was on hospital records, harmed her because it fed into the "women cry rape for revenge" myth, made her look like a liar, and turned the public suspicious. As Levin said, "The problem with this case was the woman was very bizarre. Her story changed several times. She denied things on that witness stand that everybody in the courtroom knew were true: The welfare, her boyfriend living at her house, the previous rape thing. She could have admitted all that stuff and it wouldn't have hurt her case as much as it did to deny it."

One of the most damaging stories to the victim printed during the first weeks of the trial was a jailhouse interview with defendant Victor Raposo, which Impemba had conducted a year earlier but had not published. A week after the damning Medeiros interviews had hit the headlines, Impemba received a note from Raposo, who was being held in the local county jail, saying he wanted to tell his side of the story. Impemba had just been promoted to assistant city editor at the *Standard-Times*. He went down to the jailhouse with a photographer, without telling anyone else, and did the interview.

Ragsdale, Impemba's editor, said he first heard about the interview when he received a phone call from the courthouse. "It was our court reporter on the phone saying the judge was all excited and was about to issue a gag order against us for the jailhouse interview." Raposo's attorney, fearing that the interview would incriminate his client, had asked the judge to prevent its publication. Ragsdale fought the gag order on principle, but when he saw the interview he refused to publish it anyway. "I thought the interview was fatally flawed," Ragsdale told me. "Impemba didn't challenge Raposo. In this kind of a case an interview should be a dialogue between two people. It shouldn't just be 'I am taking your word for it.' It was what I call a marshmallow interview."

Impemba, naturally enough, disagreed. "This was an interview that took place over a two-to-three-hour period—it wasn't as though I was just listening to whatever he was trying to say," he recalled. "I kept trying to trip him up. . . . I gave a lot of thought to that particular interview. I went up with the thought that he's probably just going to use us as a vehicle, but I came away believing him—not a hundred percent—but to a large degree."

Impemba's willingness to believe Raposo was not shared by his editor. Ragsdale refused to publish the interview and even hid the transcripts and tapes "in a place that was so secretive they wouldn't have found it for another 200 years," he said. When Impemba left the *Standard-Times* to work for the *Boston Herald*, however, he brought a copy of the interview with him—a copy Ragsdale had not even known he had. The *Herald* ran the interview with Impemba's byline under the splashy headline,

> **BIG DAN SUSPECT: SHE LED US ON**
>
> **Big Dan's Suspect Tells How Woman Asked Them For Sex**
>
> In a dramatic, exclusive interview, a Big Dan's defendant said the young woman pleaded for sex on a pool table after "getting all friendly" and drinking heavily.
>
> Victor Raposo, 23, one of the six men on trial for rape, told his side of the story . . . a story that differs dramatically from the one told . . . by the New Bedford mother of two.
>
> "They make this girl sound like a goody two shoes and she's not.
>
> "She told me how cute I was . . . She said I looked like her old man. She kept coming on to me . . ."
>
> Raposo said the young woman came to the bar for sex and asked defendant Daniel Silva repeatedly to take her home with him for sex. (3/1/84, pp. 1, 4.)

In the interview, Raposa predictably contradicted the victim's story: She asked Silva for sex; she "urged" Silva to take her to the pool table so she could be "comfortable;" she told a woman in the bar that "she hadn't had sex in a while" so was clearly "looking for it;" Silva was too drunk to penetrate her, so there was no real rape; no one cheered or yelled in the bar, so the victim was lying; the whole incident lasted about twenty minutes, not two hours; she did not run to the men in the truck crying "I've been raped," but started flirting and "making out" with them, too; the bartender was not a reluctant witness but a participant; and Raposo himself did nothing. The tone of Raposa's statements can be seen in this passage:

> "John [Cordeiro] asked where the chick was. Before Danny [Silva] put her on the floor she was on the bar stool making out with him. The bartender was from behind grabbing her and she wasn't resisting."

As soon as this interview was published, a furor arose between the *Standard-Times* and the *Herald.* Ragsdale accused Impemba of stealing the interview, which he said belonged to the *Standard-Times,* while Impemba claimed it was his property. The feud is not relevant to the focus of this book, but the interview was important for another reason: Despite the questionable circumstances in which it was obtained—at Raposo's request, in the jailhouse, and apparently without much challenge by the reporter—it was quoted by the *Providence Journal,* the *Globe,* the *Washington Post,* and the *Portuguese Times.* The end result was that Raposo's version of the story succeeded in getting a great deal of coverage, even though much of it was highly suspect.

The Trial Coverage

How well the defendants' claims succeeded in discrediting the victim in the eyes of the public was largely controlled by how each paper played them. To get an idea of the overall gist of the trial coverage, I took a look at the headlines during the first sixteen days of the trial.

The *Boston Herald's* headlines added up to six slanted against the victim (for example, "HALF-NAKED WOMAN SMOKED POT: OFFICER TOLD"; "ALLEGED RAPE VICTIM 'AGREED TO MAKE LOVE'—LAWYER"; "SHE WAS 'POISONED WITH ALCOHOL')" and two in her favor ("THREAT TO KILL WITNESS TOLD AT RAPE TRIAL"; "PAIR CONFESSED RAPE ROLE: OFFICER").[41] The two other headlines were mixed: "BARMAN: 'I SAW THE WHOLE THING' Witness recalls brutal rape of 'flirting' woman" (3/1/84, p. 4); "BARMAN UNSHAKEN: 'SHE WAS RAPED' But small details don't match woman's version" (3/2/84, p. 2).

Among the other papers, the counts were not much more balanced. The *Providence Journal's* headlines were more discreet than were the *Herald's* and too unremarkable to be worth reproducing here, but I counted nine headlines in favor of the victim and three in favor of the defense—the only paper to have more headlines for her case than against it. The rest of the *Journal's* headlines were neutral. The *Standard-Times* was even-handed, running six anti- and six provictim headlines. The *Boston Globe* was the most noncommittal in its wording, but it nevertheless ran only two headlines in the victim's favor and four against her. The *Washington Post*'s headlines were the most sensational after the *Herald*'s, and included four sympathetic to the victim and six against her. *The New York Times* ran two heads that made the victim look bad, and one that was favorable. The *Portuguese Times* and the *L.A. Times* ran only two headlines each, both slanted against the victim's case. In summary, thirty-one of the headlines contained statements detrimental to the victim and twenty-six reflected evidence supporting her story. This antivictim slant was further bolstered by the proliferation of stories about the hostility of the courtroom crowd:

> FOR MANY SPECTATORS AT THE BIG DAN'S TRIAL, THE VERDICT IS IN
> "I truly don't believe this kind of thing could happen in this day and age," declared Daniel Dakin, a 36-year-old defense plant worker . . . "I believe the most these guys can be charged with is gross stupidity for doing what they did in a public place." . . .
>
> Like Dakin, many of those waiting sympathized with the six defendants and several added that they felt the men were also suffering from the attention being paid to the trial. . . .
>
> Kim Encey, 18, of Fall River, said of the victim, who has spent 14 hours on the witness stand, "I don't believe her story one bit, and I don't feel sorry for her either. At first she said 12 to 15 guys attacked her, then it was six, and now she says two? Come on.
>
> "I was raped, and I can tell you, I know I was asking for it, and I think this lady was too." Encey said she had also been watching the trial on cable TV instead of her favorite soap opera . . .
>
> Alice Santos, a New Bedford teacher . . . said, "I would like to believe that any decent woman has the right to go into any establishment she pleases, but the fact is a decent woman would not go into any bar to buy cigarettes. Or if she did go into a bar to buy cigarettes, she would go right out." (Terry Minsky, *Globe*, 3/1/84, p. 23)

> BIG DAN'S COURTROOM CROWD PICKS HEROES
> "I'm for the guys more than the girl," said 19-year-old Ernie Santos of Fall River, a floor-sander. "I mean, what was she doing there in the first place? I think she was looking." . . .
>
> "I'm of Portuguese origin," said Louise Cariero, 20, of Fall River, "and a lot of our people feel the girl shouldn't have been in Big Dan's in the first place." (*Providence Journal*, 3/3/84, p. 5.)

This last story also quoted two people sympathizing with the victim, but the predominance of antivictim statements and the comparison of the trial to a soap opera revealed how little the people in that courtroom understood that rape is not sex, that women would no more "look for it" than they would look to be murdered, and that the behavior of a woman never excuses a rapist. As a *Washington Post* reporter put it: "At times during the Big Dan's rape case this week it was not clear who was on trial—the woman who claimed she was gang-raped in a New Bedford bar, or the six men charged with the crime."

(Ruth Marcus, 3/4/84, p. A2.)

The Verdicts and the Portuguese Protest

> TWO BIG DAN defendants were convicted yesterday of raping a 22-year-old mother of two on a barroom pooltable while customers cheered them on. (*Herald*, 3/18/84, p. 1.)

The jury in Vieira and Silva's trial had decided to believe the victim despite the slurs against her and despite the best efforts of a team of defense attorneys to discredit her. Furthermore, the jury opted for the most serious charge—aggravated rape.

A triumph, but a thin one, for the crowd outside the courtroom instantly exploded with fury—against the verdict, the jury, the district attorney, and, most of all, against the victim herself. The result was that the bulk of the stories, even in the light of the verdict, reflected the crowd's antagonism: "A man who identified himself as a friend of Vieira's hollered to reporters, 'The ....—she's the one that should go to jail." (*Herald*, 3/18/84, p. 6.); " **'Why don't they bring that girl out in handcuffs!' someone shouted. 'Get her too!'** " (*Standard-Times*, 3/18/84, p. 2.)[42]

The protesters' objections boiled down to the issue that had permeated the case from the beginning: the victim versus the Portuguese.

Four days after Vieira and Silva were convicted, the verdicts in the trial of the remaining four were decided. The *Herald* announced the news with misplaced sympathy: "TEARS OF TWO RAPISTS" (3/23/84, p. 1). The verdict was split. Two of the men, Cordeiro and Raposo, were found guilty of aggravated rape. The other two, Jose and Virgilio Medeiros, the only defendants charged with joint enterprise, were acquitted. As reflected by the headline, the news of the verdicts was accompanied by a flood of sympathy for the defendants. Along with photographs of the two convicted men crying were stories in all the papers about the "shock and outrage" of the Portuguese community—not at what had been finally proved to have happened to the victim, who was, after all, a member of that community herself, but at what had been done to the defendants.

> A hero's welcome greeted Jose and Virgilio Medeiros as the two vindicated Big Dan's defendants bounded out of a Fall River courthouse as free men . . .
>
> Outside, cheers and applause erupted from the crowd as the innocent men ran to a waiting car with scores of reporters and cameramen behind them. (*Herald*, 3/23/84, p. 5.)

Virgilio Medeiros, who in his pretrial interview had described the victim crying and pleading with the men to leave her alone, now stood on the steps of the courthouse and said, "She led them on, there was no rape in that bar. No. Never."[43] And: "Everybody should be considered innocent because what happened wasn't a rape. The woman was the one who started everything."[44]

On the night of the verdict, a gigantic demonstration erupted in support of the defendants: "8,000 march against 'bias' they say Big Dan's fueled" (*Providence Journal*, 3/24/84, p. A20.)[45]

People marched carrying signs: "Where is Justice?' "Was She Willing?" "Justice Crucified. March 17, 1984." Others were quoted saying the jury had been biased by publicity and ethnic prejudice, that the judicial system had failed, and that it had all been the victim's fault:

> "If she had been home with her children this would not have happened." (*Providence Journal*, 3/23/84, p. A22.)
>
> "She is the one who deserves the prison sentence." (*Globe*, 3/24/84, p. 18.)
>
> "She should get punished too. If they raped her, she was the aggravator . . . I'm sorry to say it, but I think it was her." . . . "I am Portuguese and proud of it . . . I'm also a woman, but you don't see me getting raped." "They did nothing to her. Her rights are to be home with her two kids and to be a good mother. A Portuguese woman should be with her kids and that's it." (*Standard-Times*, 3/24/84, p. 3).

The *Globe* summarized the mood.

> The thread of comment running through the crowd was that the victim in the case, not the defendants, should have been punished. A new Bedford priest attending the march said, "The girl is to blame. She led them into sin."
> (3/24/84, p. 18.)

The question at this point is what could the press have done to avoid furthering this persecution of the victim? The signs were there, the quotes were there, and the hostility of the crowd was unmistakeable. Ragsdale said, "We were powerless to control what was taking place in the newsmaking situation out there."

Yet, perhaps the papers were not so powerless. They certainly had to report the demonstrations and placards and quotes maligning the victim, but they could also have sought out her supporters, outside the community if necessary, to counterract some of the invective. In addition, they surely could have avoided some of the other errors they made when covering the trial; such as the imbalance of the headlines, the preference for antivictim quotes, and the tendency to present defense attorney's allegations against her as fact. The papers also committed other avoidable errors. After the first verdict, for example, they continued to allude to the victim as "alleged" in their coverage of the second trial, even though the rape had been ascertained by one jury. Ragsdale said he thought the "alleged" had become such a habit by then that it had slipped in by mistake, but Downing and Ellsworth said it was there for legal reasons.

"Legally speaking a rape cannot take place if there's consent," Ellsworth said. "She would have only legally been a victim had she not consented to *each individual defendant*. It's certainly a strange idea. There was never any doubt in my mind that she was a victim, but legally speaking that had yet to be proven at the second trial."

Legally required or not, the continued labeling of the victim and the rape as "alleged" had the effect of further undermining her credibility. It could have been counteracted by reminding the reader that the first jury had decided there was a rape, but that the guilt of the remaining four men had not yet been determined.

Upon the announcement of the second verdicts, the press made another mistake by paying an inordinant amount of attention to the grief of the defendants' friends and relatives, but little attention to the reaction of the victim or her family. Only her lawyer was quoted, saying she was "satisfied" with the verdicts, but felt sorry for the convicted men's families. I asked the reporters how much effort they made to get the victim's side of the story. "Everybody wanted to talk to her," Kukielski said. "Everybody was calling her lawyer and asking him for an interview. He was saying no, not now, but down the road maybe. She also moved. People didn't know where she was." Kukielski added that the victim was hard to write about. "First of all, she was a rape victim. We don't normally write about rape victims. Second of all, we couldn't find her. She didn't have a job, so you couldn't go and talk to employers about her. . . . So you weren't left with much hard information except some mention in the yearbook."

Impemba had a different view. "I think we could have done more," he said. "Maybe we weren't as exhaustive as we should have been, trying to get to her or her family. Maybe a different tack could have been approached—through a women's group or rape support group."

The fact is, little real effort was made by the press to counteract the antivictim sentiment that was flying about after the verdicts. Once in a while an editorial, a letter, or a column was printed, but most of those were about the plight of rape victims in general, not about the sufferings of this particular woman. As for not being able to find people to talk about her—that is hard to believe. The victim may not have been employed, but she would have known other mothers, neighbors, and people in the area. Reporters could have gone to playgrounds near her home to seek out women who knew her, to stores where she shopped, or to neighbors who had known her and her family for their entire lives. After all, the victim came from a family who had been in New Bedford for three generations. There must have been some people on her side who would talk, if not about the case, then at least about what the woman and her family were like. There were certainly feminists and rape crisis counselors and other rape victims all over the country who could have spoken sympathetically about her particular ordeal. Not enough effort was made to get her side of the story, and no effort was made to help the public see her as an ordinary person.

The Posttrial Coverage: A Fifth Sentence

After the trials and demonstrations were over, the community remained enflamed about the case for some time. The Portuguese still felt wounded, criticism of the justice system was still rampant, and the anger was still being expressed in the form of vilifying the victim. The press, therefore, continued to be faced with the challenge of how to cover the story without being sucked into the community's antivictim mood.

The press first failed to meet this challenge when, only three days after the verdicts, the victim was hounded out of town by threats to her home and family. Her lawyer was quoted saying, "There were five sentences in this case—one of them exile," but the tragedy was given minimal coverage, even though all the reporters and editors were aware of the harassment against her at the time.

"I remember there were reports that she was hounded in a supermarket that we didn't cover," said Charig.

Ragsdale added: "People would go to her house. They found out where she and her parents lived. They would throw things at the house and damage it. She became a double—triple—victim. . . . There was a real blood-letting in this community. It was the closest I've come to seeing mob hysteria. It was awful."

In spite of this knowledge, the *Standard-Times* ran only two small stories on the victim's exile, with no mention of these violent incidents. One of the stories was by Catherine Gabe, who interviewed the victim's nephew:

> RAPE VICTIM'S FAMILY: "IT'S TIME TO GET OUR LIVES BACK TOGETHER"
> In most of the contact with the media, he has been the intervenor, shielding his aunt from the attention.
>
> The role has not been an easy one for the youth to play. Yesterday, he was calm, though his voice was a bit shaky. However, a few weeks ago . . . he lashed out at the press.
>
> "Our entire family is Portuguese," he said. "We didn't make an issue of it—everyone else did. But people say we discriminated (against) them." . . .
>
> All he will say is that his aunt, whose name The Standard-Times has declined to publish, has moved out of state. (4/7/84, p. 1.)

The *Globe* ran only one story about the victim's flight. The *Portuguese Times* gave it a tiny story under a headline using her name. The *Washington Post* only mentioned it in one paragraph at the bottom of a story about the sentences. The *L.A. Times* failed to mention it at all. The only reporter to give her exile major attention was Estes of the *Herald*, who wrote one story about it headlined "BIG DAN VICTIM FLEES TOWN." In it, Estes wrote that the victim had been "threatened and harassed" and quoted some of the threats.

> "She's a dead girl," said a young woman standing outside the massive Fall River courthouse.
>
> "She asked for it and they gave it to her," said Anna Laurendeau

> of Fall River. "What do you expect? They're not animals. They're human beings. They're not queers. They're men." (3/27/84, p. 1.)

The *Herald* story went on to mention an "unsubstantiated rumor" that some people were taking up a collection to hire an assassin to kill the victim, but none of the other papers ever reported the substance of the threats against the victim.

Why did the papers neglect the victim's exile? Why was this essential part of the story ignored? Why was the opportunity missed to point out just how extreme and vindictive the reaction to her had become?

One reason, for the *Standard-Times* at least, may have been that the paper had to appease its readers. None of the *Standard-Times* reporters said as much, but it was clear from reading the clips that the paper was worried about the criticism it had received from its Portuguese customers. After all, New Bedford is 60 percent Portuguese and the *Standard-Times* is a New Bedford paper. This may explain why the posttrial coverage focused so much on the grief of the defendants and their families and so little on the plight of the victim. The paper was catering to the concerns of its readers.

Charig gave another answer on behalf of the *Standard-Times:* "We were conscious throughout the coverage of her being a victim. We decided not to name her and we avoided writing any stories that would identify her or lead other people to her identity." This argument is understandable, but given the unusual amount of hatred and blame directed at the victim, it weakens. Normally, I would not advocate dwelling on the personality and life of a rape victim, but in this case, when she was subject to so much slander, the papers should have pursued a more balanced view of her. As it was, they missed the most unique and troubling aspect of this entire story: the posttrial persecution of a rape victim.

After ignoring the victim's exile, the local papers committed a second error while awaiting the sentences. They ran a series of stories about the fears of the convicts, while continuing to remain virtually silent about the plight of the victim: "Stiff sentences feared in rape at Big Dan's" (*Standard-Times*, 3/25/84, p. 1); "Big Dan's rapist fears jail violence" (*Herald*, 3/26/84, p. 9). The number of stories expressing pity for the convicts increased as sentencing approached, but virtually no stories quoted anyone in the community expressing pity for the victim. Yet, even though the majority of people in New Bedford seemed to have committed themselves to the defendants' side, there were men and women in the area who sympathized with the victim, as the occasional column, editorial, or letter revealed:

> It's appalling that the men in the bar couldn't see alternatives to rape, such as directing her out of the bar and calling the police, if necessary, to keep her out. If someone in the bar had pulled a gun on a patron, the bartender certainly would have called the police to prevent violence. The violent crime of rape could have been prevented just as well.
>
> (Letter from Ellen Kellner, *Providence Journal*, 4/14/84, p. 19.)

> In reference to the recent verdicts in the Big Dan's rape trial, I think the Portuguese people are missing the point. They are forgetting that if the crime was committed, whether it was Portuguese, Irish, Italian or whatever, they are guilty. . . . My husband is of Portuguese descent and we don't feel any resentment towards the verdicts at all. What happened still happened.
>
> (Dawn Morris, *Providence Journal*, 4/3/84, p. A9.)

Outside of New Bedford, in more progressive Boston, there was even a rally protesting the victim's treatment one month after the convictions, sponsored by the Women's Committee of The Rainbow Coalition and the Cambridge Women's Center. It was covered only by a small AP story.

> "Every day of the Big Dan's trial was an assault on all women," said Margaret Cerullo, one of the 30 protesters at the rally. "What the trial said to women is that if you are raped, you go on trial." . . . "It's true that this woman's life has been completely ruined, she had to move away and everything, but the men were convicted," Ms. Stephen said of the Big Dan's case.
>
> (Associated Press, *Standard-Times*, 4/22/84, p. 6.)

By ignoring those sympathizers, the papers not only contributed to the continuing neglect of the victim, but misrepresented the community.

When the sentences were announced at the end of March—nine to twelve years for Silva, Cordeiro, and Raposo, six to eight for Vieira—protest resurged and again the press erred by concentrating on the local view that the convicts were the victims in this case: "Crowd hurls death threat at D.A. Pina, cheers four rapists" (*Standard-Times*, 3/27/84, p. 1). Once again, the press ran stories quoting people libeling and threatening the victim without offering her recourse or balance.

After the sentences were announced, a new issue arose to infuriate the community—the question of whether the convicts would be deported—and this led to even more stories sympathizing with the convicts and ignoring the victim.

> LETTERS PLEAD ON BEHALF OF BIG DAN'S CONVICTS
>
> Nearly 500 people have written to . . . ask Judge Young to block the deportation of two men convicted in the Big Dan's rape trials . . .
>
> They are letters like these:
>
> "Dear Judge Young. Please do not send Jose and Victor back to Portugal," said Ligia DeValles, an otherwise unidentified first-grader. (*Providence Journal*, 4/23/84, p. A3)

One story focused on Victor Raposo's illegitimate son, who had been born to his girlfriend three years before the trial. Raposo's lawyer, Judith L. Lindahl, said that he was "the father of a U.S. citizen" and is "as acculturated as you or me."[46] This was a wonderful demonstration of the double standard at work: The convict's unwed parenthood was used to depict him as a family man and upright citizen, while the victim's unwed parenthood was used to paint her as a prostitute.

The deportation furor was particularly ironic in the light of the victim's flight. The community was up in arms about the possibility of the rapists being exiled, but indifferent to the fact that she—as much a member of the community as were the men—already had been.

Once the postsentencing furor was over, several papers ran summaries and analyses of the case that further contributed to the persecution of the victim by continuing to question her story, in spite of the guilty verdicts. They criticized her initial accounts of the rape, questioned the number of people in the bar, and once more brought up doubt about whether anyone really had cheered.

> BIG DAN'S: QUESTIONS PERSIST
>
> STORIES STILL DIFFER ON HOW MANY WERE IN THE BAR
>
> With the completion of the trials and the sentencing of the four convicted men last week have come doubts about the authenticity of that original [story].
>
> One defense attorney and several members of the pro-defendant Committee for Justice charged that when a jury recently acquitted two men charged as accessories, it rejected the notion that men in the bar were cheering—an essential ingredient to the shock felt here and across the nation.

> Others, however—including the district attorney and the victim—are sticking with the cheering story . . .
>
> The story appeared . . . one day after the woman ran half-naked and hysterical from the bar . . .
>
> In that first report, she gave an account that was so lurid and grotesque it *belied belief.* (My emphasis.)
>
> (Levin, *Standard-Times*, 4/1/84, p. 1)

Levin followed these statements—and his unfortunate disinterment of the words "half naked" and "hysterical"—with a recapitulation of the crime and its coverage, at one point even referring to the rape as "alleged." He then once again ran though the differences between the victim's initial account and the version the juries had settled for.

> The victim said at the trial that she was raped—by intercourse and other means—four times . . . but other witnesses said three men at most raped her . . .
>
> The victim reiterated on the witness stand that she believed someone had a knife during the rape, but she could not recall details.
>
> No other evidence of a knife was presented during the trial . . .
>
> Police originally received varying accounts from the woman and from other witnesses—some accounts saying as many as 20 men were in the bar . . .
>
> However, testimony of people in the bar named only nine men.

In this story, Levin paid no attention to the early accounts he had described to me, indicating that there had been a crowd of people in the bar who had disappeared once the police had been called. He also failed to mention the fact that the victim said she was so traumatized at the time that she could not count how often she was assaulted. Furthermore, he did not quote anyone pointing out that, to a rape victim, nine men *is* a large crowd, and that being assaulted by three men is as traumatic as being assaulted by four. The discrepancies between the victim's perception of what had happened to her and the defense's account was presented, even at this late date, as evidence of the dubiousness of her story. It took a reader to point out the unfairness of this:

> Trying to belittle the victim because she may have been raped fewer times than she had thought, or there might have been fewer men cheering on her attackers, is disgraceful. If you or I had been forced into such abuse for an hour or two, we, too, might lose track of details.
>
> (*Providence Journal*, 4/3/84, p. A9)

The *Standard Times* was not the only paper to run the victim through the mill yet again after the trial and sentencing were over.

> First reports of the event led us to believe that a number of men had actually raped the victim and that a crowd—perhaps dozens—had looked on. . . . The large cheering crowed turned out to be a great exaggeration. (*Washington Post* editorial, 3/27/84, p. A22.)

> [A]s the trials of the six men charged in the Big Dan's Tavern case finally unfolded here . . . it became increasingly clear that what happened the night of March 6, 1983—however reprehensible and sordid—bore little resemblance to the initial tale reported by the news media. (*L.A. Times*, 3/21/84, p. 1.)

This posttrial nitpicking had a lasting effect on the public mind, as was revealed more than four years later in a *Wall Street Journal* review of the movie inspired by the case, *The Accused*. In the review, the critic, Julie Salamon, stated, "That was the case in which bystanders purportedly cheered while a woman was gang-raped on a pool table. It turned out there weren't really any heckler accomplices."* Salamon probably was referring to the *L.A. Times* clip or just her memory, but she seemed unaware that the existence of the crowd was never disproved and that many people involved in the case said there had been cheering. She and other writers questioning the cheering also neglected another fact: Big Dan's bar was so small, essentially one room the size of a Mom and Pop grocery store, that no one could have been inside during the rape without seeing it. Even if the only men who had cheered were the four convicted of the rape, the others in the room must have watched it, a fact that would have been disturbing to the victim, even if it did not result in convictions of joint enterprise in a court of law.[47]

If the community was still discussing the validity of the "facts" in the case the papers certainly had to cover that, but they need not have taken such a one-sided approach, giving so much space to the defense's

*The article also made another inaccurate statement about the case: ". . . the New Bedford attackers were too overcome by drink and, perhaps the anxiety of public performance, to technically complete the rape." Semen was found in the victim's vagina, and four men were convicted of aggravated rape, which includes penetration. Salamon is remembering the arguments of the defense attorneys rather than the version the juries believed, which demonstrates the power of attorneys and the newspapers reporting them to dictate public memory. "Film: Barroom Horror Story; Mafia Fable," by Julie Salamon. *Wall Street Journal*, 10/88.

view and so little to the prosecution's. As Ruth Marcus of the *Washington Post* had pointed out a month earlier, the victim was being put on trial—only this time, after the verdict was in.

The End of the Story

On December 14, 1986, two years and eight months after the trial, Maria Bianco was killed in a car crash in Florida, where she had fled after the rape. She was twenty-five, and she left three children behind, her son of twelve and her two daughters, aged six and four.

Carole Agus of *Newsday* did one of the best stories on Bianco's life and death. She went to the trailer park where Bianco had moved, deep in the Florida countryside, interviewed her friends and neighbors, and talked to a Californian librarian, Bernadine Abbot, who had bought rights to Bianco's life story. Agus's biography revealed how terrible the persecution of Bianco had been—the story that the press had missed so glaringly. Here are some excerpts.

> When the verdicts came in, there were street demonstrations for the defendants and against her, people shouted and pounded on cars, and the death threats came not from anonymous strangers but from people she knew . . .
>
> "They threatened to bomb her house," said Abbot. "She was literally run out of town . . ."
>
> So she fled. Three days after the trial, March 1984, she grabbed the two youngest of her three children and moved into the mobile home in The Redlands that belonged to her boyfriend's father, Bernard Lavalle. She would soon be joined by her boyfriend, Peter.*

(No reporters during the case had mentioned Bianco's son or that she'd had to leave him behind; another tragic consequence of her persecution. She had left him, Agus discovered, because she did not want to take him out of school. He lived with her grandparents.)

> [The woman] driving through the Redlands at top speed, veering from lane to lane, was a very different Maria from the one who testified at the trial. The reporters at the trial had observed how calm and self-possessed she had appeared. Now her hands shook, her speech ram-

*The names of the victim's children and other relatives, which were given in full in the story, are changed here to protect their privacy—au.

> bled, friends said. Her voice soared crazily into the upper reaches, so that in normal conversation she fairly shrieked at people . . .
>
> "She was so scared they would come and kill her, she thought they were following her," [said George, her best friend]. "When she drove she didn't just look at the rear-view mirror, she stared at it."

Agus went on to describe Bianco's life.

> "She felt like she was trapped here," [George] said. "She didn't like it here. She tolerated it. She hated the fact that she had to stay here. She kept talking about a big house her grandparents had in New Bedford. She wanted to go home." (*Newsday*, 12/30/86)

By day, the neighbors said, she was a good mother—quiet, loving, domestic. At night, however, she would go out, get drunk, and take cocaine. It once got so bad she was put in a drying out hospital for three months, but even there she would not tell the counselors of her problems. They considered her "very depressed."*

Just before her death, according to Agus, things had been looking up. Her boyfriend "Peter" had been offered a job in Kansas, Bianco had been working on an assembly line in a factory, and they had saved enough money to buy new clothes for the girls and a special Christmas present for her son.

> Later that Sunday, Maria's car went out of control, ending her life on Quail Roost Drive. A few days later, a photographer asked her daughter Geraldine if anyone was home. The little girl's arm was broken in the accident and she struggled to ride a blue-and-pink plastic Powder Puff tricycle. "No," said the little girl. "My mommy is dead."

Bianco's body was found to contain three times the amount of alcohol used to define drunk driving.

Discussion

Even though the Big Dan's verdicts were hailed by the press as a triumph for feminists and proof that a woman "doesn't have to be a saint to get

---

*In an interview with the author, Greta Rideout said she also drank heavily and was paranoid for a time after the rape by her husband and the trial. "I kept thinking John was coming after me," she said. This reaction is not uncommon among rape victims even when they have not been run out of town by their neighbors—au.

raped," as the *Boston Herald* put it,[48] Maria Bianco should go down in history as one of the worst-treated rape victims of the decade. She was vilified by her community, which threatened her life and drove her out of town; and even though the press treated her well before the trials, she was so neglected during and after them that defense attorney smears were allowed to dominate newspaper pages without balance, and her enemies were able to grab headlines without a murmur in her defense.

The reasons Bianco attracted so much hostility are not hard to ascertain. She had every one of the eight biasing ingredients listed in Chapter 1 against her: She knew the assailants (it was never clear whether she knew any of them before the rape, but she spent enough time with them in the bar to count in the public eye as knowing them—she certainly was not jumped by complete strangers); no weapon was used (the early accounts of the butterknife never came up in court); she was of the same race, class, and ethnic group as the assailants; she was young; she was attractive, and, above all, she deviated from the norm of a "good woman" by being alone in a bar full of men, drinking, when the attack occurred.

Any section of the public is liable to see these ingredients as discrediting a rape victim, as the defense lawyers knew when they relied upon them to undermine her story in court, but the Portuguese community took the victim-blaming to an extreme. The press at the time tried to analyze their hostility by quoting anthropologists and locals describing Portuguese culture as extremely traditionalist and machismo, but, as Ferreira said, those analyses only further infuriated the community, making it feel maligned and patronized. Sociologist Lynn Chancer, who studied the antivictim reaction of the local Portuguese women, supported that complaint by pointing out that a traditionalist view of women as belonging in their homes and to their men exists in many cultures, and criticizing the media for making it sound as if the attitude was exclusively Portuguese. Ferreira made the same point: "In American culture, too, if you see a woman go into a bar in a combat zone, what are you going to think about her?" Chancer also blamed the press for inflaming the ethnic issue by failing to mention that the victim, like her assailants, was of Portuguese descent. She wrote: "Had the victim's ethnic background been part of the media's story, the community would have been hard pressed to focus on ethnic discrimination to defend the rapists, and Portuguese women might not have had to choose between identification with the victim as woman and identification with the rapists as Portuguese."[49]

I disagree with Chancer that the media ignored the victim's ethnic background. It was mentioned several times. The *Providence Journal*, for example, quoted the victim herself mentioning it during cross-examination at trial, something that would have been broadcast by cable television:

> Miss Lindahl asked Miss Bianco if she had told one of the police detectives that the men in the bar "were all greenhorns . . ."
> "If that was the case, I am also a greenhorn," Miss Bianco replied. "I'm just as much Portuguese as they are." (2/29/84, p. A14.)

The *Boston Herald* also mentioned it on the same day in a rare profile of the victim headed, "She remains a mystery," by Gayle Fee: "The 22-year-old woman was born, raised and lived all her life in the North End of New Bedford, and like most of that city's residents, she is of Portuguese descent." (2/29/84, p. 12.)

The flaw in the reporting of this case was not so much in ignoring the fact that the victim was Portuguese as in ignoring the chance to portray her as a human being rather than a symbol: victim to the feminists, vamp to the locals—and here I do agree with Chancer that this was the fault of the press. Once the defense attorneys and the suspects pulled out the rape myths to discredit the victim, the press fell in line and perpetuated those myths in the pages of its newspapers, enhancing them by the use of her name coupled with the graphic description of her sexual assault.

I also agree with Chancer that the press was indirectly responsible for the Portuguese turning against the victim. Without Portuguese reporters or speakers, the local American papers were unable to portray the community in a nonstereotypical way, unable to find people who had not blindly turned against the victim, and unable to win the trust of the victim's family and friends in order to represent her side. The result was that the case polarized into the liberal American media versus the New Bedford Portuguese, which filled the local people with such a sense of injustice that they turned on the victim as a scapegoat. This was not entirely the press's fault, but it was certainly exacerbated by its failures.

In many ways, the press itself became as much a part of the Big Dan's story as did the victim and the defendants. By using the victim's name, by describing the trial with hitherto never-used explicitness, by profiling the defendants' community, and by running column after column expressing feminist views of rape and self-criticism, the press drew so much attention to itself that the community reacted as much to it as to the crime. As a result, the media came in for a lot of blame in postcase analyses, some of it undeserved, much of it well earned. With all this criticism in mind, I asked the reporters on the case what they thought, in retrospect, of their coverage of Big Dan's.

Ellsworth of the *Journal,* who is now a lawyer, said she thought that her paper had done a good job and that she was particularly impressed with the *Standard-Times* reporters: "They were these unassuming, quiet, relatively unsophisticated people compared to the out-of-town press. They would just sit in the press room and not say a whole lot and write stories that were better than anything else anyone was putting out." She was less impressed with the out-of-town press: "I remember being appalled at the patronizing, nasty attitude that some of the out-of-town reporters had about the defendants. About the victim, too, but primarily about the defendants. . . . I couldn't actually hear the trial sometimes because these guys and women were making jokes and yuk-yuking. I said to myself, 'How hypocritical. Here are these nice liberals moaning and groaning about what happened to this poor victim, and what they really feel is that the defendants are trash, the victim is trash and this is a big circus." Ellsworth added that she did not think that condescending attitude showed in the reporters' stories, but it is possible that the Portuguese thought otherwise, which might have contributed to their resentment toward the American press and, by proxy, the victim.

Estes, who still works for the *Boston Herald,* said this about her paper's coverage: "That was a period of time when editors here didn't have a lot of qualms about anything. Rupert Murdoch had just bought the paper. Now it's transformed, but we had Murdoch-style editors then. They were trying to make an impression and no holds were barred.

"Some of the other papers mocked our headlines. Our presentation might have looked as if we were overblowing the story. But except for the headlines, I don't remember writing anything I felt bad about."

When I shifted to the question of whether the press had treated the victim fairly, the reporters answers were more ambivalent. Impemba of the *Standard-Times* said he thought the paper could have done more for her side. Other reporters agreed that they had not always been fair to the victim, but they attributed that to their being overwhelmed by the volume of information in the case, as had the reporters on the Rideout trial. Kukielski of the *Providence Journal,* said he did not know what else his paper could have done on the victim's side, but wished his paper had stepped back more from the case: "I would have liked to do more analysis along the way. When I look back over my clips, I remember how the story was shooting off like a skyrocket in all different directions. I wish there had been more opportunity to put these things in context."

A solution to this confusion could have been to assign someone to do a weekly news analysis of the story. The analysis could have been done by an editor, a columnist, an ombudsman, a reporter not on the case, or a guest writer with some expertise on the subject of sex crimes. The analyst could have explained the technicalities of the charges, the myths of rape, the methods of attorneys, the history of discrimination against the Portuguese, and could have kept an eye on the balance of the reporting. It is possible that an aloof, outside eye could have prevented the reporters from dwelling so unfairly on the antivictim side and from allowing their class prejudices to inflame the Portuguese.

Charig, one of those "unassuming" reporters Ellsworth praised, had this to say about the Big Dan's case and its coverage: "I've never seen a case where everybody came away so hurt and so disillusioned. . . . I've covered a lot of court cases and I don't think I have seen one where there was less sense of justice. So many lives were torn to shreds.

"As a woman, I have wondered a number of times if she had never reported the rape, if she had just walked away and said, 'It's bitterly unfair this rotten thing happened to me but I'm going home naked now,' I wonder if she might not have been happier in the long haul. She lived it over and over, people hammering away at her, at her life, at the quality of her life. She was driven out of the community. Everywhere she turned the thing was right in front of her.

"One can look at the circumstances which surrounded her death in Florida and either say, 'What can you expect from someone like that?' or one could say, 'Ok, we finally drove her to a lifestyle that led to her death.' "

Maria Bianco's treatment by her community was so blatantly unjust that it elicited widespread reaction after the case. Women's groups and feminists demonstrated and wrote about it for months following the trial.[50] A sociologist conducted a study of why Bianco was so hated by her neighbors.[51] Essayists and editorial writers analyzed the Portuguese hostility in magazines and newspapers.[52] The bias against her instigated a re-examination of rules governing the media's access to trials. The use of her name inspired a governmental investigation into rape coverage.[53] And, finally, the movie loosely based on the case, *The Accused*, portrayed the victim with much of the sympathy that had been so lacking in the press at the time of the case.[54]

As a result, the Big Dan's case will not be forgotten. It revealed the raw underside of American society—the conflict between men and women, the suspicion of everyone toward victims, and the mutual hatred between settled Americans and those seen as foreign, lower-class, non-white, or "other"—and it revealed the way those elements can seduce and bias the press. The themes of class, race, and gender prejudice come up again and again in sex-related crimes, as will be seen in the next two cases, and they point to a reason why these crimes are so significant as mirrors of our society: They are not just stories of isolated, bizarre cases, they are stories that lay bare the forces underlying all our social interaction. As such they are essential for the press to cover wisely and well.

· 5 ·

"How Jennifer Courted Death"
The 1986 Killing of Jennifer Levin

Near the end of a long, hot summer in 1986, New York woke to a series of salacious headlines about the killing of an eighteen-year-old woman in Central Park. In no time at all, Jennifer Dawn Levin, the victim, and the circumstances of her death were being raked over the coals as the *New York Post,* then still owned by Rupert Murdoch, *The Daily News, New York Newsday,* and *The New York Times* competed for reader attention.

For the first few hours after Levin's body was found by a jogger early in the morning of August 26, a Tuesday, the press assumed a rape-murder by a stranger: "WOMAN FOUND RAPED AND SLAIN IN CENTRAL PARK" (*Post,* 8/26/86). "At first we thought it was just a homeless dirtbag who had strangled her," said Bill Hoffman, who covered the story for the *Post.* Even so, the case held plenty of attraction for the press.

"I remember the morning the case broke, we were listening to the police radio," said Hoffman. "We heard the words, 'Central Park, young white teenager, gorgeous and strangled,' and it was like TNT was planted under our rear ends—everyone flew out of here like bats out of hell. It was sex, tits and ass, and a strangling—we knew it would sell."

Shortly thereafter, a friend of Levin's, nineteen-year-old Robert Chambers, was declared by police to be the killer. He had not only been seen leaving a bar, Dorrian's Red Hand, with Levin early that morning, but had been seen, it later turned out, hanging around the body and sitting on a wall by the park, clutching his knees.[1] Once the police had him, he confessed.

Chambers's confession was designed, naturally enough, to blame Levin rather than himself for her death. He described her propositioning him for sex, luring him to the park, seducing him, and tying his hands behind his back with her underwear. "She had her way with me," he said. He told police that Levin had pushed him to the ground, sat on his chest facing his feet, and squeezed his testicles so hard that he had to pull her off him. He grabbed her by the neck and flipped her over his shoulder—and that, he said, was how he had accidentally killed her. The police officers taking the confession laughed.[2]

The prosecution's version was quite different: Levin and Chambers, who had slept together before, went to the park after a night of talking in the bar, had a quarrel and he, either out of drug-induced fury or simple lack of control, punched her, knocked her over, picked her up by her neck and dragged her along the ground, strangling her in the process. Then he rearranged her clothes to make her look as if she had been sexually assaulted by a stranger.

For some time, the press was remarkably inclined to accept, or at least to emphasize Chambers's side of the story: "JENNY KILLED IN WILD SEX"—the *Post* three days after her death (8/28/86); "SEX PLAY 'GOT ROUGH' "—the *News,* the same day. On the following day: "SUSPECT DEATH WAS ACCIDENT DURING SEXUAL TRYST IN PARK"—*Newsday;* and "SUSPECT CALLS PARK SLAYING ACCIDENTAL"—*The Times.**

"The thing about this case was the defense, the rough sex business," said Arthur Brown, metropolitan editor of the *Daily News,* who was city editor at the time and responsible for assigning the Levin coverage. "He brought their sexual relationship and her sexuality into the issue . . . Because he made that an issue, it gave [the press] a reason why [it] would ever tell anyone about this stuff."

The press also decided it was worth telling "about this stuff" because they found out that the two teenagers were "preppies" with posh

*In Linda Wolfe's book on the case, *Wasted,* she reported that Jack Litman, Chambers's attorney, was furious at these headlines, perhaps realizing that their victim-blaming slant would turn public sympathy away from him and his client. He had not, he shouted at a *Post* editor, used the phrases "rough" or "wild sex," which the paper had attributed to him. The editor replied, "My headline writer just took a bit of literary license," but from then on, the phrase, "rough sex" was to appear in all the papers, repeatedly, and became inerasably associated with the case. Linda Wolfe, *Wasted: The Preppie Murder* (New York: Simon and Schuster, 1989.) p. 197. Linda Fairstein, the prosecutor, said Litman did use the phrase "rough sex" at Chambers's indictment.

addresses—Chambers lived with his mother on East 90th Street, one of the toniest neighborhoods in the city, and Levin lived in a fancy loft in SoHo with her father and step-mother. They were both white, they both went to expensive private schools, and they were both part of a rich, independent crowd of teenagers who hung out at certain bars buying drinks on the strength of their altered drivers licenses, partying until the early hours of the morning.

"[When] it started emerging that this was a girl who'd been in a bar the night before, and it was a preppie bar and rich kids, it of course became *really* fascinating," said Stuart Marquez, rewrite man for the *News*. "There's this fascination with the rich who have their troubles because it makes everyone feel, 'They're no better than us.' "

Hoffman of the *Post* put it even more succinctly: "The story had three basic elements of a classic tabloid story: sex, good looking people, money. When you combine those three elements, it's irresistable."

Between Chambers's explicity sexual defense, the press's fascination with class, money, and looks, and the narrative convention about sex crime victims, Levin, by four days after her death, was irrevocably labeled a "sex victim" who had sought her own demise:

"SAD FAREWELL TO SEX VICTIM" (*Post*, 8/29/86).

"HOW JENNIFER COURTED DEATH" (*News*, the same day).

That idea of Levin having provoked her own death was never shaken, even when the tide of public opinion turned against Chambers and his lawyer just before the trial. It was because of this blame-the-victim slant that the Levin case became a *cause célebre* among feminists and press critics. In the November after she died, the "Justice for Jennifer Task Force" was formed to monitor the press coverage of the case. The Task Force issued a statement asserting that Levin's death "has been overshadowed by an inordinate interest" in her accused killer, and added, "We believe Jennifer Levin has been maligned by innuendoes, misinformation, and outright distortion."[3]

Samuel G. Freedman of *The New York Times* summarized these objections in a story that could as easily have been written about the Big Dan's case as Levin's, revealing how little had changed in the two years since the woman I have named Maria Bianco had been driven out of town.

> SEXUAL POLITICS AND A SLAYING: ANGER AT CHAMBERS'S DEFENSE
> In many ways, those who have watched the progress of the Levin case say, it has come to resemble less a murder prosecution than the most

> volatile sort of rape trial—one in which the victim's reputation, not the question of whether she was assaulted, is made the primary issue. (12/4/86)

It is because of this case's resemblance to a rape trial, and because of the point made by Freedman in this quote, that I have included it in this book.

The Case

The story of what exactly happened between Chambers and Levin was never completely sorted out, even after the trial; however, according to news sources, it went like this:

Robert Chambers, nineteen, was drinking in the East Side bar, Dorrian's Red Hand, on the evening of August 25, a Monday, where he had arranged to meet his current girlfriend. He was apparently in a gloomy frame of mind, had been late for the meeting, and then had ignored his girlfriend after he arrived. They ended up quarreling and she was overheard telling him to find someone else. Chambers said later that he was upset that night because he had heard of the death of a friend.

Jennifer Levin, eighteen, arrived at Dorrian's after Chambers. She came with three friends with whom she had just had dinner, and was by all reports in a happy, celebratory mood because she was about to go off to college that week. She and Chambers knew many of the people in the bar.

Levin and Chambers had dated three times before, and had slept together. Various reports had Levin saying she did not particularly care for Chambers's personality, but thought that he was a good lover. Other reports suggested she had a crush on him. Chambers, meanwhile, was said to have at first really liked Levin, and later to have lost interest in her as he became involved with someone else.

At one point in the evening, a friend of Levin's later said in the trial, Levin approached Chambers for a possible flirtation or liaison. At first Chambers was not interested, but later he spent several hours talking to her alone at a table. The two of them eventually left the bar together at 4:30 A.M. They went into a pocket of Central Park behind the Metropolitan Museum of Art, and all that is known for sure is that Chambers then strangled Levin to death.

The Reporting

The "Preppie Murder," as Levin's killing came to be called, was covered by proportionally more men and fewer women than any other case in this book. Among the daily newspapers I examined, male reporters dominated the coverage. *The New York Times* put twelve men and three women on the case, the latter of whom wrote only one story each. The *New York Post* put twenty-one men and six women on the story, all the women except one in rewrite or "legwork" roles—newspaper jargon for reporters who gather facts but do not write the story. The *Daily News* had seventeen men and only two women on the case, both of whom also wrote only one story each. *Newsday,* although the most balanced with fourteen men to ten women on the case, gave the bulk of the coverage and all of the most important stories to men. To some extent, these numbers may have reflected the male–female ratio in the newsrooms at the time, but not wholly. Hoffman said the gender ratio in the *Post* newsroom was about equal, for example, and theorized that fewer women were put on the story because they did not "make enough noise" to get the assignment. The main explanation for the disproportion, however, is that newsrooms still traditionally give crime stories to men. In this case, the total count was an overwhelming sixty-six men to twenty-one women.

Men also wrote the biggest magazine stories on the case, in *New York* and *People.* The one *Village Voice* article on it, a cover story, was written by a woman, however, as was the book about the case, *Wasted: The Preppie Murder,* by Linda Wolfe.[4]

Hoffman admitted that the preponderance of male reporters on the daily papers may have contributed to the bias against Levin. "The media is male dominated," he said, "and every male reporter collectively clutched his own genitals when he heard about her squeezing Chambers's balls. Male reporters said, 'I'd push her off, too, and if she died that's too bad.' " Hoffman may have been overstating the male reaction here, but the fact remains that no reporter could deny the press's initial preference for Chambers's version of the encounter.

Because this case happened in New York, where there is more competition among the media than in any other U.S. city, the coverage of this story was markedly different than it would have been anywhere else. The number of reporters assigned to it was larger, the tabloid influence bigger, and the day-to-day coverage more intense than even in the Big Dan's case. This chapter, therefore, is not only a look at the way Levin's murder was covered, but at the way the New York press, particularly its tabloid press, functions.

The First Two Days: Reluctant Romeo and The Hot Date

Levin's body was found on the night she died and, by the next day, August 27, every police reporter in town knew who she was and who had been accused of killing her.[5] The press flocked to the story in droves, for the case was perfect New York material. It not only took place in the city's beloved playground, Central Park, but involved glamorous, East Side teenagers, people from the very families to whom *The New York Times* caters and whom tabloid readers are assumed to envy. Right from the beginning, therefore, the press leapt to all sorts of extremes to fit the teenagers into a newspaper dream: gorgeous, rich, and upper class.

> BOTH TEENS LIVED THE GOOD LIFE
>
> Bobby Chambers and Jenny Levin lived Manhattan's good life in ways enjoyed only by the most privileged and protected. They also walked together into the darkest of horrors.
>
> He was tall and handsome, wealthy and intelligent; a star athlete idolized by other boys and adored by the girls. She was tall and beautiful; a bright, bubbly, young woman about to start college and pursue a career.
>
> They traveled in circles with rich young jet-setters who attend expensive schools, live in the finest apartments, drive the fastest cars and get nearly everything they want . . .
>
> (Stuart Marquez, *Daily News*, 8/28/86.)

The papers were merely indulging in one of their journalistic clichés—that pretty, rich people are more interesting than plain, poor ones—but the effect was already to cast doubt on Levin's credibility. The reason, as mentioned in Chapter 1, is that when a sex crime victim is considered attractive she receives *less* sympathy for her attack, whereas when a suspect is labeled attractive, he receives *more* sympathy regarding his innocence.[6]

The glamorization of Chambers, which began the very day after Levin's body was found and he was arrested, was particularly extreme and inaccurate. He was almost never mentioned without the epithet *handsome,*—sometimes "extremely," "extraordinarily," or even "breathtakingly handsome,"—a description that accompanying photographs hardly bore out. In addition, the press greatly exaggerated his accomplishments and popularity. The *Post* was the most blatant, labeling him a "reluctant Romeo" and going to press with the cover headline, "LADIES' MAN HELD IN SLAYING," the day of Chambers's arrest. Inside, under the head, "Preppy suspect was the cream of the crop," the *Post* described Chambers as a " 'friendly, energetic' youth who seemed to have opportunity after opportunity fed to him on a silver spoon." His former school headmaster was quoted as saying, "He was an up-and-comer—a society boy. He was bright, tall and very handsome. If you met him, you'd like him."

New York Newsday, which at that time was new in town and struggling to compete with the other tabloids, at least mentioned that Chambers was not a good student and was "dismissed" from one school, but it, too, was unable to resist exaggerating Chambers's glamor and reluctant Romeo image—an image mostly created from the quotes of only one young woman:

> **PRIVILEGED CHARACTERS**
>
> The man arrested for Jennifer Dawn Levin's murder wasn't one of those against whom Upper East Side parents guard their children. The suspect wasn't a street person, or someone armed with a knife or gun. According to the police, the person they had to fear all along was one of their own.
>
> And Robert Chambers was emphatically one of their own, a nineteen-year-old who charmed his way into at least one expensive prep school and was the breathtakingly handsome soccer player on whom legions of high school girls had a crush . . .
>
> "He was my idol," said Cory Mervis, eighteen, standing outside York, where she graduated in June. "Everybody used to follow him around. I would faint when I saw him. It was, 'My god, there's Robert Chambers.' " (Sandra Widener, 8/28/86.)

Later reporting belied virtually every one of these statements. Far from being "idolized by other boys," as the *News* had claimed, Chambers was regarded with suspicion by most of his friends who knew he stole and had drug problems. Far from being "up and coming," he had been expelled from three private schools, had dropped out of college, had been treated unsuccessfully for a cocaine habit, was a notorious liar, and was later indicted on several counts of burglary. Those "legions of high school girls" boiled down to a mere handful. He did not even come from a rich or genuinely "preppie" family.

While Chambers was described as handsome, he was also called charming and full of promise. Levin, however, was described mainly in terms of her sexual appeal, reflecting society's habit of judging men by their achievements and women by their looks.[7] Underneath the "cream of the crop" headline in the *Post* eulogizing Chambers, for example, was the head, "The type of girl you'd want to date," referring to Levin. In the story, her boss was quoted calling her

> "an all-American girl you just couldn't help falling in love with."
>
> "She was so beautiful, so gorgeous," said Eric Barger, the manager of Flutie's restaurant in the South Street Seaport where the college-bound teenager worked as a summer hostess. "She's the type of girl that, once you saw her, you'd want to go out with her," said Barger. (*Post*, 8/27/86.)

Newsday followed this same approach, describing Chambers as charming and Levin as unfaithful:

> Chambers, by all accounts, a charming young man who police said has the build of a linebacker, had dated Levin two or three times during the past three weeks, police said.
>
> Levin had a steady boyfriend and had also dated Michael Dorrian, the restaurant owner's son, according to friends and detectives.
>
> (Richard Esposito, 8/28/86.)

The story did not mention that Chambers also had more than one girlfriend.

Even the adjectives used underlined the difference in the way Chambers and Levin were written about: Chambers was called "intelligent" while Levin was only "bright," he was a "star athlete," while she was merely "bubbly." He was a maturely handsome "youth," she was only a "girl." He was always called "Chambers," she was frequently called "Jenny." This inequality was constant throughout the case's coverage.

These stories were all playing upon society's double standard about men and women: A man who is popular with women is admired ("Ladies' man"), while a woman popular with men is slurred (Levin's many dates). Levin had been dead for less than twenty-four hours, and the newspapers, or at least the sources from whom reporters were getting these quotes, were already squeezing her into a sex crime victim's stereotype: attractive, sexually active, available, "the type of girl you'd want to date"—the bad girl of the "women provoke rape" (or in this case murder) myth: the vamp.

On the second day of the case, August 28, Chambers's confession came to light. He admitted that the many scratches on his face and chest, which he had first said were made by a cat, were made by Levin. More significantly, he admitted that he had killed her by accident, but he pleaded innocent to the charge of second degree murder. With his confession came his soon-to-be-famous contention that he had killed Levin accidently because she had hurt him during sex play. The confession did nothing to change the approach of the tabloids. They ate his story up, continuing to glamorize him and denigrate Levin. The *Post*, for example, ran the suggestive headline, "JENNY KILLED IN WILD SEX." Inside, under the echo "WILD SEX KILLED JENNY" was a story on the same page headed, "Drinking buddies rally behind Mr. Nice Guy." (8/28/86).

The *Times* jumped into this fray two days after Levin's death, with a series of articles focusing on the lifestyle of the two preppies and their friends. In the first, "Darkness Beneath the Glitter: Life of Suspect in Park Slaying" (8/28/86, p. A1, B7), reporter Samuel G. Freedman seemed to promise a welcome relief to the idolizing descriptions of Chambers that had been filling the tabloids.

> For Jennifer Dawn Levin and Robert E. Chambers, Jr., life was private schools, fancy apartments, foreign vacations, and underage drinking at a preppy hangout called Dorrian's Red Hand. But for Mr. Chambers, it was also unemployment, academic futility, and signs of cocaine abuse.

There followed a summary of the case, after which it became apparent that Chambers was not the only one whose "darkness' was to be revealed.

> And as Mr. Chambers was waiting to be arraigned last night, the details of both his life and Miss Levin's began to emerge—details that contradicted Mr. Chambers's golden-boy image and revealed a naïveté beneath Miss Levin's worldly exterior.

To describe someone who has been murdered during a sexual encounter as "naïve" is subtly suggestive. The subtext is that a naïve person does not know something she should have known, that she was too out-of-touch to protect herself. The word *naïve* indicates a foolishness that the word *innocent* does not. To then describe that same person as having a "worldly exterior" covering up her naïveté is even more damning, for it suggests that she acted sexually sophisticated but did not mean it; Freedman was unintentionally suggesting that Levin was at best a phony, at worst a tease.

In the very next paragraph, Freedman stumbled upon Chambers's reluctant Romeo image:

> Mr. Chambers, in the recollection of friends, possessed charisma and mature good looks rare for a nineteen-year-old. He stood six feet four inches tall, weighed 220 pounds and was a gifted athlete, who had played for three years on the soccer team at York Preparatory School, 116 East 85th Street.

[If Chambers had not been white, rich and "handsome" and yet was accused of murder, one can imagine how these attributes would have been turned against him.]

> "Nothing less than total success," said the caption beneath Mr. Chambers's photograph in the York yearbook, "Diversions 1984."
>
> Mr. Chambers had a particular touch with young women. Mr. Dorrian, the bar owner, said: "He didn't have to chase girls. They chased him."

The story went on to give a short biography of Chambers, his life with his divorced mother, his membership as a cadet in the elite Knickerbocker Greys, "a drill team for the children of prominent families"; his brief sojourns at three private schools, his dismissal from the College of Basic Studies at Boston University, and his involvement with drugs "at one time." At the same time Mr. Dorrian was quoted calling him "the nicest kid you'd want to meet" and the worst people would say about him was that he was "lackadaisical," an "underachiever" and that he was not a master of self-discipline.

> If anything, he seemed to try to coast on his good looks and charm—and, in academic settings, not always with success.

When Freedman turned to Levin, it was with these words:

> Miss Levin, meanwhile, was a young woman who "was always happy," said Eric Barger, the manager of Flutie's . . .

Barger described Levin as a cheerful, hard worker, followed by this paragraph:

> "She was a lovely, lovely little girl," Mr. Dorrian said. He said Miss Levin's regular boyfriend, whom he recalled only as "Brock," was vacationing in Europe this summer. Miss Levin had dated several different co-workers from Flutie's, according to Mr. Barger.

The sudden jump from being a "lovely little girl" to her boyfriend being away, and then to her dating co-workers not only suggested that Levin was unfaithful, but promiscuous. After a brief description of the school Levin attended, making the point that it was inferior, "an institution that tries to prepare mediocre or troubled students for middle-level colleges," came the final paragraphs:

> Miss Levin's father, Steven, said yesterday that his daughter was "always the straight kid of her crowd," and that "maybe she was too trusting." Her stepmother, Arlene Levin, added that the young woman might even have been considered "a prude."
>
> Still, Mr. Levin acknowledged that his daughter "liked to go out at night." Mr. Dorrian said she came into his bar two or three times a week. And amid Miss Levin's belongings at the murder scene, the police found a learner's driving permit giving her age as twenty-two.
>
> It had been her passport into Dorrian's Red Hand.

Here, the story's innuendo reached a peak. The father "acknowledged"—a word that suggests reluctant confession—that his daughter liked to go out at night, making that liking sound shameful. She was then said to have been in possession of a false ID, as if that was an exceptional crime rather than one all her friends committed. In addition, that ID was described as being her "passport" into the "Red Hand," as if that murderous-sounding place was a den of iniquity that related directly to her death rather than a regular hangout for all her friends—as if, indeed, she had knowingly risked her life by going there. Perhaps the *Times*'s headline should have been, "How Jennifer Courted Death."

The reason I dwell upon this one story at such length is that its effect was to cast Levin in just as negative a light as had the tabloids, but it did so more subtly, and thus more insidiously. Everything about her behavior, none of which was so unusual for an eighteen-year-old of her set, was presented as shocking and, by implication, blameworthy. Freedman told the reader that Levin was naïve under her worldly exterior, that she went out with a lot of men and was unfaithful to her boyfriend, that she attended an inferior school, and that she had altered her ID so she could drink underage at Dorrian's Red Hand—in other words, he fit her smack into the "bad woman" narrative. I do not mean to suggest that he should have whitewashed her, but by telling the reader nothing about her family, her other friends, her hobbies, or other aspects of her life, he offered nothing to counterbalance the negatives. The result was that this profile that was supposed to expose Chambers's "darkness" did almost as much to condemn Levin. It is no wonder that her parents were so eager to depict her as "straight," "trusting," and a "prude"—they were already defending her against the vamp image.

Above all, the story begged a question no one at the time raised: Why was Levin, a victim of a crime, not a perpetrator, being being put on an equal footing with Chambers in this story? What had her intelligence, schooling, dates, or boyfriends to do with her murder? Indeed, why was she being scrutinized at all? Her very presence in this story served to condemn her because it implied that her behavior had as much to do with the crime as did his—that she shared responsibility for her fate. The fact that the story opened with the words, "Both the victim and the suspect in the strangling death Tuesday of an eighteen-year-old woman moved in the same Manhattan circle of rich and privileged young people . . ." put Levin in the same boat as Chambers and made Freedman sound as if he was out to expose her as much as him. To check my impression, I asked Freedman why he had portrayed Levin so unflatteringly. He said he was reacting to the sentimental coverage by the tabloids.

"The tabloids had started to come out with stories that were all, if I remember correctly, very much sob stories about Jennifer, who was this brilliant, promising student who had had her life snuffed out," he said. "But I was not one to take on faith the fact that anyone who went to a private school in New York was brilliant . . . because to me that was too much of a class bias. Those schools were about money, not about intelligence. . . . And that one Jennifer Levin went to was considered the bottom of the barrel of the prep schools . . .

"I got attacked for [saying] that, because it became equal to saying that because she wasn't a great student she deserved to be killed, which of course was hardly my point. But I thought that, given that she was killed, and given that she was now in the news, was no reason to romanticize her academic record." (Checking over the coverage during these first days of the case, the only "sob stories" I found about Levin were those quoting her family and friends at her funeral. There, her uncle called her "innocent" and referred to her fun-loving, lively personality. No one said anything about her being brilliant.)

Freedman also admitted to holding a certain prejudice against Levin's type and crowd. "This was one of the few times when I almost thought I shouldn't do a story, almost asked to be taken off it because I felt so offended by the lifestyle that these kids lived. I was concerned that I could not report without being too judgmental . . . Then I guess I went through a psychological metamorphosis. I went from the initial feeling of being repulsed by the life of privilege these kids lived—I guess because my own sympathies are much more working class—to feeling a great sympathy for them, and realizing that at that age they are more victims than victimizers. I began to feel that perhaps they had been victimized by the inattention of their parents."

I also asked Freedman whether he thought those phrases he had quoted about Levin, "naïve beneath her worldly exterior," a "prude," and "too trusting," hinted that she was a tease. "Oh no," he said quickly, "I didn't mean it that way at all. The reason I used those phrases in the story was more the issue of parenting. I felt that either her parents had been terribly disingenuous—either they know their daughter goes out until 3:00 in the morning and are trying for their own benefit to cover their asses by saying, 'Oh no, she was such a good girl she was in fact prudish'—or they're terribly naïve themselves about what their daughter's life was. And that's why I put that in. To me it didn't have any particular sexual context at all. . . . The reason my reporting was so different than the *Post* or the *News* is that I didn't pick up that angle on what role sex played in it at all."

Freedman clearly did not intend the innuendoes in his story. He did not consciously mean to hint that Levin was "bad" or that she should be blamed for her own demise. Yet the implication was there in both the structure and the language of the article. Freedman had fallen into the rape narrative.

The Third Day: Jennifer—Drink and Sex

The day after the "wild sex" headlines, Levin's funeral was held and, at the same time, Chambers's confession was released. The juxtaposition of these two events was unfortunate for Levin. The *Post* yet again labeled her with the headline, "SAD FAREWELL TO SEX VICTIM," referring to her funeral, while inside, right next to quotes from her mourning friends and family calling her "innocent" and "pure" was the head, "JENNY TIED ME UP, INSISTS CHAMBERS." The opening paragraph read:

> Central Park murder victim Jennifer Dawn Levin tied her accused killer's hands behind his back with her panties in a weird sex ritual before she was killed, the suspect, Robert Chambers, told police.
>
> (Cy Egan, 8/29/86, p. 3.)

In another edition of the *Post* that day, under a huge headline, "INSIDE MIND OF PREPPIE," the paper went to its furthest extreme yet in glamorizing Chambers, featuring reams of quotes about how charismatic and charming he was. Under the subhead, "Girls constantly threw themselves at his feet," was this story:

> Robert Chambers, the accused Central Park murderer, was a reluctant Romeo, constantly being besieged by women, friends say.
>
> "He didn't have a way with women," said Larry Greer, a former York prep school classmate. "Women had a way with him."
>
> Tim Packard, who has known Chambers for eleven years, agreed.
>
> "He had girls constantly throw themselves at his feet," he said.
>
> "But in order for him to go to bed with a girl, he really had to like her."
>
> "Robbie" was actually shy with women, according to former girlfriends. (8/29/86.)

The story went on to paint a picture of Chambers as qualifying for sainthood. "Greer agreed that his friend 'didn't have an angry bone in his body' . . . 'I never heard him raise his voice—ever.' " When his cocaine habit was mentioned, it was only to compliment him, inaccurately, on how he had ended it: "One former girlfriend said Chambers was proud of how he kicked a cocaine habit about a year ago." The cumulative effect of those *Post* stories, the very day his confession was released, was to make Chambers sound like the victim—a shy, gentle boy pursued by sexually aggressive girls—while Levin sounded like the assailant, chasing men and tying them up in "weird" sex rituals.

On the same day as the *Post* was reporting Levin's funeral and the "weird sex ritual" quotes, the *News* went to press with an "exclusive" bearing the much criticized headline, "HOW JENNIFER COURTED DEATH." Inside the paper, under the head "THE LAST HOURS," reporter Paul La Rosa described, from hour to hour, how Levin had spent her last evening. The opening paragraph: "She was in a party mood last Monday night. Summer was ending, her first year of college beckoned and Robert Chambers was on her mind . . ." La Rosa related that Levin went to a Mexican restaurant with three friends, had a fun, chatty time, was in a "great mood" and did not do much drinking. Then, in the fourth paragraph, was the line, "Another topic of dinner conversation was Robert Chambers." There followed an account by one of those friend saying that Chambers had told her the night before that "he really liked Jennifer but wasn't sure she liked him," that signals had crossed between Levin and Chambers, and that missed telephone messages had led Chambers to feel "she had lost interest." Finally came the passage, "In truth, the girl friend said, Levin confided to her pals that she had enjoyed sex with Chambers immensely."

The story then went on with the rest of the evening, describing the night in Dorrian's, the meeting of Chambers and Levin, and Levin's cheerful goodbye as she left the bar with him.

The bias in this "LAST HOURS" story is not immediately obvious. Levin's friend described her affectionately, La Rosa portrayed her actions as relatively innocent, and the paper seemed to be merely paying tribute to the last unsuspecting hours of a girl doomed to die. Compared to its headline, the story seems inoffensive. It is less so, however, when its implications are considered. Why was all this attention being paid to the last hours of Levin, who was merely a victim, and not to the actions of Chambers that night? Something could have happened to him that had put him in a dangerous or desperate mood—why did no one look into that? The attention to her actions and not his made the *News* look as if it was examining *her* motives, as if she were the accused criminal.

La Rosa said that he thought the reason the paper concentrated on Levin's last hours rather than those of Chambers was more to do with luck than intention. Stuart Marquez, a rewrite man, whose byline appeared on many *News* stories about the case, agreed: "People are more willing to talk about people who are dead. If you have any secrets that you don't want the world to know, don't get murdered. Because if you get murdered, detectives go through your whole life and they talk to the press, and all your little secrets come out. I think that's what happened."

Arthur Brown, the *Daily News* editor responsible for assigning stories at the time, confirmed that his reporters had more difficulty getting information about Chambers than they did about Levin. With a cynical twist, however, he added: "Her friends have nothing to lose by talking—they get to be a celebrity for a day. On the other side are his friends, who've got an interest in not revealing what they know. We had a lot of difficulty getting people to talk about what Chambers was doing that day, except through the lens of Levin's friends. We felt 'Let's do him, let's find out what he's like,' but those people just did not cooperate in any way."

If, as Brown said, details about Chambers's actions the day of the killing were not available, then the paper should have paused to consider its obligation to be balanced. Running a story about a victim's last hours before her death and not those of her killer automatically laid blame at her door, as the headline writer obviously realized. Why the *News* exercised such bad news judgment was revealed by La Rosa's explanation of how the story came about.

"It was a tip through somebody at the paper. The source of the story was a *Daily News* editor's daughter's friend. . . . It was supposed to be from the very beginning that she would only talk if she wasn't identified. . . . But we had a lot of credence because of who she was."

This is an example of how the excitement of the chase overrides any consideration of ethics. The *News* had an inside source, an "exclusive" as it proclaimed on its front page, and that was all it needed to run with the story without stopping to consider whether it might cast unfair innuendoes against Levin or, by proxy, seem to favor Chambers.

The headline to that story, "HOW JENNIFER COURTED DEATH," which was not written by any of the reporters on the case, was one of the main reasons the *News* came under criticism from Levin's family and the public. All the *Daily News* reporters and editors I interviewed independently brought up their distaste for it. "In the first few days . . . our paper wrote a headline that I found somewhat offensive and other people found offensive," said Marquez. La Rosa agreed. "Yeah, 'courted death,' that was a little unfair. There was a lot of that 'she was asking for it' at the time. What was she doing out so late? What was she doing drinking when she shouldn't have been? Obviously she was no 'good girl.' Not that I agree with it, but there was a lot of that."

As La Rosa pointed out, according to the moral guidelines that are invariably applied to sex crime cases, "good girls" do not do any of the things Levin did that night: They do not stay up late in bars, they do not drink underage, they do not go to Central Park with a boyfriend, they do not talk about, let alone enjoy sex, and, above all, they do not chase men. Levin was condemned for all these things, by implication in the press and more overtly during the trial. Yet, it certainly can be argued that none of Levin's actions were reprehensible or even unusual. What was she doing in that bar? No more than all her set did; it was a place she knew well, full of her friends, where she was known—in some ways, she was playing it safer by going there than almost anywhere else, other than home. What was she doing drinking underage? All her friends drank, there was no evidence she had been drinking excessively, and, in any case, her drinking was unrelated to the crime. Why did she go to the park with Chambers? There was nothing particularly foolish in going to the park with a six-foot, four-inch sometime lover she had no reason to distrust—at least she had not gone alone or with a stranger. Why did she talk openly about enjoying sex? She was speaking to intimate friends and this was 1986, not 1886. Finally, it should be said that in the 1980s, condemning a woman for pursuing a man was out-of-date and hypocritical. As Hoffman of the *Post* said: "It was just a girl with a couple of drinks in her who went off to the park for a bit of petting—something we've all done. . . . She just went off with the wrong guy."

The Second Month: Underage Drinking and Neglectful Parents

When the press was not covertly condemning Levin's behavior, it was engaged in an extraordinary amount of moralistic tut-tutting about the lifestyle of her entire set. It did so out of the time-honored journalistic impulse to find a moral lesson in every crime,[8] the same impulse that led columnists to dwell on the Kitty Genovese analogy in the Big Dan's case. No paper was as fixated on this quest as the *Times*.

Unlike the Rideout and Big Dan's cases, Levin's murder did not point to an obvious aspect of our society about which to moralize. The case did not test new legal ground, nor did it paint a picture of disintegrating urban mores. The Levin murder seemed a freak, nothing more than individual tragedy. The *Times*, therefore, always searching for a worthier reason to cover crime than mere curiosity, had to reach for a moral lesson in which to couch the case and with which to justify its extensive coverage. Samuel Freedman found it on the third day of the case: "Underage Drinking Sparks a Tragedy and Debates" (8/29/89, p. B3).

The story focused on the underage crowd who regularly drank at Dorrian's, and quoted officials lamenting how hard it was to prevent bars from selling alcohol to minors. In a passage a few paragraphs down came the tie-in with Levin, which probably inspired the headline:

> According to law-enforcement officials, Mr. Chambers, nineteen years old, told the police he had several drinks at Dorrian's before leaving

> the bar with Miss Levin at 4:30 A.M. Tuesday. Jack Dorrian, who said his wife owns the bar, said Mr. Chambers was such a regular at the bar that his mother often called to check on her son's well-being.

The story implied that Chambers's drinking was connected to the murder, and the headline suggested the same about Levin, assertions for which there was never even a hint of proof. Yet underage drinking and the decadent lifestyle of East Side preppies became a theme the *Times* would not let go of for weeks. Six different articles about it and the use of fake IDs were published over the next two months, including a particularly odd one by another reporter, Daniel Goleman:

> **DEPRESSION TIED TO SOME EXCESSES IN YOUTH**
>
> Throughout life there is a search for meaning and identity, but it is in late adolescence, roughly from the late teenage years to the early twenties, that the search, and the experimentation that accompanies it, is fraught with particular peril. The dangers are many—unwanted pregnancy, drugs, crime, violence—and the consequences potentially fatal, as the much-publicized murder of Jennifer Dawn Levin demonstrates. (9/9/86, p. C1.)

Is Goleman saying here that Levin's murder was a consequence of teenage experimentation? Look at the scenario this passage suggests: Chambers is a rich, neglected teenager. He tries cocaine. He tries hanging out in a bar and drinking. Then he meets a pretty girl and tries strangling her. All merely part of "experimenting." Or, was Goleman suggesting that Levin tried "experimenting" by going off with Chambers, and ended up strangled as a consequence? By putting Levin's strangling into the same category as drunken driving or experimentation with drugs, Goleman hinted that she had consciously taken a risk that turned out to be fatal—that she had, indeed, "courted death."

My objection to these stories about the lifestyle of Levin, Chambers, and their friends is that they, once again, seemed to be dividing the blame for Levin's death equally between her and Chambers. The stories implied that her death was not a result of Chambers's personal problems—his temper, perhaps, or his bottled-up anger, his drug dependence, his lack of control—but a result of unsupervised partying and teenage experimentation, something Levin was guilty of, too. I do not object to the idea of doing stories on neglected teenagers and underage drinking, but the journalistic habit of having to link stories to a current event—"the news peg"—resulted here in absurd logic and another weight set on the balance against Levin. The mistake the *Times* stories made here is analogous to the mistake reporters made about the ethnic issue in the Big Dan's case. By linking stories about the Portuguese quality of the neighborhood with the rape, the press sounded as if it were saying the rape occurred because the defendants were Portuguese. Likewise, by linking the teenagers' lifestyle to Levin's murder, the press sounded as if it were saying that the murder happened because of that lifestyle and not because of any mistake on the part of Chambers.

When the *Times* was not blaming drink or teen-age experimentation for her death, it turned to blaming Levin's parents. The following article, again by Freedman, illustrates how far the *Times* was stretching to find moral lessons in the case.

KILLING IN PARK RAISES DIFFICULT QUESTIONS FOR AFFLUENT PARENTS

> The events have served to illuminate a subculture of sophisticated, affluent teenagers regularly partying and club-hopping long past midnight. And much as a suburban car accident that kills several high-school friends forces families there to confront the problem of drunken driving by teenagers, the Levin case has raised some peculiarly urban questions.
>
> Is it harder to rear children amid the glitter and vice of the big city? Is it inevitable to lose control of a nineteen-year-old? Or have some parents in demanding, high-paying professions substituted money for affection and freedom for supervision? Have they abdicated their role as parents to surrogates? (9/11/86, p. 1.)

Here the *Times* took the opportunity to universalize this case by shaking a finger at its readers and saying, "This could happen to you! You people with your money and your divorces and your careless attitude toward your kids—look what can happen!" In the article, Freedman pointed out that both Levin and Chambers came from broken marriages, and quoted several psychologists and the like on the importance of stability, love, and authority at home. By doing so, he was putting not only the alleged murderer in the category of neglected children, but also the victim. He revealed his intention in his last paragraph, after a description of the Red Hand's owner and his happy family: "Whether or not [Mr. Dorrian's family] was the ideal family, it was at least an intact one. That suggests what experts say is one of the few lessons that can be drawn from the Levin murder case." Freedman's thesis was right there: The "lesson" of this case was that if parents neglect their kids, it can lead to tragedy, even murder. Furthermore, as he phrased it, this lesson applied as much to Levin's parents as it did to Chambers's.

Freedman said he turned his attention to these affluent parents because he was so shocked by the way they ignored their kids. He had wanted to lead his story with the fact that Levin had been away from home for three days before her death without ever contacting her parents. "I was amazed at that," he said. "I remember arguing with an editor about it. He said, 'But she's eighteen, she's legally an adult,' and I said, 'I don't care if she's eighteen, I'm amazed that eighteen-year-olds can just go off to the Hamptons for three days and then come back and go out partying and the parent doesn't seem to want to know.' "

He lost the battle to use Levin's three-day absence as his lead, but more and more he saw neglectful parents as his theme. "One thing I learned covering other stories about the death of teenagers is that death itself doesn't mean anything other than someone dying," he said. "The larger meaning is what does it say to parents and teenagers who are alive about how they will behave? . . . There did seem to be a lesson here in terms of parents of affluent kids around the country—why are you so relaxed about the way your kids behave, why aren't you being grown-ups for them? That was the issue that would stick in people's minds about the case."

Freedman was right. Neglectful parents was the issue that stuck in people's minds. A variety of newspapers and magazines soon followed his example and began shaking their fingers at affluent, working parents. In the magazine *America,* for example, under the head "Teach the Children Well" (9/20/86), an op-ed piece intoned:

> Jennifer Levin's unlikely and untimely death emphatically reminds us that even the most blessed and successful teen-agers need the patient, painful, persistent and awkward efforts of their parents to develop discernment in today's confusing moral climate.

While Freedman and his followers were scolding Levin's parents, other reporters were scrutinizing Chambers's, in particular his mother, who was portrayed as a pushy social climber. Indeed, the mother-blaming became so blatant that reporter Nina Bernstein of *Newsday,* one of the few women covering the case, later dubbed it the "monster mom" theory, and mocked it in a pretrial piece a year later.

> Like a movie running backward from a sordid final scene, the Chambers family history emerged in a jumble of distorted images. They were

> images of wealth, of status, of social connections relentlessly sought and deployed by a domineering mother who loved her son too much for his own good.
>
> That picture of Phyllis Chambers is still being advanced by sources close to the prosecution as jury selection drags on. Indeed, the idea of a "monster mom" seems to serve prosecutors almost as a counterweight to the female stereotype that defense lawyers selected for the victim by presenting Jennifer Levin as a sexually voracious vamp.
>
> (12/3/87.)

There is nothing wrong with writing articles about neglectful parents, or with the urge to find universal lessons in an individual crime. Indeed, crime news has little meaning if it is not seen in the context of a larger picture, be that pattern crimes, history, or social criticism. The trouble is that, given the time and depth limitations of the press, the urge to universalize often results in superficial and somewhat absurd generalizations. In the Levin case, the stories seeking a universal moral had the effect of blaming everyone but Chambers for her murder. The criticism of Levin's lifestyle as well as Chambers's put her in the same boat as her killer, thus seeming to make her equally responsible for her death, and the parent scolding articles had the effect of blaming her parents and his instead of him. If Levin had wandered into Dorrian's Mr. Goodbar-style, to get a drink and pick up a man, had met Chambers there for the first time and been killed by him, then perhaps the stories examining her parent's lack of supervision might have had some validity. Given the facts, however,—that Dorrian's was a comfortable and familiar hangout and Chambers a sometime lover and friend—the linking of her lifestyle to her murder was far-fetched and unfair. It was what newspaper jargon calls "a reach."

October and November: Chambers as Coverboy

The press's tendency to blame everyone but Chambers for Levin's death continued to be in evidence throughout the months after her body was found—even, rather extraordinarily, after Chambers's indictment for the burglary of three Upper East Side penthouses in October. The parents, drink, status, and money all came under fire. Most of all, however, Levin herself was blamed. Arthur Brown of the *News* attributed the blame of Levin to Chambers's line of defense: "He made her into this kind of sexually greedy, sexually hungry, loose-living person," he said.

The press, however, had invented its own version of this scenario, one that went far beyond Chambers's accusations or manipulations by his lawyer. The *Village Voice,* which had been fairly quiet about the case so far, ran a long cover story by C. Carr in October reacting to the bias against Levin headed, "WHO'S ON TRIAL?" "The Chambers/Litman story is that of a 'bad girl' who gets what she deserves and a helpless man defending himself from her sexual voraciousness."[9]

The antivictim slant of those first weeks of stories was so blatant that most of the reporters I interviewed admitted to it. Even tough-talking Hoffman of the *Post,* who was one of the two main reporters responsible for story about Levin being "the type of girl you'd want to date," agreed that the press was biased. "There was a shade of sexism in the story during the first six or seven months of coverage," he said. "We seemed to believe Chambers's story that he was tied up and that his genitals were hurt, that he was raped and that's why he killed her. We had that outrageous headline, 'She raped me' in huge type, outlined in red [this came out on Nov. 13]. We got a lot of criticism for that."

In a long cover article on the case, published in *New York* magazine on November 10, author Michael Stone tried to remedy this anti-Levin slant by taking a close look at Chambers, his life, and problems. The story was given front page play, with the headline, "EAST SIDE STORY," blazoned across the cover in tall, white letters on a black background. A clean, coiffed, and preppily dressed Chambers stared out at the reader, his arms folded, his face serious, but slightly rueful. Inset was an unflattering black and white snapshot of Levin in dark glasses, and under her were the words, "Robert Chambers, Jennifer Levin, and a death that shocked the city."

Although through no fault of Stone's, the story was already squewed in Chambers's favor. The glamorous photograph and the headline's nod to *West Side Story,* even if intended ironically, made him look like a celebrity, a member of that revered class to be gawked at and envied. The message was: "Here I am, a handsome preppie with movie star status, looking right at you. You know people like me can't really commit murder, don't you?" This cover, in highly questionable taste, played right into the narrative convention for sex crimes: Handsome, white, upper-class men only victimize women when driven to it.

Stone opened by setting the scene in Dorrian's—teenagers drinking, party atmosphere, everyone having fun. He introduced Chambers as a silent, romantic stereotype.

> At the edge of the gaiety, one Dorrian's regular, a tall, handsome nineteen-year-old named Robert Chambers, sat at the bar, drinking beer

> by himself. Chambers is a good drinker, his friends say, and he can be aloof. But that night, he seemed particularly moody, at times looking straight ahead and ignoring the festivities around him.

Next Stone reported that Chambers's "pretty sixteen-year-old" girlfriend came in, but he ignored her. (Note the condescending "pretty" versus the mature sounding "handsome.") They quarreled and she was heard telling him to find someone else. Then followed the first mention of Levin:

> Another pretty student, eighteen-year-old Jennifer Levin, may have overheard the exchange. She was high-spirited and popular, and she'd been interested in Chambers for some time. They'd had a few flings, and she'd confided to friends how sexy she thought he was. Levin now told the other girl that she wanted her boyfriend, and over the next three hours, friends saw Levin flirting and talking with Chambers at the bar.

Here Stone showed Levin behaving like anything but a "good girl." The phrase "Levin now told the other girl that *she wanted her boyfriend*" was particularly condemning, for it made her sound frankly aggressive and sexual. If Stone had written that she was "interested in" or "attracted to" Chambers, Levin would have sounded less course. Stone told me that he chose his vocabulary, when not directly quoting, to reflect the language of the teenagers he was interviewing, but whether this word "wanted" came from her friends or Stone's interpretation is open to question.

Stone followed this description with the phrase: "Less than two hours later, Jennifer Levin was found dead in Central Park." He then described the state of Levin's body and Chambers's confession, following with this passage:

> The death of Levin and the charge against Chambers stunned and baffled the city, and raised questions about the way children grow up in New York, about underage drinking in public bars, and casual sex in Central Park. How, people asked, could an apparently innocent teenage tryst end in death?

This paragraph closely echoed one of Freedman's leads in the *Times*, and instead of raising natural questions about Chambers, such as whether he was violent, unstable, had a history of uncontrollable temper, had ever hurt previous girlfriends, or simply why he killed, it raised the same irrelevant questions that applied as much to Levin as to Chambers.

Stone then went on to put together the story of the fatal evening. The article covered eleven pages of the magazine but reflected the same pattern I had discovered in the newspapers—Levin was described in terms of her looks and sexual appeal *four times* more often than was Chambers, and she was characterized as the more sexually aggressive of the two: "she had casual affairs with other boys;" "She was very flirtatious, definitely outgoing;" "she commented on his sexual prowess;" and, in reference to her boss, "So she just grabbed him by the shoulders . . . and she made him fall in love with her." Contrast those descriptions to this one of Chambers, recalling the reluctant Romeo image from the tabloids:

> Chambers's tall good looks—he's six four and about 220 pounds—and secretive manner made him something of a legend among the younger private-school girls. A friend recalls that girls from surrounding schools used to camp out on the steps of the brownstone where he lived. He hated to be pursued that way, the friend says, and in fact, Chambers was always more comfortable hanging out with his male friends. Still, there was a sensitive side to him that he revealed to girls he liked. He also had a hard time letting go of old girlfriends. The girl who broke up with him while he was at Choate says that years later he was still pursuing her.[10]

The mention of Chambers pursuing his old girlfriend was particularly ironic because it was presented as sensitive and loyal, whereas Levin's pursuit of Chambers was portrayed as sluttish and annoying:

> Some time after his girlfriend had walked away, Levin began flirting with Chambers at the bar. Drifting around the room, she again told friends that she wanted to go home with Chambers, and she commented on his sexual prowess. At one point, she talked to Chambers again and then came back and reported the exchange to LaGatta and another friend. She said she'd told him, "The sex we had was the best I've ever had." The comment apparently irritated Chambers. "You shouldn't have said that," Levin said he'd responded.

(At the trial it came out that Levin had said this in front of another person, embarrassing Chambers.) This passage made Chambers sound like a victim again, hunted for sex, although he in fact engaged in much of the same sexual and social behavior as did Levin. Look at who was doing the pursuing in this description of the way Levin and Chambers first met:

> Levin and Chambers first met at Dorrian's on a night toward the end of June, according to Betsy. "He was sitting about four tables away from me," Betsy says, "and he kept looking over and smiling . . . and finally he said to me, 'I just want to tell you I think your friend is so beautiful.' He said he wanted to talk to her, but that he couldn't do it in public, that he had a girlfriend. I told him he should just go up and talk to her, and he said, 'I can't. Tell her to meet me outside.' "

Stone and his fellow reporters, and the friends of Levin and Chambers also used the word *flirt* many times when referring to Levin, but not to Chambers. *Flirt* is a word that is exclusively used for women and that, in the context of a sex crime, is particularly condemning because of the "bad woman" narrative. "Some time after his girlfriend had walked away, Levin began flirting with Chambers at the bar," wrote Stone. Chambers, too, however, was in the bar late at night, drinking underage. He, too, was being unfaithful during the times they went off together. He, too, talked to Levin for hours, just as she talked to him.

On the subject of language, I asked Stone in an interview why he described Levin so often in terms of her looks and sexuality. He replied: "Those adjectives were not manipulated by me. Those kids tend to see their friends in very superficial terms. It's very important to kids how they look—all kids—but especially amongst that group. It was always a major part of their descriptions of her, and of him as well."

This may be true, but my point here is to show how our language lends itself to biased reporting about female sex crime victims. Stone and his colleagues may have been unable to avoid quoting Levin's friends using words like "pretty," "flirtatious," and "bubbly" about her, but they did not have to use the words themselves. Yet they did, frequently.

As the story progressed, and Stone got into speculation about the tactics of the trial and the probable outcome, his depiction of Levin as sexually aggressive began to blend into blatant blame-the-victim language:

> Later, however, Levin joined Chambers at the bar in what friends say looked like a serious conversation . . . as dawn approached, Chambers and Levin continued to talk quietly at the bar while Levin played with the ice cubes in her glass. Friends say she appeared to have sobered

> up, and later, the toxicologist report is said to have concluded that Levin's blood contained minimal levels of alcohol.

She had sobered up? What about him? Chambers's level of alcohol or drugs were never mentioned in the story, yet Levin's drinking was given the kind of attention it would merit if she'd been convicted of drunken driving, or if *she* had been the one who had committed a crime. Why did Stone mention Levin's sobriety and not Chambers's? Why did he not ask his sources whether Chambers had appeared drunk?

The answer lies in a passage near the end of the piece:

> It's possible that Levin *triggered* Chambers's anger *through her persistence* or through inadvertently causing him pain. Their struggle may then have escalated in a series of actions and responses, with Chambers holding ever more tightly to Levin's throat in an effort to *control* her.
> (My emphasis.)

The statement that Levin "triggered" Chambers's anger "through her persistence" was uncomfortably akin to saying a woman "provokes" a man's rape. Levin, with all her flirtatiousness, her "bubbly" vivacity, her drinking, and her outgoing aggression, was portrayed here as someone a man would want to control. Meanwhile, the article had earlier quoted several people describing Chambers as "passive," as a non-fighter, as someone who walks away from conflict ("Tulenko remembers Chambers as a 'wimp, not capable of violence.' " '. . . he's meek, really passive.' ") Now, however, he was suddenly *controlling* this wild girl with a deadly grip around her neck. The message was clear: Levin was so pushy and so irritating that she drove Chambers to violence.

Stone ended his long article with a clearly sympathetic, pro-Chambers scene:

> In a brief press conference at Litman's office on October 1, Chambers made his only public comment about the death of Jennifer Levin. "I regret that nothing I can say or do can undo the terrible *tragedy that has occurred,*" he said, reading from a statement. Later, he told friends that as he had stood against the museum wall, watching squad cars arrive, *he'd felt he was in a dream,* a terrible nightmare from which he still sometimes expects to awake. Until that morning, Chambers had led a privileged existence, his misdeeds and failures patched up or taken care of. But as dawn broke around him, a vision of the *lifeless girl he'd embraced* only minutes before must have *tugged at his conscience:* Jennifer Levin was real, and so was her death. (My emphasis.)

According to Stone, Chambers was remorseful. He was in a dream. A tragedy spontaneously "occurred," he did not make it occur. A lifeless body appeared, as if out of nowhere. He "embraced" her moments before, rather than strangled her. Finally, his conscience was bothering him. Chambers appeared a passive victim of circumstance.

Stone, like the other reporters I interviewed, took on this story with the best of intentions. He had, he explained, been writing for some time about the lifestyle of these rich, neglected teenagers, knew some of them well, and in fact had been approached by them about the case. I asked him whether he agreed that linking stories of the two teenagers' lifestyles to the killing implied a cause and effect. He said he did not.

"I don't believe for a minute that Levin died because of these things," he said. "Kids don't go around strangling each other because of changes in social norms."

When I asked him why he wrote the story, he said; "To elucidate the context in which these kids lived and the things in Chambers's life that brought changes to his condition. To try to understand why someone had not seen that this was an extremely troubled kid headed for a crisis, who was about to explode. . . . The points about Chambers were not a justification for what he did, but a look at the way he was growing up."

If this view of Chambers as not merely an unfortunate boy who had fallen unwittingly into tragedy, but a troubled youth "about to explode" had been as clear in the printed story as it was in Stone's spoken words, it could have gone a long way toward redressing the imbalance of reporting on this case. Yet, apparently, it took the trial, public disgust with the way Levin had been treated, and public outrage at Chambers's light, five-to-fifteen-year sentence to make the press look at Chambers in a less than flattering light. Contrast the descriptions of him I have quoted earlier to this passage about Chambers from a posttrial *People* magazine.

> In an hour-long statement video-taped at the police station, Chambers comes across as 6′4″ of bad attitude, insisting petulantly that he was the blameless victim of an "insane" Jennifer Levin. He expressed little concern for her, and no grief.[11]

"She Raped Me": Pretrial Moves and Litman's Manipulations

The portrayal of Levin by Stone and others as a sexually hungry, aggressive young woman who had driven Chambers to violence was not entirely a result of her friends' quotes and the reporters' interpretations. It was also, of course, a reflection of Chambers's defense.

In November, the videotape of Chambers's confession was released, and with it came one of the most extraordinary headlines of the entire case: "CHAMBERS: I WAS RAPED" (*Post,* 11/13/86).

Chambers had actually given three different accounts to the police when he was arrested. First, he had said, he knew nothing about what happened to Levin after leaving her at Dorrian's Red Hand, and that he had been scratched by his cat. Then he had said that he had walked down the street with Levin and that she had scratched him "for not returning his affections," then left. Finally, he had brought out his rape story.

> According to this third account, Levin scratched him and then tied his arms behind him with her underpants. On the videotape, Chambers says: "She was raping me. I told her to stop and she wouldn't." At that point, the defendant said he freed his left arm, reached around her neck and pulled her off of him. According to the autopsy report, Levin died of strangulation. (*Newsday,* 10/17/87.)

The effect of this account, aside from making the police laugh on tape, was mixed. On the one hand it fed the Chambers-as-victim image that had been promoted so far by the press. On the other hand, the "I was raped" headlines turned public sympathy away from Chambers because no one could buy the idea that a 120-pound, five-foot-eight woman could rape a 220-pound man of six foot four. It was at this time, just before the trial, that a group of women led by Rose Jordon founded the "Justice for Jennifer Task Force" and that feminist groups such as the National Organization for Women began to object to the press's treatment of Levin. These groups were not only protesting the portrayal of Levin as a rapist, but the fact that Chambers's lawyer was Jack Litman.

Litman was notorious for a 1977 case in which he had defended Richard Herrin, who had hammered his girlfriend, Bonnie Garland, to death in her sleep for trying to leave him. In that case, Litman had painted Garland as promiscuous and Herrin as driven mad by grief, and had won his client a conviction of manslaughter rather than murder. Afterward, Litman admitted to a reporter that he had tried to sully Garland's character intentionally. "It was necessary to taint her a little bit," he had said, "so the jury would not believe, as the parents wanted them to, that she was this ingenue who fell in love for the first time [with] this wily man."[12] Feminists protested this tactic at the time, forming some of the first victim's rights groups in the country. Ever since, Litman had been known as a man who specializes in blaming the victim. Indeed, a new phrase was coined at Chambers's trial—"Litmanized"—which meant being blamed for one's own victimization. He was, however, also known as a sharp and accomplished lawyer.

Predictably enough, therefore, during the pretrial months beginning in November, Litman made a move that was obviously designed to smear Levin's character. He filed a request to see Levin's diary before the trial, arguing that it chronicled her "kinky and aggressive sexual activities."[13] The diary quickly became labeled a "sex diary," a phrase that some said came from Litman while others said came from the tabloid headline writers. The judge looked at Levin's diary and said it was no such thing, but merely the ordinary diary of hopes and dreams that any teenager might keep. He denied Litman his request, but Litman had done his damage by suggesting an image of Levin as a sexual collector—and the press proved itself unable to resist his manipulations:

> " 'SEX DIARY' KEPT BY JEN?" (*News*, 11/14/86).
>
> "JENNIFER KEPT SEX DIARY" (*Post*, 11/14/86).

Again, this tactic of Litman's had mixed results. Like the "she raped me" claim, it bolstered the rape myth image of Levin as a bad woman who provoked her demise, but it also angered the feminists who were watching the case and, in turn, the press—a reaction prosecutor Linda Fairstein had foreseen and was apparently pleased about.[14] Nearly fifty Guardian Angels picketed Chambers's house to protest Litman's pursuit of the diary. "I think that was the turning point, when we began to look at the other side," said Hoffman of the *Post*. Indeed, the "sex diary" move turned public sympathy away from Chambers so noticeably that, once the trial began, Litman backed off and relied on more subtle attacks on Levin instead—so subtle that some critics missed them altogether.[15] The result was that the trial garnered less criticism from feminists than had Litman's pretrial moves.

The Trial

Chambers was brought to trial on January 4, 1988, a year and a half after Levin's strangled body had been found in Central Park. He was charged with two counts of second-degree murder. One count accused him of intentionally killing Levin, the other of showing "depraved indifference to human life." The jury consisted of eight men and four women, and the trial was attended by both families, a crowd of spectators, and a legion of reporters. Cameras were banned in the courtroom. (He was simultaneously tried for his burglary charges in a different court, but this received little coverage.)

In contrast to the Rideout and Big Dan's trials, support for the victim at the trial was more than a token presence. The Guardian Angels, led by Lisa Sliwa, picketed outside the courtroom, decrying the anti-victim tactics of the defense. Levin's family and friends came to court wearing "Justice for Jennifer" buttons until Judge Howard E. Bell ordered them to take them off. NOW members were present and loquacious. Slashing victim Marla Hanson[16] and the father of Bonnie Garland came to lend their support for victim's rights and Levin's family. Levin's uncle, mother, and father all spoke up for her, issuing moving and eloquent statements to the press that helped garner sympathy for Levin, exposed Litman's tactics, and sharpened public criticism of him and Chambers. Furthermore, Linda Fairstein, the lead prosecutor on the case, was herself the head of the sex crime unit in Manhattan's District Attorney's office and a veteran of rape cases and was well aware of Litman's tactics and the "bad girl" narrative that would be brought to bear on Levin. As she said in an interview with *Newsday*,

> " 'Rough sex' probably were the two words most commonly associated with this case. That was Litman's phrase at Chambers's arraignment. That phrase became a catchword we had to fight."[17]

In many ways, this trial was an example of what both the Rideout and Big Dan's trials had needed more of—a feminist presence. The Chambers trial was therefore something of a test case to see how much that presence could discourage blame-the-victim tactics by the defense and victim-blaming by the press.

In her opening statements, Fairstein directly attacked the "Jennifer courted death" and "Jenny killed in wild sex" line of the defense by denying that the killing was a sex crime at all:

> Sex played no part in the violent struggle more than sixteen months ago in Central Park . . . a prosecutor asserted yesterday to a Manhattan jury.
>
> "We say there was no sex that morning—only violence, only death . . . Jennifer Levin died in a violent struggle." . . .

> Fairstein charged that Chambers' statements were nothing but "a preposterous story that makes a vibrant eighteen-year-old girl the agent of her own death." (*Newsday*, 1/5/88.)

Fairstein's version was that Chambers and Levin had quarrelled, that he had punched and attacked her, and had repeatedly strangled her until she died. He had then dragged her body along the ground and arranged her clothes to make the attack look like a sexual assault by a stranger.

Litman countered Fairstein's opening arguments by saying that Chambers's version, as given in his final confession, was the truth and that Levin's death was "a tragic accident," and by bringing up Levin's sexual aggression with this disingenuous statement: "No one here is faulting Jennifer Levin for aggressively pursuing or sexually pursuing Robert Chambers." (*Newsday*, 1/5/88). The trial went on for eleven weeks. The prosecution called twenty-six witnesses—forensic experts, friends of Levin, joggers, and police officers who had seen her body. The defense called only five, most of them medical experts who contradicted the prosecution's evidence. The trial contained many emotional moments, such as when the Levin family cried in the courtroom while Chambers's parents looked on stony-faced, and Chambers himself paled, wept, and otherwise visibly responded to testimony. Even the attorneys quarrelled, refusing to speak to each other for days at a time. The jury also had its tribulations, fighting with each other, trying to get out of the case, breaking into tears. The highlights of the trial were:

- Prosecution witnesses said that Levin's body had been covered with bruises and wounds, indicating that she had been in a violent struggle with Chambers and that she had tried to escape. The defense countered that the wounds were caused by improper treatment of her body by police and that she had died instantly.
- The prosecution said Levin's neck wounds were caused by the material of her blouse, which Chambers had twisted into a noose and with which he had repeatedly strangled her. The defense contended that they were caused by Chambers's watchband during his brief choke hold on Levin.
- The prosecution produced a medical expert to say Levin had been strangled for too long to have died in the way Chambers claimed. The defense produced a medical witness who disagreed.
- The prosecution's medical witness also said that one of Levin's

eyes was swollen shut, indicating that she had been punched. Later evidence showed that Chambers had sustained a fracture in a bone of his right hand, which the prosecution considered proof of that punch. Chambers said he hurt his hand on a rock, which was backed up by the defense medical witness, who also said her eye had closed only as a result of postdeath reactions.

- The press leaked information that Levin had been wearing diamond earrings the night of her death that had not been found on her body—a motivation Fairstein hoped to suggest for her killing. The earrings were never recovered, however, so this argument was dropped.
- The prosecution called a friend of Levin's to the stand, who testified that Levin had been chasing Chambers the night of her death, and that Chambers had formerly been infatuated with Levin—testimony that the press turned lurid.

"LAST DRINK & TALK OF SEX" (*News,* 1/15/88).

"JENNY'S DATE WITH DEATH" (*Post,* 1/15/88).

- Both sides spend many days attacking the credibility of each others' medical witnesses.

Even with the watchful presence of NOW and the "Justice for Jennifer Task Force," as the trial stretched on more and more of the testimony was about Levin's behavior and sex life. Suggestions were made that she had been on diet pills, which Chambers said made her "very strong." More of her friends testified about her drinking and sexual interests. One of the witnesses, who had been a source for a *Mademoiselle* magazine story in which she had been quoted saying that Levin was "physically flirtatious" in Dorrian's, denied on the stand that she had said any such thing.[18] Meanwhile, the court heard no testimony about Chambers's drug taking or sex life. This imbalance, which so weighed against Levin, was largely a result of the attorney's inability to find witnesses willing to talk about Chambers. Fairstein, whose own witnesses had damaged Levin's image with their testimony about her interest in Chambers, later told *Newsday* that she blamed the press for the lack of teenage witnesses:

"It was incredible to know that every day there were thirty to fifty reporters sitting behind us in the courtroom who were evaluating and criticizing everything that we did. As far as [that] having an effect on the trial itself, I think there were a few possible witnesses who were scared away . . . if this trial had no press coverage, we probably would have had more cooperation from the parents of potential teenage witnesses."[19]

Soon after Levin's friends had testified about her actions the night of her death, the jury viewed the videotape of Chambers's confession and, once more, the "she raped me" claim was in the headlines: "She was having her way with me without my consent . . ."[20] Chambers declared. His choice of that Gothic novel phrase revealed how deeply the preconceived narrative about sex crimes runs—he reached for the first cliché that occurred to him.

By the end of the trial, the jury and the public had heard an extraordinary amount of contradictory and gruesome evidence, much of it focused on the physical aspect of the murder—how long Levin had been strangled, how she had actually died, and how her bruises and wounds had been caused. The attorneys' closing statements, therefore, were suitably dramatic. Fairstein put two photographs on display for the jury, one showing Levin smiling and happy on the night before her death, the other showing her partially clothed body askew and bloody on the ground, and argued that Chambers had killed her intentionally and out of anger. Litman calmly proclaimed that the prosecution had found no motive for the killing, that Chambers was telling the truth, and that it had all happened because Jennifer had pursued him "for sex." Litman's strategy of portraying Levin as a promiscuous, man-eating girl was never clearer than in his closing statement: "It was Jennifer who was pursuing Robert for sex . . . that's why we wound up with this terrible tragedy."[21]

Chambers Cops a Plea

The jury deliberated for nine days, amid much publicity and speculation. One juror accused another of being a racist; three of them wrote desperate notes to the judge, asking to be relieved; and they kept coming back to court requesting more evidence and more witnesses. Meanwhile, outside the courtroom, representatives from NOW, the "Justice for Jennifer Task Force," and Women Against Pornography held a press conference urging the jury to find Chambers guilty.[22]

Then, suddenly, all the jurors' efforts were preempted. On March

25, Chambers took a plea. Because the jurors seemed headed for an impasse, and because that would have resulted in a mistrial requiring another trial to be begun from scratch, Litman had offered a plea bargain. After some fierce negotiations with Fairstein and her team, the terms were agreed upon: Chambers would plead guilty to first-degree manslaughter, and to second degree burglary, but not to murder; he would be allowed one night at home with his mother before going off to jail (he had originally asked for six weeks, but Fairstein and the Levin family would not allow it); and he would have to do what he had never done—admit in court that he had killed Levin. He did so reluctantly—the judge had to ask him to say it three times—but the deed was done, the Levin family somewhat appeased, and Chambers sent to jail.

LEAVING HOME FOR A NUMBER AND CALL
CHAMBERS BEGINS SENTENCE

After walking through a taunting crowd shouting "Murderer, murderer," Robert E. Chambers, Jr. was driven to jail in a Cadillac yesterday.

By the end of the day, Chambers was officially known as inmate number 30088-400006 in the Rikers Island prison . . .

Twenty beret-wearing members of the Guardian Angels, who kept an all night vigil proclaiming support for victims' rights, chanted, "They're coming to take you away, ha, ha" as detectives arrived to take Chambers into custody. (*Newsday*, 3/27/88.)

Chambers was formally sentenced on April 16, 1988, nearly twenty months after killing Levin, and he received the expected time of five to fifteen years, his sentence for the burglaries to be served concurrently. If a jury had found him guilty of the same charge he had accepted for the plea bargain, he could have been sentenced to a maximum of twenty-five years. If a jury had convicted him of second-degree murder, the top count of his indictment, he might have faced life. As it was, legal experts predicted he would serve ten years, and be eligible for parole in five.

At the sentencing, Chambers tried to apologize for the first and only time:

AN APOLOGY AND THEN TO PRISON

Chambers, 21, wearing a double-breasted, navy blue blazer with charcoal gray pants, said, "For two years, I have not been able to say I'm sorry. I've not been able to say anything. And I now wish to have my

> feelings known. . . . To Jennifer, nothing I can do or say will ever bring her back. But I'm sorry." (*Newsday*, 4/16/88.)

The last word of the case, however, really belonged to Levin's father, Steven, who made a stirring statement to the press after Chambers was sentenced and packed off to jail.

> "There is not a day that is not spent forcing down overwhelming feelings of despair, anger, and horror. . . . What do you do with these feelings, how do you channel this anger? If we don't find a way it will eat us alive."[23]

Then, in another story, he was quoted addressing the trial and the point of this chapter:

> The father of Jennifer Dawn Levin yesterday criticized the criminal justice system for accepting the "rough sex" defense, saying that with enough money and bizarre lies, defendants can get away with blaming the victims for their own deaths.
>
> "It's become open season on women. . . . Kill your date, trash her reputation, and pay big bucks to get away with murder."
>
> (*Newsday*, 5/11/88.)

The Last Chapter: Page One Ward

The lightness of Chambers's sentence surprised and infuriated much of New York. As James Kunen wrote in *People* magazine,

> As the news swept over the city, many New Yorkers swiftly reached a different verdict: Chambers had choked the life out of Jennifer Levin and gotten off with a slap on the wrist.
>
> Had the jurors been stymied by a lack of proof that Chambers intended to kill? Or had defense attorney Litman succeeded in playing to a belief on their part that a young, sexually active girl is somehow responsible for whatever befalls her? From the beginning, the victim had been on trial.[24]

As a result of the anger about his sentence, Chambers's handsome hero image was at last laid to rest. A homemade video was released to the public, showing him cavorting with three scantily clad women and pretending to strangle a doll while saying, "Oops, I killed it," at a time when he was supposed to be under supervision by a priest, waiting for trial for his killing of Levin. Also, the press finally allowed itself some fun at his expense when covering his time in the "Page One Ward" of Rikers, where he hobnobbed with other celebrity prisoners such as Joel Steinberg, the man who beat his wife, Hedda Nussbaum, and killed their six-year-old adopted daughter, Lisa: "Robert E. Chambers, Jr., has learned that it is not such a great thing to be young, handsome and convicted in New York." (*Newsday*, 4/8/88.) The change in attitude toward Chambers was nowhere as apparent as in the previously mentioned *People* story:

> The two [teenagers] were widely depicted as a pair of pampered children whose mutual tragedy was a symptom of upper-class parental neglect. In fact, the description fit neither Chambers nor Levin.
>
> Levin was rich, but she lived as if she were not. She worked after school and on vacations . . .
>
> Chambers was not rich but lived as if he were. . . . His only real success was with young women, for whom he held a fatal attraction . . .
>
> [A] passing bicyclist discovered Jennifer Levin's twisted, battered, half-naked body lying beneath a tree. Directly across the road sat Robert Chambers, watching. A passerby would later testify that Chambers looked as though he'd been in "an industrial accident," his face was so badly scratched . . .
>
> At first he denied even having left the bar with Levin. He said the deep scratches on his face, chest, and abdomen had been inflicted by his cat and that the open wounds on his hands were the result of an accident with a sander. Finally, after seven hours of questioning during which he never asked for a lawyer, Chambers admitted that he had gone to the park with Jennifer Levin, where, he claimed, he had "accidentally" killed her when she "molested" him.[25]

This language is not without its objectionable sensationalism, but it is interesting to note how much innuendo is cast here against Chambers. Levin was rich but noble enough to work anyway, while Chambers lived a life of pretension. Levin worked hard, while Chambers did nothing but exercise a "fatal attraction" for young women. Her body was found as if it had been savagely beaten; he was covered with wounds, as if she had fought for her life. Finally, he had the audacity to accuse this poor victim of "molesting" him. *People* magazine has never been known for its objectivity, but this piece nevertheless illustrates how innuendo could have been used earlier against Chambers as it was against Levin, had the press been so inclined.

After his stint with the celebrities, Chambers was moved to the Great Meadow Correctional Facility in Comstock, New York, where he was to serve his time as an ordinary prisoner. The attention to his case, however, continued. The story was turned into a two-hour television movie, called *The Preppie Murder*, which Chambers was not allowed to watch because he was in solitary confinement for using marijuana.[26] It was also written up by Linda Wolfe in a best-selling book, *Wasted*.

Wolfe's book was a thoroughly researched, anecdotal account of Levin's and Chambers's lives. Her thesis was that these children were victimized by the fast, moneyed, irresponsible lifestyle of their parents and peers. She also suggested that Chambers was much more dependent upon drugs than had been revealed by the daily press. Wolfe concluded her book by summarizing all the possible scenarios for why Chambers killed Levin:

> Robert, I knew, had always been looking to blame his own transgressions on someone or something outside himself. Thinking about the milieu in which he had come to manhood, I began to feel that in one sense something outside himself *was* to blame—that he was the by-product of the drug epidemic that swept through American youth in the 1980s. If so, then clearly Jennifer Levin was a victim of that drug epidemic. Because whatever happened in Central Park—whether Robert killed her because he wanted to steal from her in order to buy drugs, or because he experienced with her a drug-induced hallucination that she was attacking him, or because he wanted to have sex with her but was impotent as a result of the depressing action of drugs, or because something she did or said set him off into the kind of intense rage that drugs notoriously produce—one way or another, his use of drugs played a role in her death.
>
> I didn't feel that this excused Robert. What I felt was that, although I had listed and limned in my pages all the things that made him and Jennifer special, they were not, ultimately, unique. They resembled hundreds of thousands of American teenagers. And from their story it would be right on target to conclude that there, but for the grace of God and the reach of the epidemic, did go our own children.[27]

Like Stone, Freedman, and, indeed, Jack Litman himself, Wolfe chose to see Chambers as one of "us," or at least as one of "our children." That was the aspect of him that most appealed to the press and that made the press so eager to depict him as handsome, charming, and ultimately blameless. Yet, had Chambers not been white, good looking, an Upper East Sider, and of the same race and class as most of the mainstream press, then these attempts to explain how he had gone wrong would never have been made. The press so identified with Chambers that it bent over backward to find excuses for him. The facts that he had psychological problems, that he lied to his friends and family, that he stole from girlfriends right after sleeping with them, that he was an unreformed cocaine-user, a convicted burglar, a con-man, and a killer were glossed over again and again, right to the end of the entire case.

In an interview with *Newsday's* Mort Persky, Wolfe was less forgiving toward Chambers than she had sounded in her book. ". . . I think he was a much more dangerous and violent person than the press has portrayed him. . . . He had no respect for the people around him. Robert was an ugly piece of work." (8/17/89.)

In that same interview, Wolfe also painted an interesting scenario of what she thought might really have happened that night in Central Park.

> "They go off and she's saying, 'I'm leaving for college and I hope I'm going to see you.' She's trying to hold onto him, so she's being charming and kittenish and she does want to have some kind of sexual experience. But he isn't coming on. And she gets mad and says something insulting. He erupts and he screams at her. And she says, 'You led me down the garden path. You were the best sex I ever had. How can you treat me like this? You're just nothing!' Now he's even more enraged and he starts hitting her. She tries to run away, and he socks her in the eye and knocks her down. They tussle on the ground, he drags her along the ground, and in the process he gets his arm around her neck. And that, I think, is very close to what really happened."

Discussion

The coverage of the "preppie murder" was the best example yet in this book of how the press tends to depict crimes according to the preconceived narrative like cookie cutters shape dough. Levin was the "voracious vamp," as Nina Bernstein put it, who had "pursued" Chambers for sex, driven him mad with taunting and pain, and provoked him to such rage that he had killed her: She had "courted" her death in a quest for "wild sex"—the classic "women provoke" myth. Meanwhile, Chambers was a handsome, silent-hero type, who had been driven beyond his usual passive nature by this "wild" woman into a "terrible tragedy" that had hardly been his fault at all. That was how the crime was narrated, not only by the tabloids, but by *New York* magazine and, to a lesser extent, by the *Times*. Even after the trial, when the papers had toned down this stance and tried to be more fair to Levin, the narrative still sometimes held sway. It was reflected in the sentencing, many thought, in the posttrial fascination with Chambers, and even, to some extent, in Linda Wolfe's book.

Questions, therefore, arise. Why did Levin, more than any other victim I've looked at and in spite of the feminist presence, fall subject to the preconceived narrative at the hands of the press? Why, at the beginning of the case, did the press go to such lengths to attribute her murder to anything but Chambers himself? Why was there virtually no mention of his bad mood or potential to explode? Why was so little made of his burglaries, his cocaine use, his lying and his expulsion from school after school? And why did the press criticize Levin at first and glamorize Chambers? The answer to all these questions lies in the fact that while Levin fit the preconceived narrative about sex crimes, Chambers, unlike the defendants in the Big Dan's and Rideout cases, did not.

As said, Levin, had all the "bad girl" ingredients listed in Chapter 1 against her, except ethnicity (she was Jewish and Chambers is of Irish descent): She was killed by someone she knew, a weapon was not used, she was of the same race and social class as Chambers, she was young, she was attractive, and she had been drinking and flirting late at night in a bar before her death. Even though her case was not one of rape, it had so many parallels that these ingredients biased the press against her as much as if she had been a rape victim. As La Rosa of the *News* said, she was clearly not perceived as a "good girl."

Meanwhile, Chambers was the opposite of the criminal stereotype. He was not lower class, like John Rideout, or poor and foreign, like the Big Dan's defendants. He was not seedy, ugly, weird, or nonwhite. Instead, he was so unlike the narrative convention's version of a criminal, so much the good-looking white guy who went tragically wrong, that the press was deeply reluctant to see him as a murder suspect. He was too handsome, too rich, too Irish, too much like the readers of the *Times*, and too much like their sons to be a criminal. As Hoffman of the *Post* said, "It took a long time for the press to realize what a total scumbag Chambers was." Chambers threatened the press's assumptions that guys like him do not murder girls, at least not on purpose and not without undue provocation, so the press bore the attitude that the murder must have been provoked and must have been a mistake, the kind of mistake that could happen to anyone. Chambers's attorney, Jack Litman, said as much himself to the *Times:* "The sad part of this story is that this could happen to anybody's kids."[28] He was not talking about Levin's death. He was talking about Chambers.

The *Village Voice* article by C. Carr mentioned earlier brought out another element that might explain some of the bias against Levin:

> This ["bad girl"] version of events also plays right into anti-Semitic stereotypes. Imagine the story going over as easily with Chambers a Jew and Levin an Upper East Side Catholic girl. It's no coincidence that Litman involved the Catholic church in Chambers's defense right from the start—getting bail application letters from a priest and the archbishop of Newark, then arranging for Chambers to live in an Upper West Side rectory once he was out on bail. It all feeds into the image Litman wants: Robert Chambers is the former altar boy, while Jennifer Levin is the sexually neurotic Other. (10/27/87, p. 2.)

Eleven days after Levin's death, another young woman was murdered in a sex case, in the town of Potsdam, New York. The story was given a small box in the Metropolitan section of the *Times* and is worth looking at for its contrast to the Levin coverage.

> RAPE AND MURDER SCAR INNOCENCE OF POTSDAM
>
> The victim was Katherine M. Hawelka, a 19-year-old Clarkson sophomore, described by fellow students as energetic and serious. (9/5/86, p. B1).

The *Times* used the word *innocence* in the headline, while it only ever allowed Levin "naïve"; Hawelka was described as "energetic" rather than Levin's "vivacious," and as "serious," rather than "bubbly." The contrast illustrates again the strength of the biasing ingredients against sex crime victims. Levin had seven of the eight ingredients against her, but Hawelka had only three: no weapon was used, she was young, and of the same race as her assailant. Unlike Levin, Hawelka did not know her killer; she was not described as "pretty," she was not doing anything that defied traditional female roles, and she was not of the same ethnicity or class as her killer—so she did not fit the image of a vamp. Unlike Chambers, however, her assailant did fit the stereotype of a sex murderer—he was lower class, seedy looking, and had a prison record. Therefore, because he did not threaten the established clichés about who murders, and because she fit the "virgin" image rather than the "vamp," the press had no need to look to the victim for blame.

During my interviews with the reporters and editors responsible for the coverage of the Levin case, I found a dichotomy between what they were willing to say to me and what they practiced in print. Many expressed sensitivity to the arguments regarding Levin's unfair treatment, but at the same time were defensive, even proud of their coverage. "The story was blown up into incredible proportions, but in my opinion it deserved every bit of coverage it got," said Hoffman of the *Post*. "We're in the business of selling newspapers and the public thirsted after that story. It was one of the most fun stories I've ever covered, and I've been reporting for eleven or twelve years now. You'd see the words, 'Preppie Murder' and jump for joy that you were involved in it. As a tabloid newspaperman, you thirst for a story like that. You know people love to read it, that it will get big play. Even if you're writing garbage, as long as people read it is the main thing."

Those who were willing to admit to the sexist bias of their reporting, like La Rosa and Marquez of the *News* and Hoffman of the *Post*, seemed unwilling to consider change. For example, when, I asked Hoffman if his love of tabloid journalism clashed with his evident sensitivity to feminist issues, he replied, "It is a conflict. But my answer is that tabloids shouldn't stop writing about women that way, they should just write more about men in the same way. Everything should be wild and flashy. The most tragic thing a paper can do is to bore you. There's enough competition already for your attention, especially in New York—cabs, TV, noise, homeless people asking for money. A paper has to be louder than that and say, 'Hey, hey, hey, come over here!' "

Most of the reporters and editors I talked to were more willing to admit to the race and class prejudice in their approach to the Levin case than to its sexism. Arthur Brown of the *Daily News* said, "There was a lot of second guessing and press guilt with this stuff. You are always worried, are you being led only by your baser instincts? It gets into complicated social, legal, even racial questions. Does a rich white girl killed in Central Park have more value than a poor black girl killed in Fort Greene Park? But this case was not so much about race as class . . .

"We're not writing for the National Law Journal. A sex related crime with an overtone of class and wealth and decadence sells."

Five days after Levin died, the *Post* showed its awareness of the racial bias in its coverage by publishing a piece headed, "The four 'other' slayings," written by Judie Glave, one of the few women to have a byline in connection with the case. It read:

> Jennifer Levin was among five persons killed in the city Tuesday but only her strangling in Central Park and her trendy life style were subject to intense publicity.
>
> In the Bronx, a world away from the privileged life Levin enjoyed, two men and two women also became victims. (8/31/86, p. 7.)

The story went on to summarize the cases, all murders by people known to the victims, and to quote people saying that "no one cares about the Bronx," a pretty clear euphemism for "no one cares about black and Hispanic crime." As aware as the reporters were about the class and racial biases of their attention to the case, however, they seemed to accept them as a given. As Hoffman bluntly put it, "If it had happened in Harlem or Flatbush, the story would have been pissed on."

Given the years in which this case took place, 1986–1988, it might be surprising to some that the preconceived narrative about sex crime victims held such sway. After all, feminist education about rape had been going on so long that even vigilante groups like the Guardian Angels were joining feminists in decrying the mistreatment of victims, and, as I have said, the case was monitored more closely by feminists than any other case in this book. Linda Wolfe mentioned one interpretation of why, in spite of all this feminist awareness, the myths still had the power to smear Levin.

> "The Chambers case . . . played on what may have been the antifeminist backlash of the time by saying that female sexuality had gotten out of control, that Jennifer was the one doing all these super-aggressive things. Women had emerged into a certain openness about their sexuality, and now Chambers was saying, "They can hurt us.' "[29]

One year after the end of Chambers's trial, another case about Central Park hit the headlines in New York. It was a case that was to put the press's attitude toward feminism to the hardest test of all.

· 6 ·

The Jogger and the Wolfpack

The 1989–1990 Central Park Jogger Case

In April 1989, the most gruesome of all the 1980s sex crimes to hit the national headlines occurred in New York's Central Park:

> WOLF PACK'S PREY
>
> FEMALE JOGGER NEAR DEATH AFTER SAVAGE ATTACK BY ROVING GANG (*Daily News*, 4/21/89. p. 1.)

The victim was a white woman in her late twenties, wealthy, well-educated, up-and-coming, an investment banker, and a jogger. The suspects were a gang of black and Hispanic teenage boys roving the park at night looking for trouble. Not since Kitty Genovese had a case hit the conscience of New York so hard.

"The story was New York," said Hap Hairston, then city editor of *New York Newsday*, later city editor of the *Daily News*. "It was upwardly mobile New York attacked by the not so upwardly mobile; the working class attacks the upper class. It was every white Manhattanite's nightmare to be attacked by a group of black kids."

The crime was a tabloid shocker even without its class and race ingredients because of its brutality. The victim was not only set upon and raped by at least six youths (six were brought to trial, but it's likely there were more), but beaten unconscious with a lead pipe and a rock and left for dead in a puddle of freezing mud, one eye socket smashed to a pulp, her skull gashed, and her body battered, cut, and bloody. She had lost so much blood and her pulse was so low that doctors expected her to die.

Before I launch into an examination of the case it is important to set the crime in its historical context. The Central Park rape occurred in the midst of a set of racial incidents that had been claiming New York headlines for months: In 1986–1987, the media was focused on the Howard Beach, Queens, case of a black man, Michael Griffith, chased to his death on a busy road by a gang of hostile whites; a year later, the media had become obsessed with black teenager Tawana Brawley of upstate New York, who accused several white policemen of raping her, scrawling racist insults on her body, smearing her with dog excrement, and shoving her into a plastic garbage bag. Just before and during the first of the three trials of the Central Park suspects, the papers had been covering clashes between blacks and whites in Bensonhurst, Queens, and the subsequent trial for black, fourteen-year-old Yusef Hawkins's racially motivated murder by whites in that neighborhood. Later, during the trials, a boycott by black customers of two Korean groceries in Brooklyn hit the headlines, revealing a long-held resentment between blacks and the new immigrants. Spike Lee's film *Do the Right Thing*, which took a frank and pessimistic look at race relations and anger in New York, came out at the same time as the attack on the jogger; white mayor Edward Koch was replaced by black mayor David Dinkins during the year between the rape and the trial; and Nelson Mandela visited New York at the same time as jury selection was completed for the first trial. In other words, race—black–white relations—was *the* story in New York at the time of the jogger case, the major concern of the city, the biggest claimer of headlines and attention; so much so that *Newsday* ran a front page story on the topic a few days before the beginning of the first trial:

> Race Relations New Key Concern: *24 Percent Surveyed Cite Tensions as Top Problem. *Issue Now Rivals Drugs As City's Biggest Worry. *Increase Tied to Boycott, Bensonhurst Murder Trials.[1]

As soon as the racial difference between the jogger and her assailants came to light, therefore, the story was slotted into a racial profile. Whether this crime really could or should have been explained in terms of race is a question I will explore here.

The Case

The story that emerged from the defendants' confessions (the jogger was never able to recall the crime) and police accounts was as follows:

A gang of up to thirty-six youths, most of them teenagers, some as young as thirteen, gathered at about 9 P.M. on Wednesday night, April 19, 1989 in the northeast corner of Central Park. Their purpose, it seems, was to go into the park looking for trouble—to mug, rob, scare, chase, and beat any victim who crossed their path. They roved through the park, sometimes in one big group, sometimes fragmented into smaller ones, attacking people. At various times during the evening, between 9 and 11 P.M., they robbed and beat up a homeless man, attempted but failed to accost a couple riding a tandem bicycle, and assaulted two male joggers, hitting one over the head with a metal pipe, knocking him out, and beating the other one severely. Somewhere between 10:00 and 10:55 P.M. they found their first lone female victim: a jogger.

The gang jumped her, grabbed at her, hit her, tore at her clothes, and sexually molested her as she fought back. Using a lead pipe and nearby rocks, they beat her to unconsciousness, crushing the bones around her face, and raped her. Some of them cut her legs with a knife, others grabbed at her body. They left her for dead. Hours later she was found in a puddle at the bottom of a ravine. Five of the youths were arrested on reports from the earlier victims and released. After the jogger was found, they were rearrested, along with three other youths, and held for questioning.

Out of that night of arrests came some of the most gruesome and dramatic confessions the papers had laid their hands on for years. The youths confessed on videotape and, in some cases also on paper, to grabbing the woman, fighting her, beating her, and raping her, and they told the story apparently without remorse. Later, the validity of some of these confessions came into question, but at the time they served to deepen the shock of the city and the public's horror of the crime. Eventually, six youths were officially charged with rape, attempted murder, sodomy, and assault, and tried in three separate trials.

The Reporting

The Central Park jogger case became a national story almost overnight, and was followed closely by every paper and television station in New

York and by many from around the country. As the national stories were generated primarily by New York reporters, however, I have concentrated on the New York papers for my study of the coverage of this case: *The New York Times, New York Newsday,* the *Daily News,* the *New York Post,* the *Village Voice,* and the city's two major black-owned and oriented newspapers, *The City Sun* and *The Amsterdam News.* I have also looked at magazine coverage of the case by *Newsweek, Time, U.S. News & World Report, The Nation, New York* magazine, and at women's magazines such as *Glamour* and *McCall's.*

As in all the cases examined here but the Rideouts', the story was predominantly covered by men and by whites. Each of the mainstream papers gave the story "blanket coverage," assigning an enormous number of reporters to cover it. Here is a breakdown of the gender and racial ratios among the bylined stories about the case before the trial:

Name of paper	Total reporters	Men:Women	White:Black
Amsterdam News	9	8:1	0:9
City Sun	4	3:1	0:4
Daily News	31	21:10	22:9
Newsday	35	22:13	29:6
New York Post	35	19:16	34:1
New York Times	20	13:7	18:2
Village Voice	10	4:6	2:8
Total News Reporters	144	90:54	105:39

In general, men outnumbered women almost two to one, and whites outnumbered blacks by almost three to one.

I asked editors and reporters on these papers if the overwhelmingly white and male ratios reflected the ratios in their newsrooms, and received different answers. *The New York Times,* which hires the fewest female reporters of all New York newspapers, put slightly more women on the story than would have reflected the newsroom's ratio at the time, and slightly fewer minorities. A *Times* editor told me that the paper had two black reporters contributing to the stories without bylines, but even so that made a total of only four blacks out of twenty reporters on the story. Both the *Daily News* and *Newsday* had fewer women on the story than they had in their newsrooms because, as reporter Nina Bernstein explained, the story was a crime story and most crime reporters are still men. The *New York Post* boasted the best male–female ratio on the story and in the newsroom, but has the worst record in hiring minorities—only one black reporter, Pamela Newkirk, covered the jogger case. The *Village Voice* was exceptional because it intentionally assigned black writers and women to the story. The jogger stories in the *City Sun,* which has a female editor, and the *Amsterdam News,* both politically weighted weeklies, were written primarily by men.

The First Day: The Victim and the Park

The very first headlines about the case revealed the main aspects of the crime that initially attracted the press—the same factors that had made the Levin case a big story three years earlier: The seriousness of the attack, the symbolic value of Central Park as New York's playground, and the class and looks of the victim:

> NIGHTMARE IN CENTRAL PARK
> Teen wolfpack beats and rapes Wall Street exec on jogging path. (*Post,* 4/21/89, p. 1.)

Right away, the tabloids approached this crime with a "Beauty and the Beast" theme. In the first headlines and leads, they labeled the victim by her fancy job and salary, and her attractiveness—Beauty. In the same headlines and leads they labeled her attackers as her opposites: savage, animalistic, degraded—the Beasts.

> A 28-year-old investment banker who regularly jogged in Central Park was repeatedly raped, viciously beaten and left for dead by a wolf pack of more than a dozen young teenagers . . .
>
> The young woman whose life was jeopardized by marauding teenagers, lived the way most of us dream. . . . In her yearbook photo she appears as a pretty blond in a turtleneck sweater with an engaging smile and eyes gleaming with promise. . . . She was headed for the big time: New York, Salomon Brothers, Wall Street.
>
> (*Daily News,* 4/21/89. Note the archaic language of "pretty blond.")

> She was an investment banker on the fast track to vice president, an attractive, well-liked woman who strove to keep in shape despite grueling 12-hour days in the Wall Street scramble . . .
>
> The victim, a native of Pittsburgh, adopted the career of an investment banker, *trading social life for a six-figure salary.*
>
> (*Post,* 4/21/89. My emphasis.)

The press's characterization of the victim as an "investment banker" received an interesting reaction from the public. In many ways it was an improvement over the traditional descriptions of rape victims as nothing but "pretty coeds" and "attractive divorcées" so common in the 1960s and 1970s, for at least it labeled the woman by her job and achievements rather than only by her looks or status vis-à-vis a man. Nevertheless, objections to it were raised, especially by critics in the black community. Black victims of crime are not graced with such flattering, nonsexist labels, said the critics, so the fact that the jogger was only revealed racism and class-worship among the press, not any tendency to be fairer to women.[2]

Less unusual were the descriptions of the jogger as "attractive" and "pretty" by the *News* and *Post*, descriptions that no one criticized. The men who were attacked during the same rampage that victimized the jogger were not described as attractive or pretty, or even as handsome, ugly, or unattractive. Their ages and occupations were given, and the height and strength of one of the men was mentioned as surprisingly not having daunted the assailants, but no judgment was made as to their looks or sex appeal. If the men had been raped, would this have been different? "Attractive, blond, male high school teacher raped by gang of marauding youths." The habit of describing female sex crime victims as attractive, invoking the "she provoked it" myth, is so ingrained that editors and reporters even indulged in it in this case, when their sympathies were overwhelmingly with the victim, without noticing or being noticed.

The first day characterizations of the jogger as an innocent, up-and-coming "Beauty" and her assailants as wolflike "Beasts" was to set the tone for all the reporting to come, and for all the angry objections to it as well.

Why Jog at Night?

"One of the first things people thought of when they heard about the crime was, 'Why would she be in the park at night?' " said Jim Willse, editor of the *Daily News*. "It's a standard New York thing not to be in the park at night. There are even jokes about it. 'Do you know the way to Central Park?' 'No.' 'Then I'll just mug you here.' "

The question of what the jogger was doing in the park at night placed the press in a dilemma, albeit a probably unconscious one: How much to indulge in a traditional blame-the-victim impulse and how much to show mercy to this poor, comatose victim? Unlike the Levin and Big Dan's cases, the victim had not put herself in a sexually risky situation—she had not stayed up after hours drinking in a bar and flirting—

but on the other hand, she had broken a standard New York taboo: she had gone into the park alone at night. How were the papers to handle this?

The *Daily News* took the least subtle approach. In the same issue as its first day cover story, "WOLF PACK'S PREY," was a full-page spread headlined "Why jog at night?" The story, by Sharon Broussard and Alfred Lubrana, consisted mostly of quotes from joggers and cyclists in the park declaring that the jogger had taken a foolish risk. Like all the stories on this subject that appeared that day, the point was made that, statistically speaking, Central Park has less crime than any other area of New York, but the story nevertheless focused on people's fears.

> "Even with the lights, you have to realize it's a war situation," said Lofton, who lives near the park. "The enemy can come up from the hills on the side and catch you. You should never run late."
>
> (*News*, 4/21/89, p. 29.)

Newsday ran a story on the first day that also played up the risk the jogger had taken by using the word *failure* to describe her actions.

> Wildofsky and other experienced Central Park joggers, as well as police and city park officials, stress a *failure* to use common sense and precaution could turn a jogger into a victim. (4/21/89. My emphasis.)

On the third day, *Post* editor Jerry Nachman also pointed out the jogger's "failure" to protect herself.

> In the rapidly-thickening pages describing the condition and treatment of this victim of a Central Park night, there is no chart entry listing a proximate cause of what put her on the critical list.
>
> If there were, it might read: "Patient suffered from cultural insufficiency. She was apparently unaware of, and hence *failed* to vaccinate herself against the clinical hazards of a place called New York."
>
> (4/23/89, p. 5. My emphasis.)

The cumulative implication of these stories (and there were more in *Newsday* and *Newsweek*) was that if the jogger did not exactly deserve what happened to her, she certainly "failed" to prevent it. No doubt this is how many people reacted upon hearing the story, for no one could deny that jogging in the park at night is risky. I do not expect the press to have covered up that fact, but the papers could have sought a wider balance of opinion to counteract these blaming quotes. Jim Willse, editor of the *Daily News,* was unmoved by this suggestion. "To construct the story as putting the onus on the jogger is just ridiculous," he said. He was not, however, taking into account the initial impulse of any reader, as mentioned in Chapter 1, to protect him or herself from fear of crime by thinking, "It was her fault." Nor was he taking into account other views, such as that the jogger was not at fault for being in the park—the assailants were for attacking her.

That there were contrasting opinions about the jogger's "failure" to protect herself is proven by stories that appeared in other papers. The *Times* was the most remarkable for its lack of blaming quotes. In its first day edition about the case, it ran a story by Constance L. Hays headlined, "Park Safety: Advice From Runners," which featured suggestions about running in numbers and avoiding areas of the park, but also ran quotes defending the rights of women to run wherever they want.

> "I am personally very angry," Mr. Lebow said, "because women should have the right to run any time. I feel guilty telling women not to do certain things, when in this day and age we should not be telling them not to do anything." (4/23/89.)

Joan Morgan, a black writer, gave another view of why the jogger was in the park in a *Village Voice* column.

> Some who knew her have suggested that she was simply not the type to be hedged in by limitations or to accept being told that she could not do something because she was female. I can dig that. I know women like that. (5/9/89, p. 39.)

Andrea Kannapell, a white writer, carried that thought further in her *Voice* piece entitled, "SHE COULD HAVE BEEN ME; *28 and White.*"

> What was she doing in Central Park at 10 P.M. that Wednesday? She'd been there before; she had proved to herself that the stories of unfaceable danger were lies, proved it by going back. We're like test pilots sometimes, testing the limits of safety within our lives. But if women didn't push the edges of the envelope, we'd never even get off the ground. (5/9/89, p. 37.)

When I mentioned the lack of victim blaming in the *Times'* stories to reporter Michael T. Kaufman, who covered much of the jogger case for the paper, he took it as a criticism rather than a compliment. His view was that the only reason the *Times* did not get those blaming quotes was because its reporters tend to unwittingly select their sources to reflect points of view acceptable to liberal *Times* readers. "Even if you were to go to Bay Ridge and go into a bar and sit down and strike up a conversation, the responses will be conditioned to a great extent by knowing you're from *The New York Times*," he said.[3]

So, according to Kaufman's explanation of what he called "autoselection" by journalists, *Times* reporters quoted people with liberal and feminist points of view, while the tabloids went after the working-class, conservative, traditional views. Yet an essential, although difficult, part of any reporter's job, whichever paper he or she works for, is to reach for balance. On a political question these reporters would presumably have made the effort to go to both sides, so why did they not for this story? One answer might be that they did not look for quotes defending the jogger's right to be in the park because that view was too radical—it sounded too feminist. As has been documented by Doris Graber and other press critics, most of the press automatically upholds the status quo, and the status quo for women is that they do not have the freedom to take the risks that men do.[4] Jimmy Breslin's column in *Newsday*, which appeared on the first day of reporting this case, made the latter point clear:

> The young woman who ran with such exhilaration through the night *could not, with all her schooling and all her success in a brilliant financial office*, envision a kid like this, who at age 13 or whatever knows enough to cover his face before getting out of a cop car. If she realized that the other New York throws out kids like this by the thousands and thousands, no, the tens and tens of thousands, she wouldn't have been running alone at night in a park. (4/21/89. My emphasis.)

Breslin's column not only questioned the jogger's judgment in "running alone at night," but also attributed that bad judgment to her privileged class. The idea that the jogger, in all her privilege, knew no fear became a recurrent theme in the tabloids. As a result the stories often had a punitive tone to them: She thought her privilege protected her from danger, and look what happened! This tone reached a peak in a story by Andrea Peyser and Jim Nolan in the *Post:*

> **SHE DIDN'T KNOW FEAR**
>
> **POPULAR EXEC ON HER WAY TO THE TOP** (4/30/89, p. 3.)
>
> From her salad at lunch to her nightly jog in Central Park, the woman maintained her routine religiously. Self-discipline was the thing that kept her strong, that gave her an edge in an unpredictable world . . .

> At the drop of a barrel, she would be off to Texas or Louisiana, a diminutive "li'l gal" telling the courtly Southern gentlemen how to handle their money.

Then the story got down to the matter promised by the headline:

> Just another night. She got into her T-shirt and laced up her Saucony running shoes, like so many nights before, and headed for the park. It's not safe, people always told her. She laughed. This woman who could hold her own in the Wall Street jungle—who accomplished so much so young through sheer determination and discipline—wasn't afraid of what lurked in the shadows. She would jog.

The very next paragraph, like a Grimm's fairy tale, dealt out the punishment for such audacity.

> Within a few hours, the woman's well-ordered existence would change forever.
>
> Raped and beaten in a senseless, random attack by a gang of young thugs, her stellar life would hang by a thread. *The woman who was so secure in her routines, so confident in her safety, became—possibly for the first time—completely helpless.* (My emphasis.)

This story neatly illustrates a point mentioned in Chapter 2, made by Hall, Brownmiller, and others:

> Women have been raped by men, most often by gangs of men, for many of the same reasons that blacks were lynched by gangs of whites: as group punishment for being uppity, for getting out of line, for failing to recognize "one's place," for assuming sexual freedoms, or for behavior no more provocative than walking down the wrong road at night in the wrong part of town and presenting a convenient, isolated target for group hatred and rage.[5]

The *Post*'s declaration that the jogger was "possibly for the first time completely helpless" suggested that a woman of privilege knows no fear until her overconfidence brings punishment upon her—a warning to "uppity" women if I ever heard one.

"Wilding"

By the second day of the case, April 22, the suspects had been arrested and identified and the focus had shifted from the victim to them. Right away, from that day on through the next two weeks, stories poured out about the chilling and remorseless manner in which the suspects had confessed the brutal crime—further evidence for their characterization as "the Beast."

The focus on the suspects began with the media's discovery of the word *wilding*.

> **"WILDING"—THE NEWEST TERM FOR TERROR IN CITY THAT LIVES IN FEAR**
> New Yorkers learned a new word for fear yesterday.
>
> It's called "wilding"—a street term even high-ranking police officers hadn't heard before.
>
> Like something out of "A Clockwork Orange," packs of bloodthirsty teens from the tenements, bursting with boredom and rage, roam the streets getting kicks from an evening of ultra-violence . . .
>
> Like an animal, which has caught the scent of blood, the mob—boyed by the excitement of the chase—gets out of control.
>
> (*Post*, 4/22/89, pp. 2–3.)

After striking the pose of respectable, out-of-touch whites learning to their horror about this "street" (i.e., black) term, the *Post* went on with this deceptively ingenuous statement.

> Cops learned the term when interviewing suspects, who clued them in to the fine art of wilding.
>
> It goes on mostly in Harlem and Brooklyn, police said.

Who lives in Harlem and Brooklyn? Almost more than any other aspect of this case, the fuss over the discovery of the word *wilding* marked the press as overwhelmingly white. All the papers made much of the phrase, in horrified and superior tones, ignoring the discussion among the few black voices that managed to be heard above the hubbub that perhaps the word had been misheard or had never existed at all.* The press made it clear with its amazement at this foreign word that it regarded the accused as beings from a different world, even a different species, than the rest of its readers.

Once everyone knew who the suspects were and where they lived, reporters swarmed into their neighborhoods in East Harlem to find out

---

*Barry Michael Cooper, a black investigative reporter who wrote about the suspects for the *Village Voice*, quoted members of the black community saying they had never heard of the word *wilding* and they thought the white police and press had confused it with the suspects' mentions of the song, "Wild Thing." (*Village Voice*, 5/9/89.)

all they could about "wilding," the youths, and the crime. As a result, readers began to hear explanations for the crime that seemed to reveal a shocking casualness and brutality among Harlem youths. One of the first such stories was by Richard Esposito of *Newsday*.

> Otis Cross says he knows the frenzy of "wilding" and the feeling of knocking a man to the ground and beating him while running through the upper reaches of Central Park with up to 50 other youths . . .
>
> Standing in front of his building in East Harlem yesterday, Cross, 18, said wilding is a way to relieve the boredom and release the tension after a night of "drinking and smoking reefer." . . .
>
> The motive, he says, is not profit, or racism.
>
> "They was just bored," says Cross . . .
>
> Cross says he understands why his younger neighbors and friends went wilding Wednesday night, but thinks they went too far.
>
> "I still think after everything they should have went for her. I say, 'hit her up,' but they shouldn't have raped her. That's bad."
>
> (4/22/89.)

Public horror increased when the press described the suspects' confessions.

> **AN OUTRAGE**
>
> Exclusive: Thug's chilling account of Central Park rape
>
> Eight jailed suspects laugh, joke and brag: 'It was fun'
>
> (*Post*, 4/23/89, p. 1.)

> **RAPE SUSPECT'S JAILHOUSE BOAST:**
>
> **'SHE WASN'T NOTHING'** (*Daily News*, 4/23/89, p. 1.)
>
> **ONLY ONE WAS SORRY** (*Daily News*, 4/24/89, p. 1.)

All the papers ran a considerable number of stories about the teenagers' lack of remorse, but none emphasized it as much as *The Daily News*. The *News* filled two issues with long, full-page stories about the cold-heartedness of the arrested teens, about the way they laughed and sang "Wild Thing" in jail, and about how they wolf-whistled at an "attractive" policewoman. Timothy Clifford, a *Newsday* reporter on the case who had also covered Robert Chambers's trial, said he thought that the youths' remorselessness added to the press and public's fascination with the crime: "The idea that the suspects went to the park allegedly with the intent to prey on people and that this was considered a sport of a sort—I believe there are quotes from them saying it was fun—there was a lot of horror about that. The idea that this was considered a night's entertainment!"

The Issue of Race

Amid the wonder about the word *wilding* and the horror about the youths' casual attitudes toward the crime came the first questions about whether race had anything to do with the rape. Paradoxically, the initial mentions of race were all in the form of denials.[6]

> Colangelo said the sexual assault and crime spree do not appear to be racially motivated.
>
> In statements to detectives, the youths said the sexual assault was committed because, "it seemed like the thing to do at the time."
>
> (*Newsday*, 4/21/89.)

One of the suspects was later reported to have said something about getting a white woman, but that phrase was never confirmed. At any rate, the police stuck to their original interpretation of the crime and refused to ever label it a crime of racial bias,[7]* a decision some columnists later saw as more political than accurate, an attempt to tone down the racial tension in the city. While the papers were busy filling their pages with denials that racial hatred motivated the crime, however, they were simultaneously inflaming the issue, partly because the sheer number of pieces devoted to the subject kept shoving the issue to the forefront, and partly because of the lack of understanding with which many writers tackled the topic. In an editorial that appeared in the *Post*, for example, racism seemed to be defined merely as denying the poor material goods.

> In material terms, these young men have far more and live far better than most of the people in the world; they certainly have more than did most Americans during the Great Depression.
>
> Indeed, any attempt to explain this crime spree by referring to the supposedly deprived circumstances of the accused should be recognized as an attempt to rationalize unconscionable crimes.
>
> (*Post*, 4/25/89, p. 26.)

*In New York State at the present time, a crime of bias does not include crimes against women. If rape were defined as a crime of bias—against women—it would be interesting to see how that would affect its treatment by law—au.

Particularly guilty of inflaming the racial issue was the *Post's* columnist, Pete Hamill. Look at this reasoning he set forth for why the case was "racial" in his third-day column under the headline, "A SAVAGE DISEASE CALLED NEW YORK."

> "It's a terrible thing," said a 44-year-old black man named Raymond Dufour. "Thing like that happens, it breaks everybody's heart. . . . And, you know, they gonna make it a race thing, too, that's the worst part. Bunch of young animals do this, some people gonna blame a whole damn race . . ."
>
> He was right, of course; race will be part of it because the remorseless young predators were black or Hispanic. (4/23/89, p. 4.)

Hamill missed Dufour's point entirely—that the case will be used to denigrate all blacks—and twisted it into saying it would be racial simply because the suspects were black and Hispanic. Hamill went on to fulfill Dufour's prediction with this statement:

> These kids . . . were coming downtown from a world of crack, welfare, guns, knives, indifference, and ignorance. They were coming from a land with no fathers. They were coming from schools where cops must guard the doors. They were coming from the anarchic province of the poor.
>
> And driven by a collective fury, brimming with the rippling energies of youth, their minds teeming with the violent images of the streets and the movies, they had only one goal: to smash, hurt, rob, stomp, rape. The enemies were rich. The enemies were white.

This column infuriated many blacks. By lumping all poor kids together, all the youth of Harlem and Brooklyn, their criticism went, Hamill was making it sound as if all black youth—indeed, all the poor—were this violent, this brutal, this full of hatred. He was suggesting that all black teenagers could rape.

I dwell on the extremism of Hamill and the *New York Post* because of the role they played in infuriating the black community. Reading over the early criticism by black writers in the *Amsterdam News*, the *City Sun*, and the *Voice*, as well as in letters printed in all the papers, it seems clear that their outrage was ignited primarily by the *Post*, to a lesser extent by the *Daily News*, and then generalized to include the other papers.[8] Compared to the *Post* and the *News*, *Newsday* hardly mentioned race at all, and the *Times* did so even less, although it did feature a few patronizing articles about the terror of Harlem streets.[9] I asked Hap Hairston of *Newsday* why that paper did not play up the racial aspect of the crime as much as the other tabloids. He replied: "There's two reasons. I'm black, and my deputy who handled the case is a woman. And we've worked together for ten or eleven years. I don't think *Newsday*'s eye is the same as the eyes at the *Post*, and I don't think *Newsday*'s editors are classical tabloid type editors. The other thing is that there's a significant number of blacks in the newsroom and when the racial aspect of the case came up, there were people to discuss it with. It wasn't all white males making a decision. One of the women who edited the copy, one of the night editors, is a black woman. When you have minorities and when you have women, there are sensibilities that happen that don't happen when it's all white male oriented."

In the light of Hairston's comments, I asked the editor of the *Daily News*, Jim Willse, who is white, if there had been discussion among black reporters and editors on his paper about the issue of race and how to cover it. He said, "No, it was not a particularly political issue in the newsroom." He then explained why the *News* devoted so much space to the question of race in the jogger story.

"We didn't start it. It became an issue when it was raised by the Harlem community. Any time a crime involves more than one race, certain questions must follow and one is how the media is covering it. The story is just there, so we do it. Are we consumed by whether the crime was racially motivated? I don't know. But in any crime like this the police look into if this is a bias case and the answer has something to do with how much coverage the racial aspect gets. In the jogger case I think race was just as much a part of the story as the sexual nature of the crime."

In contrast, Mike Pearl, who has covered courts for the *Post* for the past twenty-three years, denied that race had anything to do with the case, even though his paper played it up as if it did. He also said that his paper has "trouble" hiring blacks. "This is not a racial case," he said. "Even though the victim was white and the accused are black, the district attorney's office and the police department's bias unit has insisted up and down that there's nothing racial about the case."

Several editors, including Kaufman of the *Times*, told me that they received more angry phone calls about this case than any other they had ever covered, and that many of those calls were racist.[10] So, even though some of the papers tried to avoid blowing up the racial issue, the editors were aware that it was out there in the public mind, and this awareness clearly affected their coverage as the case went on.

The Suspects Profiled

At the same time as the papers were waffling about race, portraits of the individual suspects began to emerge. The most thorough of these were written by Michael Kaufman in the *Times,* Sheryl McCarthy and Nina Bernstein in *Newsday,* and Barry Michael Cooper in the *Village Voice.*

Kaufman's profiles were published first, less than a week after the case broke, under the head, "Park Suspects: Children of Discipline" (*Times,* 4/26/89, p. 1.) The gist of the story was that, contrary to the stereotypical portrayals of the suspects by people like Pete Hamill, the youths in this case were not victims of the worst kind of life, consumed by anger and hatred, but children from relatively respectable and stable homes.

> Some were the children of broken homes, and certainly all bore daily witness to the abounding pathology of drugs, drink and poverty. But four lived in a building with a doorman, and one went to parochial school. One received an allowance of $4 a day from his father, while another had just received a "A" on a report he had written. . . . One played tuba . . . another was described by teachers and classmates alike as a talented sketch artist . . . .
>
> "I deal with kids in trouble, these kids were not trouble" the principal [of a junior high where two of the boys were enrolled] said.

The story went on to give a two-to-three inch profile of each of the eight suspects. The first three were tried together, amid much publicity, during the summer of 1990. Each was charged with rape, attempted murder, sodomy, and assault:

Antron McCray, fifteen, was described as having a stable home with both parents, as being fond of baseball, and as having a strict father. A friend mentioned he liked to joke, but "was a little wild."

Yusef Salaam, fifteen, a student at a Catholic school, was described as having a concerned, religious mother who had enrolled him in a Big Brother program.

Raymond Santana, age not given in this story but elsewhere reported as fourteen, was described as "charming," with a sense of humor and successful with girls. "He was one of our nicest kids," said the director of his small, experimental public school.

The next two were tried together at the end of 1990, on the same rape, attempted murder, and assault charges as the others.

Kevin Richardson, fourteen, was described as a musician and a sharp dresser but "not a bad kid," more of a follower than a leader.

Kharey Wise, sixteen, was described as having a learning disability and as being shy, reserved, and mild-mannered. His mother was a born-again Christian.

The sixth defendant. *Steve Lopez,* fifteen, was tried alone in 1991, during the last trial of the case. He was described as being shy and a loner, who "wanted people to like him." His mother was worried about him being subject to negative influences. Lopez was charged with raping and beating the victim with a lead pipe, and was named by several of the other suspects as the leader and main rapist in the attack.

The other two suspects were never brought to trial for assaulting the jogger.

Michael Briscoe, seventeen, was described as going to church every Sunday with his grandmother and being a devoted basketball player. He had a police record for robbing another teenager. (Briscoe was eventually tried only for the assault of one of the male joggers.)

Clarence Thomas, fourteen, was described as someone who "never looks for fights." He went to an alternative high school and lived with his mother and sister. (The charges against him were dropped because the police did not charge him in time. Some said he was being kept as an inside witness.)

"I got kudos for that story from a columnist in the *Washington Post,*" said Kaufman. "He wrote a piece in which he said that kind of story is fine for breaking the stereotype of the wolf pack. I felt it was important that the kids become distinctive, even as evildoers."

The *Newsday* story on the suspects, which ran two days later, accented the troubles of the youths more and went into more depth than did Kaufman's, but it basically conveyed the same message that the kids came from surprisingly stable homes and lives. Nina Bernstein, who had written some of the better stories on the Levin case, worked with partners on two stories about the suspects. She said she wrote the profiles largely in reaction to the kind of stereotyping of the youths that Hamill and others were purveying in the tabloids with their "wolves" and "mutants."

"The initial impulse was to expect to find out horrible things about these kids because the crime was so brutal," she said. "The crime had assumed a mythic quality, both a racial one and a class one, that these were have-not kids having a kind of revenge because of all the horrible things that had happened in the city under Koch and the Reagan era.

"Then you go out and ask questions of people and find the tendency among neighbors, friends, schoolmates, teachers to say, 'This was a good kid.' It would have been very easy to go with the flow of the mythology and say these were bad kids, but it was important to be saying things were not as simple as they first appeared."

The story in the *Voice*, which ran eleven days later under the head, "CRUEL & THE GANG: Exposing the Schomburg Posse," was entirely different. Written by Barry Michael Cooper, who has since won attention as the writer of the film *New Jack City*, it revealed a startling discovery: Contrary to the preceding reports, several of the youths arrested in the jogger case were not good guys gone wrong at all, but were notorious troublemakers. Cooper described how he researched the story.

"I went back into the neighborhood and talked to a few people I knew from childhood. We grew up around the same block. I said, 'Listen, man, are these kids really so angelic and all of a sudden they went bad? And this friend said, 'Man, these guys are freaking notorious.'

"It turned out that a crew of them, at least three out of the accused [Steve Lopez, Kharey Wise, and Kevin Richardson], were well known around the Schomburg Plaza, houses in their neighborhood. They came in, they broke glass, they fought with a lot of the residents, and they were cursing at older people. So the people there were expecting to see these kids go on to big lights and big crime and big jail.

"When I found this out I said, 'Bammo, this is it! This is real, man. These kids aren't choir boys. They're maniacs!"

Cooper's story ran for several pages. In it, he quoted many residents citing accounts of violence on the part of the three boys mentioned earlier and Michael Briscoe. According to residents, the youths had beaten up other teenagers in the housing complex and one of the teen's mothers. They had threatened the security guard and some of the parents. They had thrown glass bottles over the wall into an area where babies and toddlers were playing. They had broken windows and robbed people. "I believe they came from good parents," said one of the women in the housing project, "and that they were probably nice boys in the building, but once they got outside they were *very different people.*"

(5/9/89, p. 32.)

The discovery that these youths were not the angels gone wrong that the mainstream press had portrayed did not explain away the crime, or change the basic reasons for it, but it did help make clearer the difference between boys of a violent disposition, prone to rape, and the decent citizens of the black community. Cooper said making this difference clear was his main motivation for doing the story. "My whole thing was to say, don't try to broadstroke all black men as a wolf pack and wilding animals," he said. "These were bad kids. Lay blame where it's due."

Cooper's revelations had little effect on the mainstream press's coverage of the suspects. Even though Cooper received quite a bit of attention for his story—WCBS and Channel 5's Fox News did stories based on it, he was invited to appear on television to talk about it, and it was mentioned by the *Post*—the tendency of many establishment editors and reporters was to shrug it off as "fringe journalism." Hap Hairston, for example, was not impressed: "Everybody was at the Schomburg houses, everybody was in East Harlem doing portraits of these kids. The *Voice* did it their way and the newspapers did it a lot more concisely. I don't think the reporting or writing was any better. I'm not even sure it was significant journalism."

Nina Bernstein, who worked on *Newsday*'s version of the portraits, was less defensive. "Why didn't we get what the *Voice* reported? All kinds of reasons. It was a mob scene with a million other reporters trying to get the same thing, and people either grinning before the cameras or slamming the door in your face. I had problems covering this story as a white woman. And there was a lot of pressure to get the story fast."

Paul Fishleder of the *Times* put down the missed story to simple lack of time. "Things turn out to be more complicated than they appear to be at first, but when you're in a hurry and under the pressure of deadline, the first picture always turns out to be the simplest and often not all that true."

Cooper had a different answer for why he got this story and the other reporters didn't. First, he pointed out, it was not only a matter of time, because he did the story over one weekend. Second, he had an inside source he could use to cultivate trust among the people at the housing projects. Third, he was approaching them as a fellow African-American and former resident of Harlem. Finally, he has developed a low-profile, low-pressure approach to reporting designed to win the trust of sources.

The reason the dailies missed this story boils down to two points: pack journalism and the lack of black reporters. The *Times* used two black reporters to ask questions, apparently, but they had the onus of being from a white establishment paper, which may have put off their sources. *Newsday* had one black reporter researching and writing the story, Sheryl McCarthy. The story, however, was mostly covered by white reporters from white newspapers who were descending on the neighbors in hoards: not a situation likely to elicit trust. Furthermore, many of the dailies made a common mistake in journalism—going to official sources such as teachers and principals for information instead of to ordinary people.

The fact that the press missed this story had a significant effect on the reporting of the case. The supposed respectability of the suspects confused the press because it contradicted the "weird loner" rape myth, which people rely on to explain the crime in lieu of being able to blame the victim. If even nice boys like these commit gang violence, the thinking went, how can we explain what happened? As a *Times* article put it, "If children so seemingly normal went so horribly wrong, the obvious question is Why?"[11]

Racism Versus Sexism: The Search for Answers

Throughout the case, even up to the start of the trial, the white and black press kept running articles trying to analyze why the youths had committed this heinous crime against the jogger and the other victims in Central Park that night. They looked for answers in race,[12] drugs,[13] class,[14] and in the ghetto's "culture of violence."[15] They tried to blame the crime on rap music,[16] on the lack of fathers in the boys' lives,[17] on the lack of a death penalty,[18] on Mayor Koch,[19] on television and the movies,[20] on schools,[21] on boredom,[22] on teenage lust,[23] on peer pressure,[24] and even on the full moon.[25] Even though some of these explanations had partial validity, especially for the attacks on the other victims (although many were absurd), they were woefully inadequate as an explanation for the attack on the jogger because the press never looked at the most glaring reason of all for rape: society's attitude toward women.* Because the press failed to look in the right place, it kept failing to come up with answers.

---

*The American Jewish Committee study found that in the first two weeks of coverage, there were only *six* references to the attack as a crime against women. Also, in an opinion piece on the topic in *Commentary* magazine, Richard Brookhiser wrote an entire essay about the media's attempts to find explanations for the crime, and never mentioned it as a crime against women once. Indeed, his piece read as if it were all about the violence and not about a gang rape at all. "Public Opinion and the Jogger." *Commentary*, July 1989, pp. 50–52.

> 1 WEEK LATER, QUESTION REMAINS: WHY DID WOLF PACK ATTACK?
> It's mostly all there. We all know who, what, when, where, and how.
>
> But no one answers the real question. Why?
>
> (Jerry Nachman, *Post*, 4/27/89, pp. 4–5.)

In the *Times:*

> What caused such savagery? How could so many teenagers lose all sense of morality, even of compassion? The public lunges for explanations.
>
> Drugs.: . . . Police have ruled out drugs as a factor.
>
> Greed: The police rule that out, too. The wolf pack stole nothing more than a sandwich.
>
> Race: . . . three of the victims were also black or Hispanic . . . the park group did not display the crude racial animus of the Howard Beach group, who attacked blacks simply because they had wandered into the neighborhood.
>
> Poverty: . . . Reporters find that some of the suspects come from stable, financially secure families. . . . Only one suspect has a criminal record.
>
> Then what is the explanation for this explosion of savagery? . . . The question demands more than the quick reassurance of a label. Glib answers bear a price. For one thing, without fuller understanding, the incident could inflame racial tension. For another, labels distract from real answers. How could apparently well-adjusted youngsters turn into so savage a wolf pack? The question reverberates.
>
> (4/26/89, p. 20.)

Articles like these appeared in every paper and many magazines and none of them showed the slightest understanding of the history and prevalence of violence against women. Instead, when addressing the question of why the gang had raped the jogger, and had done so with such brutality, the editors and reporters writing these stories acted as if no one had ever explained or studied gang rape. This revealed that none of them had read any of the literature on rape that has been available since the mid-1960s. Upon questioning those editors and reporters, I found that they had not even bothered to call up a rape crisis center to ask why these "well-adjusted" youths would attack a woman. They had never stopped a woman, or a man, on the street to ask why they thought the boys raped the jogger, even though they did ask people if they thought race lay at the root of the crime. They had never gone to the file index in their local library and looked up "gang rape" or thought to add misogyny to the list of drugs, greed, and so on. They had never listened to their own female reporters: "I think first and foremost it was a sex crime. You can talk about breakdown of families and racism, but the fact is they wouldn't have done that to a man!"—Natalie Byfield, reporter for the *Daily News*. They never even bothered to refer to their own op-ed pieces:

> Like the proverbial fish who cannot describe water, Americans see everything but gender at work in the April 19 assault. . . . Given more than 30 years of research on rape, our myopia is hard to explain . . .
>
> [W]hen was the last time you heard about a gang of teenage girls raping and beating a man in Central Park? To get to the roots of this particular brand of violence, we need to [go] beyond race and class to look at gender relations in the United States.
>
> (Jane Hood, sociologist, *Times*, 5/16/89, p. A23.)

Gang Violence and Rape: Women as Objects of Prey

It is necessary at this point to step back from this specific case and do what the press failed to do at the time, define and explain gang violence and rape. Why these boys did what they did, contrary to the press's frequent claim, was no mystery. The dynamics of group violence and rape are well understood by psychologists, criminologists and sociologists.[26]

For an explanation of the mob's attack on the male victims in the park, the press only had to look at the many studies of gang behavior published in popular and academic books. Criminologists have long established that males in groups show off to each other and prove their worth by outdoing each other in acts of daring and violence. Group dynamics work to bury individual morals and qualms. Mass hysteria and excitement sweep people up in the chase and the fervor of the moment—witness Hitler's sway over crowds, mob violence, looting, and riots. Teenagers are particularly prone to mob hysteria and peer pressure and tend to target their standard enemies: other gangs, adults, those who have more power, money, or privilege than they—and women.

For an explanation of the attack on the jogger, which was the subject that most obsessed the press, reporters only had to look at the many governmental and private studies on gang rape.[27] One third of all rapes are committed by a group of two or more men; gang rape is overwhelmingly committed by teenage boys on a lone female, and is likely to involve more sexual humiliation, beating, and torture than single-assailant rapes, although it is less likely to result in the death of the victim; and victims are picked for their availability, not for their looks or personality.[28] The majority of rapes are committed within races: whites against whites, blacks against blacks,[29] and most gang rapists are white, just as most people in this country are white. (This was a fact rarely brought up in the jogger case.[30]) "Group rape involves intense and prolonged humiliation for victims. Verbal insults, beating, and sexual humiliation (besides the rape) are likely to occur . . . there is a complete lack of consideration for [the victim's] dignity and well-being."[31] These words, written by Menachim Amir in one of the earliest studies of rape twenty years ago, could have been describing the jogger case.

In spite of the plethora of information available about gang rape during the jogger case, one of the only informed comments about it published at the time was written by Jane C. Hood, the sociologist quoted earlier.

WHY OUR SOCIETY IS RAPE-PRONE

> In a society that equates masculinity with dominance and sex with violence, gang rape becomes one way for adolescents to prove their masculinity both to themselves and to each other . . .
>
> In a study of 150 subsistence societies, Peggy Sanday, an anthropologist, found high incidences of rape to be associated with militarism, interpersonal violence in general, an ideology of male toughness and distant father–child relationships.
>
> Rape-free societies, on the other hand, encourage female participation in the economy and political system and male involvement in child rearing.[32] (*Times*, 5/16/89, p. A23.)

In conclusion, contrary to the uninformed assumptions of most writers on the jogger case, rapists are not usually drug addicts or hardened street criminals. Men do not rape for drug-related reasons, nor is gang rape confined to the poor and the dark-skinned. Rapists rape out of hostility to women, and a sense that they have a right to women's bodies, attitudes that pervade all classes and colors.[33] As Amir pointed out in his study, a negative attitude toward women is a necessary component of rape: "Let us consider for a moment the state of mind of the individual group member who is already aggressive, has certain attitudes toward women, and hence is prepared to participate in group rape."[34] To Amir, it was obvious that any rapist would have "certain attitudes" toward women, and those attitudes are to regard women as objects to be taken at will, as creatures less than human, as trophies for whom there is no need to feel compassion or remorse. Kharey Wise, one of the defendants in the jogger case, exemplified this attitude perfectly when he said in his videotaped confession, "I can imagine raping a woman, but not beating her up."[35]

Other studies of rapists and male attitudes toward women have confirmed that callous attitudes toward women go hand in hand with sexually coercive behavior. In 1987, two psychologists recruited 175 male college sophomores for a study of "male sexual fantasies." The majority of those men admitted to having used coercive tactics to "get sex." Seventy-five percent said they had used drugs or alcohol to persuade a date to have sex with them, more than 40 percent had used anger, 20 percent had used force, and 13 percent had threatened it. The researchers concluded that "the socialization of the macho man, if it does not directly produce a rapist, appears to produce callous sex attitudes toward women and rape . . ."[36]

This "callous" view of sex and women, these studies have shown, is not unusual.[37] It is merely an extension of the attitude condoned by society at large and mirrored by the press, as was demonstrated again and again in the coverage of the jogger case. The view was reflected by the neighborhood man who said, "they should've just raped her," by the suspects' friends who suggested the youths attacked the jogger out of boredom, and by the opinions of various columnists, editorial writers, and interviewees that the boys attacked the jogger because it was a spring night, or because a school holiday was coming up, or because they were merely feeling their oats. It was reflected by Pete Hamill's statement, "This was a savage little pack that came out of the darkness of a spring night, eventually to take what they couldn't get through work or money or love: the body of a woman."[38] It was reflected by the *Times* editorial's failure to include "society's sanction of violence toward women" in its list of possible reasons for the rape. It was reflected by the *Post*'s editorial saying, "Teen-age gangs tend to select their victims on the basis of race, religion, ethnicity or ostensible sexual orientation," while leaving out gender.[39] It was reflected by the mainstream press's inability to even bring up the issue of sexist violence, let alone handle it in detail, in their coverage of this case.* Finally, it was

---

*In *The New York Times*, for instance, a background story on the attack by David E. Pitt, headed, "Gang Attack: Unusual for Its Viciousness," offered an analysis of violence among youth groups, but failed to mention their antifemale attitudes even once. Even the sociologists and psychologists interviewed for the article did not mention this glaring element of gang rape. (4/25/89, p. B1.)

reflected by the fact that only women columnists and alternative papers and magazines such as the *Nation*, *Ms*, and the *Voice* recognized the gender issue at all.

The reason these sociological and feminist explanations for the attack are so important is that they could have prevented some of the racist reactions to the case. If the press had reminded the public that gang violence and rape is committed frequently by men of all races and classes—especially by male-centered, competitive groups such as soldiers, fraternity boys, college athletes, and bike gangs—then there might have been less tendency to see these particular suspects as exceptional monsters and mutants, less tendency to reach for trivial explanations, less tendency to see the crime solely as a reaction to a racism that defined the suspects' lives, less tendency to make it sound as if only black men rape, and, above all, less tendency to deny the role of sexism in rape.

White editors and reporters, however, were not the only ones unwilling to discuss violence toward women in our society. Many black editors and writers were just as reluctant.

The Black Press: Anger and Accusation

That racial tension had been inflamed by the coverage of the jogger case was immediately apparent in the very first stories about the crime published by the two main black-oriented papers in New York, *The City Sun* and *The Amsterdam News*. Both papers, which are weeklies, took a very different stand on the jogger case than did the white-dominated dailies.

The City Sun's first move was to blast a huge headline on its front page that parodied the *New York Post*'s of a few weeks earlier:

IT'S AN
OUTRAGE!

Under these gigantic words, which took up most of the tabloid-size cover, was an editorial by the *Sun's* editor, Utrice Leid, a woman. Leid began, like the other writers in both papers, by condemning the attack and expressing sympathy for the victim, but she quickly passed on to the real target of the piece: racism in the white media.

> The same media that refused to print or say that Tawana Brawley was raped had no difficulty summarily in stating so in the case of the Cen-

> tral Park victim. The same media that demanded Brawley "prove" her sexual assault made no such demands in the Central Park case. The same media that had no difficulty identifying the underaged Wappingers Falls teen-ager by name, invading the sanctity of her home to show her face and even televising seminude pictures of her while she was in the hospital have been careful to avoid identifying the Central Park woman. . . . The same media that would not accept a Black female teenager's story that as many as six white men sexually assaulted her have no journalistic difficulty stating as fact that Black boys sexually assaulted the white woman in Central Park. They tell us that only young Black men go "wilding," young white men never do.
>
> (April 26–May 2, 1989, p. 1.)

Leid's complaints were echoed frequently by defense lawyers, the families and neighbors of the accused, and by black commentators everywhere, and several of them were valid. There was racism in the phrase *wilding*, as discussed earlier, as well as in the lack of mention that white "wolf packs" rape, too. Leid, however, made a mistake, as did many others, in equating the Central Park jogger case with Tawana Brawley's.

As explained in the Big Dan's chapter, there are two kinds of rape cases, legally speaking. The first is a rape that definitely happened—the question is whether the police have the right suspect. The second questions whether there was a rape at all. The Central Park case was the first kind of rape, for medical evidence provided all the proof police needed to know that the rape had happened: The victim was found naked, unconscious, and beaten to a pulp, and sticks and dirt were found in her vagina. That is why the word "alleged" was never used by the mainstream press to describe the victim or the rape. Tawana Brawley's case, however, was the second kind of rape: She had been found in a garbage bag, her clothes torn, her body smeared with excrement and racist words in ink, but doctors found no evidence that she had been injured, let alone raped—in fact, they suspected her of faking her injuries before she had spoken to anyone or had accused white men of being her assailants.[40] The legal question in her case, therefore, was not so much who had committed the rape, but whether it had happened at all. That was why Brawley's rape, like the victim's in the Big Dan's case, was constantly labeled "alleged." The answer to Leid's first challenge is, therefore, that the fact of the jogger's rape was not questioned because there was physical and medical proof of it. There was no such proof in Brawley's case.

The next point Leid made—that the media identified Brawley and not the jogger—can be explained, too. It is normally newspapers' policies to withhold the name of a rape victim, especially a minor, if requested to do so by the victim or her family; however, in Brawley's case her family released her name voluntarily. They not only released her name, but her aunt, who had been her surrogate mother for much of her life, actively sought publicity for the case, calling up television and newspaper reporters and spelling Brawley's name for them over the phone, right after Brawley was released from the hospital and before most of the press knew about the story.[41] I agree with Leid that Brawley was exploited by the media, especially by the tabloid photographers, but she was exploited with the consent—even with the active, willing, and eager participation—of her family and advisors.

Unfortunately, these facts about Brawley were widely forgotten by the time the jogger case came to light, and so the impression was left in many minds that the two cases were analogous and thus provided neat, easy proof of the unequal treatment by the media and the law of whites and blacks. Not all black writers, however, accepted this view.

> When a woman as courageous and committed as *City Sun* editor Utrice Leid blazons the headline IT'S AN OUTRAGE! above a front page editorial that reads like a pathetic whine of sour grapes over Tawana Brawley, we witness how skewed political priorities can overcome the capacity for compassion.
>
> (Greg Tate, *Village Voice*, 5/9/89, p. 33.)

The *Amsterdam News*'s first stories on the jogger were as full of anger as were Leid's. In defiance of press conventions, the paper printed the jogger's name on the front page, in the lead of its very first story.[42] In an editorial explaining why in a later issue, editor-in-chief Wilbert Tatum declared that he was redressing the racist injustice of naming the black suspects and not the white victim. (Although I believe it is fair not to name rape victims, I agree that there is an inherent inequality about naming the accused, who are, after all, innocent until proven guilty. I will discuss this matter further in the Conclusion.) To call the policy of naming rape suspects racist, however, ignored the fact that this is done to all such suspects, regardless of their race. Tatum's editorial went on:

> The *Amsterdam News* took a great deal of unwarranted, stupid flak from daily and local newspapers last week because we named the name of the rape victim in Central Park. The criticism, to our way of thinking, was total hypocrisy and came about as a consequence of terminal

> racism on the part of some few writers in the white media who have for years tried to convince us of their liberalism. . . . These liberals, in all things except race and sex, saw no problem at all with naming Black children who got themselves caught up in the form of terrorizing for which the Black community has apologized on bended knee; and for which those guilty will be prosecuted. (5/13/89, p. 14.)

(Note the passive tone of "got themselves caught up in," as if these "children" took part in the crime unwillingly.)

Other than Tatum's furious antiliberal and anti-Koch diatribes, most of the *Amsterdam News*'s early coverage of the case consisted of long editorials and columns expressing the views I listed earlier about why the youths committed the crime—all views, like those in the white press, that entirely missed the gender explanation. Some of the stories, like Tatum's editorials, were so angry that they verged on denying that the crime had happened at all. Alton Maddox and Rev. Al Sharpton, for example, were quoted telling the listeners of radio station WLIB that "they doubted there was a rape victim comatose at Metropolitan Hospital."[43] After naming the jogger in one issue of the *Amsterdam News*, Tatum twice called her an "alleged" victim two issues later.[44]

The purpose of all these stories, extreme as they sometimes were, was to discuss racism and to bring up a list of accusations against the white media and police. Many of these accusations were valid and deserve to be dealt with point by point:

- *The press was racist to repeatedly use animalistic descriptions for the suspects. Such phrases would not have been used for whites.*

Although the *Post* and *News* have been using the word *wolf pack* to describe gang attacks by people of all races for years, I agree that the animalistic descriptions were abusive. In a quantitive study of the first two weeks of the crime's press coverage, the American Jewish Committee found that the suspects were described in "emotional negative language" 390 times, using 185 animal images such as "wolves," "pack," and "herd."[45] The *Post* alone used *three animal images* per day during the period studied. The peak of this kind of invective was reached by Pete Hamill, in his column defending wolves four days after the rape.

> I thought about wolves in the wake of last week's atrocity in Central Park. Those who have been charged with the crimes have been called "animals" by cops and ordinary citizens. They have also been described

> as a "wolf pack." I think this is an insult to animals in general and wolves in particular. . . . Wolves would not . . . cripple a female member of their own species, knocking her unconscious, and then take turns having sex with her comatose body.

Hamill went on to say that only humankind would commit such an atrocity, and in particular a new species of man, a "mutant," a "bizarre new form of life." And from where did he say this mutant has sprung?

> "[It] has developed in the parish of urban despair, particularly where so many housing projects have been converted into seminaries of anarchy. . . .
>
> This mutation might be the result of prolonged resort to drugs, welfare and television; it could be the last brutalized vestige of the evils of slavery. (*Post*, 4/25/89, p. 4.)

Hamill was clearly talking about the poor black man.

- *The press was racist to paint all black youths as being as bad as the assailants.*

As said earlier, I also agree that many writers, such as Pete Hamill, Jack Newfield, and Pat Buchanan generalized negative pictures of the suspects to all black men.[46] Even the *Times* indulged in this: "Grim Seeds of Park Rampage Found in East Harlem Streets,"[47] a headline certainly not written with the feelings of decent Harlem residents in mind. Michael Maren, a writer for the *City Sun*, addressed this bias:

> The news is written by, intended for, and about middle-class whites. . . . It may be passive rather than active racism but its effects are as damaging. Most disturbing, however, is the way the media enthusiastically leaps into that rift, giving white America what it expects rather than teaching them what they should know. (5/24–30/89, p. 33.)

- *The press was racist to ignore the sympathy for the victim expressed by the Harlem community.*

This criticism, too, was valid. Little mention was made of a vigil held at the hospital for the victim by Harlem mothers and teenagers. Instead, reports like this were printed: "But in the grim neighborhoods north of the park, youngsters showed little sympathy for the beaten woman." (*Newsweek*, 5/1/89, p. 27.) The only evidence *Newsweek* had to offer for this generalization was a quote from one twelve-year-old boy, who said the victim deserved what she got by not protecting herself with Mace or a man.

- *The press was racist to pay so much attention to the crime while ignoring similar crimes against black or Hispanic victims.*

As I revealed in the Levin chapter, reporters and editors of the mainstream papers admit readily that the white-dominated media pays more attention to crimes against whites than those against minorities.[48] There was a brief flurry of media attention to a black woman who was raped and thrown off a roof in May 1989,[49] and Donald Trump even made a show of visiting her in the hospital, but that coverage was more aberrant than normal, a reaction to this very criticism. One exception to the general neglect was a story by Don Terry, a black reporter, in *The New York Times*.

> A WEEK OF RAPES: THE JOGGER AND 28 NOT IN THE NEWS
>
> From poor women, whose suffering rarely makes headlines, to bankers on the fast track, to little girls in pigtails, vulnerability to rape is shared by all women and girls, experts say.
>
> In the week in which a white investment banker was brutally beaten and raped . . . there were 28 other first-degree rapes or attempted rapes reported across New York City, police said . . .
>
> The victims that week ranged in age from 8 years old to 51.
>
> "Sexual violence happens to women of every racial and ethnic and economic background," said Brooklyn District Attorney Elizabeth Holtzman . . .
>
> "The Central Park attack was treated as extraordinary . . . [but] it happens all the time." (5/29/89, p. B1.)

Michael Kaufman of the *Times* commented on this coverage: "Shortly after the Central Park rape and the black criticism there were a few rapes of black women that did get prominence because I think we were sensitized. There was the woman on the rooftop. And then that sort of disappeared after a time simply because, I suspect, it's commonplace and not news."

I doubt the black community would be too pleased to hear that rape of its women is too commonplace to be news. This definition of news is clearly white.

Further evidence supporting the criticism that the press neglects crimes against minorities came up with two other stories: The gang rape and murder of Kimberly Rae Harbour in Boston, which occurred in October 1990, during the jogger trials; and the St. John's University sodomy case in New York, which occurred in April 1990, just as the first jogger trial was about to begin.

Harbour, a twenty-six-year-old sometime prostitute, was set upon by eight youths in a field near a housing project on Halloween night. They beat her up with a tree limb, repeatedly raped her, and stabbed her over 130 times, leaving her to die.[50] In spite of the similarity of the crime to the jogger case, the story received scant attention and was only revived later, in order to point out that inattention. The fact that Harbour was both black and a prostitute, and that her assailants, most of them juveniles, were also black clearly had a lot to do with the neglect of her murder.

The St. John's case was also a gang-rape, only this time the accused were white and upper-middle-class and the victim was black and foreign-born. In many ways, this case, which also received little press attention compared to the other cases in this book, made a much better contrast to the jogger rape than did the Brawley or Bensonhurst cases.

The story of the St. John's case was as follows: The alleged victim, a student at St. John's University, a Catholic college in New York, accepted a ride home from a fellow student in one of her classes. The student told her he needed to drop by his house to get money for gas and invited her in. She accepted. He offered her a drink, and in some accounts forced alcohol on her, although how that was done was not clear at the time. While she slipped in and out of consciousness as a result of drinking too much, he and five other men sexually abused her and forced her to engage in repeated oral sex.

Once the woman escaped from the house, she did not report the assault for some time, which is usual for traumatized victims of sex crimes. Eventually, however, with the support of counselors, she did report it. Six students were arrested and charged with sodomy and other sexual abuses. They pleaded not guilty to all charges and were set free without bail. They were not allowed to return to college. The trial was not held until June 1991, when three of the defendants were acquitted. Two others pleaded guilty to reduced charges, and the sixth took a plea bargain but confessed to the substance of the charge: that he had taken her to his house, had got her drunk on vodka, and had forced oral sex from her without her permission. (*The New York Times*, 2/12/92, p. B3.)

Much was made in the few stories on this case of the fact that the accused were college jocks, members of the Lacrosse team, and that they were white, well-groomed fraternity boys. Very little was made of the fact that the victim was black—for weeks many people, especially the readers of *The New York Times*, were not even aware of the victim's race because it was not mentioned until the last paragraph or two of the story. Compared to the Central Park case, the press seemed to be hiding the fact that the assailants and victims were of different races—indeed, during the trial, the victim's race was not mentioned by the *Times* at all until her brother stood up in court and made an issue of it, claiming that the assailants had hurled racial epithets at her as they raped her.[51] Only the *Amsterdam News* seemed to see the double standard at work here.

> A veil of silence seems to have descended upon the case of the young Black coed who is alleged to have been sodomized and/or raped by several white men who are Lacrosse team members at St. John's University in Queens. . . . All of the men in the St. John's case are white college students, presumably adults. Yet, they have not been named. One gets the feeling that, somehow, different standards are being applied and there is not the kind of media pursuit of this story that there would have been had the woman been white, and her attackers Black. (4/28/90, p. 14.)

(Note that the woman here is called a "coed," while the men are allowed "college students." The *Amsterdam News* may be alert to racism, but it is persistently blind to sexism.)

By May 1990, the accused in the St. John's case had been named, and their ages all given at twenty to twenty-three. There was still a huge difference, however, in the coverage between this case and the jogger's. Not only was the question of whether race motivated the crime never raised but the press, especially *Newsday* and the *Times*, decided to use the case as a chance to discuss gang rape, sexual assault by athletes, and the abuse of women by fraternities and other college male groups.[52] In other words, the press was giving the kind of background information to explain this crime that had been so sorely missing in the Central Park jogger case. The fact that the press was willing to examine gang rape and violence against women in this case, as well as to a small degree in the Big Dan's rape, where the assailants were also white, but not in the Central Park case, where the assailants were black, reveals the racism inherent in sex crime coverage: When the assailants are white, the press is willing to explain gang rape in terms of the male ethos. When the assailants are black, the press looks instead to stereotypes of the violent black underclass.[53]

• *The press was racist to treat the suspects as guilty from the start.*

There is much evidence for this. Compare the way the press first treated Robert Chambers, calling him handsome and charming and sought after by girls, to this headline about a suspect in the jogger case, still not brought to trial: "PRIEST BAILS OUT PARK PUNK" (*Post*, 6/9/89, p. 1). There was also: "JOGGER WILL FACE WOLF PACK: Brave Move By Battered Woman" (*Post*, 10/10/89, p. 1.) It is a myth that the press covers crime and trials without bias—the tabloids in particular tend to try people in the press, and they do so to whites as well as to blacks. As even Paul Fishleder of the *Times* said: "Of course there's truth in the accusation that the press tries and convicts the suspects. That's kind of the way it is with all these stories, especially in a place so media-saturated and crazy as New York." In the jogger case, however, the press was particularly merciless to the suspects. Look at this description of the first three defendants to go to trial by black columnist Bob Herbert of the *Daily News:*

> This is not a pretty trio. Yesterday they sat together at the left-hand corner of the defense table. Some grown-ups had tried to dress them like divinity students or something, but it didn't work.
>
> McCray, 16, is little, a tiny-headed, frightened, wimpish pipsqueak who looked for all the world like a black Joey Fama.[54]
>
> Salaam, also 16, was tall and awkward. . . . His resemblance to a divinity student fell apart as soon as you looked at his ankles. His socks were the color of pistachio ice cream.
>
> Santana, 15, is the only one of the three whose family has been unable to make bail. Apparently they've also been unable to get him a sports jacket, so he sat through yesterday's proceedings in his shirt-sleeves . . .
>
> Right now it will take a very big effort to keep McCray, Salaam, and Santana from going down for the count.
>
> As they clearly do not have the stamina or the courage of the woman they are alleged to have attacked, you can expect them to go down quietly. (6/26/90, p. 4.)

• *The press was racist to profile the accused and release the names of their schools and addresses. This would not have been done if the accused had been white. The press did not do that to the Howard Beach or Bensonhurst suspects.*

The answer to this accusation is more complex. It is not necessarily true that the press would not have painted the accused in such detail if they were white—witness the stories about the accused rapists in the Big Dan's rape (although, even in the Big Dan's case, the rapists were members of a minority group, Portuguese immigrants) and the flattering profiles of Robert Chambers. In most notorious crimes, the suspects are profiled relentlessly. On the other hand, the accused in the Howard Beach and Bensonhurst racist mob murders were not described in the insulting language used for the jogger's assailants. To give another example, in the St. John's University case mentioned earlier, the accused were hardly described at all; they certainly were not called "punks."

On the whole, the black community had many valid criticisms of the way both the law and the press handled this case. Unfortunately, though, the *Amsterdam News* and *City Sun* chose to express their anger in the form of turning against the victim, just as the *Portuguese Times* had done in the Big Dan's case. As a result, these papers turned their backs on their women readers and on fairness. They ignored the view expressed by people like Eva Rodney, a black reader who wrote to the *Post:* "I pray for the full recovery of this young lady and, as a female, I feel that, black and white, we have to fight together against rape." (5/10/89, p. 28.) Instead, they printed stories that were deeply insensitive to women and particularly to the jogger. One of the worst was by Peter Noel in the *City Sun* headed, "Rape & Class: From Scottsboro To Central Park," an attempt to link the Central Park case to the kind of racism that resulted in the false accusation of the nine "Scottsboro boys" of rape in 1931.[55]

> The worst nightmare of New York City's white male-dominated press corps had become unflinchingly real: a bunch of horny Black kids had committed one of the gravest taboos. They raped a white woman. This "wolfpack" of "uptown project babies" operating, as they prefer to do, under the cover of night, feasted wantonly on The American Ideal—a beautiful body, as white as milk, of ideal smoothness, a tiny body with round hips and pert buttocks, soft wide thighs, slender calves, firm and high breasts. (May 3–9, 1989, p. 1.)

Even if Noel was trying to be ironic here, describing the jogger this way, even jokingly, as she lay beaten and comatose in the hospital made him sound vengeful, as if he wanted to humiliate her further—as if, perhaps, the rape and the fact that Harlem youths were arrested for it were her fault.

Noel went on to accuse white columnists Dennis (not Pete) Hamill and Jimmy Breslin of racism, and to drop the jogger's name whenever he could (I counted nine uses of her name in this one story), but the bulk of his story was a detailed interview with the mother of suspect Michael Briscoe. Noel's reporting did not stand up to much scrutiny—he seemed to have swallowed whole the story of the accused youth's innocence, without a hint of skepticism—but, on the other hand, the mainstream press was not too skeptical of the police and prosecution's side of the story, either. It could be argued that there was a place for a story like Noel's, since the rest of the press was equally imbalanced with its presumption of guilt. Noel's compunction to make denigration and resentment of the victim part of his story, however, was the piece's tragic flaw. Noel's misogyny certainly outraged *City Sun* reader Annette Gordon-Reed, who wrote a letter about it that was published in a later issue.

> With regard to Mr. Noel, I understand that his purpose was to reiterate that America has a racist history and present. But the flippant tone used at the beginning of the piece to describe the serious violation of another human being was sexist and insulting to Black people. Rape is a nightmare. That whites may not feel that about the rape of Black women is obviously the point of the criticism of the press' reaction to the Central Park incident. But it is certainly possible to attack the prejudices of the white media without diminishing the horror of what happened to the female jogger. (5/24/89–5/30/89, p. 33.)

Luckily, this antivictim approach by the two black weeklies was not acceptable to everyone, as the next section will show.

The Second Month: Alternative Voices

While the mainstream press was squabbling over whether the Central Park rape was racially motivated and the black press was busy denigrating the victim and accusing the white press of racism, the alternative papers set to work in a different direction. Specifically, the editors of the *Village Voice* devoted the bulk of an entire issue to the case:

> Reactions to the recent Central Park assault are being played out in the city's media—black and white—and by our would-be leaders, from Al Sharpton to Donald Trump. As accusations between the races take center stage, the universal outrage against rape gets pushed into the wings,

> and the voices of women and the black community go largely unheard. In these pages, black writers speak out on violence and sexism run amok within, and the lash of racist hysteria without.
>
> (5/9/89, p. 25.)

The issue featured eight writers, all of whom tackled the media's response to the rape, the community's reaction, and the significance of the case to women and blacks. (Cooper's story about the suspects, cited earlier, was also in this issue.) The writers criticized both the white and black press for ignoring the sexual violence in the crime.

> The extent to which this case of gang-rape is an expression of sexism run amok in the black community remains ignored by the black press . . .
>
> Rape is a universal crime. No one has to wander around bewildered that these youngbloods did this without being under the influence of crack, or that some were choirboys, went to good schools, had two parents in the home, and even a little spending change in the pocket. Boys from good homes commit rape all over this planet every day and there ain't no mystery why. Male aggression and violence against women are accepted practices in nearly every culture known to man.
>
> (Greg Tate, 5/9/89, p. 33.)

Lisa Kennedy expressed outrage at the assumption that blacks would be on the suspects' side just because they are black, and described the difficult position black women were put in regarding the case:

> Rape is part of the fabric of our communities too. As a black woman, I find myself in a schizo state of mind, my body fragmented beyond thought: woman or black? . . . To bad-mouth the youths means taking a chance that my language might be used against blacks. If I remain silent . . . then again I am in danger. (pp. 35–36.)

Joan Morgan wrote about the abuse that women receive all the time, from men of all ages and races:

> There is much less tolerance for racism than sexism in the black community. . . . We live in a pro-rape culture . . .
>
> Where did these kids come from? How could they have done this? The answer isn't so mysterious. They're susceptible children who receive messages from their environment. They watch the brothers verbally harass women on the street and get away with it. They listen to their favorite rappers wax macho and sexist. They watch television and

movies in which "No" from a woman means at least "Maybe." And they live in a community that has been traditionally afraid to address the issues of sexism and rape. (p. 39)

These opinions, however, were heard rarely in the mainstream press, which remained steadfastly blind to the issue of sexual violence. Instead, it found new fodder for headlines and heartstrings: the jogger's health.

The Rest of the Spring: The Jogger as Heroine

Except for brief pieces on the arraignments and indictments of the suspects and their high bail, most of the stories about the case over the next few months concerned the jogger's health. The press was fascinated because, initially, doctors had expected her to die. That prognosis changed to permanent brain damage, but once she emerged from her coma she surprised everyone by recovering well enough to talk and walk. She left the hospital for a rehabilitation center and, after that, went back to New York to resume her work. By the time the trial began, the public still did not know the extent of her recovery—one late report said she had sustained some neurological damage and memory loss and still spoke and moved awkwardly—but in general the tone of the press was one of awed respect.

The tabloids paid the most attention to the jogger's medical progress, devoting sensational front page headlines and full-page spreads to her every blink and word ("JOGGER GIVES A 'HIGH FIVE,' " front page of the *Post*, 5/2/89; "HER FIRST, SHAKY STEPS," front page of the *News*, 5/16/89) and their tone was always sympathetic and admiring—a far cry from the tone used to describe the Big Dan's victim, Jennifer Levin, and Greta Rideout. Indeed, the jogger was depicted as a kind of heroine of the moment, an angelic, spirited young woman fighting for her life. The most negative thing said about her was that she was obsessed with running and seemed to have a tendency toward anorexia. Here is a list of the kind of vocabulary used to describe the jogger (each phrase is a direct quote from a newspaper or magazine):

> Investment banker. Attractive. Well-liked. Perfect neighbor. Fantastic girl. Everyone loves her. Bright. Well-mannered. A girl with "most likely to succeed" written all over her attractive, patrician face.[56] Rising corporate star. Young and attractive. A strong woman. Athletic. Fight-

> ing spirit. Innocent. **Golden Girl.**[57] Bubbly. Upbeat. Brave. Has a zest for life that is impossible to quench.[58] Pretty. Articulate. Courageous. Gifted academic. Talented athlete. Stood out for her intellect and charm.[59] Spirited and spiritual. **Lady Courage.**[60]

The words were sometimes condescending ("bubbly" or "bright," rather than intelligent; "girl" rather than woman), the usual tendency to call a victim "pretty" and "attractive" was present, and they reflected some class resentment ("patrician face," for example); however, they were overwhelmingly positive, emphasizing her achievements and courage. The American Jewish Committee's study found 114 positive words about her in the first two weeks of coverage alone.[61] She was not called "worldly" or a "prude," as was Levin. She was not described as a sexy tease, as were the other victims in this book. She was not described in terms of her sexual appeal or sex life except, again, by the small faction of black demonstrators at the trial (to be described later). Most revealingly, she was allowed to be *innocent*—the word that was so glaringly missing in the coverage of the other victims. In short, the jogger was slotted into the "virgin" image rather than the "vamp."

The Case for the Defense: Police Violations and Blaming the Boyfriend

Along with the stories about the jogger's health, a few reports began appearing that questioned the prosecution's evidence. The prosecution had obtained samples of blood, hair, fingernail scrapings, and the like from the accused youths and the jogger, and the results were eagerly awaited, especially as this was the first case in New York for which DNA tests had been used to identify rapists. The results, however, were inconclusive. Bloodstains on four of the defendants' clothes were found to match the victim's blood type in general, but the DNA testing of semen yielded no link to the suspects—the only semen found had been on her underpants, rather than on her body, and that had turned out to belong to her boyfriend. No weapon had been found, either (later, the prosecution was able to produce a rock that had been used to hit her.) The prosecution's only real strength, therefore, was the collection of grisly confessions the suspects had made on videotape and paper. The confessions thus became the focus of the defense's attack.

The initial line taken by the defense was that the police had arrested the first black children they could find in Central Park and had forced them to confess. Another argument was that the police had abused the rights of juveniles under sixteen not to be questioned by police without a parent or guardian present. Later, even more drastic accusations were made against the police and Assistant D.A. Elizabeth Lederer, the lead prosecutor on the case:

> One of the defendants in the Central Park rape case testified yesterday that a detective took him to the crime scene and tried to force him to put his hand in the blood of the jogger . . .
>
> Alternately holding his head in his hands and then looking up with undisguised anger, Mr. Wise said he had been repeatedly beaten and coerced by the police into signing two incriminating written statements and into confessing to a role in the attack in a videotaped statement. (*Times*, 11/18/89, p. 31.)

The defense also tried to make much of the semen link with the jogger's boyfriend, deliberately using a phrase that evoked the Levin case.

> Defense Attorney Colin Moore . . . said the new bombshell strongly indicates that the victim and her boyfriend were involved in *rough sex* in the park that resulted in bloodshed.
>
> (*Amsterdam News*, (2/2/89, p. 1. My emphasis.)

The flaw in Moore's argument was twofold: the jogger's underpants were torn off and tossed away *before* she was raped, so the fact that they bore none of the defendants' sperm was no surprise. Also, the majority of rapists do not ejaculate anyway, so a sperm link is not necessary to prove rape.[62] This blame-the-boyfriend line, however, was not to be forgotten.

> Delores Wise, the mother of a defendant, Kharey Wise, jumped to her feet from a spectator bench and identified the victim by name.
>
> "She was raped by her own damn boyfriend," Mrs. Wise shouted . . .
>
> "This has gone too far; my son has been in jail a whole damn year . . . and that woman, she's back jogging, she's back working, and she's back with her boyfriend." (*Times*, 3/17/90, p. 31.)

Meanwhile, a more cool-headed examination of the weaknesses in the prosecution's case was being developed by *Village Voice* investigative reporter Rick Hornung. His story came out in February 1990, and was headlined, "THE CASE AGAINST THE PROSECUTION." The story cast doubt, in convincing detail, on the behavior of the police who arrested and questioned the youths.

> Everyone agrees that the confessions are the cornerstone of the case, but what has not been reported until now is that the police engaged in highly irregular conduct to obtain the admissions—conduct so improper that it has put the case at serious risk . . .
>
> [A]t least one high-ranking police officer has had second thoughts about his role in the investigation . . .
>
> "In the rush to collar these kids," admits the officer, "we played fast and loose with the law." (2/20/90, p. 32.)

The mainstream press's reaction to this piece varied. Most of the reporters I talked to admired it, but not Mike Pearl of the *Post*, "That was bulldinky," he said, "written by a reporter who obviously didn't know what was going on and who had bought some bill of goods that one of the defense lawyers was saying. I don't think the prosecution or the police fouled up the investigation."

Nor, it turned out, did the judge. On February 24, Justice Thomas B. Galligan of State Supreme Court in Manhattan ruled that the "incriminating statements" made by the defendants could be admitted in court, that the police had not violated their rights as juveniles, and that there was no significant evidence that the confessions had been coerced at all.[63]

The fact that the defendants' confessions were allowed in this case, while some of the confessions by white youths in the Bensonhurst murder of Yusef Hawkins had been thrown out by a more liberal judge, added fuel to the fire of those accusing the justice system of racism. So when the trial was postponed because new forensic evidence was found—semen on a sock lying near the jogger's body—the defense and the black press were more infuriated than ever.

> Whoever believes that these young Black males raped a woman and then took the time to find a sock several feet away in the dark and ejaculate into the sock, possesses the kind of imagination more suitable for "Star Wars" than for a case in which twelve persons tried and true will have to make a decision. . . . This very delay . . . will probably serve as one more piece of the mental documentation being prepared by Blacks, Hispanics, and poor whites in this city: the story of the failure of the criminal justice system.
>
> (*Amsterdam News*, 4/7/90, p. 12.)

Once it was discovered that the semen in the sock matched none of the defendants' blood types and added nothing to their cases, the trial for the first three defendants, Yusef Salaam, now age sixteen; Raymond Santana, now age fifteen; and Antron McCray, now sixteen, was reset to begin on June 13, 1990. All three were charged with rape, attempted murder, sodomy, and assault on the jogger, as well as with assault on one of the male victims, John Loughlin.

Cameras and Her Name

With the new trial date set, two issues were raised that also had been pertinent to the other cases in this book: Whether to allow cameras in the courtroom, and whether to reveal the victim's name.

> Justice Thomas Galligan said the ages of the defendants and the nature of the charges against them, which he called "lewd and scandalous," made camera coverage "inappropriate."
>
> (*Newsday*, 6/11/90, pp. 5, 29.)

Unlike in the Big Dan's case, and perhaps partly because of that judge's regret at having allowed cameras in the courtroom, the victim and the suspects were to be spared the daily grind of being photographed and taped. All sides, except the press, were pleased: The prosecution because many of the witnesses had said they were nervous about appearing on camera and because the victim's privacy and identity could be better protected; the defense because of the ages of the suspects.

The issue that gained the most coverage at this stage, however, was whether to use the victim's name. *Newsday* and the *Times* ran long stories on the question that revealed an interesting range of views.[64] Wilbert Tatum, publisher of the *Amsterdam News*, said he was ready to use the jogger's name again, as he had done earlier, if he thought it was "appropriate" and called the rest of the media's refusal to name her "hypocrisy and poppycock."[65] The publisher of the *City Sun*, Andrew Cooper, differed from Tatum this time by saying that, although he did not regret having published the jogger's name earlier, he was strongly against doing so again. (His reporters, however, did not abide by this rule. In an October story on the second trial, Kimberleigh J. Smith used the jogger's name five times.[66]) In general, however, because the media did not want to violate the jogger's family's wishes that her name be kept private, and because they honored the policy of protecting rape victims' identities, they agreed in tandem not to name her. Jerry Nachman of the *Post* gave a concise reason why:

> "What we want to avoid is, a year from now, she buys a blouse from Bloomingdale's and hands her credit card to the clerk who says, 'Oh, yeah, you're the one who got gang-raped in Central Park.' "[67]

Amid all this good will, however, which Edward Kosner, editor of *New York* magazine, called "old fashioned, but . . . kind of nice,"[68] there was the same willingness expressed by editors in the New Bedford case to buckle under and name the jogger if everyone else did. As the *Newsday* piece on naming put it, "If any of the media were to break ranks and publicize the jogger's name, it would undoubtedly cause others to rethink their policy and possibly follow suit."[69] In other words, that "old fashioned" consideration for the jogger and her family would go to the winds for the sake of pack journalism.[70] In practice, though, the barring of cameras and the willingness of the media to hide the jogger's identity were further indications of the care with which the press treated this victim right up through the trials.

The First Trial: Racism or Rape?

The trial of the first three defendants, Salaam, Santana, and McCray, lasted six weeks, from June 25 to August 9, 1990. At first the coverage was slim, but by the end the New York papers had generated hundreds of pages on the trial. The coverage continued to revolve around the same issues that had come up before: Had the confessions been coerced? Had the suspects' rights been violated? Above all, was this a case about racism or rape?

During the first three weeks of the trial, the prosecution was clearly winning all the shots. The opening arguments began with a close to hour-long account by Assistant D.A. Lederer of the grisly details of the crime that once again sickened readers over their breakfasts.

> **JOGGER TERROR**
>
> They saw a young woman whose hair was matted with blood and mud, who was naked but for a jogging bra, cold to the touch.
>
> She was tied up with a blood-soaked shirt that bound her mouth, her neck and her wrists. There she lay in the mud, thrashing back and forth and groaning. (Front page, *Newsday*, 6/26/90.)

The press reported that the bones around one of the jogger's eyes had been smashed to bits, that she was found with her eye staring unseeing out at the night . . . and amid all this horror it quoted the defendants talking about getting on top of her, punching and smashing her, shouting "Shut up bitch" at her, taking turns. . . . By the time the defense attorneys stood to deliver their opening statements, they had a hard road to travel. According to columnists Dennis Duggan of *Newsday* and Bob Herbert of the *Daily News*, they traveled it badly, relying on weak arguments and sliding into what Herbert called "gibberish."

> By the end of the day, trial-wise reporters were nudging each other and rolling their eyes as the defense lawyers laid out a predictable array of arguments, including police brutality, racism and even the media as reasons not to convict their clients.
>
> (Duggan, *Newsday*, 6/26/90, p. 35.)

The defense attorneys' case did not improve. The judge denied their attempt to declare two of the defendants, McCray and Salaam, too unintelligent, unstable, and vulnerable to resist being coerced by police. Semen (their own) was found on two of the youths' clothes. The lawyers' arguments about police racism and coercion did not seem convincing. The only thing on the defense's side was that the succession of witnesses who were called by the prosecution to testify about their attacks by the roving gang could not identify any of the three defendants.

Meanwhile, the male columnists were *still* going on about the mystery of the crime, and still missing the point of violence against women. In a column describing the testimony of David Lewis, one of the victims of the Central Park rampage, Duggan of *Newsday* made this comment:

> The three defense attorneys . . . studied the blow-up [of David Lewis's injuries] intently. The thought must have occurred to them and to the jury which studied the two police photographs that the 31-year-old Lewis was lucky indeed to have escaped the awful nightmare inflicted on the jogger. (6/28/90, p. 3.)

Duggan seems not to have realized that *all* the male victims that night were spared the jogger's "nightmare," not because of luck, but because they were male.

If Duggan and his colleagues were subtly sexist by ignoring the rape aspect of the crime, the *City Sun* was blatantly so. During the same week as the opening of the trial, the *Sun* ran a long essay by Clinton Cox that amounted to a ferocious diatribe against not only feminists, but white women in general, echoing the blame that had been directed at white women since the days of lynching.

> **FEMINISM: APING THE ANTICS OF THE GOOD OLD BOYS**
>
> For three or four years, it seemed that society might actually be serious about letting Black women and men compete on an equal basis with whites in the job market. But a funny thing happened on the way to the equal employment office: white women . . .
>
> Suddenly, white women, who never had been turned away from hotels because they were white women or forced to ride in the back of the bus because they were white women or hanged from trees because they were white women, were labeled an oppressed "minority." . . .
>
> This isn't the first time in American history that the white-feminist movement has slowed or blocked the Black struggle for equality. (6/27–7/3/90, p. 5.)

Cox ignored the fact that white and black women have been and are the victims of discrimination, violence, and murder because of their gender all the time—the FBI conservatively estimates that a woman is raped every six minutes in this country,[71] battery by men is the leading cause of injury to women,[72] and reports came out during the first trial of the jogger case indicating that 75 percent of American women have been or will be the victims of violence in their lifetimes.[73] Rather than step into the murky pool of comparing women's oppression with that of blacks, however, I will only say that Cox's vengeful piece was emblematic of the post-Scottsboro conflict between black rights and women's rights, resulting in a line the *City Sun*, the *Amsterdam News*, and the defendants' supporters were increasingly to take as the trial went on: attacking the victim.

The Black Protesters

During the trial, a group of a dozen or so black protesters began turning up in court every day. Their aim was to protest racism in the judicial system by discrediting the prosecution, the jogger, and the other victims of the gang rampage.

> Yesterday, they hissed Loughlin [one of the male victims of the rampage]. The day before, they hissed another victim of the marauding

> gang, Gerald Malone, calling him "bastard" for attempting to fend off his attackers. (Amy Pagnozzi, *Post*, 6/29/90, p. 4.)

Influenced by the Rev. Al Sharpton, Vernon Mason, and the black media, the protesters touted an extreme antivictim, antiwhite line throughout the case. They did so loudly, shouting and demonstrating outside the courtroom, snickering and jeering inside.

> "What was she doing [in the park]?" they shouted, following Assistant District Attorney Elizabeth Lederer as she left Manhattan Supreme Court at lunchtime . . .
>
> "She went up there to score drugs," they screamed, often repeating the jogger's name.
>
> "Where's the jogger's boyfriend? Where's the rape evidence?" (*Post*, 7/13/90, p. 5.)

By the third week of the trial, all the papers were covering the protesters. Indeed, a sort of war began between the "heckling mob," as the *Post* called them, and the newspaper columnists. Bolstered, perhaps, by a knowledge that those views belonged to extremists, not to the majority of their readers, the columnists made it clear that they considered the antijogger views hate-mongering and monstrous. In the Big Dan's case, reporters had to worry about the large proportion of Portuguese among their readers who felt slighted by the treatment of the suspects; however, in the jogger case, the mainstream reporters, black and white, saw no such responsibility. That, plus the fact that the mainstream press was so ready to identify and sympathize with the jogger in her "virgin" image, enabled the papers to remain steadfastly protective of her.*

*Erika Munk, who had been writing feminist pieces about the case for the *Voice*, wrote about the protesters in a *Nation* editorial. The piece again brought up the ongoing conflict between black activists and white women. ". . . The black press initially raised many good questions . . . and then—forced by a pro-defense momentum it had itself helped to create—started to promulgate theories that were unanswerable because they were absurd: The jogger went to the park to buy drugs, to sell herself, to meet a lover, to be sacrificed in a full-moon satanic ritual; she was never raped at all. If the Central Park defendants were to be made heroes by Sharpton, Mason, and Farrakhan, they had to be not only the victims of unequal justice but innocent; not only innocent but accused of a crime that had never happened. Father Lawrence Lucas, a black priest active in the defense, told me, 'The sexism here is in reverse. This gal Lederer [the prosecutor] is trying to up her career on the backs of innocent young black males, which is what this society is all about.' " "Race and Rape," *The Nation*, 10/8/90; pp. 368–69.

The war between the mainstream press and the black protesters reached a peak when, during the fifth week of the trial, the prosecution produced a surprise witness: the jogger herself.

The day the jogger took the stand was the high point of the whole trial and revealed, as had nothing else, just how sympathetic to her the mainstream press was. Every reporter at the courthouse milked the drama for all it was worth—the wounded, virginal figure facing her assailants gently, calmly, and apparently without ire. Her behavior fit the brave, victimized heroine perfectly, like something out of a Gothic novel. Even the fact that her picture could not be shown helped, because it freed the reporters to describe her more subjectively than they could have with cameras. "Then there was the matter of her eyes, the right larger than the left, and both wide, wide open, as if the attack that nearly killed her was happening all over again." (Charles Carillo, *Post*, 7/17/90, p. 4.)

Newsday, which devoted six pages to the story of the jogger's day in court, loved the drama in columnist Jim Dwyer's lead so much it used it on the front page: "She was a walking crime scene." The *Post* and the *Daily News* each ran four full pages on the jogger's appearance, emphasizing her courage and calmness on the stand. Even the *Times*, which had been giving scant attention to the case in recent weeks, devoted a front page story and a whole second page of its Metropolitan section to her testimony. In general, the media's admiration of the jogger was expressed by this *Post* headline: "LADY COURAGE" (7/17/90, p. 1.).

In fact, the jogger testimony was somewhat anticlimactic. She told the packed courtroom that she could not walk steadily, had double vision, and had lost her sense of smell. She answered the prosecutor's questions about when she had last had sexual intercourse with her boyfriend (a line of questioning necessary to determine when the boyfriend's semen had gotten on her clothes). She also testified, however, that she had no recollection of the attack, an admission the defense later tried to claim as a triumph. The defense refused to cross-examine the jogger, well aware of how unsympathetic it would look to hammer away at such a fragile, courageous, and sympathetic figure.

To the angry demonstrators, however, the jogger's appearance in court was only another chance to attack her credibility—as the *Post* reported with glee.

JEERING SPECTATORS ADD INSULT TO HER INJURIES

Seeing is not always believing—at least to the clique of pro-defense spectators at the Central Park jogger trial.

> Yesterday, after the jogger's dramatic appearance moved a packed courtroom, they still refused to see her as a victim.
>
> Instead, they ridiculed and taunted her as she left the courthouse in a white van with tinted windows.
>
> "She's an actress! That wasn't the jogger! Where's the jogger?" said one man . . .
>
> "More racist lies!" he shouted . . .
>
> "Why don't you find her drug dealer that she went to the park to meet?" barked a strapping, T-shirted antagonist . . .
>
> "Why are they trying to lynch these boys? Lynch the boyfriend! Lynch all her boyfriends! She had many of them."
>
> (7/17/90, p. 4.)

In line with the protesters, the only paper to remain unimpressed by "Lady Courage" was the *Amsterdam News.*

> **JOGGER'S COURT PRESENCE FAILS TO SWAY OPPONENTS**
> **SPECTATORS JEER WITNESS, THEY CALL HER STORY A LIE.**
>
> (7/21/90.)

In that same issue, Tatum, the publisher, wrote an editorial under a headline that was to catch the imaginations of the defendants' supporters for weeks to come: "The legal lynching." As he had been doing all along, Tatum questioned the evidence and criticized the white press for not doing the same thing, but once again he spun off from important questions to extreme accusations:

> The truth of the matter is that there is a conspiracy of interest attendant in this case that dictates that someone Black must go to jail for this crime against the "jogger": and any Black will do. *The rationale being the belief that Blacks are interchangeable anyway, and that if these particular Blacks that are on trial didn't do it, they could have, or alternately that they have done something equally horrible in the past that we didn't catch them for or that they will do something in the future that will harm the body politic. Therefore, we have them now, so let's convict and punish them now. It is of no real consequence whether or not they are guilty of this particular crime.* (7/21/90, p. 37.)

This editorial received quite a bit of contemptuous coverage in the white press. Amy Pagnozzi attacked it in her *Post* column, pointing out the irony that, in the very same issue that Tatum accused whites of seeing blacks as interchangeable, the front page photograph of defendant Antron McCray was misidentified as being of Raymond Santana.[74]

When the black protesters were not casting aspersions on the jogger, or making wild accusations about the racism of every white in New York, they and the black papers were bringing up some valid points. One of these was that the videotaped confession of suspect Raymond Santana, released to the press the day after the jogger's appearance in court, sounded highly suspicious—so much so that white columnist Carole Agus of *Newsday* was also moved to question the prosecution's entire case.

> There never was a 14-year-old working-class kid that ever talked the way Santana is supposed to have talked to the police that night:
>
> "We met up with an additional group of approximately 15 other males who also entered Central Park with us . . ." it [the videotaped confession] says at one point. "We all walked southbound in the park in the vicinity of 105th Street." . . .
>
> We who are watching this trial . . . are waiting to see if there is any believable evidence that will connect these kids to the crime.
>
> So far, we haven't heard any. (7/18/90, p. 25.)[75]

Agus's point, however, and other important questions about the validity of the prosecution's case, kept on getting buried in the battle between the black demonstrators and moderates, and between the black and white press.[76] All during the case that battle continued, with the tragic result that neither side was tackling the important question at hand: Were the suspects getting a fair trial? One of the only writers to address this question without hysteria was Sheryl McCarthy, a black columnist for *Newsday*. She wrote an incisive column summarizing the dilemmas—the bloody facts of the crime on the one side, and the history of blacks unjustly accused and executed on the other—and brought up the lack of physical evidence, the lies the police told on the stand, and the lies they told the defendants in order to get them to confess. She also tackled the real meat of the trial: Whether to believe the confessions.

> But then there are the videotapes. They assault the senses like a horse's kick. Antron McCray's was played last week. In it he sat calmly, in the presence of both parents, and described the attack in detail—the charging, beating, the sexual assault, his kicking the jogger and his own feigned rape of the jogger just to impress his friends. On the videotape, he did not look frightened or stressed out, starved, or worn out by fatigue. He told the story in his own words and he named names.
>
> (7/23/90, p. 24.)

William Glaberson, a white reporter at the *Times*, was another of the few reporters to question the fairness of the trial without hysteria. Earlier, he had criticized the defense for not coordinating their strategy, presenting a sound plan, or arguing their cases well.[77] Then, in the wake of widespread criticism of Robert Burns, Salaam's defense attorney, he raised another essential question: How could these suspects be guaranteed a fair trial when they were represented by poor quality lawyers, assigned to them by the public defender system? That question, which Tatum and others had also raised, was a pertinent one to this trial, although it did not apply to Burns himself, who had been hired by Salaam's mother as a family friend. Indeed, by the second month of the trial, the question of whether poor blacks could find fair representation at the hands of the criminal justice system had become urgent enough for even Erika Munk, one of the primary feminist writers on the case, to concede that race had by now become as much a part of the trial as gender.

> This rape is famous not because of either victim or accused, but because it fleshed out the white middle class's worst fear—that the young black poor will take their revenge on privilege, success, and confidence . . . and [it] fleshed out black fears, too, of white stereotypes and racism's double standards. (*Village Voice*, 7/17/90, p. 11.)

By the end of the first trial, the views of the press were clearly in two camps. The black press maintained that no one in the case was to be trusted—the police had coerced the confessions and lied on the stand, the jogger had lied about her boyfriend, the white press had covered up facts and slandered the suspects with racial stereotypes, and the suspects were innocent martyrs. The white press took the view that the suspects were guilty thugs, the demonstrators crazed by racial resentment and the jogger a noble victim.[78] The clash echoed the historic confrontation between black activists and white feminists over interracial rape that has been raising hackles since the days of lynching, Scottsboro, the civil rights movement, and Eldridge Cleaver. As Susan Brownmiller wrote, "The crossroads of racism and sexism had to be a violent meeting place. There is no pretending it doesn't exist."[79]

The Jury Deliberates

By the end of the trial, the jury had heard forty-three witnesses, had seen 182 exhibits, and had listened to six weeks of testimony. Each of the three suspects was charged with thirteen different crimes and the jury had to understand two tricky facts about New York law: that the defendants could not be convicted by their own statements without corroboration or additional proof, and that a person can be convicted of rape for abetting a rape, even if he did not actually penetrate the victim. (In the New Bedford case, penetration had to be proven to convict for rape—a very different requirement that was responsible for the more sexually graphic testimony in that trial.)

For the next ten days the jury deliberated in secret, while the press filled their pages with summaries of the trial, reactions to Tatum and the black protesters' points, and calls for various kinds of punishment. Tatum ran an editorial slamming the white press for being "mean, vindictive, vile, venal . . . totally biased, often unprofessional and certainly not objective when it came to reporting this trial." (*Amsterdam News*, 8/11/90, p. 12). Pagnozzi wrote a column defending the press and referring to the antagonism between Tatum and the *Post*, which had become a kind of game by then. Meanwhile, the tabloids continued to run unflattering columns about the defendants that revealed an unabashed presumption of guilt.

Finally, on August 19, the verdict came in. As the *Daily News* put it in huge letters on their front page: GUILTY. The jury decided that the three teenagers were guilty of rape, assault, and all the other charges except the most serious—attempted murder. The defendants were cleared of that, one jury member later explained, because they had been carrying knives and, if they had intended to kill the jogger, they would have done so. Others said the murder charges were dropped because the jury felt the teenagers were too young to have known what they were doing.

After the verdicts, the coverage did not slow down for days. Interviews with jurors, posttrial analyses, repetitive profiles of the jogger, and rehashes of the black–white issues continued to fill pages of the New York papers every day. The defense lawyers and supporters decried the verdicts, cried racism once again, and vowed to appeal. The real posttrial highlight, however, came with the sentencing, when Yusef Salaam stood to hear his sentence and decided to show off. Salaam read a long rap poem protesting his innocence and martyrdom at the hands of a racist criminal justice system, which he had written after first being arrested, and compared himself with Malcolm X, Dr. Martin Luther King, and Nelson Mandela. The press could not resist mocking this self-aggrandizement, the *Post*, predictably, most of all with a screaming headline two inches high:

SALAAM BALONEY! (9/12/90, p. 1.)

The first three defendants in the trial were sentenced to the maximum possible time for juveniles—ten years. They were to be eligible for parole in five.

The Second Trial: The Powerful versus The Powerless

The second trial began on October 22, 1990, nineteen months after the attack, and lasted six weeks. It differed from the first mainly in that one of the two defendants, Kharey Wise, was eighteen by that time and could face an adult sentence of nineteen to fifty-seven years. Kevin Richardson, the other defendant, who had been only fourteen at the time of the rape, was now sixteen.

The second trial received less attention than the first—the *Times* virtually stopped covering it at all, except for the occasional highlight. This neglect was probably a result of the press's fatigue with the case and of concentration on other events in the news—a second Bensonhurst trial, the divorce of Ivana and Donald Trump, the trial of mafioso John Gotti, and the warming up to the Persian Gulf war.

The trial opened with a clash between the two defense lawyers. Colin Moore, Wise's attorney, an outspoken, fiery man determined to play up the racism in the case and to prove there was no rape, declared his intention to call the jogger to the witness stand once again and to cross-examination her relentlessly about her sex life. He also publicly referred to her as a 'bitch." This alarmed Richardson's attorney, Howard Diller. " 'My opinion is that to cross-examine her would be so detrimental to a fair trial that I may move for a mistrial at the point,' Mr. Diller said. 'It would only result in her being pitied by the jury and I don't need that.' "[80] Partly as a result of this clash, Richardson's family tried to replace Diller with C. Vernon Mason, an activist lawyer who had made a name for himself along with the Rev. Al Sharpton and Alton Maddox during the Tawana Brawley case. The judge refused to allow the change.

The first dramatic moment in the trial occurred when Wise broke down in the courtroom. After hearing Assistant D.A. Lederer accuse him of holding the jogger's legs down and "playing" with them while others raped her, he burst out screaming, "She's lying!," and began to sob, shake, and, according to some, to foam at the mouth. He was calmed, but the incident in an odd way humanized one of the defendants for the first time. In general, Wise was seen as unlucky because his crime was relatively mild compared with the others and yet, because he was only a few months older than they, he faced the harshest sentence.[81] His breakdown also led to an interesting revelation:

> "He is under a lot of pressure," [Wise's attorney] Moore said later. "When the inmates at Rikers, where he has been held for 18 months now, heard over the weekend that the Reverend Al Sharpton wasn't coming to this trial because he thought these defendants might be guilty, they got on his case and gave him a rough time."
>
> Sharpton denied yesterday that he ever said any such thing. In fact, late yesterday afternoon he said he wouldn't attend this jogger trial because "I don't know if they are guilty or innocent the way I knew that Antron McCray was innocent."
>
> (Dennis Duggan, *Newsday*, 10/23/90, pp. 3, 25.)

On the whole, the defense fared badly. For example, when Moore tried to rely on the usual rape trial tactic of discrediting the victim by suggesting that her wounds were trivial and her sex life responsible for her attack, his attempts were mocked. His failure to win these points testified both to the sympathy the jogger's injuries had won, and to the strength of her "virgin" image.

> Jurors in the Central Park jogger rape and assault trial laughed, shook their heads and rolled their eyes as defense attorney Colin Moore suggested that the female jogger's injuries were "piddling."
>
> (*Newsday*, 11/1/90, p. 5.)

Meanwhile, the black papers continued the prodefendant stand they had taken in the first trial. The *Amsterdam News* began running stories on the trial by Vinette K. Pryce that suggested that the trial was unfair, attorney Diller inadequate, and Moore the only one on the right track. The *City Sun* printed a large headline playing with the question of who were the real victims in this case, the "powerful" jogger or the "powerless" defendants: "THE JOGGER TRIAL'S INNOCENT VICTIM" (11/14–20, 90, p. 1). The "victim" was Kevin Richardson's mother.

The white tabloids, meanwhile, were being as antidefendant as the black press was pro. The *Post* ran the story of Wise's two videotaped confessions a day and a half before the tapes were shown in court—"news before it happens," as Guy Trebay called this move in a *Voice* article.[82]

> "THIS IS MY FIRST RAPE"
>
> In a damning videotape confession to be played today, jurors at the Central Park jogger-rape trial will hear suspect Kharey Wise tell authorities: "This is my first rape . . . and this is going to be my last." . . .
>
> "They told me to pull down her pants, so I pulled down her pants. Steve [Lopez, who has not yet been tried] called me a punk because I ain't doing it . . .
>
> "I wasn't doing what they were doing. They were on top raping her for pleasure. I was just playing with her. They were f——— her, I was just playing with her legs. . . ."
>
> Asked if he touched the jogger any higher, Wise said, "I was about to" but didn't "because I could see the expression on her face."
>
> (*Post*, 11/15/90, pp. 1, 5.)

By the day of the closing statements, November 28, the defense had little strategy left but to claim racist coercion. Witnesses had corroborated both the defendants' involvements, Wise's mother had been banished from the courtroom for calling the lead prosecutor a "snake" and yelling at her to "shut up," other witnesses had backed out of testifying, and the videotapes stood out as powerful confessions, as they had done in the first trial. In their closing statements, therefore, Diller relied on the coercion defense and Moore called once again upon Scottsboro and the history of black men lynched because a white woman—or a white man on her behalf—had cried rape.

> Mr. Moore acknowledged that the woman was the victim of a "horrible and terrible" attack. "But does that justify a blood lust for the first black and Hispanic the police could put their hands on?" he asked. "Do we want a recurrence of those days in the South when black men died in trees simply for looking at white women?"
>
> (*Times*, 11/29/90, p. B3.)

Assistant D.A. Lederer countered these statements one by one, ending with the point, "This is not a case of black, white, and Hispanic. It is a case of right and wrong." (*Newsday*, 11/30/90, p. 5.)

After twelve days of deliberations, the jury of seven women and five men, four of them black, four white, three Hispanic, and one Asian, who declared later that they had never discussed race in connection with the case, came out with verdicts that surprised everyone. Wise, whose two confessions had been considered the most damning, was found not guilty of attempted murder or rape, but was found guilty of sexual abuse and assault. Richardson, whose videotape was less incriminating, was found guilty of all eight counts against him. That made him the first defendant in the case to be found guilty of attempted murder. His mother was so shocked by the harsh verdict that she fainted and had to be revived with oxygen.

Posttrial stories cited the jurors as saying they had been easy on Wise largely because they were, after all, suspicious of his two videotaped statements. In the first, Wise had claimed to have only watched the rape from behind a tree. In the second he said he had been lying and had in fact held the jogger's legs while the others raped her. The jury suspected this change may have been a result of police pressure. They also, various reporters speculated, might have been affected by the knowledge that Wise was facing a longer sentence than the others. After all, he had cried out in court, "I'm facing fifty-seven years over this."

Richardson, on the other hand, was convicted on the grounds of forensic evidence more than the videotape. Pubic and head hair matching the jogger's had been found on his underpants, which were also stained with grass and mud, putting him pretty clearly at the scene. As one juror rather colorfully put it, "Pubic hairs don't just fly through the air."[83]

Analysts agreed that this trial, even more than the first, had been about race.

> "It was a classic racial courtroom drama," famed criminal defense lawyer William Kunstler said. "White woman, black alleged rapists. All-white prosecuting team. Black defense attorneys. Hand-picked white judge. The cancer of racism is so deep that you can't avoid it, even in the laboratory of a courtroom."[84]

Even though Kunstler failed to mention the racially balanced jury, the families and friends of the two defendants clearly agreed with him. Right after the verdicts were announced, their anger erupted outside the courtroom and they attacked reporters, called A.D.A. Lederer a "whore" and a "bitch," and accosted white bystanders with the epithet "white racists." Joan Didion wrote a story on the case for *The New York Review of Books* that summarized the polarization this case had highlighted between blacks and whites, the poor and the rich of New York:

> One vision, shared by those who had seized upon the attack on the jogger as an exact representation of what was wrong with the city, was of a city systematically ruined, violated, raped by its underclass.

> The opposing vision, shared by those who had seized upon the arrest of the defendants as an exact representation of their own victimization, was of a city in which the powerless had been systematically ruined, violated, raped by the powerful.[85]

On January 9, 1990, the defendants were sentenced. Richardson received the maximum for a juvenile, five to ten years. Wise received five to fifteen, considerably less than the eight to twenty-six years he could have faced.

The Third Trial: An Anticlimax

The importance of the videotaped confessions to the prosecution in the jogger case was never as apparent as during the third and final trial of the lone remaining defendant. Steve Lopez, who was seventeen by the time of the trial, was the only suspect not to have made a confession, videotaped or oral, and without it, the prosecution's case fell apart.

Lederer had been going to rely on a stream of witnesses against Lopez, for even though he had been named the most brutal and the central figure in the rape of the jogger by the other defendants, by law none of their statements could be used against him. All the witnesses backed out, however, saying they feared for their safety, were afraid of self-incrimination, and that they did not want to risk the wrath of the Harlem community.[86] The jogger, too, told Lederer that she wanted to get on with her life and avoid appearing at a third trial. The only remaining evidence against Lopez was a single blondish hair that could not even be forensically linked to the jogger.

In January 1991, Lopez thus took a plea bargain, avoiding all mention of the attack on the jogger. He was sentenced to one-and-a-half to four-and-a-half years for "acting in concert with others" in striking the male jogger, John Loughlin, with a pipe. He was to serve his sentence in a youth correctional facility. Meanwhile, all news about his trial and reactions to this last peculiar anticlimax of the jogger case were pushed off the pages by the advent of the Persian Gulf War. Two years and nine months after the jogger was attacked in Central Park, the case was finally over.

Discussion

Unlike Greta Rideout, the Big Dan's victim, and Jennifer Levin, the jogger was treated with reverence and discretion by the mainstream press. Her name was never disclosed, except once by WCBS inadvertently, followed by an apology, and a few times by the black-oriented media for reasons explained; her sex life and morals were subject to minimal scrutiny; the only aspersions cast on her character were by a few extremists; she was repeatedly described in glowing, positive terms; and, on the whole, she was not even subject to much blame for the crime, even though she had broken a New York taboo by jogging at night alone in Central Park. Why did the press show such mercy? Had it at last learned to respect rape victims? Had feminism triumphed?

The answer is both yes and no. Yes, the press had been more sensitive than usual in its treatment of a rape victim, but the reason they spared her was not due to any feminist enlightenment. They spared her because, unlike the other victims in this book, she had the majority of those eight damning rape-myths in her favor.

Unlike the other victims, she did not know her assailants and could not be construed as knowing them, thus was less easily blamed. Unlike in the other cases, weapons were used—and brutally. Unlike the other victims, she was not, as the press continually emphasized, of the same race and class as her assailants; she was of the dominant race and class, the same race and class as the editors and owners of the mainstream newspapers. Unlike Greta Rideout and the New Bedford victim, she was not of the same ethnic group as the assailants—they were "the other" in every way. Unlike the other victims, she was not engaging in disreputable behavior when she was attacked. The only ingredients against her were that she was young and "pretty," although the latter was played down by all but the most old-fashioned of writers because the attack was not covered as a sex crime, where the looks of the victim traditionally matter, but as a rampage of class against class, race against race. No, the rape myths permitted the jogger to be perceived as a good woman, so she was allowed her innocence and dignity.

Yet, the press's selection of the virgin image over the vamp was not without its price. Because the preconceived narrative would not allow the press to portray the jogger as having enticed her assailants beyond endurance, it had to slot the youths into the alternative "weird pervert" cliché instead. And it did so, eagerly. From the very first day of the coverage, the press leapt on the image of jogger as Little Red Riding Hood in the woods, attacked by wolves, and described the suspects as monsters, animals, and mutants. In doing so, the press came to sound more and more racist. The racial conflicts arose in this case, therefore, not because of the nature of the crime but because, by choosing the virgin myth of sex crimes, the white press forced itself into racist clichés about the suspects to which the black press and community naturally had to object. (The coverage of this case also revealed that invectives against the "black underclass" are becoming more and more tolerated in the white press as an expression of America's exasperation with its crime.)

Once race had come up, it reawakened the painful memories of interracial rape in this country. As Brownmiller wrote in 1975,

> By pitting white women against black men in their effort to alert the nation to the extra punishment wreaked on blacks for a case of interracial rape, leftists and liberals with a defense lawyer mentality drove a wedge between two movements for human rights and today we are still struggling to overcome this historic legacy.[87]

In the jogger case, this struggle was enacted all over again. It pitted black activists, who had the view that accusing black men of raping white women is the ultimate expression of racism, against feminists, who had the view that all women should be free of rape and that rapists should be severely punished. Black women, meanwhile, were caught in the neglected middle.

The other reason this case came to be seen as a racist issue was simply because no one would recognize it as sexist. I asked the reporters and editors on the case, who had interviewed experts and people in the street if they thought racism was at the root of the crime, why they had not asked a single person if attitudes toward women might play a part.

Mike Pearl, court reporter for the *New York Post:* "You'll have to talk to the *New York Times* about that. Tabloid newspapers aren't going to go into sociological explanations. I just don't think that this is a subject for a tabloid or even for a paper like the *Times.*"

Jim Willse, editor of the *Daily News:* "I can't recall why we had no coverage like that, but if we didn't do it, we didn't do it, and I don't see anything wrong with not doing it."

Hap Hairston, city editor of *Newsday* at the time of the case: "That kind of journalism is thumbsucking journalism. I don't think that kind of reporting is really legitimate. Once you write a piece about rape experts talking about why people do gang rape, there's no follow-up."

Patrick Clark, then court reporter for the *Daily News:* "That sort of explanation is more appropriate on an editorial page."

Michael T. Kaufman, deputy foreign editor of the *New York Times,* then metropolitan reporter: "I can't imagine the range of reaction to the sexual aspect of the crime would be very strong. I may be wrong but I can't think right off-hand what questions one ought to ask about that."

Nina Bernstein, who covered some of the case for *Newsday:* "If we'd had more women columnists, they could have said this was a crime against women first. But it's hard to do that without a soapbox. It points to a desperate need for women columnists."

Paul Fishleder, an editor at the *Times:* "Racism is the big story in New York. Men–women relations, or whatever you want to call them, are not."

That these reporters and editors were willing to go to sociologists, psychologists, and community leaders to talk about class and race hatred but not about the hatred of women revealed the extent to which they considered racism a subject for news stories, but saw sexism as fit only for columns and editorials. It also revealed that, as in the Levin case, these reporters and editors seemed more able to admit to their racism than to their sexism—they were apparently more comfortable talking about the sick socialization of blacks in urban ghettos than the sick socialization everyone gets at schools, fraternities, and in society at large. Yet, when the perpetrators could not be easily blamed for rape because of their class and race, as in the St. John's University case, these very same reporters and editors suddenly reversed their policies. In that case, background articles on the link between sexual violence and misogyny were run aplenty.

To be fair to these reporters, some of them, although not all, were willing to speculate about why this glaring aspect of the case—violence against women—was left out of the reporting. Kaufman of the *Times* suggested that sexism is not news any more because it does not make people as angry as does racism: "There was no thought that women would not vote for Dinkins because of this incident. If that were the case, it would have been treated differently."

Clark of the *Daily News* had a more down-to-earth explanation. "Why was the story covered in terms of race as opposed to gender? I guess because the city desk is made up of male whites. Gil Spencer [former editor of the *News*] used to call it the Wonderbread city desk."

Fishleder of the *Times* said that the gender aspect of the case may have been ignored because of the pack mentality of the press: The press began by focusing on race, "so it became easy to stick to this story as, 'Oh yes, this fits into the racism story' and do it that way."

Richard Esposito, who covered much of the case as a police reporter and who is now city editor of *Newsday,* said the gender issue was missed out of habit. "It's sometimes difficult to remember to do something you haven't done before."

Bernstein of *Newsday* said reporters did not go to rape experts for explanations because "there's a tendency in papers to be shocked and horrified again and again. The whole thing is to say a case is unusual because if it wasn't unusual, it wouldn't be news." In short, editors did not want to hear that the case was only one of many gang rapes—they wanted it to be a first, as Clark revealed when he said: "A crime like that has never happened before."

The unwillingness of the mainstream press to interpret sex crimes in terms of gender relations was further revealed in a *Newsweek* cover story inspired by the jogger case, entitled "The Mind of the Rapist." The story devoted page after page to the question of why men rape and answered without a single reference to gender roles in our society. Instead, it provided answers in terms of individual pathology and dabbled in the old "rape is sex and motivated by lust" myth.

> No single profile provides an answer to why men rape. Opportunity, emotional illness, *lust*—it happens for all of those reasons, yet often for none of them.[88] (My emphasis.)

The article also failed to discuss the number of normal, nonabused college types who rape (fraternity boys and athletes, for example) and exposed a racist bias when it showed one white and two black rapists in its photographs, even though, numerically, the majority of rapists are white.[89]

The press's lack of understanding about rape was also revealed by the inability of many reporters to describe the jogger's rape in nonsexual terms—even this particularly gruesome, bloody rape. For instance, several reporters, including Timothy Clifford of *Newsday*, kept using the word *fondling* to describe the boys grabbing the jogger's breasts and legs. Clifford said he picked the word up from prosecutor Elizabeth Lederer, but to use a word with sexual, fond, caressing connotations makes the rape sound like an act of love. The boys themselves certainly did not use that word—they used *grabbing* or *touching*. Even worse was the tendency of several reporters to use the term *having sex with* for the rape, a phrase implying consent on the part of the victim. *New York* magazine writer Michael Stone, who wrote the Chambers piece analyzed in the previous chapter, used the phrase several times in his article on the case:

> A law-enforcement officer says Lopez was the defendant who bashed the victim's face with a rock and was one of the teenagers who *had sex with* her . . .
>
> Richardson said that McCray *had sex with* the victim . . .
>
> Even then, Wise allegedly said, Lopez called him a punk because he refused to *have sex with* the jogger. (My emphasis.)[90]

Obviously, the reporters were trying to avoid the crude language the youths used themselves to describe the rape, but why not use *touching* or *grabbing* instead of *fondling?* Why not use "penetrate" instead of "had sex"? Here is a more realistic transcription of the way defendant Kharey Wise talked about the crime, from the *City Sun:*

> "Steve and Kevin both f——ed her. Ramon was holding her too and he was grabbing her tits and Antron was laughing and playing with her leg." (6/21–27/89, p. 6.)

Compare that to *Newsday's* attempt to translate Wise's confession:

> They fondled her, up to eight hands at a time, exploring her body. Wise said he ran his hands up and down her legs. (10/9/89.)

Using phrases like *fondling, exploring her body,* and *having sex* about the forcible rape of a comatose woman perpetuates the confusion of rape with lovemaking.

All in all, the unwillingness of the press to research and explain gang rape or to cover the rape of the jogger as a gender-based crime illustrates both the racism of the coverage and the backlash the United States is now experiencing against feminism, in the press and among the public. The press's racism was revealed by its insistance on blaming the rape on the assailants' color and class, rather than their gender. The press's sexism was revealed by its refusal to cover the crime with any reference to the misogyny in American society. As *Village Voice* writer Greg Tate, put it: "There's a silence around the issue of rights of women as human beings. Those rights haven't even entered the language of newspapers." Or, as a *Voice* headline on the jogger case declared, "Sexism: The Forbidden Issue" (5/9/89.) In the New Bedford case six years earlier, the press did pay attention to sexual violence as a phenomenon, providing background articles about rape, rape crisis counseling, and feminist protests, and so did the public with their huge antirape march and formations of victim support groups. There were no such background articles in the jogger case, however, and there were no such marches against sexual violence, even though this case was much more brutal than the Big Dan's rape. There was only a small demonstration in Central Park by runners, which received a minimal amount of press; another by the vigilante group, the Guardian Angels, outside the courtroom, the vigil held by black sympathizers for the jogger in hospital, and one, tiny feminist demonstration against the extremist protesters at the trial, which was covered by *only one* newspaper, *Newsday*.[91] The idea that rape is an expression of the sexism in our society, and that rape is a societal more than an individual problem was ignored by the mainstream and the black press throughout the entire jogger case. As a result, a story that should have focused on important questions about society's treatment of women turned instead into a story that irresponsibly and unnecessarily inflamed racial tensions throughout New York City.

· 7 ·

Conclusion

How the Press Should Cover Sex Crimes

During the 1980s and 1990s, the quality of sex crime coverage has been steadily declining. The press still prefers crimes against white victims while ignoring those against blacks, and although it focuses less exclusively on black-against-white rapes than it did in earlier decades, it still covers those cases with exaggerated frequency, class prejudice, and racist stereotypes, as the coverage of the Central Park jogger case demonstrated. Furthermore, the swing of sympathy away from victims in recent years has been noticeable enough to result in several organized protests and publications.[1] Many of the 1970s rape crisis centers and training programs for police and doctors have shut down; the rape crisis centers that still exist are struggling to stay afloat, having lost their previous funding from state and city interests; and the influential National Center for the Prevention and Control of Rape, which funded many valuable studies on the subject, has been whittled down and absorbed into its parent, the National Institute of Mental Health. All in all, rape as a societal problem has lost interest for the public and the press, and the press is reverting to its pre-1970 focus on sex crimes as individual, bizarre, or sensational case histories—witness the furor over the celebrity rape case against William Kennedy Smith.[2] Along with that loss of interest has come a loss of understanding.

One example of the recent reversal of understanding about rape has been the revival of the issue about whether to name rape victims. The debate resurfaced when, in the spring of 1991, a story about rape won the Pulitzer prize. Written by Jane Schorer, it was an account of the rape of Nancy Ziegenmeyer, a twenty-nine-year-old housewife and mother of three in Iowa, who was attacked in her car, where she had been sitting and studying for a real estate exam.

The story came about after Ziegenmeyer read an editorial by Geneva Overholser, the editor of *The Des Moines Register*, encouraging victims to name themselves in order to combat the stigma of rape, an argument that inspired Ziegenmeyer to go public with her case. Published in the *Register*, the story was hailed as a triumph—a frank, graphic account of the rape of a woman who had agreed to be named. Some grumblings were heard because Ziegenmeyer was white and her assailant, Bobby Lee Smith, was black—a rape scenario that bolstered an inaccurate stereotype—but on the whole the story was applauded. This was the kind of approach, Overholser and others proclaimed, that was going to finally destigmatize rape.

"Destigmatize rape" was an exhortation heard with increasing frequency in the press during 1991. It was to be accomplished, Overholser and others said, not only by providing honest descriptions of rape, but by naming victims. If the victims show they have nothing to be ashamed of, the argument went, then rape will lose its stigma.

When the next big rape case broke in the news—the alleged rape of a woman in 1991 by William Kennedy Smith, Senator Edward Kennedy's nephew, on the Kennedy estate in Palm Beach, Florida—Overholser indeed named the victim. Only this time, she named the victim against her will. (The woman's attorney said later that the victim's "low point" came when she was publicly identified.[3]) Initially, the woman had been named only by *The Sunday Mirror*, an English paper, and Florida's *The Globe*, both sensationalist, supermarket tabloids. *The Globe*, named her in its April 23 issue under the headline, "Kennedy Rape Gal Exposed"—making it abundantly clear who was considered the villain. The tabloids were followed by NBC, and after that by *The New York Times*, the *San Francisco Chronicle*, the *Louisville Courier-Journal*, and Overholser's *Des Moines Register*. The rest of the media continued to withold her name.

The media justified printing the name with four arguments. The first was offered by NBC, which declared that it would name the woman because the tabloids had done so. "We're not in the business of keeping secrets," said the network president, Michael Gartner, on NBC news. *The New York Times* and the other papers used the same reasoning, also questioning their former decision not to name the Central Park jogger.[4] This turn-about echoed the naming controversy in the Big Dan's case, where the press waxed lyrical about protecting a rape victim's reputation and privacy until one of the brethren broke rank—revealing there was no real principle at stake at all beyond following the pack. (Once the charges against Smith were formalized, the *San Francisco Chronicle* had second thoughts about naming the victim. It stopped using her name and instead referred to itself as having used the name "in previous stories."[5] *The New York Times* also stopped naming her in later stories in the wake of much criticism, external and internal, for its use of her name.)

The second argument was that naming victims lends them credibility, an argument that opened up more questions than it answered. Is a rape story really more credible when the victim's real name is used? Does the public really care, or even notice?[6] Or is a victim's name just a trophy for reporters, evidence that they can persuade victims to act against their better interests? For that matter, why is the credibility of a rape victim so suspect—could it be the old Potiphar's wife syndrome? These questions were never raised.

The third argument, largely put forth by Alan M. Dershowitz, author and professor at Harvard Law School, was that naming the accused but not the accuser is a violation of the suspect's right to be considered innocent until proven guilty.[7] (Dershowitz made the same argument in the Big Dan's case.) Although it is illogical to equate the alleged victim of a crime, as innocent as far as crime is concerned, with the person who stands accused, whose innocence is in question, this point is valid. The solution, however, is not. Rather than naming them both, a more humanitarian and fair solution would be to not name the victim at all, unless she has consented, and to not name the accused until a grand jury or similar body has determined that there is enough evidence against him to warrant a trial. In the William Kennedy Smith case, he was named before even being charged with the crime.

The fourth and most frequently quoted argument for naming was the destigmatizing one. As Isabelle Katz Pinzler, director of the Women's Rights Project of the American Civil Liberties Union was quoted as saying, "There are feminist arguments why it might not be a bad idea to name the victims. It might be a step toward destigmatizing and, by making rape less of a faceless crime, it brings home the horror."[8] In a piece about the Kennedy Smith trial at the end of 1991, *Newsweek* writer David Kaplan made the same argument: "The paternalism of not naming names reinforces the idea that rape is anything more than a terrible act of violence, that women should be shamed."[9] This idea that naming rape victims will destigmatize the crime derives from an oversimplified definition of rape. Rape is not as simple, nor as clear-cut, as being bonked over the head by a mugger. It is not like other crimes and cannot be reduced to being like other crimes, in spite of the claim of Irene Nolan, managing editor of *The Louisville Courier-Journal,* who said that "we ought to name rape victims and treat them the same as victims of other crimes."[10] The notion that rape can be treated like any other crime derives from the "rape is not sex, it is violence" slogan, a phrase that has been passed down from the first rape speak-outs of the early 1970s to be repeated blindly by every well-meaning writer on the subject. Even Schorer used it in her story about Ziegenmeyer: "Rape has nothing to do with sex, she knew, it had to do with violence."[11] The slogan, however, has ceased to mean anything. It sounds as if rape were as free of sexual content as pickpocketing—an untruth so blatant it will convince no one. Of course rape is more than only an act of violence. Of course sex is involved in rape; desire usually is not, but sex is—that is what makes it worse than simply being punched in the face. As said earlier, rape is best characterized as torture that uses sex as a weapon. Like a torturer, the rapist uses sexual acts to dominate, humiliate, and terrorize the victim. To deny the role of sexual humiliation in rape is to deny victims the horror of what they have been through. As long as people have any sense of privacy about sexual acts and the human body, rape will, therefore, carry a stigma—not necessarily a stigma that blames the victim for what happened to her, but a stigma that links her name irrevocably with an act of intimate humiliation. To name a rape victim is to guarantee that whenever somebody hears her name, that somebody will picture her in the act of being sexually tortured. To expose a rape victim to this without her consent is nothing short of punitive.

The idea that naming victims alone is enough to destigmatize rape also, of course, reveals a lack of awareness of the rape narrative that is at work against victims. If victims have those eight biasing ingredients against them, then their reputations are going to be dragged through the mud no matter what—and naming them only makes that worse. The shining example of Nancy Ziegenmeyer, held out by Overholser and others, is misleading because her case was an easy choice for "destigmatizing." She had all the eight ingredients in her favor—she was middle class, white, married with children and respectable, yet not glamorous or rich enough to inspire envy like the jogger or Levin; she was engaged in the blameless activity of studying in her car when she was attacked rather than drinking or partying like Levin and the Big Dan's victim; and she was raped by a black man. I do not wish to detract from the courage she showed in coming forth to tell her story, but had she been black, poor, in a bar, or attacked by a man of her own race or higher class, she would not have received such sympathy from readers and the press; she may not, with reason, have even wanted to take the risk of exposing her story.

Later, after Schorer had received the Pulitzer Prize for this story, it came out that Ziegenmeyer's life was not the rosy perfection it had been depicted. She was no longer married to the father of her children at the time of the rape, but was still living with him; therefore, she was not technically married after all. Schorer may have decided to cover up this fact in her story, for the very reasons I discussed in Chapter 1: she probably knew that any smirch on Ziegenmeyer's character would be unfairly used against her. Thus, Schorer was, like reporters on the jogger story, forced by the rape myths to whitewash a rape victim in order to protect her—to choose the virgin narrative. As a result, she was dishonest as a journalist even if noble as an advocate and friend of the victim. This demonstrates that the issue of whether to name the victim is merely cosmetic—sex crime victims will only really be free of destigmatization when they can be taken seriously without having to hide behind the virgin narrative.

That victims and lawyers in rape cases are subject to the same pressure as journalists to portray a victim as a virgin in order to protect her from being seen as a vamp was revealed, incidentally, by the tactics of the prosecution in the Kennedy Smith trial. No doubt aware that a truthful account of the alleged victim's sexual interest in Smith, of why she drove him home or walked on the beach with him, would result in her being immediately slotted into the "she asked for it" myth, the prosecution tried to fit her into a virgin image, forcing her to claim that her every act had been innocent of sexual expectations. The result was that because she was forced to lie about the little things—her thoughts that night—she was not believed about the big things—that she was raped. The defense therefore succeeded in creating a vamp image anyway, portraying her as a crazy, sex-hungry partygoer who could not even tell her lovers apart and who cried rape for revenge because she was angry at Smith's callous treatment of her.

To further illustrate how automatically rape victims are smeared by the press if those eight ingredients are lined up in their disfavor, one only has to contrast the way Ziegenmeyer and the jogger were treated with the way the woman in the Kennedy Smith case was treated when the story first broke. That woman was drinking and partying when the alleged attack occurred, and the accused was white and of a higher class than she—a member of the Kennedy clan, no less. Predictably, the press quickly dragged her reputation through the mud, at the same time as naming her. In a *Times* profile of her by Fox Butterfield and Mary B. W. Tabor, for example, the headline and lead alone were enough to reveal the class bias at play:

> **LEAP UP SOCIAL LADDER FOR WOMAN IN RAPE INQUIRY**
>
> The woman who has accused William Kennedy Smith of raping her at the Kennedy estate here was born into a modest working-class family outside Akron, Ohio, but moved sharply up the economic scale 10 years ago after her divorced mother remarried a wealthy industrialist . . .
>
> She had a poor academic record at Tallmadge High School, said a school official. . . . But she was popular socially and "had a little wild streak," said a woman who knew her at the time. That meant she and her friends liked to drive fast cars, go to parties, and skip classes, the friend said.

(The story went on to describe a bad car accident that left her neck as "fragile as glass.")

> "This wildness you have heard about, it wasn't the same kind of wildness as other people," he said. "She knew her time clock was much more fragile than yours or mine."

(Her rise in work to an executive was then described, along with someone calling her "very competent" and "highly thought of," but soon the story returned to her "wildness.")

> But she was still drawn to the Palm Beach area, and in 1989 had a brief affair with Johnny Butler, the son of a once prosperous family here that owned a lumber company. . . . Mr. Butler was the father of her child, friends say. It is unclear why the couple did not marry . . .
>
> Records of the Florida Department of Highway Safety show she received 17 tickets for speeding, careless driving or being involved in an accident between 1982 and 1990. In several cases she was driving more than 70 miles an hour in a 55 mile per hour zone.
>
> In 10 cases, the woman's license was suspended for failing to pay the fines assessed her for these violations . . .

(More about her driving and failure to pay fines followed.)

> During the 1980s the woman also became a fixture in Palm Beach's expensive bars and nightclubs. "She was always having lots of fun out there on the scene," said Dick Kurley, a former bartender . . .

> Another acquaintance, Nathaniel Read, said, "She liked to drink and have fun with the ne'er-do-wells in cafe society."
>
> (4/17/91, p. A10.)

This profile was a prime example of the victim-bashing I demonstrated in the Levin, New Bedford, and Rideout cases. With that same Victorian hypocrisy that is so often brought to bear on rape victims, the woman was painted as a Vamp, driving fast, partying, and social climbing—for behaving, in short, like everyone else in that fast Palm Beach set. Not until after the piece had been published did anyone question the innuendoes implicit in this story (which the *Times* editor responsible for it, a woman, vigorously denied[12]), what her driving, partying or illegitimate child had to do with the charges, whether she deserved such scrutiny, or why she was the subject of a profile while Smith was not. Ironically, on the same page as the profile, smack in the middle of it, the national edition of the *Times* ran a box headlined, "On Names in Rape Cases," ending in the quote, "But some editors now believe that failing to identify rape victims perpetuates the idea that rape is a crime that permanently damages a woman's reputation."[13] The *Times* profile made it abundantly clear that the damage to a rape victim's reputation, carried out not by the rapist but by the press, is no mere "idea."[14]

When the police finally pressed formal charges against Smith, on May 9, 1991, the press began to treat the case differently. The woman was suddenly no longer referred to only as "the accuser"* but was at last allowed "victim" or "alleged victim," and the *Washington Post*, at least, ran a widely syndicated profile of Smith, a thirty-year-old medical intern at Georgetown University Hospital in Washington, D.C. Nevertheless, that profile, written by Mary Jordan, was largely flattering, reminiscent of the early profiles of Robert Chambers. Smith was described as quiet, gentle, concerned about the poor, a lover of art and poetry, and a man who never boasted about his Kennedy connections.

> Many of his friends insist that the charges are completely unbelievable; Smith, they say, is a quiet, gentle, considerate man.
>
> "This is a man who doesn't have any violence in him," said Mitchel Sklar, the physician who has supervised Smith's rounds at Georgetown Hospital.[15]

*Newspapers often refer to victims in rape cases as "the accuser," but this is legally inaccurate. Technically, the accuser is "the people" of the state, and the victim is only a witness.

The only mention of his sex life was that he "has courted, as one friend said, a "harem of women who want to go out with a Kennedy," which, like the profiles of Chambers, made Smith sound like a reluctant Romeo. Also, the word *courted* is much more respectful than the phrase *had an affair with* that was used about the woman in the case. The profile made no mention of Smith's taste for partying, his driving habits, or whether he had ever impregnated a woman out of wedlock, allegations that should have been looked into if the reporter wanted to treat Smith the way her colleagues had treated the woman.

The one negative note in the profile was about Smith's drinking: "Others say that when Smith drinks, he often drinks heavily, and his personality can change from quiet and thoughtful to aggressive and difficult." This, however, was only another version of the rape myth, for drink cannot turn a man who would never dream of raping into a rapist, it can only release a behavior that is already there. The Jekyll and Hyde explanation for rape—that it can be blamed on alcohol or drugs instead of the man himself—is, as those who have counseled rapists have long known, only another of the many inaccurate assumptions about the crime. (Later, more negative stories about Smith came out when three other women accused him of rape or attempted rape. The evidence of these women was not allowed in court, but the press and the public gave it much attention. At the same time, sympathetic images of Smith cavorting with his puppy and smiling with his family were widely shown, while the alleged victim's turbulent life was relentlessly exposed.)

Once the trial of Smith began at the end of 1991, the press continued to back off from its early eagerness to name the victim and rendered her anonymous. Even television covered her face with blurry dots and attempted to bleep out her name when it was spoken in court, with the exception, again, of NBC and the several mistakes that occurred when her name was inadvertently broadcast. This belated courtesy made the media look particularly hypocritical and erratic and subjected it to much criticism, reviving the "name the victim" movement yet again.[16] Yet, when, after Smith was acquitted, the woman did come forth publicly, revealing her face and name, Patricia Bowman, on television and in print (her angry face was blazoned on the cover of the *Daily News* on December 19, 1991, for example, under the headline, SHE WON'T HIDE), she met with much hostility. Her act was not seen as one of courage or as a woman fighting against what she perceived as a terrible injustice—it was seen as a hypocritical and cynical move to achieve fame. (What kind of fame she could gain, given that

Smith and his defense team had sucessfully portrayed her as a crazy liar out to destroy a man, was not considered by these critics.)

As the Kennedy case and the others in this book demonstrate, while the press is still entrenched in the rape narrative, naming victims will achieve nothing but voyeuristic finger-pointing, with or without their consent. The issue of naming victims, which was written about so extensively during the New Bedford, jogger, and Smith cases, is in fact a red herring. The only way to destigmatize rape is to change the ways in which sex crimes are reported so that victims' reputations will not be automatically destroyed and the rape myths will not be automatically called upon to provide inaccurate and harmful explanations of rape. Two approaches can be taken to effect this change, an individual one, and a larger, systemic one. These suggestions apply as much to tabloids as to broadsheet newspapers, for tabloid editors must find ways to make their sex crime stories exciting that do not rely on sexist and racist clichés.

Individual Reforms

Vocabulary

Reporters and editors must be more responsible for their vocabulary. If deadline pressures prevent them from resisting clichés, they must learn new clichés. This reform has been achieved to a large extent for racial and ethnic groups: the press does not routinely call blacks Negroes anymore, or does it refer to them in unflattering, insulting ways as it did as a matter of course in the 1800s. Neither does the press refer to Jews or the Irish with the insults and stereotypes it did in Victorian times. Even *The New York Times* finally conceded to use *Ms.* instead of *Miss* or *Mrs.* If these clichés and habits were displaced, those about women crime victims can be, too. Reporters should be able to punch up a list of "Words to Watch For" on their computers when they start to write up a sex crime, a list with the purpose of reminding them to consider unintentional and unfair innuendoes, not of squelching their vocabulary. The list would include the adjectives routinely used about female crime victims and not about men, and descriptive words that make a sexual assault sound pleasurable to the victim. Copy editors and editors could use the same list and be equally responsible for screening biased vocabulary. The purpose would be to avoid vocabulary that in any way suggests the victim deserved or enjoyed the assault.

A partial list of "Words to Watch For" includes: *vivacious*, *flirta-*

tious, girl (instead of *woman*), *pretty, attractive, curvacious, blonde, bubbly, precocious, wild, pert, prudish, naïve, worldly, experienced* (in the context of a love-life), *mature, full-figured, attractive, doll-like, hysterical, divorcée, party-goer, stripped* (in the context of a sex crime), *had sex* (to mean raping or being raped), *fondled* (to mean molested).

Granted, finding the right words to describe a sex crime case is sometimes difficult. Graphic descriptions of rape, as long as they are told in clinical rather than titillating language, are much more informative than are coy or sexual euphemisms, yet the line between prurience and such graphic fact is often thin. Because of this, reporters and editors should take time to set up guidelines before they are under the pressure of a deadline. They should ask themselves if the adjective used to describe a woman's state of emotions would be used for a man's. ("Terrified," "crying" or "weeping" is less condescending than "hysterical.") They should check to see if there is a word that gets across the violence of the act more and the titillation of it less. ("Her jeans were pulled off" is more accurate and less suggestive than "stripped." "Touched" is less prurient than "fondled.") They should find out if there is a way to describe the scene that is accurate and specific, yet not "sexy." ("Wearing only a jacket and a sock" is less sensational than "naked from the waist down.") Above all, they should find ways to describe sexual assault without making it sound like lovemaking ("raped" or "penetrated" is more appropriate than "had sex with."). These words may sometimes seem less punchy and dramatic than the old clichés, but if the press is as interested in destigmatizing rape as it claims, then those clichés must be displaced.

Balance

Reporters and editors should also have guidelines reminding them to be balanced: If a victim's looks are described, then the suspect's must be also. If a victim is to be the subject of a profile, then the suspect should be, too. If a victim's sex life is mentioned, so should the suspect's. In the William Kennedy Smith case, for example, because the woman's sex life, driving habits, and taste for parties were mentioned, so they should have been for the man.

Crime and court reporters also have to be more balanced in their coverage of trials by becoming more independent of manipulation by lawyers and by conducting their own research instead of parroting attorneys. Trial reporters should have a third set of guidelines to punch up on their computers, this one called "Balanced Trial Reporting." It would remind them not to run attorney's statements without immediate attribution, especially in their leads, to explain to readers why attorneys use certain strategies, and to describe how trials really work. It would remind them to write leads that reflect a balanced view of the trial and do not consistently favor one side or another.

Finally, reporters should be aware that their role is neither to prefer the defendant's case, nor the victim's. As part of the detective role good reporters should always play in crime stories, they should not ignore signs of implausibility in the victim's story. The press allowed itself to be manipulated to an embarrassing extent in the Tawana Brawley case, for example, even though many of the reporters on the story had doubts about some of the things they were being told. Although the emphasis of this book is on protecting the alleged victims of sex crimes from further persecution, the intention is not to suggest that victims are always truthful. Part of achieving balance is to follow up holes in the victims' stories as much as in the defendants'.

Context

Reporters should set their sex crime stories in a context that will inform the public of the reality of the crime and help people protect themselves, rather than feeding fears, myths, and misconceptions. Statistics should be gathered from both the police and local rape crisis centers, as the gap between figures from these two groups is usually large. Explanations of why such crimes happen should be collected from researchers, literature, and other victims. Whether the crime is typical or unusual should be made clear. Newspapers could better achieve both balance and context if they routinely assigned an outsider—an editor, ombudsman, or reporter not assigned to cover the story on daily basis—to write a weekly analysis of the crime and the trial from a distanced perspective. In both the Rideout and Big Dan's cases, reporters and editors complained about being too overwhelmed with the daily crises of the case to gain the perspective needed to redress the injustices they were committing against both the victims and the accused. At the moment, the only writers playing this role are news columnists, who write pieces according to their whims and opinions. These are valuable but not enough. A regular, fair analysis is needed to keep press accounts balanced.

Consideration

Reporters should not exploit the victims or their families by quoting them out of context, by failing to warn them that their quotes are on the record, by including prurient, irrelevant, or unattributed facts about their private lives, by harassing them in the midst of their trauma or grief, or by writing articles that indulge in vamp, virgin, or blame-the-victim myths. Likewise, reporters and photographers should avoid giving the public information that could further endanger the victim, such as her name, address, or whereabouts.[17]

Follow-ups

To avoid the kinds of mistakes made in the Rideout case, reporters should follow up the crimes they report, letting the public know what eventually happened to the victim and to the perpetrator if an inaccurate impression has been left by the news.

Policy and Training

To motivate editors and reporters to achieve these changes, crime and court reporters and their editors must learn the rape myths and narratives that trap them into unfair coverage. When I questioned reporters and editors on the jogger case about why they had not gone to specialists in rape for explanations, some told me they thought going to rape experts and the like was a kind of namby-pamby, overintellectualized form of reporting. If they will not go to experts, then perhaps they should become experts. A reporter covering City Hall is supposed to understand local government. A reporter covering the police should know how the police department is structured and how the law for each kind of crime works. A reporter covering health or science or business or sports is equally expected to be knowledgeable in his or her field. Likewise, a reporter who covers crime, a huge percentage of which is rape and sexual assault, should understand those subjects. That means not only learning about what rape actually is and why it happens, but facing up to their own gender, class, and race biases. Such lessons could be learned if all crime reporters and their editors were required to take a quick training course in the field of victimology and sexual assault, just as the police used to have to do in the 1970s. The course could be conducted as a required part of their training, in the office or at a rape crisis center, and could be done over one week or a couple of week-ends. (When I was researching my first book about rape, I took a ten-week course in rape counseling from St. Vincent Hospital's Rape Crisis Center in New York. The class met once a week and was invaluable. Rape crisis centers and self-defense groups will often send out speakers to organizations to inform them about sex crimes. Such a program would be of great value to a newsroom.)

Also, reporters, editors, and student reporters ought to be assigned some of the major books on rape, sex crimes, incest, feminist linguistics, and wife battery, such as *Against Our Will* by Susan Brownmiller, *Rape: Crisis and Recovery* by Ann Burgess, *Conspiracy of Silence: The Trauma of Incest* by Sandra Butler, *Rape in Marriage* by Diana E. H. Russell, *Battered Wives* by Del Martin, and *Man Made Language* by Dale Spender (a bibliography of suggested reading follows later). The ignorance about rape constantly displayed in newspapers, as was so apparent in the jogger case, is not acceptable—especially when one considers the decades of research now available on the subject. The result of this training should be a clear written policy adapted by every paper on how to cover sex crimes.

Finally, on an individual level, reporters and editors must learn to take pride in reporting rape fairly and accurately rather than sensationally. Reporters must be encouraged to provide accurate information to the public about sex crimes without punishing the victim. Ziegenmeyer's story is a good example, for it won the Pultizer Prize because it broke taboos by describing in graphic and disturbing detail just how cruel and destructive a rape is, not because it named her, as some seem to think. Rape stories that inform the public and help people protect themselves should be rewarded over those that merely disturb, frighten, or sensationalize.

Systemic Reforms

Systemic changes in the way newspapers report crimes must also be made, for as much as the small and fairly practical steps suggested here may help, it may take a more drastic approach to change the age-old practice of indulging in the rape narrative.

Leave the Victim Out

The press should reconsider whether descriptions of victims and their behavior belong in crime stories at all. Perhaps write-ups on victims should be confined to obituaries, if they have been killed, and left out of crime stories altogether. Perhaps crime stories should describe only what the suspect is thought to have done, and why, and what the actual events were. If a cry of "impossible" is raised at this, I would call attention to the jogger case. The *Times* covered that case largely without mention of the victim, her life, or her personality. Instead of the denigrating profiles the *Times* ran of Jennifer Levin and Patricia Bowman, the woman in the Smith case, it gave the jogger attention in only one separate story, a rather vague profile, under the head, "Hard-Working Banker Ran to Relax, Thinking Little of Park's Dangers" (4/28/89, p. B2). Pages and pages of its coverage were otherwise devoted to descriptions of the crime, the suspects, their families, their backgrounds, their environment, and their neighbors' and the public's reactions. This coverage told the story without making the victim a part of it. Likewise, the early coverage of the St. John's University assault barely mentioned the victim; instead, it devoted attention to the suspects and to the phenomenon of rape on colleges and among athletes.

Stop Harassing Families

The press should reconsider whether the practice of contacting the victim or her family right after the crime should be forbidden, instead of routine. Does this practice cater to anything but prurient interest? What does the public get except bewilderment, hurt, or silence from these families? Why does the press assume it has the right to invade a family's privacy simply because one of its members was victimized? Perhaps reporters could ultimately write fairer and more thorough stories if they interviewed victims and their families after the first shock of the crime, and if they gave them the choice of not being interviewed at all or of being kept off the record—a choice that would inspire more respect for the press on the part of the public.

Choose Accuracy Over Speed

The press should re-examine its outdated assumptions regarding scoops and deadlines. Leave the race to be first to the electronic media, and let the print press take advantage of its form and put more emphasis on depth and accuracy than on speed. As Michael Schudson, editor of the press study, *Reading the News*, wrote, "No one in the audience gives a damn if ABC beats CBS by two seconds or not. The journalist's interest in immediacy hangs on as an anachronistic ritual of the media tribe."[18]

Worse than that, in sex crime cases the rush to be first rather than accurate can do a great deal of harm to the victim and the accused. If newspapers are concerned about competing with each other and selling papers, let them win readers with reporting that answers people's fears with facts and useful information, not with lazy clichés. If newspapers covered violence against women with understanding and insight, it might also attract that majority of elusive female readers who presently do not seem to buy papers—why should they when the papers keep telling them those "tiny lies" Joan Didion mentioned?

Diversify the Newsroom

The biases of race, class, and gender so rife in the press now can only be rectified if members of all races, classes, and both genders work side by side in the newsroom and on the editing desk, adding their unique access and understanding of their groups to the news pool. As long as the press is predominantly white, male, and uninformed about rape, sex crimes will never be covered fairly. Also, the victimization of people who are not white, rich, or glamorous must be covered more frequently.

Stop Scapegoating Sources

The press should stop blaming sources for its biases in reporting. If one set of sources persists in describing a victim in unflattering, condemning language, a reporter should turn to different sources for contrast, even if they are only counselors who work with victims or their families. Balance is a ground rule for reporting in any other field, so should not be ignored in crime coverage.

Stop Blaming the Public

The press should stop justifying sensationalist, biased, or irresponsible crime coverage by claiming that this is what the public wants. No one can change the voyeuristic tastes of the public, but a crime story about the criminal, his motives, his life, his actions, can be made just as exciting as a story about a victim (witness Dostoevsky's *Crime and Punishment* and the popularity of "who-done-it" novels). Newspapers play the role of educator, as well as entertainer and part of that role has to be reeducating the public not to fall into the blame-the-victim, antifemale clichés that further harm the victims of crime. Furthermore, the age-old excuse that "we are only giving the public what they want" is looking increasingly suspect these days: A nationwide poll released in April 1985 by the American Society of Newspaper Editors revealed that most of the 1,600 adults questioned "believe the press is exploitative: 78 percent say that reporters are only concerned about getting a good story, and do not worry about hurting people, and 63 percent think the press takes advantage of ordinary people who become victims of circumstance."[19] The press must stop blaming its exploitative impulses on a public that does not approve of them.

Stop Disregarding Feminism

Finally, the press must stop being afraid of feminism. At the moment, the mainstream press is so unwilling to consult feminist sources that it has effectively crippled its chance of covering sex crimes properly, for it is in the fields of feminist sociology, medicine and anthropology that an understanding of these crimes lies. As historian Roy Porter wrote,

> In surveying the history of rape . . . two formulations arising from the writings of feminists do seem fully justified: *(a)* rape cannot be fully understood in terms of individual rapists, but only in terms of masculine values at large; *(b)* rape is more an expression of misogyny than of pent-up sexual desire."[20]

Rape cannot be understood without mentioning the role of women and the way men are trained to see them as objects of prey. As demonstrated in the jogger case, however, the mainstream press consistently refuses to acknowledge this.

These are the steps to be taken if the press really wants to destigmatize rape. They are not impossible to achieve, for every now and then the press demonstrates it is capable of covering sex crimes responsibly, and breaks its clichés and habits to do so: *The Boston Globe* did a good job in the Big Dan's case; *The Village Voice* covered the jogger fairly, thoroughly, and with originality. As long as the press is still stereotyping sex crime victims as virgins or vamps, however, it will continue to do victims and the public irreparable harm.

Notes

INTRODUCTION

1. Richard V. Ericson, Patricia M. Baranek, Janet B. C. Chan, *Visualizing Deviance: A Study of News Organization.* (Toronto: University of Toronto Press, 1987). "The organization and processes involved in newsmaking do not exist in a vacuum, but contribute to, and are shaped by, a wider institutional and societal order." p. 27. And, "Journalism seeks commonsense understanding by reducing one type of reality to its own way of construing the world, thereby producing common social knowledge and cultural values." p. 17.

Margaret Gallagher, *Unequal Opportunities: The case of women and the media.* (Vendome, France: Unesco, 1981). Gallagher makes the point that although it is not really provable that the media shapes public opinion, the commonsensical assumption can be made that "by creating a common field of discourse . . . the media may help shape an unquestioned consensus in society about the very nature of the world." p. 106.

2. Doris Graber, *Processing the News: How People Tame the Information Tide.* (New York: Longman, 1984.) Graber and others have made the point that the media tend to confirm the status quo more than to challenge it by reflecting public opinion and therefore solidifying it.

> Given the fact that the U.S. news media see themselves primarily as reporters of events, rather than as crusaders for social change, the infrequent probing of causes and almost total neglect of remedies are not surprising. The media do not explicitly advocate any particular social

> system, be it the existing one or a totally different one. Implicitly, through accepting the assumptions on which the existing system is based, and through silence about most alternatives, they do, however, support it. (p. 73.)

3. Todd Gitlin, *The Whole World is Watching* (University of California Press, 1980).

> From within their private crevices, people find themselves relying on the media for concepts, for images of their heroes, for guiding information, for emotional charges, for a recognition of public values, for symbols in general, even for language. (p. 1.)

4. Ericson, op cit. Ericson makes the point that the press is particularly effective in shaping public opinion about crime because the media is the vehicle through which the public finds out about crime and judges its own susceptibility to it. "Most people derive their understanding of deviance and control primarily from the news and other mass media." (p. 3.)

R. Hauge, "Crime and the Press," *Scandinavian Studies in Criminology* (London: Tavistock, 1965), Vol. I. ". . . the near monopoly of the daily press as a source of crime news therefore presumably makes it an important influence on public opinion on the subject of crime." (p. 148.)

Carolyn A. Stroman and Richard Seltzer, "Media Use and Perceptions of Crime," *Journalism Quarterly*, Summer, 1985, Vol. 62, No. 2.

> There has long been a tradition in mass communication research of linking the media, particularly television and newspaper, with public opinion formation . . . public perceptions of crime are, to some extent, formed on the basis of information received from media presentations. This assumption is buttressed by studies which indicate that: (1) 95 percent of those polled cite the mass media as their primary source of information about crime; (2) the media provide details about crimes which enable users to discuss the causes of crime and solutions to the crime problem; and (3) crime, in comparison to other topics, is a well-covered topic.

Also, "Studying the ways in which journalists make sense of the world is a significant means of achieving understanding of that society." (pp. 345–50.)

5. The Rideout case was made into a television movie. The New Bedford case was the basis for the Jodie Foster film, *The Accused* and the subject of a sociological study. The Jennifer Levin case was made into a television movie and written up by Linda Wolfe in her book, *Wasted*. The Central Park Jogger case was written about in many national magazines.

6. Studies of crime in the news reported by Smith, Ditton, Duffy, and

others have found that hearsay and gossip is as important a source of information about crime among the public as is the mass media. Presumably, however, that hearsay and gossip is triggered and guided by the news, especially in a big city. Either way, these studies indicate that talk about the subject among the public is the primary influence on public opinion about crime. Susan J. Smith, "Crime in the News," *Brit. J. Criminology*, Vol. 24, No. 3, July 1984, pp. 289–95.

7. This lack of women reporters reflects the ratio in newsrooms in general. In a study of journalists working full-time in the U.S. media in 1986, researchers found that the typical journalist is a "white Protestant male who has a bachelor's degree, is married and has children, is middle-of-the-road politically, is thirty-two years old, and earns about $19,000 a year." The number of women in the media is much lower than the number in the workforce in general; in 1982–1983, 66.2 percent of journalists were male, 33.8 percent female. The percentage of women in the general workforce in 1981 was 42.5. *The American Journalist*, by David H. Weaver and G. Cleveland Wilhoit (Bloomington: Indiana University Press, 1986, pp. 12, 17, 19).

8. Approximately 7–10 percent of all rape victims are male, victims of other men, not including rape in prison. The rapists are not homosexual. Few men realize that men figure in rape statistics, as this is so seldom written about. Ellen Frank and Barbara Duffy Stewart, "Treatment of Depressed Rape Victims: an Approach to Stress-Induced Symptomatology," in *Treatment of Depression: Old Controversies and New Approaches*, P. J. Clayton and J. E. Barrett, eds. (New York: Raven Press, 1983, p. 329).

9. Timothy Beneke, *Men On Rape* (New York: St. Martin's Press, 1982).

10. Joseph F. Shelley and Cindy D. Ashkins, "Crime, Crime News, and Crime Views," *Public Opinion Quarterly*, 1981, Vol. 45, pp. 492–501. Also, Michael J. Robinson maintained that television news, in comparison to newspapers, focuses on less substantive issues and images. "American Political Legitimacy in an Era of Electronic Journalism: Reflections on the Evening News," in Douglass Cater and Richard Adler, eds. *Television as a Social Force* (New York: Praeger, 1975).

11. A content analysis of the first two weeks of the Central Park jogger case illustrates the point: "The print media differed markedly from television in considering the attack in the context of broader social problems." Linda S. Lichter, S. Robert Lichter, and Daniel Amundson, *The New York News Media and The Central Park Rape* (Washington, D.C.: The American Jewish Committee, Institute of Human Relations, Center for Media and Public Affairs, 1989, p. 4).

12. ". . . [T]he creation of news is not therefore a matter of systemic relations among journalists and their sources. It is a product of the cultural and social organization of news work, not of events in the world or the personal inclination of journalists." Ericson, op cit., p. 9.

13. S. Smith, "Crime in the News," *Brit. J. Criminology*, Vol. 24, No. 3, July 1984, pp. 289–95.

J. Ditton, and J. Duffy, "Bias in the Newspaper Reporting of Crime News," *Brit. J. Criminology*, Vol. 23, No. 2, April 1983, pp. 159–65.

14. Caroline Wolf Harlow, *Female Victims of Violent Crime* (Office of Justice Programs, Bureau of Justice Statistics, January, 1991).

15. "What's in a Middle Name?" by Joe Queenan, *Time*, Dec. 16, 1991, p. 32.

16. Jack Katz, "What makes crime 'news'?" In *Media, Culture & Society*, Vol. 9, 1987, pp. 47–75. "The press does not depict criminals and victims largely as non-whites, poor, and lower class . . ." p. 60.

17. Harlow, op cit., p. 10. The 1991 U.S. Dept. of Justice figure of 20 percent is based on interviews with half a million householders conducted between 1973 and 1987 that did not ask interviewees directly if they had been raped. The 4 percent figure was cited as a national figure by Geneva Overholser, editor of the *Des Moines Register*, in an editorial reprinted in *Quill*, May 1990, p. 17.

18. Harlow, ibid., p. 8.

19. Mike Taibbi and Anna Sims-Phillips, *Unholy Alliances: Working the Tawana Brawley Story* (New York: Harcourt Brace Jovanovich, 1989). And, Robert D. McFadden, Ralph Blumenthal, M. A. Farber, E. R. Shipp, Charles Strum, and Craig Wolf of *The New York Times*, *Outrage: The Story Behind the Tawana Brawley Hoax*. (New York: Bantam, 1990).

20. Helen Benedict, *Recovery. How to Survive Sexual Assault for Women, Men, Teenagers, and Their Friends and Families* (New York: Doubleday, 1985). See Chapter 4, "Prosecuting."

21. *USA Today*, 7/18/90, p. 1.

CHAPTER 1

1. A. Acock and N. Ireland, "Attribution of Blame in Rape Cases: The Impact of Norm Violation, Gender, And Sex-Role Attitude," *Sex Roles*, Vol. 9, No. 2, 1983, pp. 179–93.

J. Check and N. Malamuth, "Sex Role Stereotyping and Reactions to Depictions of Stranger Versus Acquaintance Rape," *J. of Personality and Social Psychology*, Vol. 45, No. 2, 1983, pp. 344–56.

R. Hall, J. Howard, and S. Boezio. "Tolerance of Rape: A Sexist or Antisocial Attitude?" *Psychology of Women Quarterly*, Vol. 10, 1986, pp. 101–18.

2. Timothy Beneke, *Men On Rape*. Op cit.

3. Lynn S. Chancer, "New Bedford, Massachusetts . . . The 'Before and After' of a Group Rape." *Gender & Society*, Vol. 1, No. 3, 1987, pp. 239–60. Chancer cites studies showing that "macho" men and traditionally oriented men and women are particularly likely to believe rape myths.

Paul McCarthy, "Rape: The Macho View", *Psychology Today*, April 1987, p. 12.

4. "Even the Victim Can Be Slow to Recognize Rape" by Jane Gross, *New York Times*, 5/28/91, p. A8.

5. The survey, taken for TIME/CNN on May 8, 1991, by Yankelovich Clancy Shulman was reported in *Time*, 6/3/91, pp. 50–51. The encouraging sign in this survey was that the younger the respondee, the less likely he or she was to blame the victim or swallow the rape myths.

6. "Sex Crimes: Women on Trial" by Eloise Salholz et al., *Newsweek*, Dec. 16, 1991, p. 23.

7. *Ms.* January/February, 1991, p. 15.

8. Helen Benedict, *Recovery*. Op cit. Introduction. Susan Brownmiller, *Against Our Will: Men, Women and Rape* (New York: Simon & Schuster, 1975).

9. Ann Wolbert Burgess and Lynda Lytle Holmstrom, *Rape, Crisis and Recovery* (Bowie, MD: Brady, 1979).

10. *New York Times*, 4/26/89, p. B24.

11. Nicholas Groth and Ann Burgess, "Male Rape: Offenders and Victims." *American J. of Psychiatry* Vol. 137, No. 7, July 1980, p. 807.

12. Nicholas Groth and H. Birnbaum, *Men Who Rape: the Psychology of the Offender* (New York, Plenum Press, 1979). In a roundup of rape research at the end of 1991, *The New York Times* reported that anger is the most common motivation of rapists, an anger usually directed at women. "New Studies Map the Mind of the Rapist" by Daniel Coleman, *New York Times*, 12/10/91, p. C1.

13. Author's interview with Nicholas Groth.

14. Diana E. H. Russell, *Rape in Marriage* (New York: Macmillian, 1982).

15. Groth and Birnbaum, op cit. Also, Russell, ibid., pp. 64–65.

16. Russell, ibid. Also, U.S. Dept. of Justice, Federal Bureau of Investigation, *Uniform Crime Reports for the United States*, Washington, D.C.: GPO, 1980, p. 15.

17. Harlow, U.S. Dept. of Justice, op cit., p. 10.

> In rapes with one offender, about seven out of every ten white victims were raped by a white offender, and about eight of every ten black victims were raped by a black offender. In rapes with two or more offenders, victims and offenders were of the same race 49 percent of the time for white victims and 72 percent of the time for black victims.

In nonstranger rape, the most common kind, 83 percent of white women and 91 percent of black women were raped by men of their own race.

18. Ibid.

19. Benedict, op cit.

20. I once received a letter from a convicted rapist who claimed his rapes were committed as revenge on his mother—again, a woman is blamed. In his letter, he explained rape thus: R, he said, stands for Revenge. A, for Aggression. P, for Penetration, and E, for Ego—au.

21. Ellen Frank and Barbara Duffy Stewart, "Treatment of Depressed Rape Victims: An Approach to Stress-Induced Symptomatology." In *Treatment of Depression: Old Controversies and New Approaches*, P. J. Clayton and J. E. Barrett, eds. (New York: Raven Press, 1983), p. 329.

22. Benedict, op cit., Introduction.

23. *Genesis*, 39. Potiphar's wife, who is never given a name in the Bible, was the mistress of an Egyptian lord, for whom Joseph was a much revered slave. She wanted to seduce Joseph but he refused her advances, not wishing to betray his kind master or to commit adultery. In a vengeful rage, the woman accused him of raping her and had him thrown into prison, where he began his famous interpreting of dreams.

24. Brownmiller, *Against Our Will*, op cit., p. 387.

25. "Sex Crimes: Women on Trial" by Eloise Salholz et al., op cit. "Research suggests that the notion that women invent rape charges is statistically unfounded and psychologically implausible. DePaul University law professor Morrison Torrey says about 2 percent of rape reports are false—approximately the same percentage as other crimes."

26. "Nowhere to Turn for Rape Victims," by Candy J. Cooper, *The San Francisco Examiner*, 2/1/91 p. A1. "But in San Francisco, Berkeley, and Richmond last year, the unfounding rate on sexual assault cases was less than 1 percent." "Unfounded" does not mean fabricated, only lacking enough evidence to warrant a court case, as Katha Pollitt of the *Nation* has pointed out.

27. Benedict, op cit. A large part of my book is devoted to documenting why women have grown afraid to report rape.

28. Harlow, op cit., p. 9. The U.S. Dept. of Justice reported that 26 percent of women did not report their rape to police because they considered it a private matter they could take care of themselves; 17 percent out of fear of reprisal by the offender, his family, or friends; and 16 percent because they had no faith in the police.

29. Feminists such as Brownmiller and Andrea Dworkin argue that the function of rape myths, like rape, is primarily to keep women in their place—to keep them intimidated and submissive.

30. This point was supported by historian Roy Porter in his essay, "Does Rape have a Historical Meaning?" In *Rape*, Sylvana Tomaselli and Roy Porter, eds. (New York: Basil Blackwell, 1986):

> But Western culture is also thoroughly misogynistic . . . And the ultimate source and sanction of misogyny is Judeo-Christianity, with its foundation myth of Eve, mere spare rib, yet the source of all sexual temptation, shame and sin; the scarlet woman justly scapegoated for the miseries of mankind (p. 233).

31. Ann Burgess and Lynda Holmstrom, *Rape, Crisis and Recovery* (Bowie, MD: Brady, 1979), p. 222.

32. Joyce Williams and Karen Holmes, *The Second Assault: Rape and Public Attitudes* (Westport, CT: Greenwood Press, 1981), pp. 135–37.

33. Brownmiller, op cit. My research also confirms this across the board, as will be reflected in later chapters.

Williams and Holmes, op cit. pp. 139–40.

34. Benedict, op cit. Introduction.

Williams and Holmes, ibid.

35. Chancer, op cit.

Williams and Holmes, ibid.

36. Benedict, op cit. Chapter 20, "The Older Victim."

37. Jacobsen and Popovich, op cit.

38. Acock and Ireland, op cit.

J. Williams, "Secondary Victimization: Confronting Public Attitudes About Rape." *Victimology: An International Journal*, Vol. 9, No. 1, 1984, pp. 66–81.

39. Dale Spender, *Man Made Language* (London: Routledge & Kegan Paul, 1980). Robin Lakoff, *Language and Woman's Place* (New York: Harper & Row, 1975).

40. Spender, ibid., pp. 15–18, 139, 145, respectively.

41. Margaret Gallagher, *Unequal Opportunities: The Case of Women and the Media* (Paris: UNESCO, 1981).

> [W]hen women are included [in the news] there is a tendency to refer to irrelevant detail about appearance, age and family status—detail which would not be included in a report about a man. Even in relation to powerful and influential women, reporting often falls into this vein (p. 77).

42. Bea Bourgeois, "She 'fainted'; he 'passed out' ", *The Quill*, Feb, 1990, p. 41.

43. Gallagher, op cit., pp. 70–78.

44. A 1989 national conference called "Women, Men and Media" released several surveys on women in the news by different groups that are available from "Mediawatch: Woman and Men," William Woestendiek, Director, School of Journalism, University of Southern California, University Park, Los Angeles, CA 90089.

45. Gallagher, op cit., p. 72.

46. Study conducted by New Directions for News, available from "Mediawatch: Woman and Men," op cit.

47. The study, conducted by the same Women, Men and Media Project mentioned above, at the University of Southern California, looked at ten leading newspapers as well as the local press. "Most Stories Are About Men," by Daniel B. Wood from the *Christian Science Monitor*, the *San Francisco Chronicle*, 5/15/91, p. B3.

48. David H. Weaver and G. Cleveland Wilhoit, *The American Journalist* (Bloomington: Indiana University Press, 1986), p. 17.

49. "Mediawatch," op cit. I would be interested to see, in future research, whether women tend to appear in the news more often as crime victims than in any other roles—au.

CHAPTER 2

1. Ericson, *Visualizing Deviance*, op cit., p. 44.

2. Katz, op cit., p. 57. "Crime news has been continually present in the metropolitan daily for about 150 years." Katz also documented that violent crime makes up about 70 percent of crime news.

Margaret T. Gordon and Stephanie Riger, *The Female Fear* (New York: The Free Press, 1989), p. 67.

3. Frank Harris, *Presentation of Crime in Newspapers* (The Sociological Press, 1932). "The category 'sex offenses' is given least consideration in the allotment of crime space [from 1890 to 1921]" (p. 78); "In 1921, the presentation of rape crimes shrinks substantially. It may now be rated in a class with 'commercialized vice' (sex) 'other' and the lowest of the property offenses" (p. 82).

4. From 1889 to 1932, 3,745 people were killed by mobs. Ralph Ginzburg, *100 Years of Lynchings* (Baltimore, MD: Black Classic Press, 1988), p. 207.

The peak between 1890 and 1885 is documented in Jessie Daniel Ames, *The Changing Character of Lynching: Review of Lynching. 1931–1941* (Atlanta, GA: Commission on Interracial Cooperation, Inc., 1942; reprinted New York: AMS Press, 1973), p. 4.

Between 1882 and 1946, almost 5,000 people were lynched. Jacqueline Dowd Hall, " 'The Mind That Burns in Each Body': Women, Rape, and Racial Violence," in *Powers of Desire: The Politics of Sexuality*, Ann Snitow, Christine Stansell, and Sharon Thompson, eds. (New York: Monthly Review Press, 1983). pp. 329–30.

5. Ames, ibid., pp. 4–6.

6. Hall, op cit., p. 334.

7. Ibid., p. 335.

8. Ames, op cit., p. 5.

9. "One of the most bruited untruths about lynching is the common statement of the lynching-apologists: 'We've got to lynch a nigger now and then to protect our women.' The records show, however, that 1,406 lynchings since 1889 [until 1933] were for homicide, while only 623 were for rape." "Mob Violence Disappearing From American Way of Life," *New York Herald-Tribune*, Dec. 3, 1933. In Ginzburg, op cit., p. 210.

10. Ames, op cit., p. 58.

11. "The obsession with interracial rape, which peaked at the turn of the

nineteenth century but lingered from the close of the Civil War into the 1930s, became a magnet for racial and sexual oppression." Hall, op cit., p. 341. My more recent examination of the press has revealed that this obsession has continued until the present day, with the possible exception of the 1970s—au.

12. Menachim Amir, *Patterns in Forcible Rape* (Chicago: University of Chicago Press, 1971), p. 44. Amir's study of rapes in Philadelphia between 1958 and 1960 found that 7 percent were interracial, 3 percent black-on-white, 4 percent white-on-black. Charles R. Hayman's 1965–1971 study in Washington, D.C., found 76 percent were black-on-black, 21 percent black-on-white. Brenda A. Brown's 1973 study of rapes in Memphis found that 16 percent were black-on-white, .56 percent white-on-black. (Brownmiller, op cit., p. 214.) The U.S. Dept. of Justice survey between 1973–1987 found that only 9–20 percent of rapes were interracial nationwide (Harlow, op cit., p. 10). The numbers vary according to the era and the population of the city surveyed, but intraracial rape remains the most prevalent everywhere.

13. Gordon and Riger, op cit., p. 76.

14. Brownmiller, op cit., p. 213.

15. Ibid., and p. 230.

16. My sources for the Scottsboro story were *Scottsboro Boy*, by Haywood Patterson and Earl Conrad (New York: Doubleday, 1950), a book maintaining the innocence of Patterson, one of the accused; *Scottsboro: The Firebrand of Communism*, by Files Crenshaw, Jr., and Kenneth A. Miller (Montgomery, AL: 1936), a book maintaining the youths' guilt, but also including detailed transcripts of the trial; and Brownmiller's treatment of the case, based, in turn, largely on *Trial by Prejudice*, by Arthur Garfield Hays (New York: Covici, Friede, 1933): ". . . they were coralled by a posse of white men who already believed a rape had taken place. Confused and fearful, they fell into line."

17. Patterson and Conrad, op cit., p. 277. Brownmiller, op cit., p. 233.

18. In 1932, the Communist Party issued "International Pamphlet No. 25" all about "The 'Rape' Lie."

> To incite the white workers against Negroes and to further build the myth of "white superiority," the white ruling class has coined the poisonous and insane lie that Negroes are "rapists." . . . The cry of "rape" is raised whenever any Negro worker begins to rise from his knees." (Brownmiller, p. 228).

19. Ibid., p. 230.

> If one case convinced the American public—and international opinion—that lying, scheming white women who cried rape were directly responsible for the terrible penalties inflicted on black men, the name of that case was Scottsboro.

20. Hall, op cit., pp. 342–43.

> Certainly, as women enter the workforce, postpone marriage, live alone or as single heads of households, they become easier targets for sexual assault. But observations like [Tracey A.] Gardner's go further, linking the intensification of sexual violence directly to the feminist challenge . . . it seems clear that just as lynching ebbed and flowed with new modes of racial control, rape—both as act and idea—cannot be divorced from changes in the sexual terrain.

Also, Brownmiller, p. 254.

> Women have been raped by men, most often by gangs of men, for many of the same reasons that blacks were lynched by gangs of whites: as group punishment for being uppity, for getting out of line, for failing to recognize "one's place."

See also, Susan Griffin, *Rape: The Power of Consciousness* (New York, Harper & Row, 1978). Not everyone agrees with these feminists that rape, or the threat of it, is a way of keeping women subjugated, but the fact remains that the fear of rape actively keeps many women from travelling alone in certain areas, countries, and times of night—au. (See Tomaselli and Porter, *Rape*, op cit., for arguments against the rape-as-controller theory.)

21. Brownmiller, p. 213. Hall and others have also drawn a link between the fear of rape as a controlling force over women and the fear of being accused of rape as a controlling force over black men: "The 'southern rape complex' functioned as a means of both sexual and racial suppression" (p. 335).

22. Jessica Mitford, *A Fine Old Conflict* (London: Michael Joseph, 1977), pp. 134–35.

23. Ibid., p. 133.

24. Ibid., p. 156.

25. Ibid.

26. Brownmiller, p. 210.

> So to *Time* and *Life*, waging their cold war on the home front, it was the Communists who killed McGee, and to the *Daily Worker* it was a lustful white woman who suddenly cried rape. There was little middle ground to hang on to in in 1951.

27. *The Daily Worker*, 3/15/51, p. 6; 3/19/51, p. 2; 4/25/51, p. 1, respectively.

28. "Free Press & Fair Trial," *Time* May 23, 1959.

29. Stephen J. Whitfield, *A Death in the Delta: The Story of Emmett Till* (New York: The Free Press, 1988).

30. Juan Williams, *Eyes on the Prize: America's Civil Rights Years, 1954–1965* (New York: Penguin, 1988), p. 43.

31. Whitfield, op cit., p. 46.

32. Ibid., p. 47.

33. Eldridge Cleaver, *Soul On Ice* (New York: Dell-Dalta/Ramparts, 1968), p. 11.

34. Brownmiller, op cit., pp. 245–49.

35. "Women Slain in Back Bay Home," *Boston Globe*, 6/15/62, p. 1.

36. "Return of the 'Phantom,' " *Newsweek*, 7/14/69, p. 24.

37. "KITTY GENOVESE KILLER IN PLEA. Seeks retrial 25 years after stabbing," *Daily News*, 3/14/89, p. 1.

38. Quoted in "Kitty Genovese: Would New York Still Turn Away?" by Douglas Martin. *New York Times*, 3/11/89, p. L29.

39. Ibid.

40. Cleaver, op cit. p. 14.

41. Ibid.

42. Tomaselli and Porter, *Rape* op cit., p. 5.

> Only recently has the issue [of rape] been brought back into public debate, and this strictly owing to successful efforts by the feminism of the seventies and early eighties, a feminism which unlike its predecessors made rape the prime focus of its campaign.

43. Noreen Connell and Casandra Wilson, eds., *Rape: The First Sourcebook for Women* (New York: New American Library, 1974).

44. Andrea Medea and Kathleen Thompson, *Against Rape* (New York: Farrar, Straus & Giroux, 1974).

45. Gordon and Riger, op cit., p. 76, 77. ". . . post-1970 articles focused on the victim or on rape as a societal problem."

46. Ibid., pp. 77–78.

47. Ibid.

48. Ibid., p. 77.

CHAPTER 3

1. From a quote in "Oregon Tests Husband–Wife Rape Law" by Betty Liddick, *The Los Angeles Times*, Dec. 3, 1978, Part IX, p. 21.

2. Ellen Goodman, "The Rideout Case. Redefining 'Rape.' " *The Washington Post*, Jan. 2, 1979, p. A19.

3. "Oregonian Wins Acquittal Of Charge He Raped Wife," by Cynthia Gorney, *The Washington Post*, Dec. 28, 1978, p. A2.

4. I refer to Greta and John by their first names in this chapter to avoid confusion, since they both use Rideout as a surname. Greta did not return to her maiden name until after their divorce—au.

5. From, "Oregon Tests Husband–Wife Rape Law" by Betty Liddick, *The Los Angeles Times,* Dec. 3, 1978, pp. IX, 1, 24, 25.

6. Evenson now goes under her married name Davies, but as all her bylines are under her maiden name, I shall continue to use it here—au.

7. *The Statesman Journal* ran six stories on the Rideout case on that one day, Dec. 21, three of them about the crush of press and TV people who had landed in Salem. Throughout the trial, both the *Statesman* and *The Oregonian* continued to run several stories a day on the media crush.

8. In my interviews with reporters and editors who worked on the 1989–1990 Central Park Jogger case, I discovered they were unwilling to even speak the words *feminist* or *sexist* aloud and instead tended to stumble in the search for a euphemism. See Chapter 6—au.

9. "Rideout still uncertain of wife's relationships," by Janet Evenson, *Oregon Statesman Journal,* Dec. 27, 1978.

10. "Wife-rape trial/Threat to husband reported." "The day before Greta Mary Rideout allegedly was raped by her husband, she threatened to use Oregon's revised rape law against him, a witness at John Rideout's trial indicated Thursday." Evenson, *Statesman Journal,* 12/22/78.

11. Ibid.

12. Several of the local reporters said the case was a major topic of conversation in Salem.

13. Kenny and other local reporters characterized the jury as traditional, rural people not sophisticated enough to be able to accept the concept of rape within marriage.

14. "Redefining 'Rape'," by Ellen Goodman. Syndicated column, 1/2/79.

15. "Bill Rideouts." Letter to editor, *The Oregonian,* Jan. 17, 1979, p. D4.

16. Helen Benedict, *Recovery,* op cit. Chapter 5, "Rape by Husbands."

17. John was also approached by movie-makers interested in his story, but Royko, like many other reporters, neglected to mention this.

18. *Washington Post* and *LA Times,* Jan. 21, 1979.

19. It is rather astonishing that Buchwald stooped as low as using *Gone With the Wind* to make his point. That film had been used so often by feminists to prove that Hollywood glamorizes rape that it had become a cliché.

20. This is only a generalized, typical pattern; there are, of course, many individual variations. Sources for this section are interviews I conducted for my book, *Recovery,* and Diana E. H. Russell, *Rape in Marriage,* (New York: Macmillan Co., Collier Books, 1982); Louie Andres, "Family Violence in Florida's Panhandle," *Ms.,* March 1984, p. 23; "Why Battered Wives Don't Leave Home," letter to the editor, *New York Times,* Dec. 29, 1983; Nancy Baker, "Why Women Stay with Men Who Beat Them," *Glamour,* August 1983, p. 367; Jane O'Reilly, "Wife Beating: The Silent Crime," *Time,* Sept. 5, 1983, p. 26.

21. Del Martin, *Battered Wives.* (San Francisco: Glide Publications, 1976.)

22. AP, *The Oregonian,* 1/9/79, p. A1.

23. AP wire copy, March 5, 1979, P.M. cycle.

24. AP, March 9, 1979.

25. "Rideout's ex-wife cites John for trespassing," *Statesman Journal*, Sept. 29, 1979.

26. "Oregon Man Gets 9 Month Term," *New York Times*, Jan. 24, 1980, p. D22.

27. "RIDEOUTS: ANATOMY OF A RAPE STORY," *L. A. Times*, Oct. 27, 1980, Part VI, p. 1.

CHAPTER 4

1. "She remains a mystery," by Gayle Fee. *Boston Herald*, 2/29/84, p. 12. Fee's piece was the only profile of the victim to appear in the daily newspapers until her death.

2. "Requiem for a Rape Victim," by Carol Agus. *Newsday*, 12/30/86.

3. The only other local paper to devote a significant amount of space to the story was the *Fall River Herald*, but I did not analyze it because of difficulties locating clips and because it is a very small paper, of less significance to New Bedford residents than the *Standard-Times* or the *Portuguese Times*—au.

4. "To be made newsworthy, a provocative theme about personal moral competence will be typically built into the story." Jack Katz, "What Makes Crime 'News'?" In *Media, Culture & Society*, Vol. 9, 1987, pp. 47–75.

5. "A unanimous tendency for all the newspapers was to concentrate on solved crimes." Stanley Cohen and Jack Young, eds. *The Manufacture of News* (London: Constable, 1973), p. 33.

6. During the early stages of reporting Daniel Silva's name was spelled Silvia by most of the papers. Silva apparently varied the spelling himself.

7. Impemba's choice of the word *white* to differentiate the reporters from the local Portuguese seems to suggest the Portuguese are nonwhite, an inaccuracy to which many, I suspect, would object.

8. Ferreira is referring to the 1989 case of Charles Stuart, who reported to police that a black man had come up to him and his pregnant wife in their car, attempted to rob them, and had stabbed her and wounded him. She and the baby died and, later, Stuart committed suicide. It is now thought Stuart killed his wife and unborn baby himself.

9. *Portuguese Times* 3/10/83. All quotes from the *Portuguese Times* have been translated from the original Portuguese to English.

10. "Two Massachusetts rape laws make real difference," by Alan D. Sisitsky, *Boston Herald*, 3/24/83, p. 20. The *Standard-Times* also ran several background pieces on rape and the women's movement throughout the month, as did the *Boston Herald*.

11. See History chapter on the 1970s coverage of rape. Also, Gordon and Riger, *The Female Fear*, op cit.

12. Menachim Amir, *Patterns in Forcible Rape*, op cit.

13. A. Nicholas Groth, *Men Who Rape: The Psychology of the Offender*, op cit.

14. Gordon and Riger discuss the impact of news reports of rape on the fear of women in their book, *The Female Fear*, op cit. Basically, their thesis is that crime stories exaggerate and misrepresent the reality of rape, feeding women's fears rather than helping them cope with the real extent of the danger.

15. *Standard-Times*, 3/14/83, p. 5.

16. "Some Are Angry at News Coverage of the Portuguese," by Alan Levin and John Impemba, *Standard-Times*, 3/20/83, p. 10.

17. "Portuguese-Americans Criticize News Coverage of Gang Rape," by John Impemba. *Standard-Times*, 3/18/83, p. 5.

18. Anti-Portuguese letters were pouring into the newspapers at this time, most of which the editors declined to publish. One exception was an issue of the *Providence Journal*, which ran a letter that read in part, "None of [the defendants] has acquired citizenship status in our country—yet. None is fit to become a citizen of this country. They are not worthy of it. They should be ordered to go back where they came from." 3/31/83, p. A11.

19. "Alleged rape weighs heavily on city's Portuguese community," *Boston Globe*, 3/17/83, p. 1.

20. "Portuguese-Americans criticize news coverage of gang rape," *Standard-Times*, 3/18/83, p. 5.

21. *The Portuguese Times*, 3/31/83. p. 2.

22. *The Providence Journal* later ran an article that mentioned this *Hustler* photo spread.

> Pina [the district attorney] said later he is "looking into" the possibility that there is some relationship between the alleged gang-rape and an article that appeared in *Hustler* magazine late last year depicting a somewhat similar incident.
>
> A *Hustler* spokesman yesterday acknowledged the magazine published photographs depicting a woman having sex with four men on a pool table, but reported that Larry Flynt, the publisher, "does not believe that *Hustler* magazine can cause people to conduct themselves antisocially." (4/1/83, p. A8.)

23. *Hustler*, August, 1983.

24. Some of these questions included:

> 1. "Do you tend to feel that Portuguese immigrants tend to stick together too much and don't try hard enough to integrate into American society? Do you think they tend to keep too much to the ways of the old country and reject American values?
>
> 2. "Do you tend to think that the Portuguese immigrants who've come here in the last fifteen years are a different class of people than those who came before and they don't fit in as well?

3. "What would you think if your son or daughter was dating a Portuguese immigrant?"

4. "Do you use the term *greenhorn* in referring to Portuguese immigrants?"

From "Suggested Questions for Voir Dire Examination of Jurors," submitted by the defendant Virgilio Medeiros and his lawyer, Francis M. O'Boy, to William P. Grant, magistrate at Bristol Superior Court, Mass., Feb. 3, 1984. Original document.

25. "Tedious Job of Screening Jurors Starts in Rape Case," by Karen Ellsworth. *Providence Journal,* 2/7/84, pp. A1–A14.

26. "Trials Begin in Big Dan Rape Case," by Jonathan Kaufman. *The Boston Globe,* 2/24/84, p. 15.

27. Ibid.

28. "Big Dan Victim's Background an Issue," by Neil Downing. *Providence Journal,* 2/15/84, p. A3.

29. "Big Dan Jury Pool Mostly Male," by Jonathan Kaufman. *Boston Globe,* 2/18/84, p. 17.

30. See the Geneva Overholser argument in the Conclusion.

31. "Cable Stations Broadcast Name of Woman in Big Dan Rape Case," by Jonathan Kaufman. *Boston Globe,* 2/24/84, p. 18.

32. "Chilling Effect of Big Dan's Trial Cited. Fearing Publicity, Some Victims Are Reluctant to Act," by Jonathan Kaufman. *Boston Globe,* 3/11/84, p. 33.

33. "Big Dan's Judge Bars Photos of Victim in Court," by Neil Downing and Karen Ellsworth. *Providence Journal,* 2/24/84, p. A14.

34. *Boston Herald,* 2/24/84, p. 102.

35. Benedict, *Recovery,* op cit., Chapter 4.

36. "She spoke dispassionately, clinically, as if she were talking about someone else's ordeal." *Providence Journal,* 2/25/84, p. 1.

37. This case occurred before DNA tests were developed that enable laboratories to match up semen samples with those of accused defendants.

38. It later came out that the victim's skin had been swabbed with alcohol before her blood was taken for a routine, postrape VD test, which could have led to incorrect results. Alcohol is normally not used for a blood-alcohol test.

39. The rape shield laws have been designed to protect victims from having their pasts dragged through the court, but in reality attorneys are deft at getting around the law. One favorite trick is to make a detrimental statement or suggestion about the victim that flouts the law, knowing that the judge will sustain the prosecution's objection to it. Even though the statement is thus supposed to be erased from the jury's mind, the jury nevertheless heard it and the seeds of doubt have been planted—au.

40. *Washington Post,* 2/28/84, p. A5.

41. *Herald,* 3/6/84, p. 7; 3/14/84, p. 12; 3/16/84, p. 16; 3/9/84, p. 10; 3/12/84, p. 9, respectively.

42. The quote was highlighted in bold print, as I've reproduced here—au.

43. *Providence Journal,* 3/23/84, p. 1.

44. *Providence Journal,* 3/29/84, p. 4.

45. Each paper gave a different estimate of the crowd. The numbers varied from 7,000 to 15,000.

46. "Judge in Big Dan's Case to Decide if Guilt Can Be Basis for Deportation," by Neil Downing. *The Providence Journal,* 4/20/84, p. A12.

47. This description is based on a visit I paid to the site of Big Dan's Tavern, now a discount bakery shop, where I went inside and spent some time guaging the size of the room—au.

48. Editorial in the *Boston Herald,* 3/23/84, p. 36:

> What the verdicts in the Big Dan's barroom rape cases . . . have said loudly and clearly is that a woman doesn't have to be a saint to be raped. And she doesn't have to be chaste as the day is long to have the right to say, "no."

The very fact that the *Herald* had to say this reveals that newspapers and the public grapple with the virgin–vamp dichotomy every time a rape case comes up.

49. Lynn S. Chancer, "New Bedford, Massachusetts, March 6, 1983–March 22, 1984: The 'Before and After' of a Group Rape." *Gender & Society,* Vol. 1, No. 3, Sept, 1987, p. 252.

50. "Women's Groups Protest Treatment of Big Dan's Victim." AP story in *Standard-Times,* 4/22/84, p. 6.

51. Chancer, op cit., pp. 239–60.

52. Ellen Israel Rosen, "The New Bedford Rape Trial." *Dissent,* Vol. 92, 1985, pp. 207–12.

53. "Impact of Media Coverage on Rape Cases." U.S. Senate Judiciary Hearings J98 No. 112, Vol. 125.

54. *The Accused,* starring Jodie Foster, was far from an accurate portrayal of the actual Big Dan's case. The movie plot revolved around a legal question about joint enterprise that did not arise in the real case, while ignoring the charges of aggravated rape.

CHAPTER 5

1. "A Witness Tells of Finding Body in Park Slaying. Woman Recalls Seeing A Man Linger Nearby." *The New York Times,* 1/8/88, p. B3.

2. Assistant Manhattan District Attorney Stephen Saracco was frankly incredulous when he heard Chambers's statement. Under the head, "Jennifer Raped Me, Chambers Told the DA," *The Daily News* reported the following

reactions of Saracco as recorded on Chambers's videotaped statement: "Wait a minute. Where are (you) from, Iowa or someplace?"; "I really don't believe what you are saying"; "If I was sitting here telling you this story, you'd be laughing." *News,* 11/13/86, p. 3.

3. "We'll Speak For Jenny, Says Fem Group," *The New York Times,* 11/19/86, p. 5.

4. Linda Wolfe, *Wasted: The Preppie Murder* (New York: Simon and Schuster, 1989).

5. As pointed out in the Big Dan's chapter, the fact that the crime was solved also accounted for its appeal to the press. Cohen and Young, op cit.

6. Jacobson and Popovich, op. cit.

7. The tendency to describe women in terms of their sexuality, while men are allowed their achievements, was a constant for Levin throughout the coverage. It reflects the point Dale Spender made in her book; *Man Made Language,* about there being many more sexual words for women than men. See Chapter 1.

8. Katz, op cit.

9. 'Who's On Trial?," by C. Carr. *Village Voice,* 10/27/87, pp. 19–26.

10. Michael Stone, "East Side Story." *New York,* November 10, 1986, pp. 42–53.

11. "Blaming His Victim, A Killer Cops A Plea," by James S. Kunen. *People,* April 11, 1988, pp. 24–29.

12. Wolfe, op cit., p. 233.

13. "Year Later, Levin Death Unresolved," by Timothy Clifford. *Newsday,* 8/27/87.

14. Wolfe, op cit. p. 233.

> Although newspaper readers and television viewers are titillated by the idea of Jennifer's diary, Fairstein thought, public opinion will probably go against Litman for demanding it. And perhaps that will scare him into thinking twice before trying to use blame-the-victim tactics in the trial.

15. One such critic was reporter Timothy Clifford of *Newsday,* who wrote a posttrial analysis that seemed to have missed Litman's tactics altogether: "A Strange Ending to an Odd Trial" (3/27/88):

> For months before and even during the trial, outraged women's groups and angry columnists insisted that Litman was going to use some sort of "blame-the-victim" defense.
>
> But it never occurred.
>
> We did not call a single witness to talk about the victim," Gioiella [a member of the defense team] said. "All of the evidence we used in

> the case was brought in by the prosecution and put at issue by the prosecution." . . .
>
> Gioiella insisted: "One thing that this trial showed clearly was that the entire public's belief that the defense in the case was going to smear the victim was never true."

Of course the defense would deny using such a tactic, but it is surprising that Clifford should have agreed. Litman's opening and closing statements about Levin "pursuing" Chambers "aggressively or sexually" were not merely suggestive—he actually said, "It was Jennifer who was pursuing Robert for sex . . . that's why we wound up with this terrible tragedy." What was that, if not blaming the victim?

16. A model who achieved fame when her face was slashed by a rejected suitor. After her trial, in which she was subject to a great deal of victim-blaming, she became active in victim's rights.

17. "The New York Newsday Interview with Linda Fairstein," by Timothy Clifford. *Newsday*, 4/28/88.

18. "Testimony: Chambers Lied," by Timothy Clifford. *Newsday*, 1/20/88.

19. "The New York Newsday Interview with Linda Fairstein," by Timothy Clifford, op cit.

20. "Chambers Jury Views Videotape," by Timothy Clifford. *Newsday*, 2/2/88.

21. Kunen, op cit., p. 28.

22. "Chambers Jury Rehears Jogger," by Timothy Clifford. *Newsday*, 3/19/88.

23. "A Sense of Relief After the Final Act," by Timothy Clifford. *Newsday*, 4/16/88.

24. Kunen, op cit., pp. 24–26. Even in this pro-Levin *People* magazine piece, the author sometimes referred to Levin as Jennifer, while calling Chambers only by his last name, thus infantilizing her.

25. Ibid.

26. "Chambers Confined to His Cell After Marijuana Found," by Clem Richardson. *Newsday*, 9/26/89.

27. Wolfe, op cit., pp. 298–99.

28. "Underage Drinking Sparks a Tragedy and Debates," by Samuel G. Freedman. *The New York Times*, 8/29/86, p. B3.

29. Quoted in *Newsday*, 8/17/89.

CHAPTER 6

1. *Newsday*, 6/18/90, p. 1. In the story, the jogger case was not mentioned, but the others I have cited here were.

2. *Newsweek* also engaged in this class-worship by describing her as: ". . . the young investment banker, who was riding the fast track through Wellesley,

Yale business school and a lucrative jog with Salomon Brothers . . ." 5/1/89, p. 27.

3. Kaufman's point was substantiated by Richard Brookhiser in an essay on the case, "Public Opinion and the Jogger," *Commentary*, Vol. 88, July, 1989, pp. 50–52. "Public opinion in the *Times* also reflects the questions its reporters choose to explore, and the people to whom they turn for answers . . ."

4. Doris Graber, *Crime News and The Public*. Op cit. p. 73.

5. Brownmiller, op. cit., p. 254. Hall in *Powers of Desire*, op cit., pp. 242–43.

6. *The New York News Media and The Central Park Rape*, by Linda S. Lichter, S. Robert Lichter, and Daniel Amundson (The American Jewish Committee, Institute of Human Relations, Center for Media and Public Affairs. Washington, D.C. 1989.) In this content analysis of the first two weeks of reporting on the case, researchers found that "race was mentioned as a possible explanation for the attack fifty-four times, more than twice as often as any other factor. But its relevance was denied 80 percent of those times." Their conclusion:

> Although the racial element was conspicuous in this story, the content analysis found no evidence that media coverage played on racial fears or hatreds. On the contrary, the question of race was repeatedly raised in order to deny its relevance to the crime, to warn against reviving racial tension, and to call for a healing process to defuse racial animosity.

This conclusion differs from mine because this study only covered the first two weeks of coverage and did not look at the *City Sun*, one of the two major black papers to accuse the white media of racism. Also, content analysis does not take into account the implications and innuendoes of vocabulary, or of the cumulative effect of story after story denying racial relevance.

7. Definitions of bias crimes contained in a *New York Times* editorial on a new bill proposed in the Senate by Gov. Mario Cuomo included two references to gender as a category of bias. "An assailant motivated by racial, religious, ethnic, or *sexual* bigotry . . ." ". . . bias based on the victim's race, ethnicity, *sex*, or sexual orientation had been a motive for the crime." (*Times*, 5/22/90, p. A26. My emphasis.) In discussions of the jogger case, however, the "sex" and "sexual bigotry" definition of bias crimes was always left out.

8. My impression is confirmed by the findings of the American Jewish Committee study of the case. The *Post* used by far the most inflammatory language and animalistic descriptions about the suspects.

9. One of the most patronizing of the *Times*'s pieces along these lines was "Grim Seeds of Park Rampage Found in East Harlem Streets," by Gina Kolata (5/2/89, p. C1). In it, Kolata interviewed anthropologists and sociologists about

what could have motivated the suspects to commit such an awful crime, and asked questions that I doubt would ever have been asked had the suspects been white—questions to do with the drug culture, broken families, and criminal records. Such questions were certainly not asked about the white college students accused of committing group oral sodomy on a black woman against her will in the St. John's University case in April 1990.

10. The hosts of talk shows also reported a plethora of angry and racist calls about the case. "There has been more anger than I have heard in my life about any individual crime," says veteran radio talk-show host Barry Gray." *Newsweek*, 5/15/89, p. 20.

11. "Wilding in the Night." *Time*, 5/8/89, p. 20, 21. ". . . why the crime ocurred became the central question that animated media coverage." *The New York News Media and the Central Park Rape*, p. 5.

12. "Race was mentioned as a possible explanation for the attack . . . more than twice as often as any other factor." *The New York News Media and The Central Park Rape*, ibid.

13. Phillipe Bourgeois, a white anthropologist who specializes in the culture of Harlem, told *The New York Times* that even though the suspects were not on drugs, the drug culture of crack around them has taught them to be ruthless. *Times*, 5/2/89, p. C1.

14. "Many, white and nonwhite alike, hastened to say the incident had more to do with class than race—a lashing out of resentful ghetto residents against privileged Yuppies." *Newsweek*, 5/8/89, p. 65.

15. Ken Auletta, *Daily News*, 5/7/89, p. 47.

> Yes, there are environmental explanations for such behavior. We shouldn't ignore hit rap songs that glorify violence. Or overlook how children can be victims of TV violence, of sexually seductive ads, of the culture of greed lionized on Wall Street. The mind blurs when reminded of all the forces that prey on ghetto kids.
>
> But don't let that blur a more tangible and immediate—and awful—truth: Those Central Park thugs were victims of a culture of violence that will not be curbed until it is discussed, honestly, openly.

16. "The kids who allegedly attacked that young lady in Central Park were acting out a song called 'Wild Thing,' said community activist Sonny Carson, a notion with which Rev. Butts agrees." Harold L. Jamison in *The Amsterdam News*, 4/29/89, p. 3.

17. "Stop Viewing Kid Thugs As Victims of Society," by Rita Kramer. *The New York Post*, 4/30/89, p. 53.

> Increasing numbers of children in inner-city black families are growing up in households without fathers—without any authority figure to set limits and establish the values and standards of conduct which must be

> internalized if children are to grow up capable of living in a free society.
>
> Without the kind of nurturing that creates conscience and builds character, the young grow up lacking a clear sense of right and wrong.

In this comment, Kramer ignores the role of mothers as authority figures and reduces them to insignificant figures incapable of teaching moral values.

18. Countless editorials and columns in the *New York Post* used this case as a chance to call for the death penalty for adults and minors, but the most blatent of these reactions was by Donald Trump, who ran a full page advertisement in the city's newspapers on May 1, crying, BRING BACK THE DEATH PENALTY. BRING BACK OUR POLICE!, in reaction to the Central Park rape. The ads were estimated to have cost him $85,000. The black community reacted with anger to the ads, considering them racist.

19. "Koch Must Resign" by Wilbert A. Tatum, editor-in-chief, *The Amsterdam News*, 4/29/89, p. 1.

20. See Ken Auletta's quote earlier about the culture of violence.

21. "The wretched schools of New York are petrie dishes, breeding thousands of stone-hearted children." Jack Newfield, *Daily News*, 5/1/89, p. 12.

22. "It's just a bunch of kids," said a man as he bundled his wife and three small children into the family car outside Los Tres Unidos. "They got nothing to do." *The New York Times*, 5/9/89, p. B1, B8.

From Jack Newfield, *Daily News*, 5/1/89, p. 12:

> The Central Park wolf pack members don't fit the stereotype. They were not crackheads. They were all in school. They didn't have guns. They had caring families. Only one had been arrested before. . . . Despite all that, these kids nearly killed for sport. They were bored, not hungry."

23. "Driven by rage, sexual lust and boredom, free-floating bands of restless youths have preyed on New York City neighborhoods for a decade . . ." *Newsday*, 4/25/89.

24. *Newsweek*, 5/8/89, p. 65.

> Behavioral experts agree that in the dynamics of a group . . . there is an undeniably subtle power [that] has the ability to validate and thereby embolden behavior. That may be especially true of teenagers, who are particularly susceptible to pressure from peers.

25. "There was a full moon Wednesday night. A suitable backdrop for the howling of wolves. A vicious pack ran rampant through Central Park." *Daily News*, 4/22/89, p. 11.

26. *Newsweek* was the only publication to give a creditable round-up of the

understanding of gang violence, and it, also, neglected the rape aspect. "Going 'Wilding' in the City." By David Gelman with Peter McKillop. 5/8/89, p. 65.

27. Manachim Amir, *Patterns in Forcible Rape*, op cit.; A. Nicholas Groth, *Men Who Rape*, op cit.; *Criminal Victimization in the United States*, 1988, U.S. Dept. of Justice, Bureau of Statistics. A National Crime Survey Report, December 1990. See Bibliography for other rape studies.

28. Ibid. Also, Helen Benedict, *Recovery*, op cit.; Harlow, *Female Victims of Violent Crime*, op. cit.

29. *Criminal Victimization in the United States*, op cit.

30. A rare exception to the omission of the fact that white men rape, too, was an op-ed piece for the *Times* by J. Anthony Lukas.

> But adolescents—black or white, poor or privileged—tend to be wild creatures, given to surges of feeling they cannot comprehend, to bouts of violence, to cruelty. That lesson is underlined by the arrest Wednesday of five white teen-agers in the affluent New Jersey suburb of Glen Ridge for the sexual assault of a mentally handicapped girl. (5/28/89, p. IV 15.)

31. Amir, ibid., pp. 193–94.

32. A more detailed account of Sanday's work on rape-free and rape-prone societies can be found in "Rape and the Silencing of the Feminine," by Peggy Reeves Sanday. In *Rape*, Tomaselli and Porter, eds., op cit., p. 84.

33. That this is so little understood was revealed by columnist Mike Royko, when he wrote about the case: "This society has flaws. It always has. But I don't know of any policies, official or informal, that encourage young men to hide in bushes and mutilate innocent women." *Chicago Tribune* column quoted in *Newsweek*, 5/15/89, p. 40.

34. Amir, op cit., p. 191.

35. "THIS IS MY FIRST RAPE," *The New York Post*, 11/15/90, pp. 1, 5.

36. Donald L. Mosher and Ronald D. Anderson, *Journal of Research in Personality*, vol. 20, pp. 77–94. Study reported in *Psychology Today*, April, 1987, p. 12.

37. Another study that showed a link between tolerance of rape and sexist attitudes was conducted by Eleanor R. Hall, Judith A. Howard and Sherrie L. Boezio, "Tolerance of Rape: A Sexist or Antisocial Attitude?" In *Psychology of Women Quarterly*, 1986, Vol. 10, pp. 101–18.

38. Hamill, *New York Post*, 4/23/89, p. 4.

39. *Post*, 10/12/89, p. 28.

40. *Outrage: The Story Behind the Tawana Brawley Hoax*, by Robert D. McFadden, Ralph Blumenthal, M. A. Farber, E. R. Shipp, Charles Strum, and Craig Wolff of *The New York Times* (New York: Bantam. 1990), p. 21.

> The examination revealed no cuts, dried blood, bruises, swelling, deep redness, or other indications of injury. There were no signs of trauma to the mouth or throat either. . . . Dr. Pena decided to forego the use of a rape-detection kit, at least for a while. There weren't enough signs to warrant it.

41. Mike Taibbi and Anna Sims-Phillips, *Unholy Alliances: Working the Tawana Brawley Story* (New York: Harcourt, Brace, Jovanovich, 1989.) Also, *Outrage;* ibid, p. 52.

42. *The Amsterdam News* printed the jogger's name in its April 29, 1989, issue.

43. *Amsterdam News*, 5/6/89, p. 8. *Newsweek* also reported Maddox's direct quote:

> I have not seen any evidence of this woman being assaulted or attacked at all. . . . What are we going to do, accept some white person's word that she's over there . . . at Metropolitan Hospital? . . . This whole thing could be an outright hoax. (5/15/89, p. 40.)

44. *The Amsterdam News*, 5/6/89, p. 1.

45. *The New York Media and the Central Park Rape*, pp. 1, 2.

46. Pat Buchanan was one of several writers in the *Post* and the *Daily News* who used this crime as a chance to inveigh against black criminals.

> Even a glance at the 1987 National Crime Survey reveals that black-on-white gang assaults, rapes and robberies are now 21 times as common as white-on-black; and black-on-white gang robberies 52 times as common. (*Post*, 3/7/90, p. 19.)

Also "In New York, and the Northeast . . . crime is primarily a black phenomenon." Buchanan, *Post*, 5/7/89. p. 43.

47. *Times*, 5/2/89, p. C1.

48. See the chapter on Jennifer Levin's murder, in which the editor and reporters of the *Daily News* frankly admit to this bias.

49. "WOMAN RAPED & THROWN FOUR STORIES." *Post*, 5/4/89, p. 13.

50. "Scant Attention Paid Victim as Homicides Reach Record in Boston," by Christopher B. Daly. *The Washington Post*, 12/5/90; "In Boston, A Slaying Reawakens Gang Fears," by Mary B. W. Tabor. *The Washington Post*, 11/28/90.

51. "Accuser's Family Calls St. John's Case Racial," by Joseph P. Fried. *The New York Times*, 6/22/91, p. 7.

52. "The Male Athlete and Sexual Assault," by Gerald Eskenazi. *The New*

York Times, 6/3/90, Sports section 8, p. 1. "Disturbing Pattern Seen in Gang Rapes," by Eillism Douglas. *Newsday,* 5/13/90, p. 2.

53. This pattern was seen again in the 1991 rape case against William Kennedy Smith. As a result of the accusation by a woman he had met in a bar that he raped her, articles abounded about "date" or "acquaintance" rape. Once again, a rape cases involving a white man revealed a press willing to explain rape in terms of the male ethos rather than in terms of stereotypes. One example was "Even the Victim Can Be Slow to Recognize Rape," by Jane Gross, *The New York Times,* 5/28/91, p. A.8. Another was a cover story in *Time,* "Date Rape," by Nancy Gibbs, 6/3/91, pp. 48–55.

54. The white teenager convicted of murdering Yusef Hawkins in the Bensonhurst case.

55. See Chapter 1 on the history of sex crimes in the press for an account of this case.

56. Jim Nolan, *New York Post,* 5/7/89.

57. Headline in the *Post,* 11/16/89, p. 7.

58. *Post,* 11/3/89, p. 5.

59. "Jogger May Break Cover," by Alison Harper. *Newsday,* 6/25/90, pp. 8, 19.

60. *Post* headline, 7/17/90.

61. *The New York News Media and The Central Park Rape,* op cit., p. 11.

62. In a medical examination of twenty-three victims, no evidence of sperm was found in half of the cases. In other studies, only 25 percent of rapists report no sexual dysfunction. Groth, *Men Who Rape,* op cit., pp. 88–91.

63. *The New York Times,* 2/24/90, p. 27.

64. "On Wednesday, one of New York's most visible rape trials will begin. Will the media use the victim's name? Should they?" *Newsday,* 6/11/90, Part II, pp. 1, 8–9; and, "Most Papers Won't Name the Jogger," *The New York Times,* 6/13.90, p. B3.

65. *Newsday,* ibid., p. 8. Appallingly, *Newsday* got Tatum's name wrong in this story and spelled it "Wilbur (Bill) Tatum." Not a great sign of respect.

66. "Defense Lawyers in Jogger Trial Take The Offensive," the *City Sun,* 10/24/90, p. 4.

67. *Times,* 6/13/90, p. B3.

68. Ibid.

69. *Newsday,* 6/11/90, Part II, p. 9.

70. A phenomenon illustrated in 1991 when the *Times,* the *San Francisco Chronicle,* the *Louisville Courier-Journal,* and the *Des Moines Register* named the woman accusing William Kennedy Smith of rape. Those papers named the woman largely because NBC and two supermarket tabloids had. See Conclusion for further discussion.

71. U.S. Department of Justice, Federal Bureau of Investigation, *Uniform Crime Reports for the United States,* 1980 (Washington, D.C.: GPO, 1981), p. 15.

72. "On the Legislative Front," *Ms.* magazine, Set./Oct., 1990, p. 45.

73. FBI statistics cited in "Victim or Not, Pattern of Life Often Altered," by Andrea Stone, *USA Today*, 7/18/90, p. 1.

74. *New York Post*, 7/23/90, p. 4.

75. In a strange reversal of roles, while Agus was putting forth the protesters' view in her column—which had usually been devoted to making pro-victim and feminist points—Mike McAlary of the *News*, hardly known for a feminist viewpoint, was taking the opposite stand. "Racism comes in many shades . . . the victim's whiteness is as inconsequential to the crime as the suspects' blackness. This was a sex case, period." (*News*, 7/18/90, p. 4.) Apparently, McAlary was so eager to refute the accusations of the demonstrators, which he found justifiably outrageous, that he was even prepared to make a feminist point!

76. A good analysis of this clash was written by Helen Thorpe in "Behind the Headlines On the Jogger Trial: Is Coverage Fair?" *The New York Observer*, 7/30–8/6/90, p. 1. Another, more opinionated analysis was by Edwin Diamond in "Black on White: Reverse Reality in the News Coverage of the Jogger Trial, Tawana Brawley, and Other Racially Charged Stories" in *New York* magazine, 8/20/90, pp. 38–42.

77. "Jogger Defense Case: Scattershot Approach," by William Glaberson. *New York Times*, 7/13/90, p. B1.

78. During the final week of the trial, another stir was caused when Tawana Brawley showed up at the courthouse, holding hands with Rev. Sharpton. "She came to see how white victims are treated," trumpeted the *Amsterdam News*, pleased to have Brawley publicly lining up with the defendants side. I and others knowledgeable about rape, however, immediately noted that, had Brawley really been a rape victim, she would likely have sided with the victim, not the accused rapists.

79. Brownmiller, op cit., p. 255.

80. "Lawyer's Threat of Mistrial Splits Defense in Jogger Case," by Ronald Sullivan. *The New York Times*, 10/15/90, p. B2.

81. Guy Trebay described Wise in sympathetic terms in a *Village Voice* article on the case.

> Kharey Wise is a small, unmenacing kid with a longish head, a compact body, and the courtroom habit of sucking his teeth. He looks like a lot of kids who don't shave too often and who wear Esprit sweatshirts and Nike pumps and hang out in neighborhood basketball courts all over the city. In a lot of ways he's an average, even a provincial kid.

Trebay went on to describe Wise's participation in the rape as something he did "so that his friends wouldn't think he was a 'punk' " and to depict him as a somewhat hapless victim of a night of gang violence, led on first by other, stronger boys to participate, then by persuasive police to confess. "Go to the Videotape: Kharey Wise Talks Himself Into a Corner," *Voice*, 11/27/90, p. 7.

82. Ibid.

83. *Newsday*, 12/12/90, p. 5.

84. "Defense Raised The Race Issue," by Emily Sachar. *Newsday*, 12/12/90, p. 6.

85. "New York: Sentimental Journeys," by Joan Didion. *New York Review of Books*, 1/17/91, pp. 45–56.

86. *Newsday*, 1/31/91, p. 32.

87. Brownmiller, op cit., p. 254.

88. "The Mind of the Rapist," *Newsweek*, 7/23/90, pp. 46–52.

89. Cited by Geneva Overholser in an editorial in *Quill*, May 1990, p. 17.

90. "What Really Happened in Central Park," by Michael Stone. *New York*, 8/14/89, pp. 30–43.

91. *Newsday*, 7/20/90, p. 5.

> A dozen feminist activists—male and female—protested outside the courtroom . . . yesterday, charging defendants' supporters are infusing the case with claims of racism that have no place in the trial . . .
>
> "There are some who would also like to manipulate this case to separate women on the basis of race and class. Rape has no color and rape has no class."

CONCLUSION

1. In 1986, a national symposium on the treatment of crime victims by the news media was held by Texas Christian University and the Gannett Foundation, instigated by growing public concern over the exploitation of crime victims by the media. That same year, the Iowa Coalition Against Sexual Abuse released a pamphlet for the media, entitled "News Coverage of Sexual Assault," intended to provide the media with guidelines that would help them avoid further traumatizing victims. In 1987, the national Organization for Victim Assistance released a pamphlet on "Victim Rights and Services: A Legislative Directory" that included a Media Code of Ethics. These publications were responses to the public's concern over the perceived callousness of the press to crime victims.

2. Gordon and Riger, op cit., p. 78.

> The frequency of articles throughout the 1970s probably facilitated the placement of rape high on the political and social agendas of that decade. Data from the last few years suggest that magazine presentations of rape may change yet again to focus on its bizarre characteristics.

3. "Rape Charge for Kennedy Nephew," Chronicle News Service, *The San Francisco Chronicle*, 5/10/91, pp. 1, 18.

4. Times Article Naming Rape Accuser Ignites Debate on Journalist Values," by William Glaberson. *The New York Times*, 4/26/91, p. A12.

5. "Rape Charge for Kennedy Nephew," op cit.

6. In the wake of the Kennedy case, a questionnaire was passed out to 243 students, aged nineteen to twenty-three, in a journalism lecture course at the University of California, Berkeley, asking them if rape victims should or should not be named by the press. Out of the 243, 161 said victims should not be named, and only nine said they should. The rest did not answer or gave indecipherable answers. The main reasons given for not identifying victims were invasion of privacy, exacerbating her trauma, and that the names would mean nothing to the public and add nothing to the story. Clearly, in this survey, the huge majority were against naming—au.

7. "Should the Media Name the Accuser When the Crime Being Charged is Rape?," by Roger Cohen. *The New York Times*, 4/21/91, p. E4.

8. Ibid.

9. "Remove that Blue Dot" by David A. Kaplan, *Newsweek*, Dec. 16, 1991, p. 26.

10. "Editors Debate Naming Rape Victims," by Alex S. Jones. *The New York Times*, 4/13/91, p. 6.

11. The Story of a Rape" [excerpt from the *Des Moines Register* article], by Jane Schorer. *Quill*, May 1990, p. 19.

12. "Times Article Naming Rape Accuser Ignites Debate on Journalist Values," by William Glaberson. *The New York Times*, 4/26/91, p. A12.

> In remarks that have been widely quoted, Ms. Golden [the *Time*'s national editor whose staff handled the article] . . . said that the details in the article were merely informative and that the negative connotations were largely in the way people read them. "I think we can trust readers to make the right judgments," she said. "I can't account for every weird mind that reads *The New York Times*."

13. *The New York Times*, 4/17/91, p. A10.

14. For an excellent analysis of this *Times* story and the coverage of the William Smith case, see, "Media Goes Wilding in Palm Beach," by Katha Pollitt. *The Nation*, 6/24/91, cover.

15. "William Smith Loses Anonymity," by Mary Jordan of the *Washington Post*. *San Francisco Chronicle*, 5/10/91, p. A4.

16. See "Remove that Blue Dot" by David Kaplan, op cit.; "Men on Trial" by John Taylor, *New York* magazine, December 16, 1991, pp. 22–28; and "Trial by Television" by Richard Lacayo, *Time*, Dec. 16, 1991, pp. 30–31.

17. Some of these suggestions are taken from *A Resource Guide: News Coverage of Sexual Assault*, a pamphlet issued by Marilyn J. Musser and Carole Meade of the Iowa Coalition Against Sexual Abuse, 1986, Illinois Hall, 25th and Carpenter, Des Moines, Iowa 50311. Some others are taken from "Media

Code of Ethics," released by The National Organization for Victim Assistance in 1988, U.S. Department of Justice, Office of Justice Programs, Office for Victims of crime, 717 D Street, N.W., Washington, D.C. 20004.

18. "Deadlines, Datelines, and History," by Michael Schudson. In *Reading the News,* Robert Karl Manoff and Michael Schudson, eds. (New York: Pantheon: 1986), p. 81.

19. "Press Gets Bad News On Its Image," *U.S. News & World Report,* April 22, 1985, p. 2.

20. "Does Rape have a Historical Meaning?" by Roy Porter. In Tomaselli and Porter, *Rape,* op cit., pp. 299–330.

Bibliography

MEDIA

Ditton, Jason, and James Duffy. 1983. "Bias in the Newspaper Reporting of Crime News." *Brit. J. Criminology*, Vol. 23, No. 2, pp. 159–65.

Epstein, Laurily Keir, ed. 1978. *Women and The News*. New York: Hastings House.

Ericson, Richard V., Patricia M. Baranek, and Janet B. L. Chan. 1987. *Visualizing Deviance: A Study of News Organization*. Toronto: University of Toronto Press.

Gallagher, Margaret. 1981. *Unequal Opportunities: The Case of Women and the Media*. France: UNESCO.

Gallup Survey. 1986. "Who Likes the Press—And Who Doesn't." *U.S. News & World Report*, Jan. 27.

Garment, Suzanne. 1987. "Can the Media Be Reformed?" *Commentary*, August, pp. 37–43.

Gitlin, Todd. 1980. *The Whole World Is Watching*. Berkeley: University of California Press.

Goldstein, Tom. 1985. *The News at Any Cost: How Journalists Compromise Their Ethics to Shape the News*. New York: Simon and Schuster.

Goldstein, Tom, ed. 1989. *Killing the Messenger: 100 Years of Media Criticism*. New York: Columbia University Press.

Graber, Doris A. 1984. *Processing the News: How People Tame the Information Tide*. New York: Longman.

Harris, Frank. 1932. *Presentation of Crime in Newspapers*. Hanover: The Sociological Press.

Heath, Linda. 1984. "Impact of Newspaper Crime Reports on Fear of Crime: Multimethodological Investigation." *Journal of Personality and Social Psychology*. Vol. 47, No. 2, pp. 263–76.

Katz, Jack. 1987. "What Makes Crime 'News'?" *Media, Culture and Society*, Vol. 9, pp. 47–75.

Klaidman, Stephen, L., and Tom L. Beauchamp. 1987. *The Virtuous Journalist*. New York: Oxford University Press.

Manoff, Rober Karl, and Michael Schudson, eds., 1986. *Reading the News*, New York: Pantheon.

Marzolf, Marion. 1977. *Up From the Footnote: A History of Women Journalists*. New York: Hastings House.

Mawby, Rob. I., and Judith Brown. 1984. "Newspaper Images of the Victim: A British Study." *Victimology: An International Journal*, Vol. 9, pp. 82–94.

O'Keefe, Garret J., and Kathaleen Reid-Nash. 1987. "Crime News and Real-World Blues: The Effects of the Media on Social Reality." *Communication Research*, Vol. 14, No. 2, pp. 147–63.

"Press Gets Bad News on its Image." 1985. *U.S. News & World Report*, April 22.

Smith, A. 1978. "The Long Road to Objectivity and Back Again: The Kinds of Truth We Get in Journalism." In G. Boyce et al., eds. *Newspaper History* (London: Constable), pp. 152–71.

Smith, Susan J. 1984. "Crime in the News." *Brit. J. Criminology*, Vol. 24, No. 3, pp. 289–95.

Taibbi, Mike, and Anna Sims-Phillips. 1989. *Unholy Alliances: Working the Tawana Brawley Story*. New York: Harcourt Brace Jovanovich.

Tuchman, Gaye, Arlene Kaplan Daniels, and James Benet. 1978. *Hearth and Home: Images of Women in the Mass Media*. New York: Oxford University Press.

Weaver, David H., and Cleveland G. Wilhoit. 1986. *The American Journalist A Portrait of U.S. News People and Their Work*. Bloomington: Indiana University Press.

SEX CRIMES

Acock, Alan C., and Nancy K. Ireland. 1983. "Attribution of Blame in Rape Cases: The Impact of Norm Violation, Gender, And Sex-Role Attitude." *Sex Roles*, Vol. 9, No. 2, pp. 179–93.

Ames, Jessie Daniel. 1942, 1973. *The Changing Character of Lynching*. New York: AMS Press.

Amir, Menachim. 1971. *Patterns in Forcible Rape*. Chicago: University of Chicago Press.

Benedict, Helen. 1985. *Recovery: How To Survive Sexual Assault*. New York: Doubleday.

Beneke, Timothy. 1982. *Men On Rape*. New York: St. Martin's Press.

Brownmiller, Susan. 1975. *Against Our Will: Men, Women and Rape*. New York: Simon & Schuster.

Burgess, Ann, and Lynda Holmstrom. 1979. *Rape, Crisis and Recovery*, Bowie, MD: Brady.

Chancer, L. 1987. "New Bedford, Massachusetts . . . The 'Before and After' of a Group Rape." *Gender & Society*, Vol. 1, No. 3, pp. 239–60.

Check, J., and N. Malamuth. 1983. "Sex Role Stereotyping and Reactions to Depictions of Stranger Versus Acquaintance Rape." *J. of Personality and Social Psychology*, Vol. 45, No. 2, pp. 344–56.

Deitz, Sheila R., Madeleine Littman, and Brenda J. Bentley. 1984. "Attribution of Responsibility for Rape: The Influence of Observer Empathy, Victim Resistance, and Victim Attractiveness." *Sex Roles*, Vol. 10, Nos. 3/4, pp. 261–80.

Griffin, Susan. 1978. *Rape: The Power of Consciousness*. New York: Harper & Row.

Groth, Nicholas, and H. Birnbaum. 1979. *Men Who Rape: the Psychology of the Offender*. New York: Plenum Press.

Groth, Nicholas, and Ann Burgess. 1980. "Male Rape: Offenders and Victims," *American J. of Psychiatry*, Vol. 137, No. 7, July.

Hall, Eleanor R., Judith, A. Howard, Sherrie L. Boezio. 1986. "Tolerance of Rape: A Sexist or Antisocial Attitude?" *Psychology of Women Quarterly*, Vol. 10, pp. 101–18.

Hall, Jacqueline Dowd. 1983. " 'The Mind That Burns in Each Body': Women, Rape, and Racial Violence." In *Powers of Desire: The Politics of Sexuality*, Ann Snitow, Christine Stansell, and Sharon Thompson, eds. New York: Monthly Review Press.

Harari, Herbert, Oren Harari, and Robert V. White. 1985. "The Reaction to Rape by American Male Bystanders." *The Journal of Social Psychology*, Vol. 125, pp. 253–58.

Herman, Lawrence. 1977. "What's Wrong With Rape Reform Laws?" *Victimology: An International Journal*, Vol. 2, No. 1, pp. 8–18.

Holmstrom, Lynda Lytle, and Ann Wolbert Burgess. 1978. *The Victim of Rape: Institutional Reactions*. New York: John Wiley & Sons.

Iowa Coalition Against Sexual Abuse 1986, Texas Christian University and the Gannet Foundation 1986.

Jacobsen, M., and P. Popovich. 1983. "Victim Attractiveness and Perceptions of Responsibility in an Ambiguous Rape Case." *Psychology of Women Quarterly*, Vol. 8, No. 1, pp. 100–4.

Jaffee, David, and Murray A. Straus. 1987. "Sexual Climate and Reported Rape: A State Level Analysis." *Archives of Sexual Behavior*, Vol. 16, No. 2, pp. 107–23.

Janoff-Bulman, Ronnie, and Christine Timko. 1985. "Cognitive Biases in

Blaming the Victim." *Journal of Experimental Social Psychology*, Vol. 21, pp. 161–77.

Jones, Ann. 1980. *Women Who Kill*. New York: Holt, Rinehart & Winston.

Lipton, David N., Elizabeth C. McDonel, and Richard M. McFall. 1987. "Heterosocial Perception in Rapists." *Journal of Consulting and Criminal Psychology*, Vol. 55, No. 1, pp. 17–22.

Martin, Del. 1976. *Battered Wives*. San Francisco: Glide Publications.

McCarthy, Paul. 1987. "Rape: The Macho View." *Psychology Today*, April, p. 12.

Medea, Andra and Kathleen Thompson. 1974. *Against Rape*. New York: Farrar, Straus & Giroux.

Myers, Martha S. A., and Gary, D. LaFree. 1982. "Sexual Assault and Its Prosecution: A Comparison with Other Crimes." *Journal of Criminal Law & Criminology*. Vol. 73, No. 3, pp. 1282–305.

Ressler, Robert K., Ann Wolbert Burgess, and John E. Douglas. 1983. "Rape and Rape-Murder: One Offender and Twelve Victims." *Am. J. Psychiatry*, Vol. 140, No. 1, pp. 36–40.

Rosen, Ellen. 1985. "The New Bedford Rape Trial." *Dissent*. Vol. 32, pp. 207–11.

Russell, Diana. 1982. *Rape in Marriage*. New York: Macmillan.

Scully, Diana, and Joseph Marolla. 1984. "Convicted Rapists' Vocabulary of Motive: Excuses and Justifications." *Social Problems*, Vol. 431, No. 5, pp. 530–44.

Scully, Diana, and Joseph Marolla. 1985. " 'Riding the Bull at Gilley's' " Convicted Rapists Describe the Rewards of Rape." *Social Problems*, Vol. 32, No. 3, Feb., pp. 251–62.

Thornton, Bill, and Richard Ryckman. 1983. "The Influence of a Rape Victim's Physical Attractiveness on Observers' Attributions of Responsibility." *Human Relations*, Vol. 36, No. 6, pp. 549–62.

Timnick, Lois. 1983. "When Women Rape Men." *Psychology Today*, Sept., pp. 74–75.

Tomaselli, Sylvana, and Roy Porter, eds. 1986. *Rape*. New York: Basil Blackwell.

Tyler, Tom R. 1984. "Assessing the Risk of Crime Victimization: The Integration of Personal Victimization Experience and Socially Transmitted Information." *Journal of Social Issues*, Vol. 40, No. 1, pp. 27–38.

U.S. Dept. of Justice, Federal Bureau of Investigation, Uniform Crime Reports for the United States, Washington, D.C., GPO, 1980, p. 15.

Walsh, Anthony. 1984. "Differential Sentencing Patterns Among Felony Sex Offenders and Non-Sex Offenders." *The Journal of Criminal Law & Criminology*, Vol. 75, No. 2, pp. 443–58.

Weis, Kurt, and Sandra S. Borges. 1973. "Victimology and Rape: The Case of the Legitmate Victim." *Issues in Criminology*, Vol. 8, No. 2, pp. 71–113.

Whitfield, Stephen J. 1988. *A Death in the Delta: The Story of Emmett Till.* New York: The Free Press.

Williams, Joyce E., and Karen A. Holmes. 1981. "The Second Assault: Rape and Public Attitudes." Westport, CT: Greenwood Press.

Williams, Joyce E. 1984. "Secondary Victimization: Confronting Public Attitudes About Rape." *Victimology: An International Journal,* Vol. 9, No. 1, pp. 66–81.

LANGUAGE

Lakoff, Robin. 1975. *Language and Woman's Place.* New York: Harper & Row.

Lakoff, Robin. 1990. *Talking Power: The Politics of Language.* New York: Basic Books.

Spender, Dale. 1980. *Man Made Language.* London: Routledge & Kegan Paul.

Index

Abbot, Bernadine, 140
Accuracy in reporting, 264–65
The Accused (film), 139, 145
Advertising, portrayal of women in, 22
Against Our Will (Susan Brownmiller), 17–18, 29, 39, 44, 77
Agus, Carole, 140–41, 236
America (magazine), 166
American Communist Party, 28, 30–32
American Jewish Committee, 208*n.*, 216, 285
Ames, Jessie Daniel, 26, 296
Amir, Menachim, 98, 211–12, 296
Amsterdam News, 33
  Central Park jogger case, 192–93, 202, 213, 215–16, 222, 227–29, 232, 235, 238, 240
  St. John's University rape case, 220
Anticommunism, 30–32
AP. *See* Associated Press
Assailants, myths about rape, 14–15
Associated Press (AP), 46, 48, 50, 55, 77–78, 81–82, 114, 119, 136
Association of Southern Women for the Prevention of Lynching, 26
Attitudes of rapists, 211–13
Balanced reporting, 260–61
Barger, Eric, 156–57
Battered Wives (Del Martin), 44, 82, 85, 263, 298
Bell, Howard E., 176
Benedict, Helen, *Recovery: How to Survive Sexual Assault*, v, 296
Beneke, Timothy, 13, 297
Bernstein, Nina
  Central Park jogger case, 184, 192, 204–6, 246–47
  Jennifer Levin rape/murder case, 166–67, 184
Big Dan's Gang Rape. *See* New Bedford gang rape case
Black press, Central Park jogger case and, 29, 213–23
Blakely, Mary Kay, 109
Blaming of victim, 15–19, 23–24
  Central Park jogger case, 194–98
  Jennifer Levin rape/murder case, 148–49, 157–58, 162–65, 167–72, 174–75, 178–79, 184–86
  Kennedy Smith trial, 255–57
  New Bedford gang rape case, 125–27, 128–33, 141–42, 145

Blaming of victim (*continued*)
Rideout-Marital Rape Case, 55, 57–58, 60, 68, 87
"Wolf-whistle murder" case, 34–35
Boston Globe, coverage of "Big Dan's" gang rape case in, 91, 94, 97–98, 104–5, 114, 116, 134, 266
editorial, 94
J. Kaufman's reporting, 113, 119
on jurors, 111
on mood of crowd after verdict, 131–32
moralizing, 94
trial coverage, 128–30
on use of victim's name, 115
Boston Herald, coverage of "Big Dan's" gang rape case in, 91, 100, 106, 10[illegible], 121, 130–31, 141–43
editorial, 93–94
Estes on, 143
on harrassment of victim, 134–35
headlines, 93, 120, 128, 130
interview with Impemba, 127–28
interview with suspects, 102–3
opening day of trial, 120–21
Boston Strangler, 37–38
Bourgeois, Bea, 21
Bowman, Patricia, 13, 18, 258
Bradley, Mamie Till, 33–34
Bradley, Roy, 34
Brawley, Tawana, 9, 190, 213–15, 239, 291*n*.78
Breslin, Jimmy, 197, 223
Briscoe, Michael, 205–6, 223
Brookhiser, Richard, 208*n*.
Broussard, Sharon, 195
Brown, Arthur, 7–8, 148, 161–62, 167, 187
Brownmiller, Susan, 17–18, 29–30, 39, 44, 237, 245, 297
Bryant, Carolyn, 34–35
Buchanan, Pat, 109, 217
Buchwald, Art, 73–74
Bruns, Robert, 237
Burt, Charles, 53, 56–60, 62, 80–81, 83
Butterfield, Fox, 256
Byfield, Natalie, 210
Cambridge Women's Center, 136
Carr, C., 168, 186
Celarier, Michelle, 76–77, 87
Central Park jogger case, 189–249
alternative press, 223–25
Black press, 213–23
defense's arguments, 226–29, 231, 239–41
editorials, 201–2, 209–11, 213–17, 221, 231, 233*n*., 235–36
explanations of causes, 208–13
facts behind, 191
first stories, 193–94
implication of victim, 194–98
jogger as heroine, 225–26
media coverage of, 191–93
race as issue, 201–4, 213–23
racist aspects of reporting, 216–23
suspects, profiles of, 204–8
trial (first), 230–39
trial (second), 239–43
trial (third), 243
violence against women and, 208–13
wilding and, 198–201
Chambers, Robert
activity on night of Levin's murder, 150, 168–69
apology by, 180–81
arrest and confession, 147–48, 174
condemnation of, after sentencing, 182–83
confession of, 148, 155, 174
criticism of lifestyle of, 155–56, 182–84
glamorization of, 152–54, 160, 167–68, 170, 172–73
guilty plea, 179–80
lack of coverage of "last hours," 161–62
sentencing of, 180–81
"sex defense" of, 148–49, 173–74, 176
at trial, 177
Chancer, Lynn, 142–43, 297
Charig, Margaret, 99, 105, 134–35, 145
Charnas, Scott, 113
Chicago Tribune, 54

City Sun, 33, 192–93, 202, 213–15, 217, 222–23, 229, 231–32, 240
Civil Rights Congress, 31
Civil rights movement, 33, 36
Clark, Patrick, 245–47
Class
  crime reporting and, 8–9, 225, 256
  in Jennifer Levin rape/murder case, 152–53, 155–56, 158–59, 182, 185
  myths about rape assailants and, 15
  victim in Central Park jogger case, 193–94
Cleaver, Eldridge, 34–35, 39
Clendinen, Dudley, 101
Clichés, 259–60
Clifford, Timothy, 200–1, 247, 283–84*n*.15
Coalition Against Sexist Violence, 111
Cohen, Richard, 66–67, 108
Commentary magazine, 208*n*.
Communists, 28, 30–32, 34
Competition in press, effects of, 7, 264–65
Consideration of victims and victims' families, 262–64
Context, importance of in reporting, 261
Cooper, Andrew, 229
Cooper, Barry Michael, 199*n*., 204, 206–8
Cordeiro, John M., 117–18, 130, 136
Cowan, Ron, 83
Cox, Clinton, 231–2
Cuomo, Mario, 285*n*.7

The Daily News
  Central Park jogger case, 189, 192–95, 200, 202–3, 221, 234
  Jennifer Levin rape/murder case, 147–49, 151–52, 160–62, 175, 178
Daily Worker, 31–32
Deadlines, effect of, 7
Dershowitz, Alan M., 116, 253
DeSalvo, Albert, 37–38
Des Moines Register, 252
Didion, Joan, 24, 242
Diller, Howard, 239–41
Dinkins, David, 190
Domestic violence, Rideout marital rape case and, 74–79
Dorrian, Mr. Jack, 156, 164–65
Do the Right Thing (film), 190
Downing, Neil, 110, 112, 118–19, 124, 132
Duggan, Dennis, 231, 240
Dwyer, Jim, 234

Editorials. *See also* Opinion columns
  Central Park jogger case, 201–2, 209–11, 213–17, 235–36
  New Bedford gang rape case, 93–94, 98–99, 105–6
Editors, gender of, 5
Ellsworth, Karen, 110, 113, 120, 124, 132, 144–45
Esposito, Richard, 154, 200, 246–47
Estes, Andrea, 120, 134, 144
Evenson, Janet, 46–48, 50–56, 64–65, 67–70, 77, 81–82

Fairstein, Linda, 148*n*., 176–80
Fall River Herald News, 114
Families of victims, 262, 264
Fee, Gayle, 121, 143
Feminism and feminist groups
  effect on reporting, 39–40, 42
  Jennifer Levin rape/murder case, 149–50, 174–76, 188
  New Bedford gang rape case, 94, 100, 111, 121, 141–42, 145
  press's fear of, 266
  Rideout marital rape case, 54, 59–60
Ferreira, Manuel Adelino, 96–97, 99, 101, 105–8, 111, 142
Fishleder, Paul, 207, 221, 246
Fleming, Anne Taylor, 108
"Florida Tobacco Roaders" case, 35–36
Follow-ups, importance of, 262
Footlick, Jerrold K., 63
Fox, Wendy, 119
Freedman, Samuel G., 149–50, 155–59, 163–66, 169
Das Freie Volk, 34

Gabe, Catherine, 134
Gallagher, Margaret, 21–22, 295

Galligan, Thomas B., 228
Gang violence, 98, 210–13
Garland, Bonnie, 174
Gartner, Michael, 252
Gender of reporters, 5, 23, 265, 269*n.*7
  Central Park jogger case, 192–93
  Jennifer Levin rape/murder case, 151
  New Bedford gang rape, 92
  Rideout marital rape case, 46
Genovese, Kitty, 38–39, 89, 93–94
Glaberson, William, 237
Glave, Judie, 187
The Globe (tabloid), 252
Goleman, Daniel, 164
Gone With the Wind (film), 66, 74
Goodman, Ellen
  New Bedford gang rape case, 109
  Rideout marital rape case, 66, 68, 76
Gorney, Cynthia, 63–65, 78, 87
Gortmaker, Gary, 48, 51–53, 55–57, 59, 81
Graber, Doris, 197, 295
Griffith, Michael, 190
Groth, Nicholas, 98, 297
Guardian Angels, 176, 249

Hairston, Hap, 189, 203, 245
Hale, Matthew, 44
Hall, Jacqueline Dowd, 25–26, 297
Hamill, Dennis, 223
Hamill, Peter, 202–3, 212, 216–17
Hanson, Marla, 176
Harbour, Kimberly Rae, 219
Hauser, Charles McCorkle, 114–15
Hawelka, Katherine M., 186
Hawkins, Willametta, 30–33
Hawkins, Yusef, 190, 228
Hays, Constance L., 196
Herbert, Bob, 221, 231
Herrin, Richard, 174
Hill, Anita, 13
"Hillside Strangler." *See* "L.A. Strangler" case
History of reporting of sex crimes, 25–42
  1930s, 27–29
  1940s, 29–30
  early 1950s, 30–33
  mid- and late-1950s, 33–36
  1960s, 36–39
  1970s, 39–42
Hoffman, Bill, 147, 149, 151, 163, 168, 175, 187–88
Hood, Jane C., 210–11
Hornung, Rick, 227–28
Horton, James E., 28
Hustler magazine, 109–10, 280*n.*22

Impemba, John, 95–96, 104–5, 126–28, 133, 144
International Labor Defense, 28
In These Times, 45, 57, 76–77, 87

Jennifer Levin rape/murder case, 147–88
  backgrounds of Chambers and Levin, 152–59, 183
  case, 150
  coverage of crime, 159–63
  criticism of Chambers in post-trial period, 181–84
  Litman and, 173–75
  media coverage of, 151–52
  moralizing about crime, 163–67
  press's refusal to blame Chambers, 167–73, 185
  trial, 175–81
Jepson, Don, 69
Jones, Ann, 298
Jordan, Mary, 257
Jordon, Rose, 174
Journalistic traditions, effect of, 8
"Justice for Jennifer Levin Task Force," 174, 179

Kane, Robert J. (attorney), 119, 120, 123
Kannapell, Andrea, 196
Kaplan, David, 253
Kaufman, Jonathan, 113, 119
Kaufman, Michael T., 196–97, 204, 218, 245–46
Kennedy, Lisa, 224
Kennedy Smith rape trial, 4, 8, 252, 255–59

Kenny, Timothy, 47–48, 50, 52–53, 69, 77, 86
on Rideouts, 65, 77
trial coverage by, 55–59, 86
Koch, Ed, 190, 208
Kolata, Gina, 285–86*n*.9
Kosner, Edward, 230
Kramer, Linda, 47, 50–51, 69, 77–82, 87
interview with Greta Rideout, 79–80
on Oregon newspapers, 46
on John Rideout, 64–65
trial coverage by, 55–58, 61
Kukielski, Phil, 106–7, 110, 114, 132–33, 144–45
on *Journal's* decision to include graphic coverage of "Big Dan" trial, 124
on naming of victim, 115, 117
on race/ethnicity policy of *Providence Journal*, 95
Kunen, James, 181
Kunstler, William, 242

"L.A. Strangler" case, 40–42
La Rosa, Paul, 160–62, 185, 187
Lederer, Elizabeth, 227, 230, 233, 239, 241–43, 247
Lee, Spike, 190
Leid, Utrice, 213–15
Levin, Alan, 92–93, 103–4, 119, 126, 137–38
Levin, Jennifer
activity on night of murder, 150, 160–61
biased coverage of, 167–72, 184–88
blame of. *See* Blaming of victim
discrediting of, at trial, 178–79
implication of, in *New York Times* article, 155–59
"last hours" story in *Daily News*, 160–63
"sex diary" of, 175
sexist descriptions of, 154–55, 170–71
Lewis, David, 231
Liddick, Betty, 45–46, 48–51, 75–76, 78, 82, 86–87
Lindahl, Judith L., 137
Litman, Jack, 148*n*., 174–77, 179–80, 185–86
"Loose women" myth, 16–17
Lopez, Steve, 205–6, 243
Los Angeles Times
New Bedford gang rape case, 100, 102, 129, 139
Rideout marital rape case, 45–46, 48–50, 61–62, 75, 78, 83, 87
Loughlin, John, 229, 243
Lubrana, Alfred, 195
Lynching, 25–28, 237

Maddox, Alton, 216
Mademoiselle magazine, 178
Mandela, Nelson, 190, 238
Manipulation of reporters, 10
Mann, Judy
New Bedford gang rape case, 108
Rideout marital rape case, 67–68, 76
Marcus, Ruth, 111, 140
Maren, Michael, 217
Marital rape statutes, 43–44
Marquez, Stuart, 149, 152, 161–62, 187
Martin, Del, 44, 82, 85, 263, 298
"Martinsville Seven" case, 32–33
Mason, C. Vernon, 233, 239
McAlary, Mike, 291*n*.75
McCarthy, Colman, 66, 68
McCarthy, Sheryl, 204, 208, 236
McCray, Antron, 204, 221, 229–30, 236
McDonough, Sandra, 47, 50–54, 63–66, 69–70, 76–77, 81
on John Rideout, 64–66
Rideout trial coverage, 57–58, 61–63
McGee, Rosalee, 31–32
McGee, Willie, 30–33
McMillan, Gary, 98
Medeiros, Jose, 102–5, 118, 130–31
Medeiros, Virgilio, 102–5, 118, 130–31
Media
coverage in Central Park jogger case, 191–93
coverage in Jennifer Levin rape/murder case, 159–63

Media (*continued*)
coverage in New Bedford gang rape case, 91–92
coverage in Rideout case, 46–47
portrayal of women in, 21–24
Men on Rape (Timothy Beneke), 13, 297
Milam, J. W., 34–35
Mitford, Jessica, 31
Moniz, Rita, 94, 100
Moore, Colin, 239–42
Moralizing by press in Jennifer Levin rape/murder case, 163–67
Morgan, Joan, 196, 224–25
Moseley, Winston, 38
Ms. magazine, 109
Munk, Erika, 233*n.*, 237
Murdoch, Rupert, 106
Muslims, 17
Myths about rape, 13–19

Nachman, Jerry, 195, 230
Naming of sex crime victims, 40, 251–54, 259
Central Park jogger case, 229–30
Kennedy Smith trial, 258–59
necessary reforms, 263–64
New Bedford gang rape case, 98, 113–17
Rideout marital rape case, 47–48
The Nation, 32, 233*n.*
National Center for the Prevention and Control of Rape, 251
National Institute of Mental Health, 251
National Organization for Women (NOW), 174, 176, 179
New Bedford gang rape case ("Big Dan's" case), 89–146
arguments of attorneys, 124–28
candlelight march by feminists, 100–101
columnists on, 108–9
death of victim, 140–41
defendants, 117–18
editorials, 94, 98–99, 105–6
explicitness of testimony, 123–24
exposure of victim at trial, 121–24
flaws in reporting, 141–45
initial reactions, 92–95
jury selection, 110–13
media coverage, 91–92
naming of victim, 113–17
persecution of victim, 130–35, 140, 142
Portuguese and, 90, 95–97, 100–102, 105–8, 111, 130–31, 142–45
posttrial coverage, 133–41
sexist description of victim, 119–20
suspects' side of story, 102–5, 127–28
treatment of victim in press, 98–100
trial coverage, 128–30
verdicts, 130–33
victim's background, 90–91
Newfield, Jack, 217
New Journalism, 49, 50
Newkirk, Pamela, 192
Newsday
Central Park jogger case, 190, 192, 195, 197, 200–201, 202–5, 207–8, 220, 229–31, 234, 236, 240–41, 247–49
Jennifer Levin rape/murder case, 151, 153–54, 166–67, 174, 176–81, 184
New Bedford gang rape case, 140–41
Newsweek, 33
Boston Strangler case, 37–38
Central Park jogger case, 217–18, 247
L.A. Strangler case, 40–41
Rideout marital rape case, 63
New York City, tabloid press in, 151–52
New York magazine, 168–73, 247
New York Post
Central Park jogger case, 192–95, 197–203, 209, 216–17, 232–35, 241
Jennifer Levin rape/murder case, 151, 153–55, 159–60, 187–88
New York Review of Books, 242
New York Sun, 25

The New York Times
Central Park jogger case, 192, 196–97, 204–5, 207–11, 212*n.*, 217–20, 227, 234, 237, 241
Genovese murder, 38
Jennifer Levin rape/murder case, 149–52, 155–59, 163–66
Kennedy Smith trial, 252–53, 256–57
New Bedford gang rape case, 100–101, 129
Rideout marital rape case, 63, 81–82
New York World, 27
Nodelman, George, 71
Noel, Peter, 222–23
Nolan, Irene, 254
Nolan, Jim, 197–98
NOW. *See* National Organization for Women

Opinion columns
Central Park jogger case, 197, 201–2, 209–11, 213–17, 221, 223–25, 236
New Bedford gang rape case, 94, 98–99, 108–9
Rideout marital rape case, 53, 66–68, 71–74
The Oregonian, 46, 48, 53, 61, 68–69, 73
The Oregon Journal, 46
Overholser, Geneva, 252, 254

Pagnozzi, Amy, 233, 235, 238
Parker, Mack Charles, 34
PAU. *See* Portuguese Americans United
Pearl, Mike, 203–4, 228, 245
People magazine, 151, 173, 181–82
Persian Gulf War, 22–23
Persky, Mort, 184
Peyser, Andrea, 197–98
"Phantom Rapist" (St. Louis), 37
Pina, Ronald A., 99, 104, 108, 136
Pinzler, Isabelle Katz, 253
Pitt, David E., 212*n.*
Policy and training, suggestions for press, 262–63
Pollitt, Katha, 293*n.*14
Portuguese Americans United (PAU), 105
Portuguese Times, 91, 96–97, 101, 111, 114, 119–20, 128, 134
Preppie Murder. *See* Jennifer Levin rape/murder case
The Preppie Murder (television movie), 183
Press coverage before 1950s
racism, rape, and, 25–30
The Providence Journal, 91, 98–99, 103, 106–7, 110, 112–19, 123–24, 128–29, 131, 136–38, 143–44
Provocation of rape, myth of, 15–17
Pryce, Vinette K., 240
Punishment, myth of rape as, 17

Queenan, Joe, 8

Race and racism
Central Park jogger case, 189–90, 201–4, 213–23, 244–46
lynchings, 25–27
myths about rape assailants, 14–15
New Bedford gang rape case, description of, 90–91
press in 1930s, 27–29
press in 1940s, 29–30
press in arly 1950s, 30–33
press in mid- and late-1950s, 33–36
press in 1960s, 36–39
tradition of racism in press, 8–9, 25–27
Race of reporters, 192, 207–8, 265
Ragsdale, James, 95–97, 105–6, 126–28, 132, 134
Rainbow Coalition, 136
Rape and Marriage: The Rideout Case (film), 83–84
Rape trauma syndrome, 14
Raposo, Victor M., 118, 126–28, 130, 136–37
Raspberry, William, 71
Reporters
ambitions of, 7, 263
gender of, 5, 23, 46, 92, 151, 192–93, 265, 269*n.*7

Reporters (*continued*)
hierarchy in newsroom and, 10–11
manipulation of, 10
opinions of, 10
race of, 192, 207–8, 265
sexism of, 9, 245–49
Revenge, myth of women crying rape for, 17–18
Richardson, Kevin, 205–6, 239–40, 242–43
Rideout, Greta
alleged "sexual problems" of, 55, 57–58
background, 44–45
as battered woman, 76–79, 84–86
interview, 85
in Liddick's article, 49–51
witnesses for, 59–60
Rideout, John
acquittal, 62–65
background, 44–45
later convictions, 81–83
at trial, 53–54, 58–63
violence of, 76–78, 84–86
Rideout marital rape case, 43–87
background of case, 44–45
conviction of John Rideout, 82–83
discretion in reporting, 46–47
divorce, 80–81
domestic violence and, 75–79, 84–85
faults of press coverage in, 86–87
film version, 83–84
first stories, 47–52
Greta Rideout on, 85
marital problems, 79–81
opinions in press on, 66–68, 71–74
pretrial coverage, 51–52
reconciliation, 69–71
trial coverage, 52–66
Rosenberg, Howard, 83
Rowan, Carl R., 66
Royko, Mike, 66, 71–73

Salaam, Yusef, 204, 229–31, 238–39
Salamon, Julie, 139
Sales of newspapers, crime stories and, 7–8
San Francisco Chronicle, 252–53
Santana, Raymond, 204, 229–30, 236
Scapegoating of sources, 265
Schorer, Jane, 252, 254–55
Schudson, Michael, 264
Sciacca, Joe, 102
"Scottsboro Boys" case, 27–29
Seiler, Michael, 61–62
Sensationalism, 265–66
Sentencing for sex crimes
in 1970s, 42
Central Park jogger case, 239, 241–3
early 1950s, 33
"Florida Tobacco Roaders" case, 36
Jennifer Levin rape/murder case, 180–81
McGee case, 30–31
New Bedford gang rape case, 135–36
Scottsboro case, 28–29
Sex, myth of rape as, 14, 17
Sexist language, 9, 19–21
during 1960s, 37
absence of, in Rideout marital rape case, 46–47
Central Park jogger case, 225–26, 247–48
Jennifer Levin rape/murder case, 154–55, 170–71
New Bedford gang rape case, 119–20
reform suggestions, 259–60
Sharpton, Al, 216, 233
Silva, Daniel C., 95, 118, 127, 136
Sliwa, Lisa, 176
Smith, Bobby Lee, 252
Smith, Kimberleigh J., 229
Smith, William Kennedy, 13, 251, 253, 255–59
Soul on Ice (Eldridge Cleaver), 34–35
Sources, bias of, 9–10
St. John's University rape case, 219–20
St. Vincent's Hospital Rape Crisis Center (New York City), 17
Standard-Times (New Bedford, Massachusetts), 91–93, 95–97, 99–101, 103–6, 114, 116, 119, 123, 126–28, 130–31, 134–38, 144
The Statesman Journal, 46–48, 56, 59, 61, 82–83
Steinem, Gloria, 89

Stone, Michael, 168–73, 247
Stuart, Charles, 279*n*.8
Studies on rape, 39–40, 296–99

Tabor, Mary B. W., 256
Tate, Greg, 249
Tatum, Wilbert, 215–16, 230, 235–36, 238
Television, 6
  New Bedford gang rape case, 92, 113–15
Terry, Don, 218
Thomas, Clarence (Central Park jogger case suspect), 205
Thomas, Clarence (Supreme Court justice), 13
Till, Emmett, 33–35
Time magazine, 31–32, 35–36, 42
Trebay, Guy, 240, 291*n*.81
Trial coverage
  Central Park jogger case, 230–43
  Jennifer Levin rape/murder case, 175–81
  New Bedford gang rape case, 110–13, 117–33
  Rideout marital rape case, 52–66
Trump, Donald, 218, 287*n*.18

United Press International, 46–48, 50, 55, 77, 86, 114

Veary (district attorney), 120
Vieira, Joseph, 112, 118
The Village Voice
  Central Park jogger case, 192–93, 196, 204, 206–7, 223–25, 227–28, 237, 248, 266
  Jennifer Levin rape/murder case, 151, 168, 186

Wall Street Journal, 139*n*.
Washington Post
  Kennedy Smith trial, 257
  New Bedford gang rape case, 92, 107–8, 111–12, 128–29, 134, 139
  Rideout marital rape case, 55, 63–67, 71, 87
Washington Star, 55–56, 70
Wasted: The Preppie Murder (Linda Wolfe), 148*n*., 183–85
Waxler, David, 112–13
Widener, Sandra, 153
"Wilding," 198–201
Will, George, 67
Williams, Clayton, 14
Williams, Dennis, 41
Willse, Jim, 194–96, 203, 245
Wire stories. *See* Associated Press (AP); United Press International
Wise, Kharey, 205–6, 212, 239–43, 248, 291*n*.81
Wolfe, Linda, 148*n*., 183–85, 188
"Wolf whistle murder" case, 33–35
Women Against Pornography, 179
Women's Coalition Against Sexist Violence, 94
Women's groups, see Feminism
Women's movement, 39–41

Young, William G., 117

Ziegenmeyer, Nancy, 252, 254–55, 263